Immersion, Identification, and the *Iliad*

# Immersion, Identification, and the *Iliad*

JONATHAN L. READY

Great Clarendon Street, Oxford, OX2 6DP,
United Kingdom

Oxford University Press is a department of the University of Oxford.
It furthers the University's objective of excellence in research, scholarship,
and education by publishing worldwide. Oxford is a registered trade mark of
Oxford University Press in the UK and in certain other countries

© Jonathan L. Ready 2023

The moral rights of the author have been asserted

Some rights reserved. No part of this publication may be reproduced, stored in
a retrieval system, or transmitted, in any form or by any means, for commercial purposes,
without the prior permission in writing of Oxford University Press, or as expressly
permitted by law, by licence or under terms agreed with the appropriate
reprographics rights organization.

This is an open access publication, available online and distributed under the terms of a
Creative Commons Attribution – Non Commercial – No Derivatives 4.0
International licence (CC BY-NC-ND 4.0), a copy of which is available at
http://creativecommons.org/licenses/by-nc-nd/4.0/.

Enquiries concerning reproduction outside the scope of this licence
should be sent to the Rights Department, Oxford University Press, at the address above

Published in the United States of America by Oxford University Press
198 Madison Avenue, New York, NY 10016, United States of America

British Library Cataloguing in Publication Data

Data available

Library of Congress Control Number: 2022950545

ISBN 978–0–19–287097–1

DOI: 10.1093/oso/9780192870971.001.0001

Printed and bound in the UK by
Clays Ltd, Elcograf S.p.A.

Links to third party websites are provided by Oxford in good faith and
for information only. Oxford disclaims any responsibility for the materials
contained in any third party website referenced in this work.

*For*

*Bridie Rose Bridie Rose*
*Bridie Rose*

1 – – – – – καὶ ἐμέ.
*Inscriptiones Graecae* IV² 2, 757

# Preface

We label "multiple correspondence similes" those similes that link different characters or objects in the narrative to different entities in the vignette in the simile's vehicle portion (the "as" portion). Ajax kills Simoesius as a man who makes chariots cuts down a tree in a marsh (*Iliad* 4.482–9). Hector awaits Achilles as a snake awaits a man (*Iliad* 22.92–6). Thinking about how these similes work in the *Iliad* requires taking a step back to think about how the Homeric poet brings characters to our attention and sets them aside. That subject directs one in turn to the numerous minor characters who populate the poem and who reflect the challenges the poet faces in activating and deactivating characters. So, as I finished up my discussion of multiple correspondence similes (Ready 2011: 220–58), I began work on what eventuated a decade later in an article on the *Iliad*'s bit players (Ready 2020). I thought I would use that piece as the starting point for a book on minor characters in ancient Greek literature. I had tucked away in a filing cabinet a hard copy of an odd paper from graduate school about minor characters in Herodotus's *Histories*: the execution left much to be desired, but the core thesis seemed worth resuscitating. As I continued my secondary reading on characters, I came across the literature on identification with fictional characters. The bibliography on identification led me to the literature on the still larger subject of immersion in narratives.

It became clear that there was more than enough to say about immersion and identification in the context of Homeric epic and that I would have to wait yet again to write on other genres. I also discovered that I had unwittingly stumbled into a field of investigation—how recipients of narratives are immersed—that a number of my colleagues in classical studies had just begun to work. This fortuitous occurrence was the first such experience in my scholarly career. My previous books have addressed Homeric similes, the nature and history of Homeric texts, and early Homeric papyri—all subjects of long-standing interest. In those endeavors, I offered new interpretations of old topics. Here I intervene in discussions that classicists and Homerists have only started to have about how the *Iliad*'s recipients find themselves immersed in the poem. Another point of difference between this book and my previous work is that here I do not concern myself until the end with the complex relationship between Homeric poetry and oral composition and oral performance. I will confess to some degree of relief in that regard: perhaps this is what it feels like to work on Greek tragedy or the poetry of Vergil where obsessions over authorship, performance context, and text fixation do not run on an eternal loop. Still, there remains a noticeable throughline running between this book and my *Orality, Textuality, and the Homeric Epics: An Interdisciplinary Study of Oral Texts, Dictated Texts, and Wild Texts* (Ready 2019a). In Parts II and III of that book and here again I seek to illuminate how people interact(ed) with and react(ed) to Homeric poetry.

As in *The Homeric Simile in Comparative Perspectives: Oral Traditions from Saudi Arabia to Indonesia* (Ready 2018) and *Orality, Textuality, and the Homeric Epics*, I assemble and put to use in this book an extensive bibliography from outside classical studies. I again show my work and introduce the reader to this material with frequent quotations from that literature. I tend to avoid paraphrase in lieu of quotation lest I stray from the precise point being made. I again follow the practice of fields outside of classical studies in limiting the number of footnotes. For the most part, I include citations in the main text in parentheses instead of using footnotes for citations: by virtue of their placement at the bottom of the page and their smaller font size, footnotes always to some degree occlude the actual work one cites. I do acquiesce to the more usual practice in classical studies by deploying footnotes for citational chains comprising six or more references. Both the quotation and the manner of citation are my way of acknowledging the degree to which I depend on previous scholarship and my way of articulating the importance of group efforts in advancing scholarship. Only a handful of discursive footnotes appear. If a point is worth making, it should merit inclusion in the main text, and as a reader I find it hard to follow the argument in the main text if I am supposed to take breaks along the way to read paragraph-long footnotes with their own arguments.

On a couple of occasions in this book as well, I write "Iliad" and "Odyssey" in roman font (see Ready 2019a: viii). With that formatting, I refer to a tradition of oral performance in which performers present what they think of as the same story. *Iliad* and *Odyssey* in italics refer to the written texts we use.

Quotations from the *Iliad* come from Helmut van Thiel's 2010 edition, and quotations from the *Odyssey* come from van Thiel's 1991 edition. I do not reproduce his lunate sigmas. I note the editors of other ancient works only if I quote, and only when I first quote, from their editions. All translations are my own unless otherwise noted.

References to current events in scholarship of this sort age badly. But surely an exception can be made for a once in a century global pandemic. On the one hand, it has been strange to write a book about immersion and identification—essentially a book about connecting (or seeming to connect) with other people and other places—when one cannot share a physical space except with those in one's bubble and cannot go anywhere. On the other hand, if ever people have come to appreciate their degree of immersion in storyworlds and of identification with characters, now might be that time. I do not have the requisite distance from this project to determine how those two factors have shaped it. Once this volume has been absorbed and is no longer cited perhaps it will have a second life as a specimen of COVID-19-era scholarship.

# Acknowledgments

I thank Fritz Breithaupt, Ruth Scodel, and Christos Tsagalis for conversation and correspondence at various stages of this project. In December 2019, audiences in Heidelberg, Rethymnon, and Thessaloniki helped me clarify my thoughts on identification as did the summer 2021 fellows of the University of Michigan's Institute for the Humanities. I am grateful to the Press's two anonymous readers for their careful attention to the manuscript, and, once again, I thank Charlotte Loveridge and the entire team at the Press for their skillful work. As ever, I am indebted to Margaret Foster for her guidance and support.

This book is freely available in an open-access edition thanks to TOME (Toward an Open Monograph Ecosystem)—a collaboration of the Association of American Universities, the Association of University Presses, and the Association of Research Libraries—and the generous support of the University of Michigan's College of Literature, Science, and the Arts and Office of the Provost. Learn more at the TOME website, available at: openmonographs.org. The Department of Classical Studies at the University of Michigan also contributed through its Frier Fund to support the open-access publication of this book.

# Contents

1. Introduction — 1
   1.1. Overview — 1
   1.2. Terminology — 1
   1.3. Previous Scholarship — 3
   1.4. Outline of Chapters — 10

### PART I: IDENTIFICATION AND THE *ILIAD*

2. The Study of Identification — 15
   2.1. Overview — 15
   2.2. The Components of Identification — 16
   2.3. The Triggers for Identification — 28
   2.4. Ancient Precedents for a Study of Identification — 34
   2.5. Character and Emotional Identification — 45
   2.6. Conclusion — 51

3. Prompts for (a Study of) Identifying with Characters — 53
   3.1. Overview — 53
   3.2. Recurring Features — 53
   3.3. Internal Narrators and Identification — 62
      3.3.1. Agamemnon on Tydeus — 65
      3.3.2. Nestor on Nestor — 71
   3.4. Conclusion — 81

4. Identification with Mortals and Gods — 83
   4.1. Overview — 83
   4.2. Identification with Mortals — 83
      4.2.1. Agamemnon in *Iliad* 11 — 83
      4.2.2. Andromache in *Iliad* 22 — 94
      4.2.3. The Funeral Games in *Iliad* 23 — 100
      4.2.4. Priam in *Iliad* 24 — 110
   4.3. Identification with Gods — 113
      4.3.1. The *Homeric Hymn to Demeter* — 115
      4.3.2. Hera in *Iliad* 14 — 118
      4.3.3. Thetis in *Iliad* 18 — 121
   4.4. Limits to Identification — 127
   4.5. The Politics of Identification — 131
   4.6. Conclusion — 142

## PART II: IMMERSION AND THE *ILIAD*

| | |
|---|---|
| 5. Ancients and Moderns on Immersion | 147 |
|    5.1. Overview | 147 |
|    5.2. Ancient Precedents for a Study of Immersion | 147 |
|    5.3. Modern Studies of Immersion | 154 |
|    5.4. Conclusion | 158 |
| 6. Spatial and Spatio-Temporal Immersion | 159 |
|    6.1. Overview | 159 |
|    6.2. Spatial Immersion | 159 |
|    6.3. Spatio-Temporal Immersion | 173 |
|    6.4. Conclusion | 193 |
| 7. Emotional Immersion | 195 |
|    7.1. Overview | 195 |
|    7.2. Suspense | 196 |
|    7.3. Other Emotions | 211 |
|    7.4. Conclusion | 220 |
| 8. Content and Form | 221 |
|    8.1. Overview | 221 |
|    8.2. Inner Life | 221 |
|    8.3. Ourselves | 225 |
|    8.4. Formal Features | 230 |
|    8.5. Conclusion | 236 |
| 9. Conclusion | 239 |
| *Works Cited* | 253 |
| *Index of Greek Passages* | 291 |
| *Index of Terms* | 304 |

# 1
# Introduction

## 1.1. Overview

Section 1.2 offers definitions of narrative, storyworld, immersion, identification, and recipient. Section 1.3 orients this investigation of Homeric immersion and identification in relation to prior scholarship in Homeric studies. Section 1.4 provides a brief outline of the following chapters.

## 1.2. Terminology

I start with some fraught definitions. We will be talking about narrative, a tricky term to define and one that we perhaps want to be careful not to define too narrowly (Ryan 2007). Jonas Grethlein posits that a narrative is "the representation of a temporal sequence involving human or human-like characters in a sequential medium" (2017a: 34; cf. Grethlein, Huitink, and Tagliabue 2020: 8). John Frow goes into a bit more detail, discerning three essential components of a narrative (2018: 106):

> a medium of representation...; a speaking voice, or some corresponding enunciative moment (the composite gaze through which we view a film, for example), which activates that medium; and the movement of persons, or quasi-persons, through space and time and relationships in a represented world.

But there are other ways to think about the term. Fritz Breithaupt proposes that a narrative is an account that audiences understand as one possible version of what happened (2011, esp. 109, 120).

Let us move on to working definitions of storyworld, immersion, and identification. We have general agreement on a definition of storyworld: "The storyworld has two components. First, there is the setting, the place and time in which the events occur. Second, there are characters, the human or non-human agents that initiate or experience events" (Hogan 2018: 133); storyworlds are "totalities that encompass space, time, and individuated existents that undergo transformations as the result of events" (Ryan 2019: 63). Immersed recipients get wrapped up in a narrative and the storyworld it depicts and lose track to some degree of their real-world surroundings. Identification occurs when recipients interpret the storyworld from a character's perspective, feel a character's emotions or at least emotions congruent with those of the character, and/or root for a character to succeed. I will go into the components of immersion and identification in much greater detail over the course of this book.

Adopting these three definitions and utilizing these three concepts is already to make choices, to take a stand, and to maneuver carefully between opposed scholarly positions. For instance, Marie-Laure Ryan aims to rebut Richard Walsh's assertions (2017) that the concepts of world and immersion are not useful for the study of fictional narrative (2018: 236–7). Note too that media scholars have applied the term "immersion" to a range of phenomena and experiences (Nilsson, Nordahl, and Serafin 2016) or that many prefer a different word entirely, speaking of absorption, aesthetic illusion, enchantment, engagement, engrossment, entanglement, involvement, or transportation. Or, as a final example, observe the hedge in my formulation "the character's emotions *or at least* emotions congruent with those of the character," a response to a dispute over the nature of our emotional engagement with characters (see section 2.5, pp. 49–50).

Less fraught but worth explicit consideration is the following. Recipients respond differently to fictional and nonfictional narratives (e.g., Vaage 2016: 26–34), but whether a narrative is fiction or nonfiction is irrelevant when it comes to these three concepts. Whereas much of the literature on storyworlds, immersion, and identification pertains to fictional narrative, it is also true that we can speak of nonfiction storyworlds, be immersed in nonfiction storyworlds, and identify with the characters in nonfiction storyworlds.[1] I make this point because I want to forestall an objection to my use of these concepts by those who think that Homeric poetry is not fiction (see section 2.4, p. 34). The debate over the fictional or nonfictional status of Homeric epic does not affect this project (cf. Scodel 2021: 56–7).

Finally, I highlight here at the start how the word "recipient" that I have already used several times contributes to the presentation. It helps one avoid the cumbersome phrase "hearer, viewer, or reader," but, more important, its capaciousness signals my concern with features of immersion and identification that do not depend on a specific medium. No doubt the nature of immersion and identification vary depending on media (e.g., Grethlein 2017a), but I target components of those experiences that arise whether one is watching, reading, or listening to a tale (e.g., Carpenter, Green, and Fitzgerald 2018: 231; cf. Budelmann 2000: 15–16; Lovatt 2013: 21). Only in Chapter 9 do I ponder how listening to and watching an oral performer of Homeric epic shaped the audience's experience of the storyworld.

---

[1] Chen, Bell, and Taylor 2016; 2017; Fitzgerald and Green 2017: 56; Roberts 2018; R. Allan 2019b; 2020; Ryan 2019: 62–3, 66; Alam and So 2020; Fernandez-Quintanilla 2020; Maloney 2020; Tyrell 2020: 48; Grethlein 2021a: 49, 55–6, 264; Goffin and Friend 2022: 135.

## 1.3. Previous Scholarship

A 1947 article in *Classical Journal* concludes with a chart purporting to show how the audience experiences varying degrees of emotional intensity over the course of the *Iliad* (Ingalls 1947). The majority of Homeric scholarship in the second half of the twentieth century had concerns other than thinking about the affective dynamics of the presentation. With attention directed to how and when the *Iliad* and the *Odyssey* were composed, energy went into determining how best to interpret them in light of those compositional mechanisms (cf. Hutchinson 2017: 145). Even those who did not worry so much about the genesis of the poems saw their job as asking after the meaning(s) or argument(s) of the poems (e.g., Redfield 1975: ix).

Occasionally, explorations of what critics termed "pathos" appeared—some longer (e.g., M. Scott 1974; Griffin 1980, esp. 104–5), some shorter (e.g., Glenn 1971: 170; Martin Mueller 2009 [1985]: e.g., 55; Davies 2002: 29). Suspense received a fair amount of attention too (Rengakos 1999; cf. Liotsakis 2021: 6), and Elizabeth Minchin considered some other ways the *Iliad* poet sought "to keep us involved in his tale" (1999: 64). Typically, however, scholarly protocols allowed for only brief acknowledgments of the experience of hearing or reading the *Iliad* and the *Odyssey* and of the impact the poems can have on recipients. For example, the *Iliad* poet's detailed descriptions of horrific wounds suggest that "he and his audience enjoy the scene enormously," and the variety in these descriptions "never bores us" (E. Vermeule 1979: 96–7). In moments of embedded focalization—the narrator grants access to a character's point of view even though the character is not talking—"the audience is brought into a closer sympathy with the character, and hence into closer emotional involvement with the tale" (Edwards 1991: 4; cf. 2002: 36). An investigation of Trojan politics starts from the observation that the poet wants audiences to sympathize with the Trojans (Sale 1994: 7–13). When the *Odyssey* poet "transforms folklore and anecdote," he produces "situations of profound human meaning that lead us back to the poem again and again" (Segal 1994: 194). Achilles undergoes "an evolution in his character which is brilliantly conceived, intuitively plausible, and profoundly tragic" (Most 2003: 75). James Redfield relegates personal reflections to the preface of his book on Hector (1975: ix, xii):

> The present book thus grew out of an interest in, and even perhaps an identification with, one hero.... I developed the analysis because I care about the *Iliad*.... We carry with us in our solitude these fictions the poets have left us, we brood over their meanings, feel joy and sorrow at the events, make of the characters our friends and enemies, and find ourselves somehow nourished by the experience.

Conversely, Nancy Felson saves for the penultimate page of her book on the *Odyssey* the following comment: "I conclude by depicting the events that occur when I *as a reader* envision the action of the poem.... I am lulled to silent awe and complacent satisfaction that the characters who have become my companions have finally reached home.... A provisional satisfaction overcomes me..." (1994: 143, emphasis in original). The final sentence of Leonard Muellner's 1996 book on the meaning of *mēnis* also stands apart in tenor and point from what comes before: "Achilles bequeaths to us the self-perpetuating artistic representation of an idealistic, disturbing, and consoling definition of the human condition" (175).

Aristotle's attention in his *Poetics* to pity, fear, and catharsis as essential components of the audience's reaction to Greek tragedy created a permission structure for twentieth-century scholarship in that subfield to attend to the audience's affective engagement, discussions that point up by way of contrast the general occlusion of such matters in Homeric studies.[2] But Homeric studies had good company: wittingly or not, it joined other branches of literary studies in limiting, even suppressing, if not exiling, discussions of how readers respond, especially emotionally, to and become immersed in narratives.[3]

Fittingly, then, we were told that to consider audience response to the Homeric epics properly one should ask after the "assumptions and responses which the works themselves seem to expect" as opposed to "the assumptions and responses which we, as contemporary readers, tend to provide" (Gill 1990: 8). Our own reactions are to be segregated and then (presumably) ignored. Or one could recognize that the characters prompt "our sympathetic interest" (Gill 2002: 97), our "sympathetic engagement" (99), and "our sympathetic involvement" (105), but this connection arises as a result of ("is a reflection of" (105), "inheres in" (152)) the careful and rigorous intellectual analysis that they compel us to perform: we become "engaged in their reasoning" (117; cf. 105, 152, 172–3) as they wrestle with "certain fundamental issues of human life" (119) and "with the questions or 'problems' which the poem as a whole explores" (97; cf. 173). A clinical, rational engagement is allowed. Those more willing to explore how the epics generate a range of affective dynamics often viewed such dynamics with suspicion. Consider Lillian Doherty's assessment of the end of the *Odyssey*: "I have not stopped taking pleasure in the reunion of Odysseus and Penelope; rather, my pleasure has become infused with an awareness that it invites me to be reconciled to an androcentric view of the world, a view in which Penelope's happiness is subordinate to and indeed defined by that of Odysseus" (1995: 40; cf. 192).

In keeping with broader trends inside and outside of classical studies,[4] priorities have shifted in the subfield of Homeric studies. Jon Hesk asks us to confront "the

---

[2] E.g., Stanford 1983; Heath 1987; Griffin 1998: 54–61; 1999: 91–2; Griffith 1999b: e.g., 43; Budelmann 2000: e.g., 23, 91; cf. Wohl 2015: 12, 168 n. 6.
[3] M. Smith 1995: 188–9; Robinson 2005: 143; Davis 2007: 20; Felski 2008: 54; 2015: 12–13, 54; 2020b: 30, 62; Ryan 2015a: 107; Grethlein 2017a: 4, 123; 2021a: 154; 2021b: 228; Douglass 2018: 112; Hogan 2018: 4; Plantinga 2018: 211; Kuzmičová and Bálint 2019: 430; Knox 2021: 12; cf. Sedgwick 2003: 144, 150.
[4] Inside: e.g., Wohl 2015: 28, 106–9, 135–6; Cairns and Nelis 2017: 10–11; Olsen 2017; Meineck 2018; Weiss 2020: 333; de Bakker, van der Berg, and Klooster 2022: 10–15. Outside: e.g., Robinson 2005; Plantinga 2009; Hogan 2018; Grethlein 2021a: 103.

difficult issue of the audience's pleasure" and how the *Iliad* "deliver[s] prurient thrills and entertaining forms of terror" (2013: 33; cf. 43). Lynn Kozak's *Experiencing Hektor* explores how and why "the *Iliad* has caught me with its Hektor" (2017: 1)—that is, how and why the poem enables audience members to connect with and care about its characters and engage with the tale more generally. Kozak attends to a number of factors that bring "pleasure" to recipients, from a challenge to their expectations (119), to a resolution of a storyline (121), to a "callback" (cross-reference) to an earlier episode (130), to their recognizing the typical pattern of a battle scene (137). Kozak introduces to Homeric studies the notion of "allegiance" wherein recipients judge the characters and experience like or dislike as a result (5-6, 8; cf. section 7.3, p. 211). This experience is one manifestation of our "engagement" with the characters (62, 111, 157; cf. 22). They also deploy the notion of "melodramatic alignment structure" wherein recipients "know more than any one character knows" (6; cf., e.g., Rengakos 1999: 323 on dramatic irony). This knowledge "increases emotional investment and anticipation of the events to come" (Kozak 2017: 92; cf. 100, 137-8, 140-1, 151, 170, 198). And Kozak traces still other ways in which the poem builds anticipation, suspense, curiosity, and even anxiety in its audience (8-9, 27, 29, 31, 82, 95, 102, 115, 143, 147, 195, 218). Focusing on the *Iliad*'s divine apparatus, Tobias Myers queries "the emotional impact [on the audience] of the devastation at Troy," "the intensity of their [the audience members] experience as they listen to the telling," and how "the poet understands himself to be hooking his listeners" (2019: 3, 33, 175). He writes, "While the *Iliad* responds wonderfully to analysis, it is aimed not at analytical critics but at audiences ready to be swept away by wonder, pleasure, terror, and tears" (59; cf. 91, 93). At the same time, Myers argues, the *Iliad* poet urges his audience to consider their emotional reactions to the tale (124, 210). Rachel Lesser discerns a triad of desires felt by the *Iliad*'s audience (2022, esp. 12-22). They experience narrative desire (wanting to learn how the story will turn out), sympathetic desire (feeling for a character and hoping all goes well for them), and empathetic desire (taking on a character's "urges, wishes, and longings" (18)). The audience can sympathize and empathize with a range of characters—Chryses, Achilles, Hera, Helen, Menelaus, Agamemnon, Odysseus, Andromache, Patroclus, Priam, Hecuba; they can sympathize and empathize with a specific character at one moment but not at another (178, 189, 213, 228). Sympathetic and empathetic desires can go hand in hand with and even enhance narrative desire (21, 30, 107, 189, 195, 200, 203, 215, 221, 229, 241), or they can conflict with it, causing at times feelings of dissonance or even dread (99, 128, 153, 178, 181, 199, 215). Liberating too is Joel Christensen's study of the therapeutic work afforded (or not) by storytelling to the characters and external audiences of the *Odyssey* (2020; cf. Grethlein 2017b: 118, 271-82). Homerists, then, have answered Gregory Hutchinson's call for "thinking more about how the poem affected listeners" (2017: 168).

This book builds on these interventions as well as on additional scholarship by investigators of the ancient world—both in Greek studies and Roman studies and in biblical studies—that starts from two facts now well-established in disciplines outside classical studies devoted to the exploration of narrative. When people read a story or when they watch a play, movie, or television show, many find themselves immersed in the tale and its world and many identify with the characters (cf. de Bakker, van der Berg, and Klooster 2022: 15–17). More than that, many consume media in order to immerse themselves in the tale and its world and to identify with the characters: they "choose" and "allow" themselves these experiences (Plantinga 2018: 195, 249) and "strive to be overcome by the objects of their passion" (Felski 2020b: 65). We can shift priorities and think about narratives as more than a series of puzzles for the critic to solve.

One can find these propositions in traditional sites of literary criticism. From her perch in English, for example, Rita Felski points to the necessity of taking seriously the majority of readers who read in an apparently "unseemly or inappropriate fashion—identifying with characters, becoming absorbed in narratives, being struck by moments of recognition" (2015: 29; cf. 191; 2008: 14, 17–18; 2020b: 25; Moi 2019: 59). We critics, she writes, should overcome our fear "of being contaminated and animated by the words we encounter" (2015: 12), and whereas our training prompts us to ask colleagues, "'But what about power?'," we should now ask, "'But what about love?' Or: 'Where is your theory of attachment?'" (17–18). Drawing especially on Bruno Latour's actor-network theory to argue that texts "make things happen" (168, 180; cf. 2020b: 21–4), Felski proposes a "postcritical reading." This approach "treat[s] experiences of engagement, wonder, or absorption not as signs of naïveté or user error but as clues to why we are drawn to art in the first place" (2015: 180). It asks, "How do works of art move us, and why? Are certain features of texts more likely to trigger empathy or recognition, absorption or disorientation? What does it mean to talk about identifying with a character?" (181; cf. Anker and Felski 2017; Felski 2020a).

Felski's clear articulations of the matter at hand and of its stakes inspire (cf. Docherty 2021), but I concentrate for the most part on other research in communications, literary studies, media studies, and psychology that provides accessible and precise definitions and models of immersion and identification as well as actionable findings on how immersion and identification come about. This project represents the first book-length application of that research to the *Iliad*. It thereby helps explain why people care about this epic poem and its characters (cf. B. Vermeule 2010) and how they actually respond to the poem. Put differently, those of us in Homeric studies who want to think about narrative immersion and identification should take as our guides researchers in those aforementioned fields who study narrative immersion and identification and especially those researchers who do so in an empirical fashion. By empirical, one refers to controlled experiments with results subject to falsification (Hakemulder and van Peer 2016: 192; differently, Margolin 2008: 9).

To be sure, several relevant contributions in classical studies that address issues of immersion and/or identification do not choose this route. Studying "images of song" found within the Homeric epics, Stephen Halliwell notes the poems' concern with an audience's "intense absorption," "rapt concentration and engagement," and "total immersion" (2011: 45; cf. Liebert 2017: 48–62; Ready 2018: 170–84; Giordano 2022: 177–83). In an earlier intervention, Halliwell addresses Plato's *Republic*: performers experience "self-likening, absorption, and identification" and "full psychological immersion" with characters (2002: 54, 79) whereas audience members experience "'sympathy' rather than 'identification'" (81; cf. 93). Nancy Felson's influential article, "Vicarious Transport: Fictive Deixis in Pindar's *Pythian* Four," finds "Pindar uses deixis with expertise and subtlety, primarily to make his audiences 'travel' across space and time.... He transports them along carefully demarcated pathways" (1999: 5; cf. Sobak 2013: 111 n. 10, 115 n. 21; Weiss 2016: 250; Neer and Kurke 2019: 37, 204, 276). Pauline LeVen queries how Timotheus's *Persians* "immerses its audience" such that it "is brought to the scene" (2014: 201–2) and experiences "mental transport" or "mental displacement" (217–18; cf. 242). A deictic shift (see section 6.3, p. 188) enacted by the use of the imperfect tense contributes to this effect (197–204). What is more, intertextual citations in the direct speech of characters endow the characters with "fictional weight" (216) and make them into entities "whom the audience can not only observe directly but also project into, in [a] form of wish-fulfillment fantasy" (209; cf. 232). Jonas Grethlein argues that ancient prose writers— Thucydides in his *History of the Peloponnesian War*, Xenophon in his *Anabasis*, Plutarch in his *Alexander*, Tacitus in his *Annals*, Polybius in his *Histories*, and Sallust in his *The War with Catiline*—deploy a range of techniques that make us feel as if we experience the narrated events or as if figures from the past come before us (2013). The use of the imperfect tense and the historical present "let the reader follow the battle as if it was unfolding right before her eyes" (34; cf. 63). Internal focalization renders the action "present" (34), gives the recipient "a sense of witnessing history as it unfolds" (36), and "puts the reader right on the spot of the action" (56; see section 6.3, pp. 182–7). Speeches by characters suggest "unmediated access to the past" (36) and "contribute to making the past of the narrative present" (64; cf. section 6.3, p. 190). Techniques for creating suspense (see section 7.2) help us feel what "the historical agents must have felt" (44). "Sideshadowing" raises the specter of something happening that does not ultimately transpire, and these potentialities put us in the shoes of the characters who do not know what the future holds (14, 45, 69). When a recipient fills in "blanks" about what happened to a character, this act of supplementing "deepens the immersion of the reader" (88). Second-person address to the implied reader "deepens the immersive quality" of a passage (99; see section 6.3, p. 187). A "spatial deixis" that tracks the movement of a character can make "the scene highly graphic" (122). Highlighting ambiguities and uncertainties regarding cause and effect and the course of events recreates for the recipient what it felt like to live through the narrated period

(154–6, 165–7). Recipients can feel themselves addressed when a character addresses in the imperative mood an internal audience: "the blending together of internal and external audiences raises the immediacy of the narrative" (260–1). A conclusion that resists closure "binds the reader into the world of the narrative" (303).

We can approach the topics of immersion and identification in various ways. Nevertheless, I take my inspiration from: Michael Power's 2006 doctoral dissertation, *Transportation and Homeric Epic*, which employs Richard Gerrig's model of transportation (1993) and Melanie Green and Timothy Brock's expansions of that model (2000; 2002) to explore how recipients respond to *Odyssey* 9 and, more precisely, to the "ambiguous" characterization of Polyphemus and Odysseus; from Rutger Allan, Irene de Jong, and Casper de Jonge's 2017 article on the Homeric epics, "From *Enargeia* to Immersion: The Ancient Roots of a Modern Concept," which looks to Ryan's 2001 book, *Narrative as Virtual Reality: Immersion and Interactivity in Literature and Electronic Media* (cf. Clercx 2018); and from five pieces by Rutger Allan that deploy a range of research on immersion from outside classical studies—the work of Ryan features as does that of Green and Brock, of Kaitlin Fitzgerald and Green (2017), of Anneke de Graaf et al. (2012), and of Werner Wolf (e.g., 2013)—to explore immersion (and identification, to a lesser extent) in ancient texts, including the Homeric epics: "Construal and Immersion: A Cognitive Linguistic Approach to Homeric Immersivity" (2019a); "Herodotus and Thucydides: Distance and Immersion" (2019b); "Narrative and Immersion: Some Linguistic and Narratological Aspects" (2020), which studies some passages in the *Iliad* and in Thucydides's *History of the Peloponnesian War*; "Metaleptic Apostrophe in Homer: Emotion and Immersion" (2022a); and "Persuasion by Immersion: The *narratio* of Lysias 1, *On the Killing of Eratosthenes*" (2022b).

I also tip my hat to Jonas Grethlein and Luuk Huitink's article, "Homer's Vividness: An Enactive Approach." To get at how Homeric epic "transports listeners and readers," "captivates the audience," and casts its "spell...on listeners" (2017: 83–4), they leave the friendly confines of classical studies and utilize an enactive approach from cognitive (literary) studies (or more properly an approach from the branch of enactivism called "sensorimotor enactivism" (Ward, Silverman, and Villalobos 2017: 370–2)). In his 2021 book, Grethlein uses the same tools to illuminate the immersive potential of the *paedagogus*'s false report of Orestes's death in Sophocles's *Electra* (2021a: 53–67). Finally, I single out two monographs in biblical studies. Eric Douglass's *Interpreting New Testament Narratives: Recovering the Author's Voice* (2018) constructs an idiosyncratic but detailed model of identification that overlaps in several of its particulars with the empirical studies of identification I will use. Douglass cites publications by Keith Oatley (1994) and Jonathan Cohen (2001), two scholars whose extensive bibliographies feature prominently in my own presentation. In *Identifikationspotenziale in den Psalmen: Emotionen, Metaphern und Textdynamik in den Psalmen 30, 64, 90 und 147* (2019), Sigrid Eder also interacts with early formulations of Werner

Wolf (1993) and Oatley (1994) and makes use of research from still other scholars whose work will appear in what follows, such as Ed Tan (1994), David Miall and Don Kuiken (2002), and Suzanne Keen (2007).

I would urge sticking to the work of researchers in narrative studies. In a chapter that culminates in an analysis of Hermes's arrival on Ogygia in *Odyssey* 5 (2019a), R. Allan turns to Rolf Zwaan's "Immersed Experiencer Framework" (2003; cf. Grethlein 2021a: 102; 2021b: 226-7). As Allan stresses, Zwaan aims to explain how we comprehend language: he does not aim to explain narrative immersion (2019a: 66). This feature of Zwaan's model presumably justifies its application to the study of narrative: if language comprehension is a matter of immersion and we are studying immersion in narratives that involve language comprehension, then we should be looking at research on language comprehension as immersive. I grant that the study of literary texts benefits from the application of embodied theories, such as Zwaan's, of how one processes language. In this case, however, I worry that if we focus on how linguistic activity writ large involves immersion, we lose sight of what is distinctive about recipients' immersion in narratives: as Wolf opines—using aesthetic illusion, his preferred term for what others call immersion—"there is a special relationship between aesthetic illusion and narrative" (2014: section 3.4). To wit, the immersed reader understands that the storyworld is not the real world; this "bifurcation" (Felski 2008: 74) or "twofoldness" (Plantinga 2018: 31) does not concern Zwaan's immersed experiencer.

This attribute of immersion in narratives has important implications. For example, one can speak of temporal immersion. Temporally immersed recipients attend to a character's past, present, and future: they focus on the relationships between events in the character's past to their present circumstances and between events in their present to possible outcomes in the future (Ryan 2015a: 99-106). In keeping with the idea that narrative offers a safe space for emotional (Oatley 2012: 51, 140; Menninghaus et al. 2017; cf. Oatley and Gholamain 1997: 267) and empathetic (Keen 2006: 220; Caracciolo 2016: 42-3, 45; Lesser 2022: 20) engagement—an idea ventured by Plato (*Republic* 605c9-606c9; Halliwell 2005: 400) and discernable in eighteenth-century writers too (Gallagher 2006: 351)— Grethlein reflects on the attraction of temporal immersion (2017a: 52-3; cf. 56):

> They [readers] confront time in the same way as in the everyday world, however, without any pragmatic strains. As in their own lives, readers have re- and protentions and harbour expectations as well as memories. Yet, the memory of what has happened is without the weight it has in real life, the anticipation of what will come without the anxiety of everyday expectations. Narrative permits us to undergo an experience without being directly affected by it. It allows us to experience the force of time and simultaneously keeps it at a safe distance.... Narrative subjects us to, and simultaneously lets us overcome, the force to which

we are exposed in the everyday world.... Readers experience time but free from its real-life implications, notably death.

Temporal immersion brings these benefits. That recipients are not actually in the storyworld and know that they are not enables them to profit from the experience of temporal immersion.

## 1.4. Outline of Chapters

This book contains two parts. Part I addresses identification. I start with identification because identification goes hand in hand with immersion and because the discussion of immersion in Part II at a couple of points builds explicitly on the findings in Part I. This first part comprises Chapters 2 through 4.

The first lengthy section of Chapter 2, section 2.2, uses the aforementioned 2017 article by Allan, de Jong, and de Jonge to begin exploring the components of identification with characters in a narrative. It directs attention to the capacious but granular models of identification crafted by researchers outside of classical studies. Section 2.3 delves deeper into the factors those researchers see operating as triggers for identification, such as the degree to which recipients find characters similar to themselves and the degree to which they deem the narrative realistic. Invoking ancient writers and commentators from Gorgias to Aristarchus, section 2.4 investigates the numerous precedents we find in ancient scholarship for a study of identification. Section 2.5 explains why I am comfortable with the terms "character" and "emotion," why I speak of modern recipients experiencing "emotional identification" with Homeric characters, and what I mean by emotional identification.

Chapter 3 initiates our study of the *Iliad* and lays the groundwork for the close readings presented in Chapter 4. Section 3.2 reviews nine features of the poem as a whole that prompt identification with its characters, from the prevalence of laudatory epithets to the abundance of well-known characters. Section 3.3 examines how Homeric characters enable their interlocutors to identify with the characters in the stories they tell: this move on the characters' part reflects the poet's own efforts to encourage the external audience to identify with his characters.

Chapter 4 studies first identification with mortal characters in four discrete episodes in the *Iliad* (4.2) and then identification with divinities in the *Homeric Hymn to Demeter* (4.3.1) and in two episodes in the *Iliad* (4.3.2 and 4.3.3). These detailed analyses bring out the various ways in which the *Iliad* cues identification with its cast of characters. Section 4.4 considers factors that interrupt the experience of identification or even impede a recipient's ability to identify with a character. These breaks and obstacles allow the recipient to recharge for another round of identification, a taxing endeavor. Section 4.5 rounds off the chapter and Part I by querying the politics of identification: it critiques identification's critics and defenders and asks what recipients get out of the experience.

Part II on immersion comprises Chapters 5 through 8. Chapter 5 provides a point of entry into the subject. Section 5.2 charts how ancient authors and critics, from Hesiod to Longinus, talked about what we call immersion. Section 5.3 offers an introduction to research on immersion in fields outside classical studies, stressing how investigators tease out the distinct components of the phenomenon.

Chapter 6 begins by exploring spatial immersion: the investigation looks at the *Iliad*'s settings, the poem's moveable objects and people, and how it handles switches in location (6.2). This section concludes with an exploration of how the poem's numerous place names help establish the storyworld. Section 6.3 examines spatio-temporal immersion. It tackles the motor resonance triggered in recipients by descriptions of characters' actions and descriptions of the actions of the objects the characters use; moments of internal (embedded) focalization; inclusive forms of address (such as "you"); similes; and different forms of speech presentation, including speech introductions.

Chapter 7 considers emotional immersion. Section 7.2 investigates suspense. It lays out the relevance of different kinds of suspense (how-, when-, what-) to the *Iliad* and then asks what makes those of us with prior knowledge of what will happen feel suspense, pointing to our attachment to characters. The section continues with a discussion of diegetic versus non-diegetic delay as mechanisms of suspense and considers similes from that angle. It closes with a brief comment on so-called metasuspense, wherein a recipient wonders how the teller will keep the story on its proper course. Section 7.3 studies first how the *Iliad* prompts us to feel a range of other emotions by triggering our propensity to judge people (and characters) and second how the poem can get us to feel emotions for ourselves, "not for others" (Ryan 2015a: 108), such as disgust.

Chapter 8 attends to matters of content and form. On the one hand, the *Iliad* immerses us by taking us into the inner lives of its characters (8.2). On the other hand, the *Iliad* immerses us because it prompts us to think about ourselves and brings to mind personal memories; recipients' familiarity with the poet's compositional mechanisms also aids immersion (8.3). Indeed, immersion can arise not only when we are enmeshed in the *Iliad*'s storyworld but also when we attend to the formal features of the poetry (8.4).

The concluding Chapter 9 begins with caveats and speculation. A narrative neither continually immerses recipients nor continually demands that they identify with the characters, and recipients' own traits and attributes influence their degree of immersion and identification. We can make informed guesses about how the Homeric poet's oral performance affected recipients' experience of immersion and identification. About other components of these experiences we can be more confident. Immersed recipients tend not to find fault with the text (counterargue), and immersion and identification have the ability to inform one's ideas and even actions after the reading or viewing experience ends. I reflect on how these factors shape(d) responses to the *Iliad* and then conclude by urging teachers of the *Iliad* to discuss immersion and identification with their students.

People have been listening to and reading the *Iliad* for over 2,500 years. What exactly enables such persistence requires attention (cf. Dimock 1997; Felski 2008: 10–11, 115; 2015: 154–5, 169). The power of the institutions under whose auspices recipients tend to encounter the *Iliad*—from the Panathenaic festival in ancient Athens to departmental curricula in modern universities—and the inertia of those institutions can only account for so much. Nor am I fond of the idea that the *Iliad* contains a set of timeless lessons that every generation needs to learn. Rather, the *Iliad*'s ability to immerse its recipients and prompt their identification with its characters provides a better explanation of its durability.

With that durability in mind, I sometimes try to reconstruct a notional archaic-era audience member's reaction to the Homeric text and I sometimes posit a transtemporal reaction. I toggle back and forth between these endeavors (cf. Budelmann 2000: e.g., 7, 64, 157; Griffith 2015: 27, 48 n. 113). There is equal value in considering how the *Iliad* resonates with ancient and modern audiences.

# PART I
# IDENTIFICATION AND THE *ILIAD*

# 2
# The Study of Identification

## 2.1. Overview

The literature on identification stresses its complex relationship to immersion. One can identify with a character but not experience immersion, and one can be immersed without identifying with a character.[1] For instance, I might at one moment identify with a character by adopting their goals but not simultaneously experience a sense of being present in the world of the tale; conversely, I can feel spatially immersed in a setting that lacks characters with whom to identify.

Nevertheless, points of contact abound. Anneke de Graaf and Lonneke van Leeuwen understand transportation (defined as "cognitive and emotional investment in the narrative") and identification (defined as "cognitive and emotional investment in the character") as two "absorption processes" (2017: 284). Jonas Grethlein avers, "The immersion of the reader can gain force from sympathy with the characters and becomes even more intense in the case of identification" (2017a: 65). Birte Thissen, Winfried Menninghaus, and Wolff Schlotz postulate that absorption and identification "presumably often coincide in fiction reading" (2018: 5). Jacqueline Thompson et al. find that "transportation also correlated with identification" (2018: 212), and Mary Beth Oliver et al. write, "Though these concepts [transportation and identification] are conceptually distinct, their empirical covariance makes them difficult to disentangle" (2019: 193): they are "empirically correlated" in one of their experiments (188; cf. Budelmann et al. 2017: 239, 245; Ma 2020: 867). Indeed, for Helena Bilandzic and Rick Busselle, one first needs to identify with a character before one can enter the storyworld (2011: 34; cf. 2017: 20; Hoeken and Sinkeldam 2014: 937). Conversely, Lena Wimmer et al. suggest, "Transportation is thought to reduce the psychological distance between readers and story characters, which *in turn* facilitates the reader's ability to take the character's perspective, share their emotions, and understand their (inter-) actions" (2021, my emphasis). When Rita Felski links with identification items typically studied under the heading of immersion—"Identifying with a character can also be a matter of cathecting onto a plot, a situation, a mise-en-scène, a setting, a style.... To what extent can an impulse to identify with Thelma

---

[1] Cohen 2006: 186; Felski 2008: 62; Tal-Or and Cohen 2010; Wolf 2013: 12; Bortolussi and Dixon 2015: 532–3; Nabi and Green 2015: 141; Calarco et al. 2017: 300; Cohen and Tal-Or 2017: 139–40; Fitzgerald and Green 2017: 51–2; Grethlein 2017a: 55; cf. Breithaupt 2019: 224.

16  IMMERSION, IDENTIFICATION, AND THE *ILIAD*

and Louise be disassociated from the sublime landscape that surrounds and enframes them?" (2020b: 87)—one again sees the difficulty in separating the concepts. Our investigation of immersion can start with an investigation of identification.

Section 2.2 surveys the components of identification. Section 2.3 delves deeper into the factors that researchers outside classical studies see as triggers for identification. Section 2.4 investigates the precedents we find in ancient scholarship for a study of identification. Section 2.5 wraps up the chapter with comments on the terms "character" and "emotional identification."

## 2.2. The Components of Identification

Homerists have used the term "identification" before. In her study of the *Odyssey*'s Penelope, Nancy Felson considers how audience members might oscillate between "an identification with and sympathy for the humanity of the suitors, on the one hand, and a desire for their death (as an aesthetic closure) on the other" (1994: 111; cf. Kretler 2020: 44–5). Lillian Doherty interrogates what it means as a modern reader, necessarily implicated in various gender and class hierarchies, to identify with, "to adopt the perspective of," Arete or Penelope or Odysseus (1995, quotation from 25). (I return to Doherty's book in section 4.5.) Helen Lovatt explores "the mix of alienation and identification" with victor and victim in the *Iliad*'s battle scenes (2013: 293–302, quotation from 297; cf. 188). Urging attention to "adopting a 'partisan' perspective" as an important component of recipients' "emotional experience," Tobias Myers speaks of recipients' "identifying with the Achaean side of the struggle: that is, feeling the Achaeans' victories and losses to be in some basic sense their own" (2019: 148, 151; cf. 154). (One can compare the following discussion of motivational identification.) Rachel Lesser talks of how in *Iliad* 1 "we may begin to identify with the hero [Achilles], sharing his nascent desires" (2022: 38; cf. 46, 48 n. 5); how we can experience "dual identification" with Hera and Achilles toward the end of that book (67); how in *Iliad* 3 one may experience "sympathetic and empathetic identification" with Helen (94); how during his *aristeia* one may experience "empathetic identification" with Achilles (215); how the meeting of Achilles and Priam in *Iliad* 24 allows us to "comfortably identify with both parties at once" (237); how during the lamentation over Hector in *Iliad* 24 audience members may find themselves "mourning in empathetic identification with the bereaved Trojans" (239). Investigators of other ancient Greek or Roman literatures have used the term as have investigators in still other subfields of classical studies.[2] For instance, contrasting archaic- and classical-era

---

[2] On Greek and Roman literature, see, e.g., Konstan 1999; Köhnken 2003; Bernstein 2004; Feldherr 2010; Gervais 2013; Elmer 2022: 195–7; Frade 2022; van Gils and Kroon 2022: 523 n. 3; Wakker 2022: 320; cf. section 1.3, pp. 6–7.

sculpture, Jaś Elsner writes of the latter's naturalism, "The viewer observes figures in a visual world *like* that which he or she inhabits, and relates to that world by means of identification.... What we look at in naturalistic art...is a world in which we might participate but cannot, to which we relate by fantasy, wish-fulfillment and imaginative contextualisation" (2006: 85–6, emphasis in original; cf. Jurriaans-Helle 2022: 250).

The present exploration will best start from a section on "identification" in Rutger Allan, Irene de Jong, and Casper de Jonge's 2017 article on immersion and the Homeric epics (41–4): the poet "provid[es] readers with a viewpoint within the narrated scene, encouraging them to identify with that viewpoint" (41). They attend to and argue the following:

- addresses to the narratee, as in "but as for the son of Tydeus, you could not determine (*gnoiēs*) whose side he was on" (*Iliad* 5.85);
- embedded focalization wherein "a narrator recounts events as seen and experienced by characters (without turning them into speakers)" (42). When the narrator reports that "swift horses were dragging him [Hector's corpse] ruthlessly (*akēdestōs*) toward the hollow ships of the Achaians" (*Iliad* 22.464–5), the adverb "ruthlessly" reveals Andromache's perspective and "the Homeric listener or reader is supposed to share Andromache's emotional focalization" (42);
- "hypothetical focalization," as in "Then no longer would a man (*anēr*) enter the fray and make light of it, whoever still unwounded by the throw or unharmed by the thrust of sharp bronze should go through their midst, and Pallas Athena should lead him taking him by the hand and check the onrush of missiles" (*Iliad* 4.539–42). To paraphrase, if one should enter the battle at that moment and be lucky enough to remain unscathed with the help of Athena, one would be amazed at the slaughter;
- "scenic narratorial standpoint," wherein the narrator "chooses to position himself on the scene, among the protagonists of the story" (43);
- apostrophe, wherein the narrator addresses a character with a second-person verb form (44). This device should be understood as a type of metalepsis: the extra-diegetic narrator "'enters' the universe of the characters."

In thinking about this list, start from the following. Els Andringa pushes the idea that one can identify "with a story setting or with a theme" (2004: 210–11, 228–9; cf. Keen 2007: 78). Ellen Esrock considers the possibility that a reader can identify with the beam from the lighthouse in Virginia Woolf's *To the Lighthouse* (2019: 280). Section 2.3's discussion of the triggers for identification touches on story setting and, in acknowledging the importance of our personal connections to what happens in a tale, subject matter (Andringa's "theme") as well. Part II's discussion of immersion has more to say about all three items: setting looms large in section 6.2's analysis of spatial immersion; subject matter is again relevant in section 8.3; and section 6.3's presentation on motor resonance will explore the possibility of feeling oneself "inhabit[ing] inanimate objects and other unnatural positions within the narrative" (Esrock 2019: 284). That said, in contrast to Andringa's and Esrock's suggestions, when researchers talk about identification, they are almost always talking about identifying with a human or human-like character in the storyworld.[3]

Note, then, that for the audience of Homeric poetry three of the items on Allan, de Jong, and de Jonge's list—addresses to the narratee, hypothetical focalization (a debatable concept, by the way: see Köppe and Klauk 2013: para. 37), and scenic narratorial standpoint—do not explicitly link us to a specific character at all. We have to do further work to determine how they contribute to identification when we understand identification (as we should) as connection to a character in the storyworld. These three techniques may serve "to stimulate the reader's sense of presence in the story world" (Allan, de Jong, and de Jonge 2017: 41)—that is, they may serve to embed us in the storyworld.[4] The "may" acknowledges the possibility—remote to my mind—that addresses to the narratee and hypothetical focalization remind recipients of their distance from the storyworld (Myers 2019: 50, 104). In any case, it has been suggested in turn that this sort of embedding "helps readers experience the events in the story as if one were inside the story, together with the character thus increasing identification" (Cohen and Tal-Or 2017: 146). These devices make it easier to identify with a character, but more must happen to get us to do so. As Jasper van Vught and Gareth Schott note, our feeling "spatially present" in a storyworld "does not mean we also experience emotions, cognitions or behaviors congruent with the character" (2017: 171). The same limitation applies when we talk about apostrophe's ability to bring characters more immediately before recipients' eyes and thereby connect recipients to the storyworld (de Jong 2009: 95; Allen-Hornblower 2016: 47, 66; Schmitz 2019: 39; R. Allan 2022a: 86). In addition, apostrophe can generate sympathy or "feelings of pity" for the character addressed, as Allan, de Jong, and de Jonge suggest (2017: 44; cf. Allen-Hornblower 2016: 48 n. 130; Schmitz 2019: 39, 46; R. Allan 2022a: 84, 86; Lesser 2022: 106), but neither sympathy nor pity equates to identification (see p. 23). The narrator's addresses to the narratee might increase identification with the narrator (cf. section 2.3, p. 32, on Oliver et al. 2019), not a character, but such addresses are so brief that they probably do not even do that.

Focalization holds more promise. Jonathan Cohen and Nurit Tal-Or note "that people tend to identify more with the character from whose point-of-view the

---

[3] E.g., Schoenmakers 1988: 150; Oatley 1994: 68; M. Smith 1995: 24; Kuiken, Miall, and Sikora 2004: 183–5; Sestir and Green 2010: 276, 283; Felski 2020b: p. xiii, 85.
[4] Cf. Ooms and de Jonge 2013: 103–4; Caracciolo 2014: 163–6; Martínez 2018: 61–9; Gleason 2020: 157; R. Allan 2022a: 86–7; see sections 2.3, pp. 31–2, and 6.2.

story is presented" (2017: 145).[5] This factor can contribute to identification more than similarities between character and recipient can and can even override dissimilarities (Cohen and Tal-Or 2017: 145; Hoeken and Fikkers 2014: 93, 95; Hoeken, Kolthoff, and Sanders 2016 (whence "override" (296)). If we understand focalization to be at the very least in the same family as point of view and perspective (Köppe and Klauk 2013: para. 3; cf. Baroni 2021), we can take focalization to contribute to identification. And if we grant that one word can reflect the focalization of a character—by no means a sure thing (Köppe and Klauk 2013: para. 26)—perhaps the moment of embedded focalization in *Iliad* 22 wherein the narrator speaks of Achilles's dragging Hector "ruthlessly" does enhance the recipient's identification with Andromache.

We must specify, however, that *Iliad* 22.463–5 by itself does not give us sufficient time to identify with Andromache. (I expand Allan, de Jong, and de Jonge's citation by one verse to include 22.463's announcement that Andromache serves as focalizer: "and him she saw (*enoēsen*) being dragged…" (see de Jong 2004: 103).) Cohen writes, "The longer an audience member is exposed to a character, the more likely he or she is to be able to imagine being that character" (2001: 259; cf. Davis 2007: 101; Breithaupt 2018: 56; Douglass 2018: 135; Ma 2020: 871). In the quotation from Cohen and Tal-Or in the previous paragraph, attend to their phrase "*the* character from whose point-of-view the story is presented" (my emphasis): the implication is that recipients identify with protagonists. One is apt to identify with the protagonist in a narrative in part because one spends the most time with them (cf. Farner 2014: 50; Douglass 2018: 139). Keith Oatley observes, "We have to know a person or a character quite well before we start to sympathize with them in their successes" (2012: 31; cf. 163–4): if mere sympathy requires time, so too will identification. One draws a similar lesson from discussions of "allegiance" in film and television studies, allegiance meaning "our allying ourselves with, focusing on, rooting for a character" (Plantinga 2010: 41; cf. 2018: 195; Vaage 2016: 5; Kozak 2017: 5–6; Felski 2020b: 96). Allegiance overlaps with identification (cf. Plantinga 2018: 44), and that allegiance takes time to emerge (Kozak 2017: 6, 20, 59, 69; Plantinga 2018: 143, 200, 202; cf. Vaage 2016: 46, 60) suggests that identification does as well. I do not deny the possibility of identification with secondary characters (but see section 4.4, pp. 128–30). Don Kuiken and Shaun Douglas speak of "alternative perspectives": "the reader identifies with or feels closer to secondary than to primary narrative personae (e.g., usually other characters, but also narrators offering ironic commentary on a primary character)" (2017: 232; cf. Keen 2007: 76, 95; Knox 2021: 152). The point is simply that identification requires time, just as feeling immersed in general does

---

[5] Cf. Plantinga 2009: 107; de Graaf et al. 2012; Farner 2014: 51, 256–7; van Krieken, Hoeken, and Sanders 2017: 4; Douglass 2018: 136; Knox 2021: 151–2; Lesser 2022: 19, 48, 203.

(Wolf 2013: 38). If identification with Andromache arises, it will not be triggered solely by the moment of embedded focalization in *Iliad* 22.463-5. Rather, as section 4.2.2 demonstrates, it arises over the course of *Iliad* 22.437-515 in which Andromache becomes the focal point of the narrative.

These comments lead us to the bigger challenge. One must go beyond the narratologist's concept of focalization to account for most of the components of, and to approach the complexities of, the concept of identification as it is understood and operationalized in other fields. Myers sets us on the right path with his observation that we do not "necessarily...sympathize or 'identify' with those [focalizing] characters in other ways" (2019: 62; cf. M. Smith 1995: 6-7, 95, 144). One might come at this topic by looking to Hans Robert Jauss's chapter titled "Interaction Patterns of Identification with the Hero" in his *Aesthetic Experience and Literary Hermeneutics* (1982: 152-88; cf. Jauss 1974; Ronning 2003: 247-9); to the literary theorist John Frow's *Character and Person* (2014), which takes its cue from Sigmund Freud's ideas about identification, and to still other work with an explicit psychoanalytic orientation, such as that of Vanda Zajko (2006) or Mark Griffith (1999a: 58-66; 1999b, esp. 36-42; 2010; 2015: 28 n. 45, 34, 46-54, 91-4, 104); or to Rita Felski's chapter that, building on Murray Smith's influential model (1995: e.g., 75, 82-4), seeks "to disentangle four strands of identification: alignment, allegiance, recognition, and empathy" (2020b: 94; cf. Plantinga 2018: 195). My investigation looks first and foremost to the rigorous and fine-grained models of identification deployed by other researchers in communications, media studies, and psychology.

For Berys Gaut, "To identify perceptually with a character is to imagine seeing from his point of view; to identify affectively with him is to imagine feeling what he feels; to identify motivationally is to imagine wanting what he wants; to identify epistemically with him is to imagine believing what he believes" (1999: 205), and one can also speak of "empathetic identification" wherein one "share[s] the character's (fictional) emotion" (208; cf. Caracciolo 2016: 39-40). For Oatley, identification arises when "we...take on something of the selfhood of an imaginary character" (2012: 17); more precisely, the recipient "takes on the protagonist's goals and plans" and "experiences emotions when these plans go well or badly" (1999b: 445; cf. 1994: 68-70; Oatley and Gholamain 1997: 268-9; Plantinga 2018: 44). For Cohen and Tal-Or identification occurs "when audience members mentally adopt a character's position within the narrative" (2017: 133): this move involves "the taking on of a character's emotions and perspective and adopting his or her goals." Cohen and Tal-Or elaborate on this definition in their review of the components of identification (2017: 134, emphasis in original; cf. Cohen 2001: 256):

> It consists of three components. The *cognitive component* describes the adoption of a character's view of things and his/her interpretation of events. The *emotional*

*component* describes the adoption of a character's feelings so that we are happy when good things happen to the character and sad when s/he is faced with tragedy. The third dimension is the *motivational component* that describes the adoption of the character's goals. As audience members, identification leads us to share the character's desire to achieve his or her goals and fear their failure.

Now, in running their experiments, most investigators provide surveys to subjects after they have read or watched a narrative (a practice criticized by Gerrig and Bezdek (2013: 106) and Jacobs and Lüdtke (2017: 80) and defended by Bilandzic and Busselle (2017: 22) and Dixon and Bortolussi (2017: 204)). They develop surveys that subjects in their experiments can understand, and these surveys in turn clarify for outsiders, such as myself, what the investigators are actually investigating. For example, adopting statements Cohen and Tal-Or have used or have proposed using on surveys to determine the degree of a recipient's identification with a character in a television show or movie (Cohen 2001: 256; Tal-Or and Cohen 2010: 415; cf. Bilandzic and Busselle 2011: 38–9), Wimmer et al. queried readers' identification with a character in a short story (2021):

> I was able to understand the events in the story in a manner similar to that in which the mother, Marjorie, understood them.
> I think I have a good understanding of the mother.
> I tend to understand the reasons why the mother did what she did.
> While reading the story, I could feel the emotions the mother portrayed.
> During reading, I felt I could really get inside the mother's head.
> At key moments in the story, I felt I knew exactly what the mother was going through.
> During reading, I wanted the mother to succeed in managing her emotions.
> When the mother succeeded I felt joy, but when she failed, I was sad.

In a discussion of the impact of reading narrative fiction, Navona Calarco et al. break down identification into a related set of components (2017: 299; cf. Burke et al. 2016: 21–6):

> Identifying with a character involves theory-of-mind (i.e., understanding the character's emotions), affective empathy (i.e., sharing the character's emotions), as well as cognitive empathy (i.e., experiencing and interpreting the narrative from the character's perspective).

Juan-José Igartua and Daniela Fiuza also speak of cognitive empathy and emotional empathy (cf. Koopman and Hakemulder 2015: 83–4), but their third component of identification is "the temporary loss of self-awareness (the receiver of the narrative imagines being the character, taking on his or her identity, and becoming merged with the character)" (2018: 503).[6] Igartua and Isabel Barrios put together the following questionnaire to query identification with Camino, the protagonist in a film (2012: 520, emphasis in original; cf. Igartua and Fiuza 2018: 510):

> *emotional empathy* ("I felt emotionally involved with Camino's feelings"; "I understood how Camino acts, thinks and feels"; "I understood Camino's feelings or emotions"), *cognitive empathy* ("I imagined how I would act if I were Camino"; "I was concerned about what was happening to Camino"; "I tried to imagine Camino's feelings, thoughts and reactions"; "I tried to see things from Camino's point of view") and the *sensation of becoming the character or merging* ("I felt as if I were Camino"; "I myself experienced Camino's emotional reactions"; "I had the impression of living Camino's story myself"; "I identified with Camino").

In a discussion of video games, Jasper van Vught and Gareth Schott posit three forms of identification (2017: 160) that arise "selectively and independently" (172): perceptual, physical, and affective. In perceptual identification, you see with your eyes solely what the character sees (170). A more capacious understanding of perceptual identification comes from Kobie van Krieken, Hans Hoeken, and José Sanders: "readers ... mentally represent what the character sees, hears, and physically experiences" in response to "linguistic references to a character's perceptions and sensations" (2017: 7). The recipient's mental representation prioritizes but is not limited to what the character sees, hears, or experiences. Physical identification finds one "identifying with visible physical characteristics of a character" (van Vught and Schott 2017: 160), such as "his size, looks, physical position, or physicality of action" (171). Affective identification consists of "an imaginative process of feeling, thinking, and acting on behalf of the character" (160). Here one is dealing with "goals, point-of-view, knowledge, beliefs, and emotions" (168). A subspecies of affective identification is "epistemic identification," wherein players think they "believe or know the same thing about the narrative situation as the character does" (169; cf. M. Smith 1995: 153).

I will neither sort the various kinds of identification discussed here into categories or hierarchies nor try to systematize them into my own idiosyncratic

---

[6] For Slater and Cohen, "the merging of the self with the character" is to be thought of as "following the experience of identification" (2016: 120): merging is a way to think about what happens when one identifies with a character and not a factor that defines identification (cf. Cohen 2014: 144–5; Cohen, Oliver, and Bilandzic 2019). To my mind, merging seems most apt for what happens to players of video games in relation to their avatars (Klimmt, Hefner, and Vorderer 2009). Oatley and Gholamain posit that "escapist reading" engenders "merging" (1997: 280), whereas "a novel that is a work of art" (275) "prevents complete merging" (280). With these scholars' use of the term "merging," one can compare Martínez's use of the cognitive linguist's concept of blending in her analysis of the "hybrid mental construct" formed between reader and character (2018, quotation from 2).

model. Each kind of identification merits analysis in the context of Homeric epic. The close readings presented in Chapters 3 and 4 rely chiefly on Cohen and Tal-Or's categories of cognitive, emotional, and motivational identification because I find them easiest to work with when thinking about the poems. Let me, however, zoom out a bit and note four things that these discussions make clear.

First, one should distinguish identifying with characters from feeling sympathy for characters, liking characters, and, finally, relating to characters. Sympathy surely conduces to identification. If "in sympathy (pity, compassion), the reader covertly expresses concern for narrative personae who are vulnerable or in need" (Kuiken and Douglas 2017: 232), it will be a small step from sympathy to identification. But it is a step nonetheless, and to sympathize is not to identify. For Bussele and Bilandzic (2009: 323; cf. 331; M. Smith 1995: 86):

> an important aspect of sympathy in narrative occurs when an audience member knows something that the character does not, for example, fearing for a character who is ignorant of impending danger. Thus, sympathy is feeling emotions for characters, but not sharing the same emotions.

Emotional identification, understood as feeling a character's emotions, does not come into play. For Raymond Mar et al., to sympathize is to "feel bad for a character whose goals are not being met" but not to "take on these goals and plans as our own" (2011: 824). Motivational identification does not come into play. Next, when these researchers talk about identification, they are not using the term as a synonym for "like." It is true that "character liking is driven by identification" (Raney and Janicke 2013: 159), but liking a character is not the same thing as identifying with the character (Cohen 2001: 253–5; Plantinga 2018: 200; Felski 2020b: 81). Moreover, when these researchers talk about identification, they are not using the term in the way we tend to use it in everyday conversation to mean that we found a character relatable to the extent that they are similar to us.[7] A good amount of scholarship adopts this commonplace understanding of identification with characters as well. When Kimberly Chabot Davis studies identification with characters by viewers of the television show *Northern Exposure* or by recipients of the versions in various media of Manuel Puig's *Kiss of the Spider Woman*, she charts how they track similarities with themselves in a character's gender or sexual orientation or personality traits or political beliefs (2007: 120, 169–75). (Disidentification in Davis's analysis involves contrasting oneself with a character (171–3; cf. Nussbaum 1995: 94 on "the unlikeness that repels identification").) Her point is that because we define ourselves in various ways we can identify with a character when we intersect in one way but not in others: for

---

[7] E.g., M. Smith 1995: 84; Lacey 2002: 102; Davis 2007: 120, 122; Carroll 2011: 165; Halpern 2013: 112, 135; Peretti 2017: 25–6, 29; Holladay and Click 2019: 157.

example, "women may identify with men (or vice versa) because they share other identities (such as race) or ideologies" (Davis 2007: 49); one recipient's "multiple and contradicting identities enabled him to experience a network of identifications with various groups" (174). For Sara Whitely, working with a model from cognitive linguistics known as Text World Theory, identification with characters arises through "acts of comparison and recognition" (2011: 27). For instance, a reader in Whitely's study identifies with a character in a novel because like the character she has recently found herself in a situation in which "someone's not speaking to you" (34). Classicists deploy this equation too. When Vasileios Liotsakis says, "We identify with our beloved protagonists on a moral level" (2021: 10), and speaks of "moral identification" (11), he means that we deem the characters to hold the same values as we do: "these personages adopt an ideological system similar to our own." As we will see in section 2.3, those in communications, media studies, and psychology consider the degree to which similarity prompts identification as they understand it.

Second, instead of tossing out the term because of the imprecise way in which literary and film theorists have tended to deploy it,[8] we should recognize the multifaceted nature of identification and specify which component of identification we have in mind when we talk about identification.

Third (and accordingly), I highlight the varied components of identification: in particular, emotional identification can be a powerful force (cf. Mouffe 2013: 96-7), but it is far from the only kind of identification one can experience (cf. Felski 2020b: 110-11). A useful parallel emerges in Fritz Breithaupt's discussion of empathy. Breithaupt understands identification "as a simple form of empathy" (2019: 139), and his definition of empathy—"the coexperience of the other's situation. Coexperiencing means projecting oneself into another's situation emotionally and cognitively" (16); "coexperience is a psychological phenomenon in which one is mentally transported into the cognitive/emotional/bodily situation of another" (11; cf. 2018: 51)—intersects in its breadth with the definitions of identification reviewed here. Like Suzanne Keen (2007: 27-8), Katja Mellmann (2010: 431), Marco Caracciolo (2016: 39-40), and M. Smith (2017: 182), Breithaupt carefully distinguishes his understanding of empathy from one that boils empathy down to "emotion-sharing" (2019: 10-11, 29; cf. Munteanu 2017: 81-2; Angelopoulou 2020: 41 n. 8; Felski 2020b: 105, 110). So too one should not limit identification to emotional engagement. Just as we feel that a chain of events becomes a story when we encounter a character with a set of goals (Hogan 2011: 83-5), I might single out motivational identification as the *sine qua non* of identification (cf. Plantinga 2018: 32, 83). One of the three conditions that Paul Woodruff posits as necessary for our caring about a character is "that he or she has

---

[8] Cf. M. Smith 1995: 4; Felski 2008: 34; Plantinga 2009: 103; 2018: 194-5; Vaage 2016: 4, 71; Kozak 2017: 5.

a goal, an aim, a passion or a project of some kind" (2008: 104) (and helpful too is Lynn Kozak's reminder that audiences feel engaged when watching a character with a "mission" (2017: 8; cf. 26, 164, 217)), but I look again to Breithaupt for support on this point. Breithaupt asks why it is so hard to identify with Donna Ana in Leopoldo Alas's *La Regenta* (1884/5) and suggests that it is because she "has no goal, not even an implied one" (2015: 448). We will identify with a bad guy, provided they have "a trajectory, outlook, or goal" (449). Those who do identify with Donna Ana, Breithaupt surmises, perhaps "invent fantastic new paths for her" (449): they identify with her because they assign her a goal. Indeed, we assign a character a goal with minimal prompting; we do not rely on the character to articulate a specific goal. If the character is a victim of injustice, we assume they want their situation to change. If the character confronts an obstacle, we assume they want to overcome it.

Still, we do not automatically identify with a character with a goal. We are more prone to do so if the goals are hard to achieve because someone (or something) stands in the character's way (cf. Nussbaum 1995: 90–1; Hogan 2018: 147–8). We need to judge the goal important: we need to determine that success or failure will have a significant impact on the character's life and we need to determine that the character can only achieve the goal in one way (Hogan 2011: 88–9). We also morally evaluate a character's goals. Carl Plantinga rejects the idea that a viewer of Alfred Hitchcock's *Psycho* allies themself with Norman Bates as he tries to do away with the evidence of his murder of Marion Crane (2018: 196):

> Audiences can sometimes root for a character to carry out a task or finish a job simply because spectators are goal-oriented or have completion compulsions. But to claim that most viewers have allegiance with Norman Bates at this point goes too far.... It cannot be the case...that simply because a character does something we have full-blown allegiance to the character.

Just because a character has a goal does not mean we experience motivational identification.

Fourth, the recipient of a narrative who identifies with a character invests a significant amount of cognitive and emotional energy in that character. That the experience of identification is so mentally taxing may explain why it only lasts for a brief period at any one time and "ebbs and flows as the narrative progresses."[9] Recipients are only willing to engage in such a rigorous mental exercise for so long—if we think that "identification...is perhaps under intentional control to some extent" (Kotovych et al. 2011: 264) or even that identification is "a voluntary

---

[9] Cohen, Wiemann-Saks, and Mazor-Tregerman 2018: 507; cf. Cohen 2001: 250–1; 2006: 185; Tal-Or and Cohen 2010: 403; van Vught and Schott 2017: 164; Knox 2021: 18–19; see also Griffith 1999b: 41–2; Whitmarsh 2022: 646.

act," "deliberately initiated" and "can be taught" (Knox 2021: 19, 157)—or perhaps only capable of engaging in such a rigorous mental exercise for so long—if we do not want to treat identification as "a conscious and controllable process" (Tal-Or and Cohen 2010: 404). Compare William Flesch's observation that we like narratives to exhibit "alternations of jeopardy and rescue or security" because we cannot tolerate constant "arousal" (2015: 379). Compare Breithaupt's argument that recipients of fictional narratives may empathize with characters precisely because they know their empathetic experience, requiring mental effort and resulting in self-loss, will come to an end (2019: 92–3, 126, 133, 167–70; cf. M. Smith 2017: 193). Just so, identification ebbs and flows because it demands so much of us and we are only interested in meeting or able to meet that demand for a limited stretch of time. Eric Douglass goes too far when he casts identification as something that persists throughout an entire narrative (2018: 129–32, 141). By the way, the circumscribed and episodic nature of identification mitigates Plantinga's concern (and that of film theorists in general (Vaage 2016: 4)) that, if we say recipients identify with a character, we deny them the ability to "negotiate the contours of the narrative independently of the character and view events in part from the outside" (Plantinga 2009: 106; cf. Woodruff 2008: 176–81). The sporadic and variable nature of identification imparts the distance Plantinga requests from the character. We will have occasion to note in section 5.3 (pp. 154–5) that immersed recipients also remain aware of themselves and keep some distance from the storyworld.

Having completed this survey, let us return to focalization. More precisely, following Tilmann Köppe and Tobias Klauk, let us query internal focalization— "what is said in the text is presented from the point of view of a particular character" (2013: para. 8)—seeing as the most fruitful explorations of focalization writ large concentrate on internal focalization (para. 4). In moments of internal focalization, narrators provide access to a character's assessment or experience of a situation: "internal focalization has something to do with revealing the focal character's beliefs, attitudes, ways of understanding and describing the world" (Köppe and Klauk 2013: para. 34; cf. de Jong 2004: 148).

To the extent that internal focalization reveals what a character sees, hears, or feels, it helps generate the looser sort of perceptual identification wherein we "mentally represent" what the character sees, hears, or feels. It can also help with cognitive identification: "the adoption of a character's view of things and his/her interpretation of events." With these specifications in mind, I can agree with Rutger Allan's comments on *Iliad* 16.104–11, wherein the Trojans pound Ajax with missiles (2020: 23–4):

> Although the scene seems to be primarily focalized by the narrator, there are also indications that the narrator's perspective is at times blended with Ajax' perspective. The use of subjective-evaluative terms such as δεινή ["terrible"] and

κακὸν κακῷ ["evil on evil"] invite us to identify with him and view the events from his perspective.

And I can agree with his comments on Lysias *Against Eratosthenes* 24-6: "by presenting the events consciously from his perspective, Euphiletus effectively encourages the audience to identify with him and his party" (2022b: 295; cf. 2019b: 148; Webb 2016: 213).

Yet in arguing that merely having a window into a character's mind prompts identification, these analyses run two risks. First, they occlude the different forms of identification. I just allowed that access to a character's mind helps generate the looser sort of perceptual identification but purposefully hedged in stating that focalization can help with cognitive identification: just because we are given access to a character's mind does not mean that we adopt the focalizing character's interpretation of events (cf. Allen-Hornblower 2016: 14)—that is, we might not experience cognitive identification. Nor does internal focalization necessarily cue emotional or motivational identification (cf. Davis 2007: 76; Vaage 2016: 5–6, 44; Felski 2020b: 94–5). We can distinguish between focalization and still other forms of identification. When a recipient experiences physical identification with a character's size or looks, their gaze finds those outward components of the character with which to identify. One remains very much in one's own head and body. Furthermore, if I feel like I am doing what a character is doing—one component of that manifestation of physical identification in which we identify with a character's "physical position, or physicality of action" (van Vught and Schott 2017: 171)—that does not mean I have somehow been transported into the character's body. I might feel as if I am experiencing what the character experiences, but that need not mean that I experience it from the character's vantage point. (I return in section 6.2's presentation on motor resonance to this idea of responding to a character's physical movements (cf. Kuiken, Miall, and Sikora 2004: 185).) For its part, the stricter model of perceptual identification—the recipient sees only what the characters sees—differs from focalization in an important way. The tendency of some to speak of focalization as a matter not of who speaks but of "who sees" (Genette 1980: 186; Nünlist 2002: 444; de Jong 2004: 30–1; cf. Wolf 2013: 47; R. Allan 2019b: 142) can make it seem as if when we encounter, say, a passage of internal focalization our vision of the storyworld becomes identical to that of the character: R. Allan writes of internal focalization as involving "a story character or anonymous spectator through whose eyes we are observing the events" (2019a: 63); or one may think, for example, that the adverb "ruthlessly" makes us see through Andromache's eyes what is happening on the plain of Troy. But in moments of internal focalization our vision of the storyworld is neither necessarily nor even likely so limited (cf. Köppe and Klauk 2013: para. 47; section 6.3, pp. 102–3); we neither necessarily nor likely see solely what Andromache sees as we would if we chose Andromache as our avatar in a first-person video game. We do not, in other words, experience strict perceptual identification. One may rather see Andromache seeing Hector (see section 4.2.2).

The second risk of concentrating intently on focalization is that doing so occludes the different factors that elicit identification. Wimmer et al. find that varying the degree to which a short story exhibits internal or external focalization does not affect recipients' experience of identification and suggest looking elsewhere for the forces behind identification (2021). Juan José Igartua and Daniela Fiuza report, "To date, there has been little research into the factors involved in the construction of characters that can increase identification…" (2018: 503; cf. Keen 2007: 93; Cohen and Hershman-Shitrit 2017: 110), but the next section aims to show that the situation is not so dire.

## 2.3. The Triggers for Identification

However obvious, the following point merits explicit declaration at the start. If recipients are to experience identification, the narrative needs to provide them with opportunities to do so (cf. Fernandez-Quintanilla 2020: 138). Analysts can look for those opportunities, opportunities to experience the various sorts of identification, such as cognitive, emotional, motivational, or perceptual identification. I stress that an opportunity is only an opportunity or a cue (cf. van Krieken, Hoeken, and Sanders 2017; Clercx 2018: 44 n. 15; Kuzmičová and Bálint 2019: 439; Webb 2020: 158, 167). Not all recipients will seize or even register every opportunity; not all recipients will follow or even pick up on every cue (cf. Keen 2006: 214; 2007: 72; Plantinga 2018: 89).

I dig deeper into the literature on identification. Similarity is frequently linked with identification (Keen 2007: 94; Chen, Bell, and Taylor 2016: 913–14; de Graaf and van Leeuwen 2017: 275; Kharroub and Weaver 2019: 659), and Cohen and Tal-Or allow that "people sometimes tend to identify more strongly with similar characters as long as the similarity is in ego-relevant domains" (2017: 144). There are several such domains (cf. Cohen and Hershman-Shitrit 2017: 113). To begin with, the ego-relevant domains of "gender or minority status" (Cohen and Tal-Or 2017: 148) or membership in a group, like "sharing a professional affiliation with a character" (141), can contribute to identification (141; cf. Kharroub and Weaver 2019: 664–5, 667). Such demographic similarities may especially enhance identification if the point of similarity is significant for the narrative itself (see Ooms, Hoeks, and Jansen 2019). Yet demographic similarities are not all important: other studies support "the possibility of identifying across identities" (Felski 2020b: 82; cf. Knox 2021: 17, 152–3). Meng Chen, Robert Bell, and Laramie Taylor discerned "no significant effect of protagonist-reader demographic similarity on identification" (2017: 707). Joëlle Ooms, John Hoeks, and Carel Jansen found that gender similarity had no effect on identification and that, although students identified more with protagonists of their same age, adults identified more with younger protagonists (2019). Cohen, Dana Weimann-Saks, and Maya Mazor-Tregerman found no connection between identification and the demographic traits of sex, nationality, age, and place of residence (2018), but they acknowledge the possibility that demographic similarities may have a greater chance of generating identification in the context of short, as opposed to long, narratives (523, 525). As Cohen and Tal-Or note of characters, "If they appeal to us in the narrative world, we may ignore their demographic dissimilarity to us in the real world and still strongly identify with them" (2017: 148; cf. Keen 2007: 70).

Researchers have also contended that recipients gravitate toward characters who share their dispositions and traits. For instance, those disposed to behave aggressively identify with aggressive characters (Eyal and Rubin 2003; cf. Sestir and Green 2010: 283), and those who score high "on the Dark Triad of personality traits (narcissism, Machiavellianism, psychopathy)" identify more with villains than those who do not exhibit these traits (Kjeldgaard-Christiansen et al. 2021). Based in cognitive linguistics, María-Ángeles Martínez's model of storyworld possible selves represents an analogous effort to get at readers' connection with characters (2018). It relies on readers' detecting "relevant matches" (120) between their own self-concepts—comprising self-schemas and possible selves—and their vision, or construction, of a character (19–27, 120). For example, Martínez interrogates her attachment as a teenage reader to the character Cyrus Smith in Jules Verne's *The Mysterious Island* (22):

> I am now aware that some of the matches with Cyrus' construct were with one of my teenage self-schemas as a cool rationalist. Other likely, simultaneous matches were with my adventurer desired possible self, and possibly also a desired, or even self-schema, leader self.

By contrast, Cohen and Michal Hershman-Shitrit conclude, "Viewers did not identify more with characters that had personalities similar to their own" (2017: 121). At best, our subjective perception that a character resembles us in personality—as opposed to more objective assessments of the actual personalities involved—is "associated . . . somewhat with identification" (123).

Similarities in still other domains matter as well if not more. One's attitudes (beliefs, opinions) are especially ego-relevant, and identification can increase if characters hold attitudes held by the recipients.[10] Cohen and Tal-Or write, "Though characters and their actions exist within the text, they are judged based on value systems that viewers and readers bring with them from their social lives" (2017: 148). Lynn Kozak rightly observes, "As we acclimate ourselves to the

---

[10] Cohen 2006: 187; Cohen and Tal-Or 2017: 141; Cohen, Weimann-Saks, and Mazor Tregerman 2018: 524; cf. Caracciolo 2014: 124; Farner 2014: 49; Douglass 2018: 137.

characters' worlds, we form allegiances with those characters not just within *our* moral framework, but also within *their* moral framework. We root for the Iliadic heroes who are good at killing because that is a standard metric of their world" (2017: 18, emphasis in original; cf. Lawrence 2013: 5; Douglass 2018: 137; Plantinga 2018: 196). The trajectory of these sentences aims to get us to recognize the importance of the storyworld's moral framework (cf. section 4.5, pp. 134–5), but Cohen and Tal-Or urge us not to forget about a recipient's moral framework. Both frameworks inform the recipient's reactions (cf. M. Smith 1995: 194–5).

Michael Slater et al. suggest that identification arises when a character "encounter[s] similar situations and conflicts that are relevant to one's [a recipient's] identity" (2014: 449; cf. Hoeken, Kolthoff, and Sanders 2016: 307), and Cohen posits that identification occurs when a narrative introduces subjects of "relevance" that "resonate with viewers' lives" (2006: 185).[11] Wimmer et al. asked participants, "'Reflecting on your own life experiences, how familiar were the events in the story to you?'" (2021). This question gets at what Slater et al. and Cohen talk about, the overlap between events in the story and events that participants have themselves experienced and that they remember because they mattered to them. Wimmer et al. found a significant positive correlation between familiarity and identification (and transportation): "participants who were more familiar with the subject...identified to a greater extent with the character" (2021). To be sure, characters in narratives tend to experience exceptional situations and extreme emotional states (Bilandzic and Busselle 2011: 33; Liebert 2017: 116; Oliver et al. 2017: 260). Nevertheless, audience members are still capable of finding points of contact, similarities, with their own lives. (In fact, for Breithaupt, "momentary feelings of similarity" arise precisely because characters experience extremes: "in these extreme situations all people would feel the same" (2019: 145; differently, Petraschka 2021: 230).)

In the end, the degree to which similarity, broadly construed, prompts identification remains unclear, and a healthy skepticism toward the equation prevails among researchers in this field.[12] One also has to treat with care the element of "character virtue" by which Cohen and Tal-Or mean "positive" attributes like being ethically upright or likeable. Recipients "tend to identify with media characters that are presented in a positive light and as having positive traits" (Cohen and Tal-Or 2017: 143; cf. Hoeken and Sinkeldam 2014; Cohen, Weimann-Saks, and Mazor-Tregerman 2018: 507; Plantinga 2018: 141–2, 195–6). Yet your devotion to your own attitudes affects your response to character virtue. If a character is, for instance, said to be likeable but does not hold the same attitudes as you do,

---

[11] Cf. Cohen and Ribak 2003, esp. 121–2; Hoorn and Konijn 2003: 257, 261, 264; Keen 2007: 79–81; Kharroub and Weaver 2019: 660, 667; Kuzmičová and Bálint 2019: 440.

[12] Cohen 2014: 146–7; Slater et al. 2014: 450; Cohen and Tal-Or 2017: 143; Igartua and Fiuza 2018: 512, 516 (at most "an *indirect* effect," emphasis in original); cf. Eder, Jannidis, and Schneider 2010: 47; Kuzmičová and Bálint 2019: 439, 446.

you are not more prone to identify with them simply because they are likeable (Cohen and Tal-Or 2017: 144). Then too characters need not be entirely virtuous to prompt identification if other components of their presentation work toward that end. Subjects in an experiment identified with a protagonist suffering from cancer regardless of how virtuous she was (Cohen and Tal-Or 2017: 143). We can also identify with villains (Keen 2007: 131–6; Vezzali et al. 2015; Breithaupt 2019: 127; Fernandez-Quintanilla 2020), and we regularly identify with charismatic anti-heroes who transgress accepted norms and act in an immoral way (M. Smith 1999: 232; 2017: 42–3; Vaage 2016; Oliver et al. 2019; Felski 2020b: 86). Some recipients may do so because the villain or anti-hero appears relatively more moral than other characters (Vaage 2016: 47, 127; Plantinga 2018: 195–6) or exhibits valued traits like allegiance to their family (Vaage 2016: 40; Clavel-Vazquez 2018: 205–6; Fernandez-Quintanilla 2020: 136–7; cf. M. Smith 1995: 222); other recipients may do so because, as I noted earlier (p. 29), they share dark personality traits with the character (Kjeldgaard-Christiansen et al. 2021).

Tal-Or and Cohen also query whether discrepancies in knowledge between character and recipient affect identification. They hypothesized that, because identification involves taking on a character's perspective (2010: 407):

> identification should intensify the more the information available to the viewer is similar to the information available to the character. That is, identification should be strongest when the viewer knows what the character has experienced in the past (knowledge that the character is assumed to possess), but does not know what will happen to the character in the future (knowledge the character is assumed to be lacking).

Contrary to their expectation, they found that identification did not decrease when recipients knew more than the character—that is, when recipients were alerted to what the character would do or what would happen to the character (411, 413–14).

Cohen and Tal-Or review as well testimony to the effect that descriptions of what characters look like and of the settings in which the characters find themselves enhance identification (2017: 146). Descriptions of what characters look like at the very least provide an opportunity for physical identification and may encourage other forms of identification. Perhaps the close-up, giving us a good sense of a character's looks, parallels an experience we only willingly have with intimates and leads us to treat the character as an intimate or good friend and respond to them accordingly (Farner 2014: 49–50). It has been suggested, to repeat (see section 2.2, p. 18), that description "of the physical surroundings helps readers experience the events in the story as if one were inside the story, together with the character thus increasing identification" (Cohen and Tal-Or 2017: 146; cf. Davis 2007: 79). In his investigation of virtual reality, Zexin Ma echoes this claim of a link between feeling oneself in the storyworld and identifying with the characters: "users were more likely to identify with the story character when they had a greater perception of sharing the same space with the character" (2020: 880). To talk of being "inside the story" or "sharing the same space with the character" is to talk of spatial immersion. I discuss spatial immersion in section 6.2 and simply note the following at this juncture. A description of a space in a narrative has to be carried out in a certain way to trigger spatial immersion. It cannot be too detailed (cf. Ryan, Foote, and Azaryahu 2016: 29; Grethlein and Huitink 2017: 71), and in fact mention of only a few key items suffices for us to forge an image of the setting. Particularly immersive are descriptions that by way of explicit or implicit references to the human body ease imageability and make the recipient feel in their body what it would be like to be in that space.

Oliver et al. (2019) reaffirm one well-documented point—identification with a character increases the more one spends time with the character ("frequent viewing" (191))—and they offer another, more intriguing conclusion: when a character directly addresses recipients, recipients feel that they have interacted with the character and having had this so-called parasocial interaction identify more with the character. One encounters here a variant on the simpler but still vital proposition mentioned earlier (section 2.2, pp. 18–19), namely "that people tend to identify more with the character from whose point-of-view the story is presented" (Cohen and Tal-Or 2017: 145).

An additional factor, perceived realism, predicts identification as well (Cohen 2001: 259; 2006: 185; Bilandzic and Busselle 2011: 44; Cho, Shen, and Wilson 2014: 833–4, 842; cf. Kuiken and Douglas 2017: 230, 233–4). Perceived realism involves external realism—the narrative matches up with the audience's "actual world experiences or expectations" (Bilandzic and Busselle 2011: 33; cf. Nilsson, Nordahl, and Serafin 2016: 126)—and narrative realism—the narrative adheres to the rules and expectations it establishes itself (Bilandzic and Busselle 2011: 33; cf. 2017: 20; Consoli 2018: 87). Bilandzic and Busselle used the following seven items, taken from a 2004 article by Melanie Green, to query external realism (2011: 37):

The dialogue in the narrative is realistic and believable.
The setting for the narrative just doesn't seem real.
People in this narrative are like people you or I might actually know.
The way people really live their everyday lives is not portrayed very accurately in this narrative.
Events that actually have happened or could happen are discussed in this narrative.
I have a hard time believing the people in this narrative are real because the basic situation is so far-fetched.
This narrative deals with the kind of very difficult choices people in real life have to make.

To gauge narrative realism, they used the following five prompts:

The story was logical and convincing.
It was understandable why the events unfolded as they did.
It was understandable why the characters behaved the way they did.
The actions and reactions of the characters were plausible.
The actions and reactions of the characters were in tune with their personalities.

At the same time, Johan Hoorn and Elly Konijn stress the need for a "mix of realistic and unrealistic features": "the presence of too many realistic features in FCs [fictional characters] may boost boredom" (2003: 253–5, quotations from 254).

For their part, Shira Gabriel and Ariana Young conclude that readers assimilate themselves to the groups featured in novels: "participants who read the Harry Potter chapters self-identified as wizards...whereas participants who read the Twilight chapter self-identified as vampires" (2011: 992). They propose that the need to belong to a group motivates readers to identify with the collectives in the books. I presume that in the case of readers of *Harry Potter and the Sorcerer's Stone* and *Twilight* we are dealing with identifying with a character for whom membership in a group is a crucial part of his identity—Harry Potter, the child wizard; Edward, the vampire—and that identifying with the character makes recipients feel as if they belong to that group too. One can extrapolate that recipients might identify with a character if a prominent feature of the character's characterization is membership in a group.

Before closing this review of the secondary literature on identification, I reference Breithaupt's work on empathy one more time. Discussions of identification should deploy an essential component of Breithaupt's model: side-taking (Breithaupt 2019: 96–103). For Breithaupt empathy arises when a dispute between two parties plays out before our eyes. We tend to take sides at such moments (for any number of reasons (102)); having taken a side, we see the dispute from the perspective of our chosen side and then begin to empathize with our chosen side. I already noted the overlaps between his model of empathy and the models of identification discussed here (section 2.2, p. 24). (I add now that other researchers on narrative empathy, such as Suzanne Keen (2007: 68–81, 93–6), discuss identification with characters.) I suggest that the chance to take a side provides a chance to identify with one's chosen side. Side-taking is yet another potential trigger for identification with a character. (My hedging here is purposeful: transportation can mitigate side-taking (Cohen, Tal-Or, Mazor-Tregerman 2015, esp. 253–4).) I stress the need for a dispute between two parties: recipients can identify equally with more than one character when the characters do not square off against one another (e.g., de Graaf et al. 2012: 811).

## 2.4. Ancient Precedents for a Study of Identification

I will come at the Homeric poems from the perspectives I have outlined in the two previous sections. I am an unabashed clumper, not a splitter (Ready 2018: 191; cf. Liebert 2017: 26–7; O'Connell 2017a: 238), and to my mind the following point made succinctly by Breithaupt necessitates this application: "fiction is so closely linked to identification and empathy that we cannot even imagine a literature without them" (2011: 120; cf. Zajko 2017: 57–8). Homeric poetry may or may not qualify as fiction (cf. Halliwell 2011: 10–12; L. Edmunds 2016: 188–9, 230–1; Myers 2019: 32), but I do count it as literature (although oralists can go on to debate whether oral literature is an apt term (Ready 2018: 22 n. 6)).

Still, we find statements like Christopher Gill's assertion that our "sympathetic involvement" with an Achilles or a Medea does not stem from "identification with a subjectively realized (and powerful) personality" (2002: 173). Gill's target here is the portion in the prepositional phrase—he argues for an "objective-participant," as opposed to a "subjective-individualist," view of personality in the literature of the archaic and classical periods—but the reader swept away by the force of Gill's argument might find themself skeptical of the possibility of identification as well. J. Mira Seo opines, "Perhaps Romans did not read texts to 'identify' with characters in some subjective, Flaubertian mode" (2013: 6), and wants to find a way of "escaping the subjective assumptions of the audience's identification with characters demanded by analogies to the novel" (6 n. 15). Some readers may feel more comfortable with the application I propose if they can be shown some points of contact between the modern research on identification and ancient responses to characters. Moreover, even if one assumes identification (as defined in this project) to be a typical and likely mode of response to the Homeric epics and to countless other narratives, as I am prone to do, one should still provide the concept of identification with a history (cf. Lynch 2015: 12). (Section 5.2 begins to do the same for the concept of immersion.)

Ancient writers and critics point to audience members' propensity to identify with characters: "'Sympathetic' or identificatory reading is often presupposed by ancient authors" (Nünlist 2009: 140 n. 20). In his *Helen*, Gorgias discusses poetry's effect on the audience (9.58–9 Donadi):

> An exceedingly fearsome shuddering and a very tearful pity and a grief desiring longing comes over those who hear it, and at the successes and failures of others' affairs and bodies (ἐπ' ἀλλοτρίων τε πραγμάτων καὶ σωμάτων εὐτυχίαις καὶ δυσπραγίαις), the soul experiences its own experience (*idion ti pathēma*) through the words.

Gorgias does more here than just "ascribe to poetry the capacity to elicit a powerful emotional response" (Grethlein 2017a: 128). One should apply the language of identification (cf. Finkelberg 2006: 69–70; Liebert 2017: 108–9;

Grethlein 2021a: 16). Gorgias's first sentence (up to "those who hear it") can be read to suggest that the fear, pity, and grief experienced by the recipient replicates the fear, pity, and grief experienced by the characters (Grethlein 2021a: 16): the recipient experiences an emotional identification in which they feel the same emotion as the character. The second sentence introduces motivational identification into the equation and suggests a different understanding of the recipient's emotional identification than the first sentence can be read to suggest. Regarding motivational identification, Gorgias asserts that recipients adopt characters' goals and cheer their victories (*eutukhiais*) and bemoan their losses (*duspragiais*) (or root against a character, bemoaning their victories and cheering their losses). Regarding emotional identification, Gorgias distinguishes the emotions we feel (*idion ti pathēma*) from the emotions exhibited by the characters (cf. Cairns 2017: 72; Liebert 2017: 110; Grethlein 2021a: 16). Although presumably not thinking of Gorgias, Keith Oatley provides what comes across as an illuminating paraphrase of Gorgias's sentence (2012: 29; cf. 37, 178):

> We feel the kind of emotions the character would feel in following a plan and entering the situations that result, but as writers and readers, we don't feel the character's emotions. We feel something that is perhaps similar to those emotions, but they are not the character's. They are our own. That's how empathy and identification work in fiction.

For Gorgias (in the second sentence) and Oatley, emotional identification involves feeling emotions congruent with those of the character but not feeling the character's emotions or feeling the same emotions as the character. I return to this distinction in section 2.5.

In Plato's *Republic*, Socrates comments on the impact of Homeric poetry and tragedy: "For the best of us, I suppose, when we listen to Homer or some other of the tragic poets representing someone of the heroes being in torment and presenting a long speech in their lamentations or even singing and striking their breasts, you know that we delight and giving ourselves over we follow along and suffer along with [the characters] (ἐνδόντες ἡμᾶς αὐτοὺς ἑπόμεθα συμπάσχοντες)" (605c9–d4 Slings). Beyond "assigning to verbal representations the capacity to trigger a strong emotional response" (Grethlein 2017a: 129), Socrates speaks of what we term identification (cf. Finkelberg 1998: 187; 2006: 66; 2022: 437; *pace* Halliwell 2002: 78, 81). Recipients experience emotional identification—hence *sumpaskhontes*. Penelope Murray rightly notes that *sumpaskhontes* points to how we "feel the painful emotions of the characters" (1996: 224 at 605d3–5; cf. Grethlein 2017a: 129; Araújo 2018: 76–7) and Carolina Araújo that "the Greeks did have a word for emotional empathy—*sumpáskhein*" (2018: 84 n. 2; cf. Lada 1993: 101–2). Plato does not have sympathy in view here (*pace* Halliwell 2002: 78; Munteanu 2012: 63). One might also align *hepometha* with the looser type of perceptual identification—to repeat, we "mentally represent" what the character sees, hears, or feels—or even with cognitive identification—"to follow" might mean to adopt the character's take on events.

In Plato's *Ion*, the eponymous rhapsode, Ion, declares, "For when I say something pitiable, my eyes fill with tears; and when I say something fearsome or terrible, my hair stands on end from fear and my heart leaps" (537c5-8 Rijksbaron). Douglas Cairns writes, "The experiences he describes are appropriate to the characters portrayed in the poems that he performs.... His recitation involves an element of identification with the poem's characters in their reactions to the events narrated" (2017: 65-6; cf. Lesser 2022: 20). Ion's report that he sees audience members "looking about fearfully" (*deinon emblepontas*) (535e2-3) signals that audience members too can experience identification with the characters (cf. Cairns 2017: 66; Lesser 2022: 20-1). The phrase evokes the retreating Homeric warrior as he anxiously peers about: Ajax "fled looking about" (τρέσσε δὲ παπτήνας, *Iliad* 11.546); Harpalion "drew back into the crowd of his companions, avoiding death, looking about everywhere (*pantose paptainōn*) lest someone graze his skin with bronze" (*Iliad* 13.648-9). Or one could understand Ion to be saying that audience members "look about fearsomely" (cf. *eneblepse deinon*, Plutarch *Life of Pyrrhus* 34.6 Ziegler and Gärtner; *eneblepse te deinon*, Plutarch *Life of Cato Minor* 68.6 Ziegler). If so, the phrase evokes the fearsome visage of the Homeric warrior: Menelaus and Paris enter the space marked out for their duel "looking about fearsomely" (*deinon derkomenoi*, *Iliad* 3.342); Amphimedon describes Odysseus initiating his slaughter of the suitors and "looking about fearsomely" (*deinon paptainōn*, *Odyssey* 24.179). The fearful glances or fearsome aspects that Ion sees in his audience reflect—to use again some of the language of identification discussed earlier—their cognitive and motivational and perhaps even physical identification with the characters he describes.

Mid-twentieth-century commentators on Aristotle's *Poetics* used the language of identification. Donald Lucas suggested that Aristotle's fear is "the suspense caused by apprehended disaster" and that we feel this fear "when we *sink ourselves in the character* and fear for them the things they fear for themselves" (1968: 275, my emphasis; cf. 142 at 53a5). James Hutton wrote, "We do not so directly fear for ourselves, but we have a genuine fear because we see a dreadful thing happening to someone like ourselves, someone with whom we *identify* ourselves" (1982: 95, my emphasis). I build on these comments. Aristotle claims that we feel pity for the one whose suffering we consider undeserved and we feel fear when watching someone who is similar to us: ἔλεος μὲν περὶ τὸν ἀνάξιον, φόβος δὲ περὶ τὸν ὅμοιον (*Poetics* 1453a5-6 Tarán). Our pity may well be inward facing: "one experiences pity when one's state of mind is such as to remember, or to expect, a misfortune like that suffered by another (to have happened/or will happen to oneself or one of one's own, *Rh.* 2.1386a1-3)" (Munteanu 2012: 122; cf. 127). As for our fear, Giovanni Ferrari dismisses the interpretation that it is directed inward toward ourselves (e.g., Munteanu 2012: 72, 136; Rapp 2015: 447). Rather we fear for the hero: we "fear on his behalf" (Ferrari 1999: 195–6; cf. 2019: 166; Halliwell 2002: 217, 217 n. 32). (Ferrari also speaks of "the audience's sympathetic fear for the character or characters that are the focus of their concern" (2019: 151) and of their "sympathetic concern for the characters they care about" (155; cf. 1999: 196).) For instance, "in Euripides' *Iphigenia in Tauris* there remains plenty *to fear on behalf of* brother Orestes and sister Iphigenia as they attempt, and nearly fail, to escape King Thoas and his henchmen, who are in hot pursuit" (Ferrari 2019: 152, my emphasis). To translate into the language of identification (cf. Finkelberg 2006: 64), our fear or concern for characters stems from our motivational identification with them. We want them to succeed, and we fear they may not. (I will return to the need for the character to be similar to us momentarily.) One might cite as well Aristotle's statement that a tragedy's chorus should "share in the struggle" (*sunagōnizesthai*, *Poetics* 1456a25–7): built into the verb, the noun *agōn* "suggests *agōnia*, the tension and anxiety that a chorus (and an audience) share with the main agents of the drama" (Mastronarde 2010: 150). Aristotle's statement, admittedly opaque (Visvardi 2015: 94–7), may point in a roundabout fashion to recipients' emotional identification with the characters, to sharing their "tension and anxiety." The *Art of Rhetoric* returns us to firmer ground: Aristotle speaks of the listener who "experiences the same emotion as (*sunomoiopathei*) the one speaking in a pathetic fashion, even if he says nothing of significance" (1408a23–4 Kassel). An orator's audience can experience emotional identification with the speaker (cf. González 2013: 535–6).

The bT scholion at *Iliad* 7.479 (Erbse) suggests that, with a description of Zeus's thundering ominously, "the poet rouses the reader beforehand and makes him feel anxious (*agnōnian*) in view of the future events" (trans. Nünlist 2009: 140). Nünlist adds, "The critic expects him [the reader] to feel an agony (ἀγωνία) similar to the one felt (presumably) by the characters themselves" (140). A T scholion at *Iliad* 23.382 makes the equation explicit in commenting on the verse "and now he [Diomedes] would have passed him or would have put the result in doubt": "he [the poet] makes the spectators share in the anxiety with them (*sunagōnian autois*)." The *autois* are the characters themselves (cf. Grethlein and Huitink 2017: 77). A scholion at *Odyssey* 4.184a1 (Pontani)—wherein Helen, Telemachus, and Menelaus weep in response to the thought of Odysseus's having lost his homecoming—posits that the poet has assigned the reaction he triggers in the audience to the characters (Nünlist 2009: 149). Nünlist extrapolates, "This note spells out what others on occasion presuppose: the reader is meant to feel the same emotions as the text-internal audience.... This may well apply to the numerous scholia that describe the characters' πάθος ('emotion')" (2009: 149; cf. Manieri 1998: 87–8). These ancient commentators note chances for emotional identification.

Demetrius discusses Ctesias's handling in his *History of the Persians* of the messenger speech in which Cyrus's mother, Parysatis, learns of the king's death

(*On Style* 216 Marini; cf. Otto 2009: 84–5; Ooms and de Jonge 2013: 105–6; Novokhatko 2021: 35–6). Because the messenger does not disclose his death right away, Ctesias "throws both the mother into torment and the hearer," or in Doreen Innes's more evocative translation, "stirred the mother's anguish, which he made the reader share" (1995: 475): καὶ τὴν μητέρα εἰς ἀγωνίαν ἐμβαλὼν καὶ τὸν ἀκούοντα. This passage, Demetrius says, exemplifies the need for "keeping the reader in suspense and forcing him to share the anguish" (trans. Innes: κρεμνῶντα τὸν ἀκροατὴν καὶ ἀναγκάζοντα συναγωνιᾶν).

In a point directed at all genres and speakers (Halliwell 2021: 480 at 24–5), Longinus finds that the proper arrangement of material "leads the existing emotion of the speaker into the souls of the ones nearby and always puts the listeners into a state of sharing it [the emotion]" (τὸ παρεστὼς τῷ λέγοντι πάθος εἰς τὰς ψυχὰς τῶν πέλας παρεισάγουσαν καὶ εἰς μετουσίαν αὐτοῦ τοὺς ἀκούοντας ἀεὶ καθιστᾶσαν, *On the Sublime* 39.3 Halliwell). He cites Demosthenes's use of asyndeton and anaphora in describing a physical assault: "through these [words] the orator does nothing other than what the one striking does: he strikes the mind of the jurors with blow upon blow" (οὐδὲν ἄλλο διὰ τούτων ὁ ῥήτωρ ἢ ὅπερ ὁ τύπτων ἐργάζεται· τὴν διάνοιαν τῶν δικαστῶν τῇ ἐπαλλήλῳ πλήττει φορᾷ, 20.2). Longinus might mean that the orator strikes the mind (*dianoian*) of the juror just as the attacker physically strikes the victim. It could, though, be the case that *dianoia* applies to both victim and juror. The attacker inflicts not only physical pain but also emotional distress on his victim, and the orator, although he cannot inflict physical pain on the juror, can structure his sentences so as to make the juror feel the same emotions as the victim (cf. de Jonge 2020: 157; Huitink 2020: 207). Longinus selects Ajax's prayer to Zeus at *Iliad* 17.645–7 to exemplify Homer's ability "to enter into [or step inside] (*sunembainein*) the state of mind of heroic greatness" (9.10; trans. Halliwell 2011: 360). He writes of the prayer, "The emotion (*to pathos*) is truly that of Ajax" (trans. Halliwell 2011: 361). Stephen Halliwell teases out the point: not only is Homer able "to emotionally participate in the moments of heroism he enacts" but readers too "feel Ajax's emotions reverberating in themselves" (2011: 363; cf. 2021: 305 at 40–2). Elsewhere, Longinus says that the poet aims to generate *eklplēxis* in his audience through *phantasia* ("mental image") (15.2). One can understand the term *ekplēxis* "to consist in a largely spontaneous (even irresistible), close emotional identification with the represented characters" (Huitink 2019: 187).

Plutarch praises Thucydides for making his readers feel the emotions of "amazement and consternation" (ἐκπληκτικὰ καὶ ταρακτικὰ πάθη) felt by those who originally witnessed, say, a battle (*The Glory of Athens, Moralia* 347a–c Nachstädt).[13] He lauds Xenophon's portrayal of the battle of Cunaxa for "always

---

[13] See Zanker 1981: 311; Grethlein 2013: 1–2, 30; LeVen 2014: 197; Sheppard 2014: 29–32; O'Connell 2017b: 144–5; Gleason 2020: 176–7; Rood 2022: 391.

making the hearer affected by (*empathē*) and equally engaged (*sugkinduneuonta*) in the actions, as if the actions were not in the past but in the present" (*Life of Artaxerxes* 8.1 Ziegler and Gärtner)—that is, for prompting the same emotions in the reader as the actual fighters felt (Sheppard 2014: 32; cf. Grethlein 2013: 54; Huitink 2020: 189). Proclus writes, "Many cry along (*sundakruein*) with Apollodorus [in Plato's *Phaedo* 117d3–6] as he wails aloud and with Achilles as he laments his friend and at such a great interval of time experience the same things (*ta auta paskhein*) as those present then" (*Commentary on the Republic of Plato* K164.2–5 Lamberton). Anonymous scholiasts contend that Demosthenes makes the audience feel the same fear and grief that he felt upon traveling through the devastated land of the Phocians (*On the Dishonest Embassy* 19.64–5; O'Connell 2017b: 131–7). Again, these authors and commentators discuss what we can label emotional identification.[14]

I cited Araújo's gloss of *sumpaskhein* as "emotional empathy" (2018: 84 n. 2), and we saw other *sun-*prefixed compounds (*sunomoiopathei, sunagōnizesthai, sunagōniān, sugkinduneuonta,* and *sundakruein*) that point to emotional identification. Additional such compounds in references to proper forms of social interaction—that is, not just references to audiences—attract our notice because they too gesture toward a shared emotional state (cf. Angelopoulou 2020: 48–9). Menelaus's slave in Euripides's *Helen* declares, "He is evil whoever does not reverence the things of his master and delight along with him (*xuggegēthe*) and suffer evils along with him (*sunōdinei kakois*)" (726–7 Diggle; cf. Aeschylus *Agamemnon* 787–93). Conversely, for Xenophon, the ruler should identify emotionally with his subjects: "But to be evident in rejoicing along with them (*sunēdomenon*) if some good should befall them, in grieving along with them (*sunakhthomenon*) if some evil..." (*The Education of Cyrus* 1.6.24.5–6 Marchant; trans. Ambler; cf. Xenophon *Symposium* 8.18.4–6). Plato speaks of a city—a collective of citizens—feeling the same pleasure and the same pain as anyone of its citizens (καὶ ἢ συνησθήσεται ἅπασα ἢ συλλυπήσεται, *Republic* 462e2; cf. Herodotus 6.39.2 N. Wilson (*sullupēthēsomenoi*)). In the *Nicomachean Ethics*, Aristotle notes one definition of a friend: "the one who is pained along with and delighted along with the friend" (τὸν συναλγοῦντα καὶ συγχαίροντα τῷ φίλῳ, 1166a7–8 Bywater). In the *Eudemian Ethics*, he speaks of a friend (*philos*) as one who feels at the same time (*sullupeisthai*) the same pain (*tēn autēn lupēn*) as another (1240a37–8 Susemihl). The Chorus in Euripides's *Alcestis* declares: "and

---

[14] I select one famous example from Latin literature. Horace writes, "If you want to make me weep, first must you yourself feel grief (dolendum est / primum ipsi tibi): then your misfortunes will pain me (tum tua infortunia laedent), Telephus or Peleus" (*Art of Poetry* 102–4 Shackleton Bailey). The actor playing Telephus or Peleus must work himself up into the appropriate emotional state so as to engender that same emotional state in the audience, but the direct address to the character—"Telephus or Peleus"—makes clear that the audience member feels an emotional affinity with the character, not the actor (see Rudd 1989: 168 at 103–4).

indeed I will bear along with you (*soi .../ sunoisō*), as a friend for a friend, a grievous pain for this woman" (369–70 Diggle). One could look beyond *sun*-prefixed compounds and beyond discussions of proper forms of social interaction: the Chorus of Sophocles's *Philoctetes*, for example, refers to a groaning in lament that prompts a groaning in lament in response (*stonon antitupon*, 693 Schein), and when Philoctetes wishes that Odysseus might feel his physical pain (*algēsis*, 792), Neoptolemus responds that he shares his mental, if not physical, anguish: "I have long since been in pain (*algō palai*), groaning for your evils" (806; cf. Visvardi 2015: 196–7). These passages along with several I have quoted in the previous paragraphs problematize Cairns's claim that "ancient Greek texts...make no grand claims about feeling what other people feel," that there is a "general emphasis of ancient Greek aesthetics on sympathy over empathy, on feeling for rather than feeling with" (2017: 73). Nonetheless, even those who favor Cairns's view and do not wish to speak of emotional identification when it comes to ancient Greek texts can find support for exploring identification from a number of other angles in the passages quoted in this section: ancient authors point to more than just emotional identification.

We can also attend to ancient scholarship's interest in factors that modern researchers see contributing to identification. I focus on two: similarity and perceived realism. In Plato's *Republic*, Socrates contends that most people cannot identify with a character marked by a "prudent and calm disposition": such a disposition is "neither easy to imitate nor when imitated easy to understand" because "the imitation becomes that of a state foreign" to the typical audience member (604e2; see Liebert 2017: 144–5). By contrast, the poet who aims at popularity depicts both "a conflicted disposition that the masses can relate to" and a range of dispositions so that "different members can identify with different characters" (Liebert 2017: 145). Put differently, recipients look for characters with similar dispositions as they themselves possess.

In his *Poetics*, Aristotle avers that artists depict characters who (1448a4–14; trans. Halliwell 1995 adapted):

> are better than we are (βελτίονας ἢ καθ' ἡμᾶς) or worse or even of the sort (that we are), such as the painters: for Polygnotus depicted better people, Pauson depicted worse people, and Dionysus depicted those like ourselves (*homoious*).... Homer represented better people, Cleophon those like ourselves (*homoious*), Hegemon of Thasos (the first composer of parodies) and Nicochares (author of the *Deiliad*) inferior characters.

Like epic poets, tragedians depict characters who are better (*beltious*) than people alive today (1448a16–18). But tragedians should also depict characters to whom we feel similar. For, to repeat, we feel pity for the one whose suffering we consider undeserved and we feel fear when watching someone who is similar to us: ἔλεος μὲν περὶ τὸν ἀνάξιον, φόβος δὲ περὶ τὸν ὅμοιον (1453a5–6). Aristotle defines this "similar" character: "the sort who neither excels in virtue and justice nor falls into misfortune on account of baseness and depravity" (1453a8–9). Recipients react, then, to characters whom they deem similar to themselves. Similarity does not mean a complete overlap (cf. Konstan 1999: 2–3). Recipients can deem similar to themselves a character whom they recognize is better than they are. This assessment shows they do not need to think that they resemble the character in all particulars to deem that character similar to themselves. Compare Aristotle's observation in his *Art of Rhetoric* that similarity can be a matter of "age, ethos, habits, position, or family" (κατὰ ἡλικίας, κατὰ ἤθη, κατὰ ἕξεις, κατὰ ἀξιώματα, κατὰ γένη, 1386a25–6) (cf. Halliwell 1986: 159–61; 2002: 229–30). Two people do not have to be similar in all regards to be considered similar. Recipients can be moved by the fate of characters who are not completely like them.

Plato's and Aristotle's positioning similarity as necessary for engagement with a character intersects with modern researchers' investigations into the role of similarity in identification. Similarity can aid identification. It can arise in any number of domains: recipients do not seek a complete overlap when considering if a character is similar to themselves. They do not need to find a character in every way similar to themselves to identify with that character. Yet one can go a step farther. If for Aristotle fear only arises in the context of our encounter with a character similar to ourselves and if we posit, as I did earlier (p. 37), that Aristotle's fear indicates a form of motivational identification, then Aristotle's discussion presages the contention that similarity contributes to the experience of identification.

Ancient critics were also concerned with what we have labeled perceived realism (which, one will recall, comprises external and narrative realism (section 2.3, p. 32)). In *Poetics* 1454a16–28, Aristotle lays out his rules for characters. Characters should be appropriate (*to harmottonta*): they must behave like one who belongs to the demographic to which they belong (Schironi 2018: 427–8). Characters should be similar (*to homoion*): "the audience has to recognize the character as someone similar and comparable to people from their own experience" (428). Audiences will compare characters either to people in their own lives or other characters they have encountered (427–8). Lastly, characters should be consistent (*to homalon*): as the plot unfolds, their actions should be consistent with one another (427–8). Aristotle then treats plots as a whole in the same way: as with characters, so too when it comes to plotting the poet "must always seek either what is necessary or what is probable, so as for a person of such a kind either necessarily or probably to say or to do things of such a kind and for one event to follow after another event either necessarily or probably" (1454a33–6). Francesca Schironi paraphrases: "A plot must consist of a necessary or probable sequence of events" (2018: 418). Moreover, possibility is not the top priority; believability is: "One should choose the impossible but probable over the possible but unbelievable" (*Poetics* 1460a26–7; Schironi 2018: 419). As for what constitutes the believable in Aristotle's framework, "something is believable if it follows from what has been stated before as a logical consequence" (Schironi 2018: 419); it does not matter "how the plot in itself corresponds to truth in the real world" (420; cf. Halliwell 2011: 211–21). Aristotle notes that epic poets have an advantage over tragic playwrights in this regard: the poet can portray the irrational (*to alogon*)—an essential component of the sought-after marvelous (*to thaumaston*)—because recipients of epic, unlike spectators in a theater, do not actually see the one doing the irrational thing (*Poetics* 1460a11–17).

The scholiastic commentary on the Homeric epics reveals other critics' engagement with these issues (cf. Nünlist 2009: 27 n. 16, 175 n. 3, 249 n. 41, 252 n. 53). Interpreters praise the poet for including realistic vignettes in which characters do things one would expect someone in such a situation to do. In a "true to life" (*biōtikos*) manner, Dione comforts, as parents are wont to do, her daughter Aphrodite after Diomedes wounds her (bT scholion at *Iliad* 5.370–2; Nünlist 2009: 279; cf. Feeney 1991: 49). Homer does well to have Astyanax recoil from the fully armed Hector: the poet "takes this from life" (λάβων δὲ τοῦτο ἐκ τοῦ βίου, bT scholion at *Iliad* 6.467; Manieri 1998: 182; Nünlist 2009: 190; cf. 151). Elsewhere the scholiasts highlight "characters who are true to life or display a behaviour which is typically human": "Achilles' behaviour is typical of a man in love..., Hector's of a peevish person... or of human behaviour in general. Paris' speech is that of a lewd and shameless person..." (Nünlist 2009: 252). In a twist on this logic, a scholion defends Achilles's lamentation for Patroclus on the grounds that "these things were customary in life then (*tōi tote biōi*)" (A scholion at *Iliad* 18.22–35a): Achilles's behavior was realistic in an earlier age (cf. Grethlein 2021a: 129). At the same time, the poet could take advantage of poetic license to depart from what we would deem realistic. A bT scholion at *Iliad* 21.269a asks, how is it that Achilles alone seems to be threatened by the flooding of the Scamander—what about all the other soldiers? The answer: "It is acceptable since it is in poetry" (Nünlist 2009: 177–8; cf. Feeney 1991: 38; Grethlein 2021a: 129).

Commentators also demanded that characters "show some consistency.... Critics either praise such consistent characterization or criticise inconsistency" (Nünlist 2009: 249–52, quotation from 249). They monitored the coherence of the plot too. The *Iliad* poet did well to have all the best Achaeans wounded and momentarily removed from the fighting before the Trojans throw fire on their ships: "because it would have been absurd (*atopon*) to set the ships on fire with them present" (bT scholion at *Iliad* 11.407–10; trans. Nünlist 2009: 25). In general (Nünlist 2009: 28):

> the Homeric scholia tend to focus on the connection between two specific passages in the text, one of which motivates the other. The former passage as it were provides the logical preparation for another passage, which is to follow later. This connection between the two passages establishes and is proof of the narrative coherence of the text under consideration.

For instance, Apollo is alone made to remain behind on the Trojan plain after the gods fight one another in *Iliad* 21 so that he can keep Achilles away from the city and prohibit the Greeks from taking Troy too soon (T scholion at *Iliad* 21.515-17; Nünlist 2009: 28-9). Another way the poet achieves coherence in plotting is by introducing a character early on if that character will play a significant part later: hence the poet mentions Patroclus as being in Achilles's company at *Iliad* 1.307 (bT scholion at *Iliad* 1.307b; Nünlist 2009: 55), and "Eurycleia is carefully introduced because she will play an important role in various scenes [scholion at *Odyssey* 1.429a Pontani]" (Nünlist 2009: 55).

Schironi zeroes in on Aristarchus's comments on these matters (2018: 429; cf. 495):

Following Aristotle, Aristarchus argued also for consistency and credibility of ἦθος: characters (usually called πρόσωπα in the scholia) should behave according to what is appropriate (τὸ ἁρμόττον), suitable (τὸ πρέπον), and proper (τὸ οἰκεῖον).... Characters were ἁρμόττοντα if they behaved as their social position, their status, their age, their present situation, or their 'mythical model' required.

With these strictures in mind, Aristarchus athetized—deemed un-Homeric but did not delete (Schironi 2018: 446; Ready 2019a: 242)—verses that he thought unsuitable for a character to speak: "It is unacceptable, for instance, to have Agamemnon dwelling on the pleasure he is going to enjoy from Chryseis back in Argos [*Iliad* 1.29-31]" (Schironi 2018: 430); at *Iliad* 8.423, Iris should not call Athena, her superior, a "shameless dog" (476); at *Iliad* 15.147-8, Hera should not tell Apollo and Iris to do whatever Zeus orders since "Zeus' orders are against her interest" (459); at *Iliad* 24.130-1, Thetis should not tell Achilles to have sex, a suggestion inappropriate for a mother to make to her son (488); at *Odyssey* 4.163-7, Peisistratus's speaking in maxims, a genre unsuitable for young men, does not jibe with his being a young man (432-3); it is strange for Alcinous to propose a marriage between Odysseus and Nausicaa (*Odyssey* 7.311-16) when he still does not know who Odysseus is (432).

Regarding plot, Aristarchus also allowed for "elements that are absurd (ἄλογα) from a rational point of view," attributing them to "poetic license" (421; cf. 443, 463; cf. Nünlist 2009: 180), and concerned himself not so much with what was possible as with what was believable and probable (Schironi 2018: 420-4). This concern prompted athetesis as well. At *Iliad* 23.810, Achilles would not invite solely Ajax and Diomedes to a feast, prioritizing them over all the other contestants in the funeral games for Patroclus (462). Odysseus could not have seen some of the shades he claims to have seen in *Odyssey* 11 because they were in Erebus and he never even entered Hades (424). In keeping with this interest in the believable and probable, Aristarchus also monitored the internal consistency of the epics' plots (425, 463). The Achaeans cannot be said to "marvel at his [Odysseus's] words" at *Iliad* 9.694: that phrase designates "the astonishment of an audience that has just heard a striking speech by someone in a position of power," but the speech that precedes the reaction at 9.694 "has no particular authority or strength" (481); the line warrants athetesis "because it is inconsistent with its context." When Poseidon removes Achilles's spear from Aeneas's shield (*Iliad* 20.322-4), the poet contradicts his earlier description of the spear's trajectory: it passes through Aeneas's shield and fixes in the ground (20.274-81) (454).

Schironi concludes (494; cf. 728):

> Aristarchus was obsessed with internal inconsistencies of every kind: in narrative, characterization, language, and style.... He would have been especially sensitive not only to internal contradictions, but also to any element which would go against what he had established to be the "Homeric usage"—both in terms of language and also in terms of content, from depicting suitable and consistent characters to avoiding unfitting "thoughts" and details.

Whereas the reader of a modern work of literature would, if so inclined, attribute any flaws in these areas to slips on the author's part, Aristarchus attributed them to generations of interpolators who marred Homer's original (and perfect) written text (484-92, 495, 736-7).

One could lengthen this survey by looking at still other ancient critics. Dionysius of Halicarnassus, for example, praises Lysias for having his characters (*prosōpa*) speak in the manner appropriate (*oikeias*) to their "age, family background, education, occupation, way of life" (*On Lysias* 9.6-8 Usher; trans. Usher 1974). Plutarch deems poetry that combines the false with the plausible (*memigmenon pithanotēti pseudos*) capable of generating amazement and pleasure (*How to Study Poetry, Moralia* 16b Hunter and Russell). But the material reviewed here suffices for my purposes. What I stress is that ancient criticism's prescriptions and proscriptions overlap neatly both with the distinction that researchers suggest recipients make between external and narrative realism—above all, the ancient scholars grant that things that cannot happen in our world can happen in narratives—and with the criteria that researchers suggest recipients use to evaluate external and narrative realism. I list several quoted earlier (section 2.3, pp. 32-3):

> The dialogue in the narrative is realistic and believable.
> People in this narrative are like people you or I might actually know.
> It was understandable why the characters behaved the way they did.
> Events that actually have happened or could happen are discussed in this narrative.
> The story was logical and convincing.
> It was understandable why the events unfolded as they did.
> The actions and reactions of the characters were in tune with their personalities.

## 2.5. Character and Emotional Identification

Before I turn to the *Iliad*, I should address what I imagine will have become matters of ever-growing concern for some readers, especially after the historicizing efforts of the previous section: my uses of the word "character" and the term "emotional identification."

I may be accused of nonchalantly tossing around this word "character." Does not that term require a vigorous contextualization? Here is my response. One can follow Uri Margolin in defining a character as "any entity, individual or collective—normally human or human-like—introduced in a work" (2007: 66; cf. De Temmerman 2014: 6; Felski 2020b: 80). From here one can (and should) explore what "individual" and "human" and related words like "person" and "self" mean and what they mean in different cultural contexts (cf. M. Smith 1995: 21; Frow 2014: 71; Felski 2020b: 89). I will not get involved in a discussion of Homeric individuality or person- or self-hood other than to say that our ability to talk about Homeric characters as, for instance, subject to learned helplessness (Christensen 2020: 47–85) or capable of ruminating (Cuypers 2002/2003: 124; Ione 2016: 45; Christensen 2020: 80; cf. A. Anderson 2019) suggests to me a degree of overlap between Homeric and modern conceptions. The important things here are that, whatever definitions (of "individual" and "human" and related words like "person" and "self") one employs and however similar to or different from one's own the definitions of those terms end up being in a specific context, one will not have altered one's definition of a character and one will still be able to say that characters can exhibit points of view on the storyworld, display emotions, and have goals—the three attributes I find most useful for a discussion of identification. They do so from the perspective of Murray Smith's "person schema," which includes, among its seven items, "perceptual activity, including self-awareness"; "emotions"; and "intentional states, such as beliefs and desires" (1995: 21). They do so from the perspective of Richard Sorabji's model of the self, with its attention to a "first-person perspective" (an "I" or a "me") and to the ownership of "psychological states" (2006: e.g., 20–30, quotations from 21–2; cf. 2008). They do so in Christopher Gill's discussions of the ancient objectivist-participant conception of personhood, as exemplified in the following statements: "... Achilles's rejection of the gifts as depending on ethical reflection about the proper goals of a human life" (2002: 125); "the three men appealing to Achilles, though using differing modes of psychological discourse, all presuppose that his emotions are informed by his beliefs and reasoning" (191). And they do so in Michiel Verheij's reconciliation of Sorabji's and Gill's positions: for example, he aims to explain "Medea's motives" and concludes, "What makes Medea such an exceptional figure is not the social code she adheres to, but her unique interpretation of this code" (2014: 190–5). One draws the same lesson from Andreas Zanker's chapter titled "Conceptual Metaphors for Mind, Intention, and Self in Homer"

(2019: 165–200), wherein a discussion of the pros and cons of Bruno Snell's influential model of Homeric concepts of mind and self does not derail his investigation into characters' thoughts and intentions in the epics, and from Mark Griffith's comments on Sophocles's heroine Antigone: "We don't have to hold any particular view as to the inherent wholeness or constructedness of her 'subjectivity', nor of her status as a unified personality, to be able to speculate and form opinions as to her (imagined) state of mind and desires" (2010: 113).

Similarly, what goes into making a character, what types of characters are out there, and what techniques of characterization are available or favored vary based on time and place (Gorman 2010). One should be on the lookout for distinctive features of ancient Greek practices regarding character and characterization (De Temmerman and Emde Boas 2018: 6–11) while simultaneously not fetishizing difference: "Granted the importance of historicizing the concept of character, the fact is that contemporary theorists tend wildly to overrate historical variability" (Gorman 2010: 174; cf. Zajko 2017: 61–4). I leave it to others to operationalize the scholarship on such distinctions because I prioritize a different set of differences. I am not interested in differentiating between Homeric and modern characters so much as I am interested in deploying and even developing various means of studying the various characters in the epics. The Homeric poems give us different sorts of characters whom we have to approach carefully with specific interpretative tools in hand, but these characters are not *sui generis*. I have, for instance, found it profitable to examine the numerous minor characters in the *Iliad* from the perspectives offered by Alex Woloch's study (2003; 2006) of minor characters in the realist novels of Jane Austen, Charles Dickens, and Honoré de Balzac (Ready 2020). Likewise, as I will discuss in sections 3.2 (pp. 60–1) and 4.3 (pp. 114–15), the concepts of transtextuality and plurimediality help one understand many Homeric characters, but those concepts come from the study of modern characters.

The concept of emotional identification requires a bit more unpacking too. In the first place, the word "emotion" suffices for my purposes (cf. Ready 2019a: 268). I make two subpoints in this regard. One, defining emotion is not an easy task (cf. Cairns and Fulkerson 2015: 1; Cairns 2016: 15–16). Patrick Hogan's "a relatively short-term motivational impulse" works (2018: 42), and critically a narrative's recipient can be said to experience an emotion even if they cannot respond to that motivational impulse by performing an action in the storyworld (Woodruff 2008: 162–4; cf. 155). Two, important discussions of emotional responses to literature place emotion in the category of affect. Charles Altieri divides affect in four: feelings, moods, emotions, and passions (2003: 2, 48; cf. Liebert 2017: 114). Building on Nico Frijda and Klaus Scherer's definition (2009), Hogan divides affect in six: emotion (or, more properly, emotion episode), mood, attitude, interpersonal stance, affect dispositions, and microemotions ("fleeting bits of expression, action, feeling, or other components of emotion episodes") (2018: 39-48, quotation from 41; cf. Plantinga 2009: 29). Contrast the following sentences (Kuiken, Miall, and Sikora 2004: 174; cf. Miall and Kuiken 2002: 233 n. 1):

> It is important, first, to distinguish feeling (the bodily sense, within awareness, of all experienced affect, including emotions, moods, and attitudes) from affect (the discrete changes in facial expression, posture, gesture, and arousal that sometimes accompany intense emotions, moods, or attitudes) and from emotions (discrete and innate psychobiological reaction patterns, such as occur in anger, sadness, and fear, independently of awareness). Emotions and affect, in the sense defined, are less likely to occur during reading than are the subtle and fugitive feelings that are not so readily named.

Here, feeling differs from affect, and feeling and affect differ from emotion. Subsequent work under the rubric of affect theory concentrates on "flows and forces, intensities and sensations" and also cleaves affect from emotion (Felski 2020b: 31; cf. Eder, Hanich, and Stadler 2019: 94). This dispute over categorization does not concern me. I review it to emphasize that the components of a recipient's experience I am after in this part of the book fall under the purview of the term "emotion." I do not address moods (e.g., Plantinga 2018: 175-89), attitudes, or sensations, for example, although I recognize they can prompt an emotion episode (Plantinga 2009: 60-1; Hogan 2018: 42) and I do explore sensations in section 6.3.

Next, I want to specify what I mean when I say (or imply) that recipients can still today experience emotional identification with a Homeric character (as opposed to cognitive or motivational identification, which I take to be less fraught). I am not thinking here of the ongoing debate over why stories about fictional or no longer existing people (or entities) can trigger emotions in us that are just as strong as the emotions triggered by alive, flesh and blood people (Ryan 2015a: 108-14; Konrad, Petraschka, and Werner 2018; Friend 2020; Seppänen et al. 2021). I focus on another debate instead.

Aware of constructivist theories of emotion (Hogan 2018: 62-79), we need to determine what the words that constitute the Greek, and, more precisely, the Homeric, emotional lexicon mean (Muellner 1996; Cairns 2003; 2016; T. Walsh 2005; Konstan 2006). But the specifics of those emotion episodes—from eliciting conditions to resulting words or deeds (Hogan 2018: 42-8; cf. Sanders 2014: 2 and *passim*)—and the specifics of the scripts and scenarios to which those words point make sense to and resonate with us (Cairns 2008, esp. 58; cf. Cairns 2003: 25-6, 28, 49; Cairns and Fulkerson 2015: 10-16; Lateiner and Spatharas 2017: 12). Just as once they are explained to me I grasp the Italian *fiero* ("intense satisfaction derived from the accomplishment of a sustained and difficult task"), the Yiddish *naches* ("pride in the achievement of one's children"), and the German *Torschlusspanik* ("the fear of diminishing opportunities as one grows older")

(M. Smith 2017: 164, 173, 210), so I have yet to come away from an analysis of a Greek emotion word thinking that I have no idea what it means to experience that emotion, however diverse or particular its components. Take, for instance, David Konstan's investigation of Aristotle's definition of *orgē* (which Konstan translates as "anger"): "there are several elements in Aristotle's account of anger that may seem remarkable: that anger entails, or is reducible to, a desire for revenge; that this desire is provoked by a slight—and only a slight; and that some people, but only some, are not fit to slight another" (2006: 43). But Aristotle accounts for *orgē*, not anger (cf. Sanders 2014: 4–5). The constituents of *orgē* can only be remarkable if we expect them to overlap with our understanding of anger. If I set aside that expectation, I can understand and even imagine feeling Aristotle's *orgē*. Konstan describes Aristotle's definition of *aiskhunē*, "shame" (2006: 260; cf. 98–105):

> We feel shame for our vices, such as cowardice, injustice, and the servility that is manifested in begging or flattering others for the sake of some advantage, and also for not having the fine things our equals have ... : like emulation, shame is a goad to maintaining one's level in society. We feel shame particularly before those who are of some account, for example people who admire us or whom we admire—or those with whom we compete. Like anger, shame is symptomatic of a society in which one's reputation in the eyes of others is crucial: one must not be seen to sink beneath the level of one's peers.

This description may hit uncomfortably close to home for many academics. Again, whatever, for example, the words *mēnis*, *kholos*, *phobos*, or *elpis* mean, I can comprehend and even feel those emotions. It does not, then, matter whether, when I say I am angry, I have the same understanding of anger as Achilles does. What matters is that when the text reports that a Homeric character exhibits what we translate as anger, I am capable of understanding and feeling what the Homeric poems designate with the word we translate as anger. We can couple the need to historicize and contextualize with the reality of universals (cf. Altieri 2003: 208–9; Cairns 2003: 12–17, 49; M. Smith 2017: 155–65; de Bakker, van der Berg, and Klooster 2022: 14–15). An illuminating parallel comes in Michael Lloyd's point about Sophocles's *Antigone*: we should determine "the implication of the words *philia* and *erōs*, but it would be impossible to understand *Antigone* without any experience of affective relations" (2018: 338). Relationships of love and hate remain discernable across time (cf. Allen-Hornblower 2016: 24).

Then, too, we are within our rights to describe what a character experiences with one of our emotion terms even when we cannot claim to be translating a specific word (Cairns 2008: 51–8; cf. Sanders 2014: 142; Lateiner and Spatharas 2017: 4; Spatharas 2019: 13, 148). Alexander Forte, for instance, detects in the *Iliad* instances of what we call surprise and shock (2018). When, for example, "trembling seized" Hector at the sight of Achilles in his new armor (*Iliad* 22.136), "one should characterize Hector's affective experience as a dynamic interplay of terror and surprise" (46; cf. Heidenreich and Roth 2020).

I have emphasized so far that the emotions of Homeric characters are intelligible and translatable. Hogan's analyses suggest a bolder explanation for why we can understand the *Iliad*'s characters on an emotional level (cf. Plantinga 2009: 82–4). Hogan studies "patterns in story structure that recur across traditions of literature and orature" (2011: 8) and imputes those recurring patterns to humans' emotional processes—more specifically, their understanding of the components of happiness. For instance, he describes the pattern of the "heroic tragi-comedy" (2003: 109–28; 2011: 129–33) and takes the *Iliad* as one manifestation of that pattern (2003: e.g., 123). This pattern is "a plot based on achieving the prototype eliciting condition for social happiness—social and political power" (2003: 110). That is, the stories adhering to this pattern do not just evince a traditional plot line: Hogan is not simply interested in crafting a folklorist's tale type. These stories also evince a recurring stance on one element of happiness—namely, that feeling oneself respected by one's peers generates happiness as does seeing one's group dominate other groups (2003: 110–11; 2011: 128, 182). These tales are undergirded by and therefore reveal "a universal prototype for happiness" (2003: 11). (A given tale can of course critique that prototype (e.g., 2011: 165).) Hogan's model points to a continuity in emotional life across time and space. The implication is that the *Iliad*'s characters make sense to us in part because what makes them happy makes us happy as well. And if we have the same understanding of happiness, we will have the same understanding of other emotions too, such as sorrow. From this perspective, we will easily comprehend the characters' emotions.

The *Iliad* poet covers a lot of ground in his explorations of his characters' emotions. We find the characters experiencing simultaneously contradictory emotions: the vexed (*akhnumenoi*) Achaeans laugh at (*gelassan*) Thersites (*Iliad* 2.270). We find the characters reacting emotionally to others' emotions: Andromache "laughed tearfully: and her husband took pity as he perceived her" (δακρυόεν γελάσασα· πόσις δ' ἐλέησε νοήσας, *Iliad* 6.484; cf. 16.2–5). We find them exhibiting emotions about their own emotions—that is, meta-emotions (Plantinga 2009: 73, 164, 182; 2018: 109, 121; M. Smith 2017: 203; Hogan 2018: 48, 101): a vexed (*okhthēsas*) Achilles curses the anger (*kholos*) that Agamemnon prompted in him (*Iliad* 18.97, 107–11; Ready 2011: 46). As the poet journeys through this emotional landscape, we can accompany him without too much trouble.

Whether I have in mind an ancient or modern recipient, I take emotional identification to mean two different things. On the one hand, it can mean feeling the same emotion as the character. Several of the researchers cited earlier adopt this definition. I add here James Harold's useful metaphor in his discussion of identification—"Your emotions are *copies* of his" (2000: 344, my emphasis; cf. 355)—as well as Katalin Bálint and Ed Tan's observation that recipients can experience "isomorphic" feelings with characters (2019: 217, 223). On the other hand, it can mean feeling something akin to the character's emotion, the operative word here being "congruent." Carl Plantinga, for instance, speaks of "*affective congruence*": "the viewer...may experience emotions that have similar orientation or valences with characters' yet are rarely, if ever, identical" (2009: 101, emphasis in original; cf. 32–3, 150, 157, 161; 2019: 165; M. Smith 1995: 103; Oatley 2012: 29, quoted in section 2.4, p. 35; S. Eder 2019: 74). For example, when Maximus in the movie *Gladiator* discovers his murdered family, "the viewer's response will be congruent in that it is oriented toward the same general object, the death of Maximus's family, even though the emotions experienced will differ in degree and in kind" (Plantinga 2009: 101). Now, Noel Carroll is skeptical of emotional identification (on the grounds that we do not feel an emotion due to a character's feeling that emotion) and is quick to point out the ways in which recipients' emotions diverge from those exhibited by a character. He wants to use the term "empathy" when we experience emotions that are "broadly similar in their general valence" to those of the character, when, that is, we experience "converging emotional states" (2011: 171–2). I would rather take a fuzzier approach to emotional identification. As we did with perceptual identification, we can posit a stricter definition—we feel the same emotions as the character— and a looser definition—we feel emotions congruent with those of the character— of emotional identification. I tend to have the stricter definition in mind when I speak of emotional identification, but the looser definition works too in the cases I discuss.

There is something disorienting for the classicist in talking about emotional identification in the straightforward way in which I do. It can, frankly, seem facile: a character feels an emotion, and a recipient feels it too. Do we spend years in graduate school to end up making such claims? Is not true rigor exemplified in complicated arguments over, say, a possible Aeolic phase in the development of the Homeric dialect? Well, we are trying to get to grips with how people respond to texts, and the simple fact of the matter is that recipients experience emotional identification. We need to get over any discomfort we may have with investigations of this apparently obvious feature of recipient response (cf. section 1.3, p. 3), and a thorough investigation of the phenomenon will require pointing to specific examples, not just saying that recipients experience emotional identification and leaving it there. I find myself in the congenial company of Lynn Kozak and Pietro Pucci: when Priam and Hecuba beg Hector not to fight Achilles (*Iliad* 22.25–91), the poet "giv[es] access to their emotions around Hektor's confrontation with Achilles as a cue for the audience's own" (Kozak 2017: 200); when Zeus claims that his heart grieves (*olophuretai ētor*) for Hector as Achilles chases after him (*Iliad* 22.169–70), "how can the heart of the reader not feel the same pity and sympathy for Hector?" (Pucci 2002: 31; cf. Myers 2019: 118; Scodel

2021: 68). So too I appreciate Eric Douglass's specifying passages in which recipients of the Hebrew Bible and Second Testament (especially the Gospel of Mark) might experience emotional identification (or emotional empathy, as he terms it) (2018: 123–4, 151, 230–1, 235, 241–2, 247, 252) and Margrethe Bruun Vaage's pointing to how we might feel the turbulent emotions of Walter White in the television show *Breaking Bad* (2016: 65, 79). Admit that discussions of other forms of identification—cognitive, perceptual, motivational, epistemic—do not generate the same hesitation or trigger the same embarrassment. Let us afford emotional identification a similar respect.

## 2.6. Conclusion

Discussions of identification need to take into account much more than focalization. Likewise, identification has several components and does not reduce to emotional ties to a character: for instance, when identifying with a character, we root for them to achieve their goals.

The factors conducive to identification are various. We can identify with a range of characters in storyworlds, including in the Homeric epics. We need to spend time with them in order to do so. We do not have to be similar to the characters and we do not even need to consider them virtuous, although we may gravitate toward those rendered positively, those who seem to think as we do and to possess similar traits, and those engaged in activities we deem relevant to our own lives and selves and consider familiar. Knowing what a character will do or what will happen to that character does not lessen identification. Physical descriptions of the characters and the setting aid identification, as do directing the recipient toward a character's point of view and ensuring the perceived realism of the character's actions and motivations. Emphasizing a character's membership in a group may enhance identification. The opportunity to take a side may do so as well.

Although they did not use the term identification, ancient readers thought through some of the issues that pertain to identification, both its different forms and its precipitating factors. This intersection encourages our project of, one, speaking of identification in the context of responses to Homeric epic and, two, applying modern research on identification to the Homeric epics. Put differently and more expansively, these ancient analyses suggest that we are on relatively firm ground in thinking that ancient recipients responded to storyworlds and to characters in some of the same ways we do. They may have arrived at different answers and judgments (cf. Schironi 2018: 728–9), but they were asking the same questions.

Finally, one need not get sidetracked over the definition of a character when studying questions of identification. Nor should one be afraid to posit a modern recipient's emotional identification with Homeric characters. Whether we are talking about an ancient or modern recipient's reaction, emotional identification should be understood to embrace both feeling the same emotions as a character and feeling emotions congruent with, but not identical to, those of a character.

# 3
# Prompts for (a Study of) Identifying with Characters

### 3.1. Overview

Chapter 4 will offer a series of close readings of passages in the *Iliad* in which recipients have the opportunity to identify with a character. This chapter joins with Chapter 2 in laying the foundation for that investigation. It surveys some of the recurring features of the Homeric epics that encourage recipients to identify with characters (3.2). It then explores internal narrators' presentations to argue that Homeric speakers try to get their interlocutor to identify with a character in their tale (3.3). One could position the internal narrator's trying to get their addressee to identify with a character in their tale as further encouraging external audiences to identify with characters: those tales join with the features of the poems discussed in section 3.2 that ease identification. I consider internal narrators' presentations for a different reason: because the poet uses the characters to show us what he himself does or aims to do (Martin 1989; Minchin 2001: 223; Ready 2019a: chs. 1 and 2), the episodes studied in section 3.3 suggest that the poet will provide opportunities for external audience members to identify with the characters. That suggestion leads us to investigate how external audiences might experience identification with the characters. Kimberly Chabot Davis sees an analogous self-reflexive equation at work in Manuel Puig's *Kiss of the Spider Woman*: that the two main characters talk about identification with characters in movies encourages external audience members to think about their own identifying with those two characters (2007: 149). In general, I rely at regular intervals throughout this book on the truism that "every text teaches us how to read it and on what terms" (Chamberlin 2015: 38).

Section 3.2, then, reviews prompts for identifying with characters, and section 3.3 reviews a prompt for the study of identifying with characters. In section 3.3's close readings as well as in those in Chapter 4, I refer as appropriate to the factors conducive to identification discussed in Chapter 2.

### 3.2. Recurring Features

Investigating the pre-history of our *Iliad*, Mary Bachvarova posits that the poem implies "an audience that identified with both sides, the Achaeans and the

Trojans" (2016: 434). Her subsequent reference to Greek speakers in the Troad suggests that she has in mind as the reason for this identification what our investigation would label demographic similarity. So too Tobias Myers argues that "the poet's audience is expected to identify with, or as, the Achaeans as a group" because the poem is presented "in Greek, by and for those who consider themselves the Achaeans' heirs" (2019: 148; cf. 121). This section highlights several other features of the Homeric poems that ease identification with characters.

First, scholarship has long recognized the characterizing force of the epithets with which the poet adorns the heroes (Martin 1993; de Jong 2018a: 35; Stelow 2020: 31–4). Wayne Booth noted that many of these epithets signal a character's innate virtue (1961: 5; cf. de Jong 2004: 137), while Michael Silk observed that they "tend to be laudatory or neutral, but not pejorative" (2004: 49; cf. Hutchinson 2017: 160). Many recipients will take various epithets—such as "courageous" (*alkimos*), "renowned for fighting" (*douriklutos*), "great-hearted" (*megathumos*), "wise" (*pepnumenos*), or even "man-slaughtering" (*androphonos*)—to signal that the characters hold attitudes similar to their own and possess virtues they value. Recall the modern research on identification that finds recipients apt to identify with characters who exhibit similar beliefs and opinions as the recipients and with virtuous characters.

Second, granted that the poet tends not to specify his characters' distinctive physical features (S. Richardson 1990: 40; de Jong 2018a: 35), we do get physical descriptions "on special occasions" (Silk 2004: 59–60):

> Agamemnon's looks are described in a series of similes (three short and one long) at the end of the unique cluster that leads up to the great catalogue of forces (II 477ff.). Agamemnon again, and the other top Achaean heroes with him, are described by Priam in the unique scene with Helen on the walls of Troy before the first duel (III 166ff.).... Hector's looks are nowhere mentioned until Achilles destroys them [22.401–3].

Yet those verses are not the only ones that help us envision a character. The poem's several arming scenes also give us a sense, however generic, of what a character looks like (see section 4.2.1, pp. 86–7). The poet labels Hector "huge with a shining helmet" (*Iliad* 2.816): Kozak asks rhetorically, "Can you see Hektor?" (2017: 31). One can also see Hector when he tells his mother that his hands are unwashed and that he is spattered with blood and filth (*Iliad* 6.266–8; Kozak 2017: 60). One can imagine the grieving Priam (*Iliad* 24.163–5; section 4.2.4, p. 110) and Odysseus in his beggar disguise (*Odyssey* 13.429–38). The poems abound with mention of characters' facial expressions (e.g., Lateiner 1995; Turkeltaub 2005) that suggest distinct images to our mind's eye. Agamemnon's eyes blaze like fire upon hearing Calchas's explanation for the plague that has befallen the Achaean camp, and he shoots evil glances (*kak' ossomenos*) as he replies (*Iliad* 1.104–5). A moment later it is Achilles's turn to "look darkly" (*hupodra idōn*, *Iliad* 1.148). When Agamemnon's heralds, Talthybius and Eurybates, stand before Achilles in silence "fearful and reverencing the king (*tarbēsante kai aidomenō*)" (*Iliad* 1.331–2), we can assign a facial expression to them and therefore more easily create a mental image of them. When Achilles tearfully (*dakrusas*) calls upon his mother (*Iliad* 1.348–51), recipients can imagine what he looks like. Agamemnon, Zeus, and Odysseus smile (*epimeidēsas*, *Iliad* 4.356, 8.38, 10.400) as do Hera, Hector, Ajax, Achilles, and Antilochus (1.595–6, 6.404, 7.212, 23.555, 23.786). Hector foams at the mouth, and his eyes blaze like fire (*Iliad* 15.607–8). Achilles grinds his teeth, and his eyes blaze like fire (*Iliad* 19.365–6). Moreover, Homeric characters are frequently on the move (Purves 2019; Hutchinson 2020: 32–77) and physically engage with the people and objects that surround them (Grethlein and Huitink 2017: e.g., 77). When told that a character is in motion or doing something to another body or object, we are apt to give that character physical attributes, to endow them with a face and a body (again, however generic) (cf. Minchin 2008b: 25). For example, when Thetis strokes Achilles with her hand (χειρί τέ μιν κατέρεξεν, *Iliad* 1.361), she takes on an appearance of some sort in the recipient's mind. Different recipients will use these cues to produce different visions, but the fact of the vision is what matters, not whether recipients share a vision. Recall that modern research on identification finds that descriptions of what characters look like enhances identification.

Third, the *Iliad* poet, as previous scholarship shows, provides cues that enable us to picture the battlefield setting in which the warriors fight, be it the Trojan plain or the Achaean camp (Minchin 2008a: 32; Clay 2011; de Jong 2012a: 29). The *Odyssey* poet, as previous scholarship shows, prompts us to imagine the varied settings of the epic (Haller 2007), including the landscape around Calypso's cave (5.58–76), the exterior and interior of Polyphemus's cave (9.182–6, 219–23), and the cave of the nymphs on Ithaca (13.102–12, 345–50) (Davidson 2002: 45–8); Alcinous's palace (7.86–102; Cook 2004) and his orchard and vineyard (7.112–31); the island off the land of the Cyclopes (9.116–41; Dougherty 2001: 129); Eumaeus's steading (14.5–16); the lair of the boar that wounds Odysseus (19.439–43; Purves 2014, esp. 48); and Odysseus's palace on Ithaca (Bassett 1912; de Jong 2012a: 23). We can attend as well, for instance, to how scattered clues in *Iliad* 6 allow us to construct images of the buildings in Troy (see section 6.2, p. 160) or to how the description of Achilles's hut helps one develop a sense of what it looks like (*Iliad* 24.448–56; de Jong 2012a: 22). In particular, the focus on the transitive bodily movements of its builders makes the hut easily imageable (cf. Grethlein and Huitink 2017: 76–7, 81–2): the Myrmidons cut the wood for it, roofed it with thatch they collected from meadows, fashioned a courtyard with a fence, and added a bolt to the door that requires three men to open and close (although Achilles could do so singlehandedly). Modern research into identification notes the importance of descriptions of settings.

Fourth, in the case of Homeric epic, one can deem realistic that which finds parallels in the actual world (external realism). The absence in the Homeric epics of "all kinds of magic or fantastic elements which the Epic Cycle displays, such as special eye-sight, invulnerable heroes, superhuman fleetness, rejuvenation, and even immortality" (de Jong 2005: 3, citing Griffin 1977) enhances external realism. Yet the Homeric poets depict a storyworld in which things regularly occur that either do not occur in the audience's actual world ever or do not occur in the audience's actual world with any regularity. The *Iliad*'s heroes perform physical feats that "men as they are now"—that is, men in the actual world—could never perform (e.g., *Iliad* 5.304; cf. Cook 2018: 118–19). The *Odyssey*'s eponymous protagonist has regular and sustained interactions with divinities, especially goddesses (cf. Cook 2018: 118, 122), of a sort denied to audience members in the actual world. On the expansive and cacophonous battlefield, warriors nevertheless deliver speeches that all their fellow fighters can hear, a departure from "verisimilitude" (Sammons 2009a: 176; cf. de Jong 2005: 17). When opposing warriors meet for a duel, they regularly recognize each other: "in view of the thousands of warriors who crowd the Iliadic battlefield, this is hardly realistic" (de Jong 2005: 15). Conversely, Michael Silk opines that in its battle scenes the *Iliad* omits the sorts of things that tend to happen in real life: "warriors win by superior valour or might: there is next to no technique or strategy. They kill or are killed, but contrary to ordinary experience they are not taken prisoner, and they are rarely wounded seriously—or if they are, the wounds rarely disable their owners for long" (2004: 50). There are also breaches in "temporal verisimilitude" that are not "historically realistic": how, for instance, can Priam require Helen in *Iliad* 3 to tell him the names of the Achaean leaders after nine years of war (Bergren 2008: 43)?

The following counterbalance discrepancies between the world of the poems and the world of their performance because they endow the poems with a high degree of narrative realism (to repeat: the narrative adheres to the rules and expectations it establishes itself). One can deem realistic that which finds parallels elsewhere in the poems. This sort of material merits the label typical (cf. Fenik 1968: 5) or stylized (cf. Silk 2004: 48, 58–9) in Homeric scholarship. The typical becomes not merely a device aiding the poet as he orally performs. By having their characters repeatedly do (and say) the same things—by relying on the typical—the poets construct a storyworld marked by routine and consistency. That normalcy contributes to narrative realism (cf. de Jong 2005: 4–5, 10). By the same logic, upon encountering a singular event in the epics, a recipient may pause over its realism. Not everything in the Homeric epics has to clear the bar of narrative realism straightaway; in fact, not everything in the Homeric epics has to clear the bar of narrative realism even upon reflection (cf. Scodel 1999: 35, 60).

The consistency of the Homeric storyworld emerges in other ways. We have learned much from generations of Analytical criticism about the faults and fissures in the epics (see Tsagalis 2020), but the poems still establish a storyworld with rules, precepts, and codes by which the characters abide. Gods and men generally adhere to the same principles in their interactions with one another, and mortals generally adhere to the same principles in their interactions with one another (e.g., Redfield 1975; Nagy 1999; Scodel 2008; Elmer 2013). As a result, although a few passages allow for (but by no means necessitate) the argument that "Homer does not feel the need to make the actions of his characters psychologically plausible" (Grethlein 2018: 83), the characters' motivations are generally clear (cf. Scodel 1999: 24, 33): critics have even explained Achilles's refusal in *Iliad* 9 to accept Agamemnon's offer and to return to the fight (Gill 2002: 136–52; D. Wilson 2002: 83; Scodel 2008: 147–8). This stability enhances narrative realism.

The factor of motivation brings us to Ruth Scodel's discussion of three strategies the Homeric poets adopt to forestall objections to the credibility of the narrative, beyond relying on their audience's "inattention" and "generosity" (1999: 15–21, 59–83). I take these strategies as mechanisms for keeping a recipient from questioning the degree of narrative realism. Scodel defines "local motivation": "an expository element or plot device that is introduced only at the moment it is needed and is not developed as the narrative proceeds" (1999: 12). How to get Odysseus ready for his meeting with Circe in *Odyssey* 10 when his patron divinity, Athena, cannot help him? Make Hermes the one to prepare him (34). Why does Achilles, usually so quick to anger, not attack Agamemnon in *Iliad* 1? Because Athena entices him not to (38). How come the Phaeacian sailors rightly land in the harbor of Phorcys on Ithaca? *Odyssey* 13.113 explains: "since they knew of it previously" (45). Why does Odysseus bring "his most festive wine in order to explore an unknown island" (not a normal procedure)? Because he had a feeling that he would meet a man "knowing neither principles of justice nor custom" (*Odyssey* 9.213–15) (47). The poet can also mitigate a breach in verisimilitude by putting an apology for the breach into the mouth of a character (13). What would possess Agamemnon in *Iliad* 2 to test his army by suggesting that the expedition disband? Because, he says, "it is in keeping with custom (*themis*)" (*Iliad* 2.73) (49). Finally, with "thematization" (14), the poet gets something of thematic value out of a seeming inconsistency (cf. O'Hara 2007: 10). Odysseus's reckless antagonizing of Polyphemus, so out of character, serves as "the beginning of an education in self-control that Odysseus will use when he confronts the suitors" (Scodel 1999: 51). These three strategies can work simultaneously or in tandem (e.g., 15, 37, 54).

I rephrase Michael Silk's observation that the Homeric poets fashion "a solid poetic reality" (2004: 56): the epics score high when it comes to narrative realism or at least present "credible impossibilities" (Scodel 1999) so that narrative realism is not questioned. Narrative realism constitutes another feature that predicts identification.

Fifth, membership in a group regularly emerges as an important element of a character's characterization. Ajax insists on the bonds of *philotēs* that connect the Achaeans (*Iliad* 9.630–1) and especially the Achaean *basileis* (9.640–2). He urges the Achaean warriors to fight for one another, even if their precise motivations differ (*Iliad* 15.561–4, 661–6). Sarpedon is first and foremost a leader of the Lycians (*Iliad* 12.310–28, 16.422). His compatriot Glaucus distinguishes emphatically between the Trojans and the Lycians (*Iliad* 17.144–59). Odysseus, Telemachus, and Eumaeus represent something of a sleeper cell working against the suitors. In *Odyssey* 24, Odysseus stands with this household in opposition to the suitors' relatives. Odysseus, Achilles, and Helen belong to a select group of elites who can converse intimately with (undisguised) gods (Petridou 2015: 41; Ready 2017: 27). I noted the research that suggests a link between identification and a character's belonging to a group.

Sixth, a component of the Homeric poems pairs readily with a component of Breithaupt's discussion of empathy. Breithaupt argues that when we see someone on a stage—be it a literal or metaphorical stage—we are more likely to empathize with them (2018: 57–8). Homeric heroes are put on stage to the extent that they constantly watch one another—indeed, they know that they are being watched (in both the present and the future: *Iliad* 6.444–6, 22.305)—and the gods watch them. The epics even thematize this staging of the mortal characters (Allen-Hornblower 2016: 18–44, 67–9; Myers 2019, esp. 29, 78–9). Keeping in mind the intersections between Breithaupt's model of empathy and identification (see section 2.2, p. 24), I suggest that recipients are primed to identify with the mortal characters because the characters are put on stage.

Seventh, a noticeable feature of Homeric poetry is what narratologists label "transference," wherein a character turns out to know something that we know but that we did not think they knew: "a character displays knowledge of something which, strictly speaking, he cannot know, but which the narratees do know; the knowledge of the narratees is 'transferred' to the character" (de Jong 2001: xviii). An example involving a minor character can suggest the frequency of transference. Eurylochus observes that some of his companions have vanished into Circe's house (*Odyssey* 10.258–60). When Eurylochus returns to Odysseus and the rest of the companions, he tries to dissuade them from confronting Circe: "she will turn you all into either pigs or wolves or lions" (10.432–3). Irene de Jong explains, "Strictly speaking, Eurylochus does not know that his companions have been turned into pigs...; as the narratees do know about the metamorphosis we are dealing here with transference" (2001: 265 at 432–4). In addition to knowing what other characters did even though they did not see them do it, a character can be aware of what another character has said even though they did not hear the speech (Taplin 1992: 149–50, 223). Achilles, for example, knows (*Iliad* 1.380–1) that the priest Chryses prayed to Apollo to punish the Achaeans (1.37–42), but Chryses uttered this prayer as he walked by himself along the shore (1.34–5). Bruno Currie captures what is going on in the scenes de Jong and Taplin discuss when he speaks of "crossing character consciousness with audience consciousness" (2016: 117). Put differently, a character unexpectedly possesses knowledge about the storyworld that we possess. Now, when we experience cognitive identification, we interpret the events in the storyworld from a character's perspective. Recipients may be more inclined to interpret storyworld events from the perspective of a character when that character knows as much as the recipients about certain actions in the storyworld. That knowledge on the character's part makes their interpretations of storyworld events more authoritative than they might otherwise be. For instance, Achilles's reference to Chryses comes in the speech in which he asks Thetis to ask Zeus to help the Trojans defeat the Achaeans (*Iliad* 1.407–12): the alignment in storyworld knowledge between Achilles and the recipient may pave the way for the recipient to agree that the Achaeans deserve this treatment.

Eighth, Homeric characters provide a model for recipients in so far as they can be said to identify with their fellows. One character's emotional state can bring others into that state. When Achilles weeps (*klaiōn*) as he recalls eating with Patroclus and speculates on the sufferings of his father, Peleus, some number of the following—Agamemnon, Menelaus, Odysseus, Nestor, Idomeneus, and Phoenix—"groaned in answer (*epi de stenakhonto*), each one remembering what he left behind at home" (*Iliad* 19.338–9; Kozak 2017: 185; cf. 19.301–2). When Achilles prays to Zeus that Patroclus push back the Trojans from the ships and return safely (*Iliad* 16.233–48), he can be said to be endorsing what he takes to be Patroclus's goal—the one Patroclus laid out at 16.44–5 ("easily, because we are unwearied, we might push back men weary from battle toward the city from the ships and huts") and the one Achilles himself laid out at 16.87 ("driving them from the ships, come back")—and experiencing motivational identification with Patroclus. Agamemnon and later Ajax declare, "Feel shame before one another in the mighty combat: when men feel shame, more are saved than perish; but when men flee, there is neither glory nor any strength" (*Iliad* 5.530–2, 15.562–4). This statement is perhaps the closest the warriors come to acknowledging not just the need for but the nature of teamwork: if you flee—that is, if you lose—I cannot hope to win; I need you to succeed so that I can succeed. A similar equation underlies the Achaeans' eagerness "to defend one another" as they march into battle (*Iliad* 3.9). From this perspective, they can be said to experience motivational identification. We will see that characters also identify in this manner with contestants in the funeral games for Patroclus (section 4.2.3).

Ninth, and finally, the *Iliad* may make use of characters that only appear in its lines—one thinks here especially of the minor characters who die on the battlefield—and it may grant to some characters, such as Hector and Patroclus, substantially larger roles than they played in other stories about Troy (Burgess 2009: 46; Kramer-Hajos 2012: 99–100; cf. R. Friedrich 2019: 212). But it also abounds in characters well known to the audience. Much work has addressed how the Homeric poet fashions his characters and, in particular, his "use of tradition for the creation of character" (Stelow 2020: 17; cf. Ready 2020: 292 nn. 43–4), and we might now focus on the audience's reception of well-known characters. Iliadic characters like Achilles, Ajax, and Nestor populated numerous other tales, as evidenced in the *Odyssey* and the poems of the Trojan War portion of the Epic Cycle (performance traditions contemporaneous with the performance traditions of the Iliad and the Odyssey; West 2013), and appeared in other media beyond oral traditional poetry, such as vases. Some acquired cult honors, such as Achilles (Nagy 1999: 9; Burgess 2009: 111–31), Ajax (Finglass 2011: 46–7; Delacruz 2021), Helen (L. Edmunds 2016: 164–87), Menelaus (Stelow 2020: 258–84), and Odysseus (Marks 2008: 97; Burgess 2019: 149).

Sarah Iles Johnston's discussion of "plurimediality" and the "accretive characters" of Greek myth and cult, such as Theseus, enables us to see the implications of this fact (2018: 156–61). Ancient Greeks fashioned their understanding of a mythic personage over time from their various encounters with portrayals of the personage (if not encounters with the personage) in various contexts, be it as a statue, a figure in a painting, or a character in a tale. Rita Felski's assessment of today's transtextual and plurimedial characters applies to the ancient world as well: "Characters...are portmanteau creatures, assembled out of disparate materials drawn from fiction and life" (2020b: 91). This point should not be overlooked. Lowell Edmunds claims, "For ancient Greeks...down to a certain point in time, Helen was a real person who lived in the days of the Trojan War" (2016: 189). Accordingly, "Helen was real and epic poetry did not create her but preserved her memory." Edmunds contrasts this understanding of Helen and of her relationship to poetry with the approach of the modern scholar: "For the modern scholar, Helen is not a historical person lying behind her poetry or artistic representation but, in the first place, the product of that representation itself" (190). Edmunds's dichotomy has its value, but, from the perspective Johnston provides, ancient Greeks created their understanding of (the real) Helen using poetic and artistic representations: their Helen was a product of those representations.

From here Johnston adds another crucial point. Manufacturing this understanding of a mythic personage required "cognitive and emotional energy" (Johnston 2018: 158) especially because the portrayal of the personage changed to greater or lesser degrees depending on the context of the portrayal (cf. L. Edmunds 2016 (on Helen); 2021: 33–5; Castiglioni 2020 and Stelow 2020 (on Menelaus)). Putting time and effort into this assemblage led one to care about the assemblage, to care about the personage; but one also cared about the assemblage, about the personage, because it was one's own construction. Johnston's logic here parallels that of Jens Eder, Fotis Jannidis, and Ralf Schneider: we get more emotionally involved with a character when we cannot quickly assign that character to an established category and instead have to fashion "a personalised mental model of the character" (2010: 36).

I extrapolate that, with its abundance of familiar characters, Homeric epic capitalized on this phenomenon: it gave audience members characters they cared about and therefore would be quick to identify with. Moreover, it had to be the case that individual recipients, although they may have had a general understanding of a large number of Homeric characters, had invested more energy in creating a vision of some as opposed to other characters and as a result had favorites. If so, they might be more apt to identify with a particular character when hearing about that character's exploits. Again, Homeric epic, with its abundance of familiar characters, provided something for everyone on this front (cf. Kozak 2017: 81, 233).

The overlaps between what researchers into identification (and empathy) talk about and what appears in an initial review of some components of Homeric epic provide proof of concept. Similarly reassuring is a 2020 study on flow—defined as "a person's state of mind when they are completely engaged in an activity"—and its importance to a positive reading experience (Thissen, Menninghaus, and Schlotz 2020, quotation from 711). The investigators found that participants experienced identification with Odysseus when reading a translation of *Odyssey* 12 (along with "flow, presence, ... suspense, and cognitive involvement") (9). They do not, however, address the different sorts of identification nor the mechanisms that enable such an experience.

It is now time to delve deeper into the poetry itself. Ultimately, only the quality of the close readings that posit recipients' identifying with Homeric characters can answer the question of whether we are right to think about identification in the context of Homeric epic. In the following readings, I usually discuss a couple of features in the text conducive to identification—be it the foregrounding of a character's perspective, description of a character's appearance, description of the setting, reference to a character's virtue or membership in a group, degree of perceived realism, and/or the possibility of taking sides—and I always nominate moments in the text as opportunities for recipients to experience cognitive, emotional, and/or motivational identification. Introspection guides my efforts in that latter endeavor. We are comfortable with introspection when our scholarship considers what a text means. We are perhaps less comfortable with introspection when, as in the present case, our scholarship explores how a text affects recipients. But comfortable with the first mode of analysis, we should be comfortable with the second. I take encouragement from the ever-increasing number of projects in classical studies that reflect on how recipients respond to a text by (implicitly or explicitly) sharing the author's own responses. Lynn Kozak writes of Hector's retreat in *Iliad* 16, "For me, it still leaves a sinking feeling, a gnawing that Hektor should not have run away" (2017: 154). They write of Hector's deliberations over whether to fight Achilles in *Iliad* 22, "Personally, I wish that Hektor would suck up his shame and get inside the city.... But there is a particularly painful pleasure in knowing that Hektor will not return to Troy" (201). Mario Telò comments on sound effects in Archilochus fragment 201: "... the sound of the word, which, like the rolling *rho*, sends forth an iambic intensity that threatens to scratch and tear the iambicist's enemies but is inevitably felt also on his audience's skin" (2020: 284). And I take encouragement from the willingness of researchers outside classical studies to share their own reactions. Here, for example, is Hogan on the moment when Romeo first catches sight of Juliet in Shakespeare's *Romeo and Juliet* (I.iv.159–65) (2018: 171; cf. Oatley 2012: 98–9):

> Romeo is expressing his initial fascination with Juliet. In the larger context of the play, I am of course aware that this marks the first stirrings of an attachment relation and a strong feeling of reward dependency through which one's wanting and liking are governed by the presence, attitudes, and behaviors of another person. As such, through its activation of emotional memories in me, the scene helps to prime my own attachment system emphatically, and even connects with my emotional memories of reward dependency. Perhaps surprisingly, I feel Romeo's delight in Juliet here in a way that I do not feel it in the more famous "balcony scene."

And here is Vaage on a scene from *Breaking Bad*: "the sequence makes me engage in what he is doing and hope that he will get the vehicle started" (2016: 85; see also Robinson 2005: 175–6; Felski 2020b: 44–5, 66).

It will not be too obvious for me to say that I do not imagine all recipients responding in the ways I propose (cf. Budelmann 2000: e.g., 22, 93; Robinson 2005: 175, 179; Koopman and Hakemulder 2015: 91; Felski 2020b: 68, 84). My reflections are merely exemplary. For instance, I will suggest possibilities for emotional identification with Agamemnon during his killing spree in *Iliad* 11, including reveling in his successful slaughter right along with him (section 4.2.1). I will not declare that recipients assuredly identify with Agamemnon at that moment (cf. Myers 2019: 153–4).

## 3.3. Internal Narrators and Identification

The *Odyssey*'s narrator reports that Phemius sang of "the return (*noston*) of the Achaeans, a grievous one (*lugron*), which Pallas Athena prescribed for them from Troy" (1.326–7). Nestor's accounts of the same subject—"a grievous return (*lugron... noston*) for the Argives" that "the bright-eyed daughter of a mighty father," Athena, orchestrated (*Odyssey* 3.132–6)—focuses on Menelaus, Agamemnon, Odysseus, Diomedes, Neoptolemus, Philoctetes, Idomeneus, and Nestor himself (3.130–95, 276–312). Phemius's account of the same subject presumably dealt with the same characters (cf. H. Mackie 1997: 80). Just so, when Telemachus says that Penelope should tolerate listening to Phemius's song because (*gar*) others (*alloi*) besides Odysseus died at Troy (*Odyssey* 1.354-5), he implies that the song tells of others besides Odysseus, and one presumes those others to be the same cast as in Nestor's accounts. We can surmise that these characters are familiar to the Ithakan audience: after all, the bard Demodocus entertains the isolated Phaeacians with a song involving Odysseus, Achilles, and Agamemnon, the "fame (*kleos*) of which extended into wide heaven" (*Odyssey* 8.74); when he and his men meet Polyphemus, Odysseus refers to Agamemnon's renown as "greatest" (*megiston ... kleos*, *Odyssey* 9.264), assuming that Polyphemus will have heard of him. Now, Telemachus titles Phemius's song "the evil fate of the Danaans" (*Odyssey* 1.350; Ready 2019a: 28) and labels it the "newest" song (1.352). What makes it "newest"? It is unlikely to be the cast of characters: it involves the usual batch of Danaans. In this case, at least, the newest song presents in new situations characters familiar to the listeners. Telemachus also declares that audiences praise the "newest" song especially (*Odyssey* 1.351-2). Audience members have formed attachments to individual characters and want to hear what happens to them next: that is why they like the newest song so much.

This idea that listeners connect with characters in some way, shape, or form overlaps with a more precise point: within the world depicted in the Homeric epics, characters seem to assume that hearers of a tale can identify with the tale's characters. I interpret in this fashion the way Athena broaches with Telemachus the topic of Orestes's vengeance (*Odyssey* 1.296-302):

> ... You must not
> keep on with childish things, since you are no longer of such an age (*tēlikos*).
> In truth have you not heard (*ē ouk aieis*) what sort of glory brilliant (*dios*)
>     Orestes won
> among all men when he killed the slayer of his father,
> Aegisthus of the crafty plans, who killed his own famous (*kluton*) father?
> You too (*kai*), friend, for I see clearly that you are beautiful (*kalon*) and great
>     (*megan*),
> be bold in order that someone even of those born hereafter may speak well
>     of you.

Athena matches up Orestes and Telemachus point for point. First, the actions inappropriate to someone of Telemachus's age bring to mind the age-appropriate actions of Orestes, Telemachus's contemporary to the extent that he too is a son of a warrior who fought at Troy. Second, Orestes merits the epithet brilliant (*dios*) and had a famous (*kluton*) father; Telemachus too (*kai*) belongs to the same class, being beautiful (*kalon*) and great (*megan*) (cf. *Iliad*

21.108-9). Third, Orestes won glory by defending his household; Telemachus should strive for glory by defending his household in the manner Athena has outlined earlier in her speech (*Odyssey* 1.272-96).

Yet the phrase with which Athena begins her paradigm suggests that Telemachus should have made these connections himself. Athena's incredulous, if not rebuking, "In truth have you not heard...?" (cf. *ē ou* at, e.g., *Iliad* 15.18, 20.188; Kelly 2007: 166) implies not only that Telemachus should have heard the tale of Orestes but also that the tale should have resonated with Telemachus: he should have identified with Orestes based on their similarities in the ego-relevant domains of age and status; he should have found it easy to adopt Orestes's goals given the similarity in their household circumstances and their attitudes to those circumstances. Nestor adopts a milder tone when he tells Telemachus and Peisistratus, "And even (*kai*) you yourselves although you are far away have heard about the son of Atreus" (*Odyssey* 3.193), but he aims to make the same point. Athena closes her speech by urging Telemachus to move beyond identification and to act as Orestes did, but she implies that identification can prompt Telemachus to "imitate" (Alden 2017: 82) Orestes.

Athena's tactic here makes sense. When Homeric characters try to persuade someone to do something, they may appeal to "honor, material, power, and justice" (Reyes 2002: 23), but researchers have also brought out the extent to which characters use the particular format of the story to persuade their listeners to think and to act in a certain way (Alden 2000; cf. Grethlein 2006: 334-7). Two articles in that vein prove especially relevant for my purposes. Vanda Zajko analyzes Andromache's speech to Hector in which she recalls Achilles's sack of her city, Thebes, and his killing of her father and brothers (*Iliad* 6.407-39). Zajko suggests that Andromache offers Hector "the potential to identify with Achilles in the role of victorious warrior" and "the potential for him to identify with her father and brothers" (2006: 90). Dana Munteanu explores how characters in epic and tragedy "offer someone in deep mourning, unresponsive, or fasting, tragic paradigmatic narratives in order to bring the sufferer back to life" (2017: 83). She contends that "the more similar the mourner perceives his or her plight to be to the narrated tragic example, the more successful the consolation" (91). I build on Zajko's discussion—with its focus on opportunities for the internal hearer to identify with a character—and on Munteanu's discussion—with its focus on how the internal recipient of a paradigm may find points of contact with the paradigm's character. Looking to the literature on identification reviewed previously, I stress how identification aids the *Iliad*'s internal storytellers in their persuasive endeavors.

Research into narrative impact finds that "highly transporting narratives have the potential to alter beliefs, attitudes, and behaviors" (Fitzgerald and Green 2017: 62) and that identification with characters makes an important contribution to this equation or effects similar changes.[1] Going beyond a debate over whether reading novels makes you more empathetic or increases your ability to gauge others' mental states (your theory of mind capabilities),[2] this literature shows how immersion and identification can change how you think about yourself (however temporarily), can make you resolve to do things differently in the real world, and can even make you take concrete steps in that direction. One can attend to how, in order to construct a persuasive narrative, Homeric taletellers provide listeners with the opportunity to identify with the characters in their tales. I will discuss Agamemnon's address to Diomedes in *Iliad* 4 (3.3.1) and Nestor's address to Patroclus in *Iliad* 11 (3.3.2).

The overarching goal of these two close readings is to claim the following: by having the characters construct tales that offer opportunities for internal audiences to experience identification with the figures in the tales, the poet illustrates what he himself aims to do with regard to his own external audiences.

### 3.3.1. Agamemnon on Tydeus

At *Iliad* 4.368–400, Agamemnon endeavors to rouse Diomedes to action by reviewing some athletic and martial feats of Diomedes's father, Tydeus (de Jong 2018b: 26; O'Maley 2018: 279–82):

καὶ τὸν μὲν νείκεσσεν ἰδὼν κρείων Ἀγαμέμνων,
καί μιν φωνήσας ἔπεα πτερόεντα προσηύδα·
"ὤ μοι, Τυδέος υἱὲ δαΐφρονος ἱπποδάμοιο,  370
τί πτώσσεις, τί δ' ὀπιπεύεις πολέμοιο γεφύρας;
οὐ μὲν Τυδέι γ' ὧδε φίλον πτωσκαζέμεν ἦεν,
ἀλλὰ πολὺ πρὸ φίλων ἑτάρων δηΐοισι μάχεσθαι,
ὡς φάσαν οἵ μιν ἴδοντο πονεύμενον· οὐ γὰρ ἔγωγε
ἤντησ' οὐδὲ ἴδον· περὶ δ' ἄλλων φασὶ γενέσθαι.  375
ἤτοι μὲν γὰρ ἄτερ πολέμου εἰσῆλθε Μυκήνας
ξεῖνος ἅμ' ἀντιθέῳ Πολυνείκεϊ λαὸν ἀγείρων.
οἳ δὲ τότ' ἐστρατόωνθ' ἱερὰ πρὸς τείχεα Θήβης,

---

[1] Igartua 2010; Mazzocco et al. 2010; Sestir and Green 2010: 282; Tal-Or and Cohen 2010: 405; de Graaf et al. 2012; Oatley 2012: 121–6; Sanford and Emmott 2012: 243–6, 260; Hoeken and Sinkeldam 2014; Koopman and Hakemulder 2015: 90–1; Hakemulder and van Peer 2016: 198–9; Slater and Cohen 2016: 119–21; Calarco et al. 2017: 305–6; Cohen and Tal-Or 2017: 136–7; Fitzgerald and Green 2017: 53, 59–62; van Krieken, Hoeken, and Sanders 2017: 3; Cohen, Weimann-Saks, Mazor-Tregerman 2018: 507; Consoli 2018: 89; Douglass 2018: 109; Mar 2018; Meineck 2018: 212; J. Young 2019: 324; Alam and So 2020: 175–6; Budelmann and Emde Boas 2020: 75; Krause and Appel 2020; Ma 2020; cf. Mar et al 2011: 829–30; Plantinga 2018, esp. 55–74; Grethlein 2021a: 102; Goffin and Friend 2022: 130.

[2] E.g., Keen 2007; 2014; Hogan 2011: 243–50; 2018: 121–8; Fletcher and Monterosso 2016; Oatley 2016; M. Smith 2017: 188–90; Oatley and Djikic 2018; J. Young 2019; Felski 2020b: 105–9; Wimmer et al. 2021; cf. Meineck 2018: 169, 210.

καί ῥα μάλα λίσσοντο δόμεν κλειτοὺς ἐπικούρους.
οἳ δ' ἔθελον δόμεναι καὶ ἐπῄνεον ὡς ἐκέλευον, 380
ἀλλὰ Ζεὺς ἔτρεψε παραίσια σήματα φαίνων.
οἳ δ' ἐπεὶ οὖν ᾤχοντο ἰδὲ πρὸ ὁδοῦ ἐγένοντο,
Ἀσωπὸν δ' ἵκοντο βαθύσχοινον λεχεποίην,
ἔνθ' αὖτ' ἀγγελίην ἐπὶ Τυδῆ στεῖλαν Ἀχαιοί.
αὐτὰρ ὃ βῆ, πολέας δὲ κιχήσατο Καδμείωνας 385
δαινυμένους κατὰ δῶμα βίης Ἐτεοκληείης.
ἔνθ' οὐδὲ ξεῖνός περ ἐὼν ἱππηλάτα Τυδεὺς
τάρβει, μοῦνος ἐὼν πολέσιν μετὰ Καδμείοισιν,
ἀλλ' ὅ γ' ἀεθλεύειν προκαλίζετο, πάντα δ' ἐνίκα
ῥηιδίως· τοίη οἱ ἐπίρροθος ἦεν Ἀθήνη. 390
οἳ δὲ χολωσάμενοι Καδμεῖοι κέντορες ἵππων
ἂψ ἀναερχομένῳ πυκινὸν λόχον εἶσαν ἄγοντες,
κούρους πεντήκοντα· δύω δ' ἡγήτορες ἦσαν,
Μαίων Αἱμονίδης, ἐπιείκελος ἀθανάτοισιν,
υἱός τ' Αὐτοφόνοιο μενεπτόλεμος Λυκοφόντης. 395
Τυδεὺς μὲν καὶ τοῖσιν ἀεικέα πότμον ἐφῆκε·
πάντας ἔπεφν', ἕνα δ' οἶον ἵει οἰκόνδε νέεσθαι·
Μαίον' ἄρα προέηκε θεῶν τεράεσσι πιθήσας.
τοῖος ἔην Τυδεὺς Αἰτώλιος· ἀλλὰ τὸν υἱὸν
γείνατο εἷο χέρεια μάχῃ, ἀγορῇ δέ τ' ἀμείνω." 400

And wide-ruling Agamemnon rebuked him
and addressing him he spoke winged words:
"Ah me, son of battle-minded, horse-breaking Tydeus, 370
why are you cowering, why do you peep about at the bridges of war?
It was not Tydeus's wont to cower in this way
but far in front of his own companions to fight with enemies,
as they say, those who saw him toiling. For not did I encounter him, nor did I see him: but they say that he was beyond all the others. 375
For in fact he came to Mycenae without war
as a guest along with godlike Polyneices, gathering a host;
for then they were making an expedition against the holy walls of Thebes
and they vigorously were asking [the Mycenaeans] to give them famed allies;
and they were willing to give them and they approved as they urged; 380
but Zeus turned them back displaying signs that boded ill.
And they when they set out then and were on their way

and they came to the Asopus with deep reeds, grassy,
then in turn the Achaeans sent Tydeus on a mission.
But he set out and he came upon the many Cadmeians            385
eating in the house of mighty Eteocles.
Then, although he was a stranger, the horseman Tydeus was not
afraid, although he was but one man among many Cadmeians.
But he challenged them to athletic competitions and he defeated all of them
easily: a helper of such a sort was Athena.                    390
And the Cadmeians, angered, goaders of horses,
led and set an ambush for him as he returned back,
fifty men: and there were two leaders,
Maeon son of Haemon, similar to the immortals,
and the son of Autophonus, Lukophontes, stout in the fight.    395
And Tydeus put an unseemly fate even on these:
he killed them all and he sent off one alone to return home:
he sent off Maeon, trusting in the omens of the gods.
Of this sort was Tydeus the Aetolian; but he bore
a son worse than he in battle but better at speaking."         400

Diomedes may be prone to identify with Tydeus because Tydeus was his father. That is an important point—familiarity increases the probability of identification—but we can attend to more specific mechanisms by and precise moments in which the account encourages identification. I preface this argument with a comment on the structure of the initial portion of Agamemnon's tale.

In verses 376–7, Agamemnon casts Tydeus as the protagonist of his anecdote. The nominative singular participle, *ageirōn* ("gather"), drives this point home: not only does the singular number forefront Tydeus's actions; not only can the leader of an expedition gather a host (*Iliad* 9.338; cf. 17.222); elsewhere the protagonist of a story assembles a host (*Iliad* 2.664, 3.47, 9.544; *Odyssey* 2.41). Having singled him out, however, Agamemnon then partially occludes Tydeus over the course of verses 378 to 383. One can take the third-person plural forms of verses 378 and 379 to refer to Tydeus and Polyneices, but Tydeus still shares the spotlight with Polyneices. At verse 380 the Mycenaeans claim the spotlight, and at verse 381 Zeus emerges. Verse 384's reference to the Achaeans suggests that verses 382 to 383 are about the movement of Polyneices's army, unmentioned heretofore, not simply the travels of Tydeus and Polyneices themselves (cf. *Iliad* 10.287; Gantz 1996: 512). Contrast Diodorus's account wherein Tydeus goes from Argos as an emissary to Thebes by himself and only upon his return to Argos does the expedition assemble (*Library of History* 4.65.4). In demonstrating the rhetorical and thematic importance of Agamemnon's rehearsal of the embassy to Mycenae, Benjamin

Sammons writes, "In the first embassy, Tydeus arrives in the company of another hero, he is treated with gracious hospitality, and his mission is nearly a success" (2014: 302). This summary overlooks that Tydeus is no longer the primary focus of the narrative in these verses. Only in verse 385 does Tydeus reclaim the spotlight. This trajectory—foregrounding Tydeus as protagonist and then enlarging dramatically the cast of characters with the consequence of partially obscuring Tydeus—may pique Diomedes's interest in Tydeus. It can make him wonder when the ostensible protagonist will reappear and perhaps primes him to identify with Tydeus once the narrative returns to him. One can compare the way the poet builds anticipation for Hector's first appearance by having other characters mention him (Kozak 2017: 25–6).

When Tydeus comes back into the spotlight, he undertakes a flurry of activities: an embassy to Thebes, an athletic contest, a return to his own side, and a fight with the Thebans lying in ambush. At each stage in this narrative, Tydeus has a goal that Diomedes can hope he achieves. The initial failure of the embassy to Mycenae can in fact augment the recipient's desire to see Tydeus succeed (cf. Oatley 2012: 31). The potential for Diomedes to experience the motivational component of identification is strong.

Several features of Agamemnon's tale encourage this identification. Agamemnon describes the Asopus river near Thebes as "with deep reeds, grassy" (*bathuskhoinon lekhepoiēn*, 4.383). *Bathuskhoinos* occurs elsewhere only in *Homeric Hymn* 9 (to Artemis) where it describes the Meles river near Smyrna (line 3 West 2003a). *Lekhepoiēs* occurs elsewhere in reference to cities, not rivers (*Homeric Hymn to Apollo* 224 West 2003a; *Homeric Hymn to Hermes* 88 West 2003a; *Iliad* 2.697). Set off by themselves in asyndeton in the second half of the verse, the one rare adjective and the other oddly used adjective attract notice. Both adjectives pertain to features of the river's banks, so they prompt a more precise image of the landscape than one might generate if they were absent: one imagines not just a river but a river flowing between banks. In addition, the specification of the "depth" of the reeds (*bathu-*)—which means that there were high reeds on the bank—really makes sense only from a viewer's embodied perspective: something can only be said to be high relative to one's own height, and one imagines standing on the bank to gauge the height of the reeds. In helping Diomedes conjure the place where the Achaeans camp and from which Tydeus sets out, these epithets enable him to feel as if he is inside the story with Tydeus and therefore increase the likelihood of identification with Tydeus.

Agamemnon presents Tydeus in a positive light: he does not scare easily, even when surrounded by potentially hostile people; shows athletic prowess; has a goddess on his side; exhibits martial prowess; and evinces piety. His presenting Tydeus in such a manner encourages identification. Looking again at that list, one could highlight his initiating athletic contests and thereby demonstrating his belief in their value and his obeying the gods and thereby demonstrating his reverence:

with these actions he exhibits attitudes similar presumably to those of the recipient, Diomedes, another factor encouraging identification.

Following in the footsteps of Lillian Doherty who observes that in *Odyssey* 14 Odysseus presents a tale to Eumaeus that the latter could classify as realistic and plausible (1995: 150; cf. 157), I consider next how Agamemnon's account of Tydeus might fare in Diomedes's eyes in terms of perceived realism. I will not distinguish in this instance between external and narrative realism. The addressee within the storyworld thinks in terms of external realism; the external audience thinks in terms of narrative realism. Put differently, what is narratively realistic for us is externally realistic for the characters.

Judgments of perceived realism consider the plausibility and suitability of the characters' actions. Three of Tydeus's actions stand out: his challenging all the Cadmeians to games; his winning all those contests; and his killing forty-nine men single handedly.

One character can challenge another individual to participate in games: Euryalus urges Laomedon to challenge Odysseus to participate in the Phaeacians' games (*prokalessai*, *Odyssey* 8.142; see Sammons 2014: 305 n. 28). But in the world of Homeric epic a hero can also issue a blanket challenge. Paris challenges to a duel any of the Achaean champions who wishes to fight him (*prokalizeto*, *Iliad* 3.19–20). Nestor recounts how the Arcadian Ereuthalion challenged all the best Pylians to a duel (*prokalizeto*, *Iliad* 7.150). Ajax notes that Hector challenged all the best Achaeans to a duel (*prokalessato*, *Iliad* 7.285; cf. 7.50). These passages inform an assessment of Tydeus's challenge as plausible on account of the homology between games and war (Redfield 1975: 206, 210; Myers 2019: 162, 182–4), the most obvious overlap being that victors acquire *kleos* in each (e.g., *Iliad* 6.444–6; *Odyssey* 8.147). As for issuing a blanket challenge in games, Epeius's declaration that he will take on any comers (*hos tis*) in the boxing match in *Iliad* 23 provides a parallel (23.667).

Five passages attest to the plausibility of Tydeus's winning every contest. Euryalus's father, Mecisteus, "defeated all (*pantas*) the sons of Cadmus" in funeral games for Oedipus (*Iliad* 23.680). The use of *pantas* there must mean the same thing as *panta* in *Iliad* 4.389: Mecisteus won every contest. Nestor recounts that at the funeral games for Amarynceus "no man at all was my peer (*homoios*), neither of the Epeians nor of the Pylians themselves nor of the great-hearted Aetolians" (*Iliad* 23.632–3). Nestor won in boxing, wrestling, running, and the spear cast; his lone defeat came in the chariot race, but the circumstances were exceptional: he was competing solo against a team of drivers, the two sons of Actor, who gained some advantage being a duo (*Iliad* 23.634–42). Odysseus boasts after he bests all the Phaeacian competitors in the discus: he could do the same (see *pantōn* "all" at *Odyssey* 8.207) in boxing, wrestling, running, archery, and the spear cast, he says, before backing off on the claim about winning a foot race (8.202–33). (The audience should recall, however, that he won the foot race at the funeral games for Patroclus (*Iliad* 23.778–9).) Finally, Apollodorus reports that Androgeus, son of Minos, "defeated all" (*enikēse pantas*) at the Panathenaic Games (*Library* 3.15.7 Dräger), and Hyginus reports that, when Priam held funeral games in honor of his dead son Alexander, the very much alive Paris "won everything" (omnia uicit, *Fabulae* XCI.5 P. Marshall; cf. Euripides *Alexander* testimonium iii lines 21–2 and fragment 62d column ii lines 22–3 Collard and Cropp).

Critics deem Tydeus's killing forty-nine men "unrealistich" (Andersen 1978: 38) and "hyperbolische" (Coray, Krieter-Spiro, and Visser 2017: 164 at 391–8): after all, they are attacking him all at once. Yet, just as Tydeus kills "all" (*pantas*) but one of his attackers (*Iliad* 4.397), Glaucus relates that Bellerophon single handedly killed all (*pantas*) the Lycians who ambushed (*lokhon*) him (6.187–90). Moreover, Athena emboldens Odysseus in the *Odyssey* by imagining what would happen if the pair were ambushed by hundreds of attackers or, if not ambushed, at least attacked all at once by hundreds of attackers: "If fifty bands (*pentēkonta lokhoi*) of mortal men surrounded (*peristaien*) the two of us, infused with the spirit of Ares for killing, even their cattle and fat sheep you would drive off" (20.49–51). Presumably, Athena imagines Odysseus doing a good portion, perhaps even all, of the required killing. Her point is that, with a goddess, such as herself, on one's side, these sorts of feats become possible. Add Diomedes's assertion that Sthenelus and he alone (Janko 1992: 328 at 97–100) could take Troy because "we came here with a god (*sun...theōi*)" (*Iliad* 9.46–9). One is presumably to understand that, when Tydeus kills the Cadmeians, he still has Athena working on his behalf as he did during the games when she served as his ally (*epirrothos*, *Iliad* 4.390; cf. 5.116 (*parestēs*)). Statius will read the episode this way: in the *Thebaid*'s retelling, Athena says that she granted Tydeus his victory over the ambuscade (uincere.../ adnuimus, 2.687–8 Gervais; see Gervais 2017: 314 at 687f.). Similarly, the reference to Tydeus's acceding to the omens of the gods (*theōn teraessi*) at *Iliad* 4.398 suggests at the very least divine attention to his fate during the ambush and perhaps even divine backing as well. With Tydeus buoyed by such support, the mass slaughter of his enemies becomes possible. As regards leaving a sole survivor—Maeon in this case—one turns to Greek myth as a whole for parallels: "The sole-survivor motif in 397 is equally conventional, cf. e.g. Lunkeus alone spared of the fifty Egyptian cousins, or Thoas of the Lemnian men slain by their womenfolk" (Kirk 1985: 371 at 393).

In short, Tydeus's actions can register as plausible. As for the matter of suitability, one returns to *Iliad* 4.390: Agamemnon's reminder that Athena looked out for Tydeus as his ally (*epirrothos*) helps explain why Tydeus specifically could perform these actions. Tydeus has all the trappings of a first-class hero— above all, divine support—and should be expected to accomplish noteworthy feats. Perceived realism is often a matter of stereotyping (Cohen 2001: 259). In Agamemnon's story, Tydeus does what a hero of his stature can do.

Judgments of perceived realism also depend on the characters' motivations. Agamemnon does not specify why Tydeus challenged the Cadmeians to athletic contests, but that readers have done so readily and easily since antiquity suggests the plausibility of the suppressed motive. The scholiasts speculate that Tydeus acted in response to the Cadmeians' mocking his small stature (bT scholion at *Iliad* 4.389b1); Sammons adds, "Perhaps he was mocked about his life as an exile" (2014: 307). Nor does Agamemnon specify why the Cadmeians are angry (*kholōsamenoi*, *Iliad* 4.391). Again, though, the ease with which one can supply a motive for their anger suggests the plausibility of the suppressed motive: either the content of Tydeus's message provokes their anger or Tydeus's dominance in the athletic contests does (Kirk 1985: 370 at 391; cf. Scodel 2008: 37). At the end of the anecdote, Tydeus lets Maeon go out of deference to omens from the gods (*Iliad* 4.397–8). Agamemnon has already rehearsed the fact that mortals act in accordance with their reading of omens: the Mycenaeans do not give Polyneices and Eteocles the troops they request once they receive signs from Zeus telling them not to (*Iliad* 4.381). Here, too, in this bit about sparing Maeon, one finds an opportunity for the recipient, Diomedes, to judge the depiction of Tydeus realistic.

These several factors enable Diomedes to identify with Tydeus. By encouraging this response, Agamemnon increases the likelihood of persuading Diomedes.

### 3.3.2. Nestor on Nestor

In *Iliad* 11 Nestor tries to persuade Patroclus to return to the fight. Nestor offers himself as an example for Patroclus to follow, rehearsing his youthful feats in battle against the Epeians (Hainsworth 1993: 296; Dickson 1995: 173, 178–9; Alden 2000: 98; Martin 2000: 54–5; de Jong 2018b: 25). Elizabeth Minchin shows how Nestor constructs an "engaging tale" marked by suspense (1991: 282). One can also trace how Nestor encourages Patroclus to identify with the young Nestor of the tale.

I focus first on perceived realism. Beginning his analysis of *Iliad* 11.735–59, Bernard Fenik comments, "Nestor's description of the battle between the Pylians and the Epeians is given in typical style" (1968: 113). Because I equate typicality with realism, I can build on Fenik's comment: Patroclus should find Nestor's description of the battle realistic on account of its typicality. I query the realism of three specific moments.

Both Neleus's refusal (*oude . . . / eia*) to let the young Nestor fight and the young Nestor's ignoring his father's wishes (*Iliad* 11.717–21) find parallels (cf. Alden 2000: 94 n. 46; Gregory 2018: 67–8). The narrator reports on the sons of Merops (*Iliad* 2.831–4):

> . . . the two sons of Merops of Percote, who beyond all others
> knew the art of divination, and he did not allow (*oude . . . easke*) his sons
> to go into battle that destroys men. But the two of them did not
> obey: for the fates of black death led them on.

We learn of Iphidamas that his grandfather "tried to keep (*kateruke*) him there [in Thrace], and he gave him his own daughter; but having married, from his bridal chamber he went after the report of the coming Achaeans" (*Iliad* 11.226–7). The narrator prefaces his account of the death of Polydorus, a son of Priam (*Iliad* 20.408–12):

> And his father did not (*ou ... eiaske*) allow him to fight
> because he was the youngest of his offspring among his children,
> and he was dearest to him, and he bested all in the speed of his feet.
> Then indeed in his folly displaying the excellence of his feet,
> he ran through the front ranks until he lost his own life.

At the start of the battle his father tried to keep him away from, the young Nestor kills Moulius and seizes his chariot and horses (*Iliad* 11.738–44). Menelaus kills Pylaemenes, and Antilochus kills Pylaemenes's charioteer, Mydon, after which he drives the chariot and team back into the mass of Achaeans: "Antilochus whipped them and drove them to the army of the Achaeans" (*Iliad* 5.576–89, quotation from 5.589); later, after Idomeneus kills Asius, Antilochus dispatches his charioteer and drives the chariot and horses back to the Achaean side: "and the horses, Antilochus the son of great-hearted Nestor, drove away from the Trojans and to the well-greaved Achaeans" (*Iliad* 13.384–401, quotation from 13.400–1). With one exception (Diomedes at *Iliad* 10.513), the Homeric warriors do not ride on horses (Walker 2016: 320–4), so to whip and/or drive horses means to whip and/or drive them while standing in a chariot they pull (see, for instance, *Iliad* 5.237 with 5.275; cf. 15.352–4, 23.500).

The highlight of the battle comes when Nestor captures fifty chariots and kills 100 men (*Iliad* 11.748–9). Fenik speaks of "exaggerations" and "the improbable number" (1968: 113), but Bryan Hainsworth observes that fifty "is Homer's standard large number" (1993: 304 at 748). This slaughter finds parallels in the *Iliad*'s other descriptions of mass slaughter by one warrior. Over the course of the battle described in *Iliad* 16.284–785, Patroclus kills fifty-four men: twenty-seven named individuals (see Stoevesandt 2004: 404–7); twenty-seven more unnamed warriors ("three times he killed nine men," *Iliad* 16.785) (cf. Arnaud 2019: 79–80). Merely by shouting from the trench that surrounds the Achaean wall, Achilles prompts such panic in the Trojan forces that "there and then perished twelve of the best men on their own chariots and spears" (*Iliad* 18.230–1). When he returns to the fight in *Iliad* 21 and 22, Achilles kills twenty-four named men (see Stoevesandt 2004: 409–12; cf. Arnaud 2019: 81–3) and slaughters an unspecified number in the river at *Iliad* 21.20–6. True, neither Patroclus nor Achilles kills 100 men, but the precise number is beside the point. What matters is that in the Homeric world a warrior can dominate the battlefield and kill a lot of opponents in a single battle, enough to make the prospect of one man killing 100 men seem within the realm of possibility. Nestor's 100 kills also need to be recognized as the logical consequence of the initial fifty. It is typical for a chariot to convey two people, one who guides the horses and another who rides alongside him (the *paraibatēs* (*Iliad* 23.132)). It is typical for one warrior to kill two men in a single chariot (e.g., *Iliad* 5.608-9, 11.91-147, 20.484-9). And, as we saw just saw, it is typical for a warrior to win a chariot as booty after the death or flight of the chariot's original occupants (e.g., *Iliad* 5.10-26, 5.216-327, 5.576-89, 13.384-401). When Nestor takes fifty chariots—and to repeat fifty "is Homer's standard large number" (Hainsworth 1993: 304 at 748)—he reasonably kills 100 men. Finally, recall Athena's attempt to embolden Odysseus—"If fifty bands (*pentēkonta lokhoi*) of mortal men surrounded the two of us, infused with the spirit of Ares for killing, even their cattle and fat sheep you would drive off" (*Odyssey* 20.49-51)—and its implication that Odysseus would be able to kill an extraordinary number of men as long as he had the goddess's support. When Nestor captures fifty chariots and kills 100 men, he has Athena on his side, as his comment at 11.721 indicates: "in this way Athena directed the contest." At *Iliad* 11.748-9, Nestor's narrative cleaves to the plausible as defined by the Homeric poems themselves.

Nestor's remark at *Iliad* 11.721 directs attention to the related topic of suitability. The perception that it is suitable for Nestor to be the one to perform the various feats he performs on the battlefield relies on his assertion, "in this way Athena directed the contest." It is suitable for Nestor specifically to excel because the goddess backs him, just as in Agamemnon's tale it is suitable for Tydeus to excel because of Athena's support.

Regarding the depiction of the young Nestor's motivations, I highlight that throughout his tale Nestor makes clear that the acquisition of spoils motivated him. He lists in detail the massive amounts of spoils (*lēida...pollēn*) that he leads the way in taking from the Epeians in the initial cattle raid (*boēlasiēi*): fifty herds of cattle, fifty flocks of sheep, fifty herds of swine, fifty herds of goats, and 150 mares along with any foals (*Iliad* 11.671-81); a few verses later we learn that he must have been instrumental in capturing the flocks' herdsmen as well (11.697). In his account of the subsequent battle, Nestor makes sure to note that he did not just kill men; he seized their chariots too (*helon diphrous*, *Iliad* 11.748; cf. 11.327). Likewise, as the Pylians cut down (*kteinontes*) the fleeing Epeians, they gather (*legontes*) the armor of the fallen as spoils (*Iliad* 11.755). Warriors do not always take the time to despoil their opponents. After Diomedes kills Thymbraeus and Odysseus kills his attendant, Molion, they leave (*eiasan*) them there and move on without taking their armor (*Iliad* 11.320-4); by contrast, they do strip their next named victims, the two sons of Merops (11.335). Hector orders his men not to strip their dead foes (*Iliad* 15.347). So one should not gloss over Nestor's reference to seizing armor at 11.755, and in fact Nestor implies that he was among those who stripped armor from the fallen. After all, he "killed the last man" (*andra kteinas pumaton*, *Iliad* 11.759)—which must mean that he killed the last man who failed to escape, not that all the Epeians were killed to the last man—and to kill the last man means to lead the way in killing: Hector routs the Achaeans, "always killing the last man (*apokteinōn ton opistaton*)" (*Iliad* 8.342); Agamemnon routs the Trojans, "always killing the last man (*apokteinōn ton opistaton*)" (*Iliad* 11.178). If Nestor led the way in killing, the act described by the first participle in verse 755 (*kteinontes*), there is every reason to think he also led the way in seizing armor, the act described by the second participle in 755 (*legontes*).

Nestor's repeated emphasis on spoils does not surprise. A critical measure of power and status in the Homeric world is the number of livestock, slaves, and prestige objects in one's possession (e.g., *Odyssey* 14.229-34, 23.355-8; Donlan 1999: 4; Ready 2010: 140-1, 144; 2011: 34-9). In general, therefore, the acquisition of spoils, both during the battle and afterward at the public (re)distribution of the booty, motivates the Homeric warrior to fight (Ready 2007). In particular, the Epeians had taken so much from them ("the Epeians owed a debt to many" (*Iliad* 11.688)) that only with a great haul of spoils can the Pylians restore the power balance both between the Epeians and themselves and, just as important, among themselves (11.703-5). Patroclus can easily judge Nestor's motivation realistic.

The passage triggers specific kinds of identification in specific ways. From the start, Nestor depicts the Epeians as the bad guys and the Pylians as the good guys. He speaks about a dispute over "cattle stealing" (*Iliad* 11.672) but picks up the action when he seizes cattle in retaliation for a prior theft (*rhusi'*, 11.674). That is, Nestor does not specify who initiated the tit for tat raids: he begins with himself and his people in the righteous position of reclaiming what is theirs from the evil Epeians. Over the course of verses 688 to 702, Nestor hammers this negative characterization home. The Epeians took advantage of Heracles's sack of Pylos and arrogantly (*huperēphaneontes*) maltreated (*hubrizontes*) and contrived outrageous deeds (*atasthala mēkhanoōnto*) against the Pylians. The severity of their transgressions matches that of Penelope's suitors, whom Telemachus characterizes in the same way—"they who maltreat and contrive outrageous deeds against me" (οἵ τέ μοι ὑβρίζοντες ἀτάσθαλα μηχανόωνται, *Odyssey* 3.207; cf. 16.86)—as does Penelope herself (*Odyssey* 17.588) along with the disguised Odysseus (*Odyssey* 20.170) and the seer Theoclymenus (20.370). To add insult to injury, Augeias, the king of the Epeians, stole Neleus's horses after they competed in games held in Elis.

The bad behaviors marked out by words from the root *atasthal-* (Cairns 2012: 35-49; cf. Alden 2017: table 4), the sort of bad behaviors exhibited by the Epeians, can make one act counter to what the gods want or even expressly decree.[3]

---

[3] *Odyssey* 1.7, 1.34, 12.300, 20.170 (reading *atasthala* with manuscripts G, O, and C), 22.416, 23.67, 24.351-2; Hesiod *Theogony* 516 Most 2006, *Works and Days* 261 Most 2006; cf. Bakker 2013: 47, 114-16; O'Maley 2014: 19-23; Scodel 2018: 12-14.

The Pylians by contrast have the gods, or at least the powerful Athena, on their side: she comes to Pylos not just to warn them to arm but to assemble the army (*laon ageirein*) herself (*Iliad* 11.714–16). If Hera's description of the toil involved in her time spent assembling (*laon ageirousēi*) the Greek host against Troy, emblematized in her own sweat and in her horses' exhaustion (*Iliad* 4.26–8), is any indication, Athena's actions demonstrate her commitment to the Pylians' cause. Moreover, with the presumed absence of any such actions by the Epeians, contrast the Pylians' propensity for sacrificing to the gods: they conduct sacrifices after the distribution of the spoils from the cattle raid (*Iliad* 11.707) and, because they are about to cross their borders (Hainsworth 1993: 303 at 727–30), before the second battle (11.727–9).

The Pylians and Nestor are the virtuous ones. Perhaps Nestor lays so much stress on this attribute to make up for the fact that he cannot rely on demographic similarity—Patroclus is a veteran warrior; the Nestor of this tale is a young man new to fighting (*Iliad* 11.684). In any case, recall again Cohen and Tal-Or's discussion of the contribution of character virtue to identification. More specifically, one would be hard pressed to resist taking the Pylians' side in this dispute and to resist viewing the story and its actors from the young Nestor's vantage point. One is apt to experience cognitive identification with the young Nestor.

Nestor also encourages Patroclus to adopt the young Nestor's goals and experience motivational identification. In verses 717–21, he discloses two related goals:

>οὐδέ με Νηλεὺς
>εἴα θωρήσσεσθαι, ἀπέκρυψεν δέ μοι ἵππους·
>οὐ γάρ πώ τί μ' ἔφη ἴδμεν πολεμήια ἔργα.
>ἀλλὰ καὶ ὣς ἱππεῦσι μετέπρεπον ἡμετέροισι
>καὶ πεζός περ ἐών, ἐπεὶ ὣς ἄγε νεῖκος Ἀθήνη.
>
>But Neleus
>did not allow me to arm and he hid away the horses from me:
>for he denied that I yet knew warlike deeds.
>But even so I was conspicuous among our horsemen,
>even though I was on foot because in this way Athena directed the contest.

First, Nestor needs to get a horse and chariot. Second, he needs to prove his father, Neleus, wrong: Neleus delighted in Nestor's success in the cattle raid against Itymoneus and the country folk (*agroiōtai*, *Iliad* 11.676) but has his doubts about Nestor's abilities in open warfare. If Nestor fails to achieve the first goal, he will necessarily fail to achieve his second goal. The specificity of each goal makes them easy to comprehend. At the same time, these are difficult goals because they require getting around the formidable obstacle of Neleus. Nestor portrays Neleus as a devoted father—he rejoices at Nestor's success in the cattle raid (*Iliad* 11.683)—and an unquestioned leader: only after he takes his share of the spoils to satiate his anger at the Epeians does he turn over the remainder to his people to divide up (11.703–5). Such a figure is not to be taken lightly and circumventing him will require some effort on Nestor's part. The adversative phrase *alla kai hōs* ("but even so," *Iliad* 11.720), used in contexts in which people overcome challenges (e.g., *Iliad* 5.482, 16.363), sums up the difficulty of each task. As I noted in section 2.2 (p. 25), one is more apt to adopt a character's goals if the goals are hard to achieve because someone (or something) stands in the character's way. A neat demonstration of the likelihood of Patroclus's adopting Nestor's goals comes when twice Nestor reports that the Epeians were "eager to destroy" Thryoessa (*Iliad* 11.713, 733): it is hard to imagine Patroclus wanting them to succeed.

Finally, Nestor provides the opportunity for Patroclus to identify with the young Nestor on an emotional level. Nestor ends the tale with a declaration of triumph: "and all prayed to Zeus among the gods and to Nestor among men" (πάντες δ' εὐχετόωντο θεῶν Διὶ Νέστορί τ' ἀνδρῶν, *Iliad* 11.761). The chiastic arrangement in the second hemistich emphasizes that Nestor received as much—or at least an analogous amount of—veneration as Zeus did (cf. *Iliad* 22.394; *Odyssey* 8.467, 15.181). The young Nestor will have reveled in the attention and, unlike Achilles, have "enjoyed (*aponēsetai*) the fruits of his own excellence" (*Iliad* 11.763). Patroclus can feel happy right along with the young Nestor.

For the most part, however, Nestor does not talk openly about his own emotions. Yet emotions run high in Homeric scenes of combat: for instance, pity compels warriors to action on the battlefield (Ready 2011: 177; Allen-Hornblower 2016: 26) as does grief (*akhos*; Cook 2003; 2009: 153–9) and anger (*kholos*; Fenik 1968: 139; T. Walsh 2005: 163–8, 175–82; cf. Scodel 2008: 49). We should not rule out a consistent emotional element in Nestor's tale. Instead, to see how the passage works in this way, we recall that Homeric epic frequently relies on implicit associations. According to the principle known as traditional referentiality, words and phrases bring with them an added value, a deeper connotation, that is to be felt even when the text does not make the implicit explicit (J. M. Foley 1991; Kelly 2007; Arft 2014). Now, interpreters of modern literature argue that characters' actions imply emotions, thoughts, and states of mind,[4] and empirical investigations demonstrate the ease with which recipients intuit characters' emotions, thoughts, and states of mind in the absence of explicit declarations (Sanford and Emmott 2012: 196–200, 207). Homerists interested in traditional referentiality occasionally look in this direction. For instance, when audience members stay

---

[4] Zunshine 2003: 270; Mellmann 2010: 428; B. Vermeule 2010: 70; Caracciolo 2014: 142–3; Ryan 2015b: 294–5; Martínez 2018: 90.

"silent in silence" after a speaker finishes talking, they reveal their "consternation at a proposal" (Kelly 2007: 85); used of a charioteer, the phrase "he whipped to drive" implies "the character's conviction in the journey's success" (98); one "looking about" (*paptēnas*) shows an "awareness of a defensive and reactive context" (265); one who "stands by" (*stē para*) exhibits "an attitude of potential or actual assistance" (272); to seize a spear (*lazeto d' egkhos*) is to reveal "the intention of using it more or less immediately" (320). To return to Nestor in *Iliad* 11: the poet does not have to have Nestor spell out his emotions because they come already implied in the actions and scenarios he describes. Further, Nestor knows that his addressee, the veteran warrior Patroclus, can deduce the relevant emotions based on those descriptions. This addendum is one logical extension of the model of traditional referentiality: we, the audience, get the underlying connotations; so too do the characters. The alternative—that the external audience get the underlying connotations and can read the minds of the characters, but the characters do not get the underlying connotations and cannot read the minds of their fellows—would be perverse, and indeed characters frequently do mind read their fellows or at least try to (see section 8.2, pp. 223–4).

Nestor says that he "took a stand among the front ranks of fighters (*promakhoisin*)" (*Iliad* 11.744). I list some other warriors who fight in the front ranks, among the *promakhoi* and the *prōtoi*, and add what the narrator implies or says about their emotional state as they do so:

- Idomeneus, "similar to a boar in might (*alkēn*)" (*Iliad* 4.253; cf. 17.281–3): *thouris*, "eager, impetuous," serves as the epithet for *alkē* twenty-five times in the *Iliad* and the *Odyssey*;
- Odysseus, "angered (*kholōthē*) in his heart at his [Leucus's] death" (*Iliad* 4.494–5);
- Diomedes, "even before eager (*memaōs*) in his spirit to fight with the Trojans. Then indeed three times as much *menos* ['a furious urge to action...surging aggression' (Clarke 1999: 111)] seized him, like a lion..." (*Iliad* 5.134–6; cf. 5.562–3, 20.110–11);
- Hector, "exulting (*blemeainōn*) in his strength" (*Iliad* 8.337), "being highspirited" (*mega phroneōn*, *Iliad* 11.296) and later, "screaming shrilly (*oxea keklēgōs*), similar to a flame of Hephaestus, unquenchable" (*Iliad* 17.87–9; cf. *iakhōn* at *Iliad* 19.424);
- Agastrophus, "on foot he was raging (*thune*)" (*Iliad* 11.341–2; cf. 20.411–12);
- Patroclus, beset by "grief (*akhos*) for his dead companion" and "angered (*kekholōso*) in your heart" (*Iliad* 16.581–5; cf. 17.591–2);
- Ajax, whom Menelaus "roused in his spirit" (*thumon orine*, *Iliad* 17.123–4).

Emotions course through the warrior who moves amidst the front ranks. One can take one's pick as to which emotion the young Nestor would have felt.

## 78  IMMERSION, IDENTIFICATION, AND THE *ILIAD*

Three features of verses 747 to 749 attract attention—the verb *eporousa* ("I leapt"), the simile "similar to a black whirlwind," and the reference to 100 unnamed victims:

αὐταρ ἐγὼν ἐπόρουσα κελαινῇ λαίλαπι ἶσος,
πεντήκοντα δ' ἕλον δίφρους, δύο δ' ἀμφὶς ἕκαστον
φῶτες ὀδὰξ ἕλον οὖδας ἐμῷ ὑπὸ δουρὶ δαμέντες.

But I leapt similar to a black whirlwind
and I took fifty chariots, and around each of them two
men bit the earth with their teeth, subdued by my spear.

Nestor will have performed these actions in a heightened emotional state. Passages that occur elsewhere with at least two of these variables—the verb *eporouō*, a simile, and a reference to a number of unnamed victims—point to the warrior's emotions. First, Diomedes attacks Aeneas even though Apollo defends the Trojan (*Iliad* 5.436–8):

Three times then he leapt (*eporouse*) desiring eagerly (*meneainōn*) to kill,
and three times Apollo struck him hard on his shining shield.
But when indeed the fourth time he rushed in similar to a god (*daimoni isos*)....

The verb *meneainō* regularly captures a warrior's murderous excitement (e.g., *Iliad* 3.379, 13.628, 15.565, 21.33). Second, Patroclus assaults the Trojans (*Iliad* 16.783–6):

Πάτροκλος δὲ Τρωσὶ κακὰ φρονέων ἐνόρουσε.
τρὶς μὲν ἔπειτ' ἐπόρουσε θοῷ ἀτάλαντος Ἄρηι,
σμερδαλέα ἰάχων, τρὶς δ' ἐννέα φῶτας ἔπεφνεν.
ἀλλ' ὅτε δὴ τὸ τέταρτον ἐπέσσυτο δαίμονι ἶσος ....

But Patroclus leapt against the Trojans intending evil things.
Three times then he leapt equal to swift Ares,
shouting terribly, and three times he killed nine men,
But when indeed the fourth time he rushed in similar to a god....

The phrase *kaka phroneōn* signals hostility (e.g., *Iliad* 7.70; *Odyssey* 17.596; R. Allan 2022a: 85). The phrase *smerdalea iakhōn* pairs elsewhere with "eager" (*memaōs*, *Iliad* 5.301–2; *emmemaōs*, 20.284–5) and with "eager and raging" (*emmemaōs*...*meneainōn*, 20.442–3). Pain (*akhos*) comes over Hector seeing his fallen charioteer, but although grieving (*akhnumenos*), he enters the fray "shouting terribly" (*smerdalea iakhōn*) (*Iliad* 8.316–21). Third, when Achilles shouts mightily (*megal' iakhe*) from the trench in front of the Achaean wall (*Iliad* 18.228), two of our relevant variables appear: two extended similes (*Iliad* 18.207–14, 219–21); twelve Trojans killed in the ensuing confusion (18.230–1). The phrase used to describe his shout attests to a roused emotional state. Upon learning of Patroclus's death, female slaves "grieving in their hearts shouted out greatly" (θυμὸν ἀκηχέμεναι μεγάλ' ἴαχον, *Iliad* 18.29), and Circe addresses Odysseus, "shouting out greatly" and "wailing" (*mega iakhousa... olophuromenē*, *Odyssey* 10.323–4) (cf. *Iliad* 17.213, 18.160). Against this backdrop, Patroclus can impute at the very least eagerness and rage to Nestor in *Iliad* 11.747–9.

One should perform a similar operation upon hearing Nestor's account of how Poseidon rescued the two Moliones "by cloaking them in a great mist" (*kalupsas ēeri pollēi*, *Iliad* 11.752). This motif of a god's using some sort of obscuring element to rescue a warrior appears six other times (Pelliccia 2021: 80–6), and on four occasions one can note the frustration manifested by or attributed to the opposing warrior. The moment in which Apollo shrouds Aeneas "in a dark cloud (*kuaneēi nephelēi*)" (*Iliad* 5.344–5) is not relevant because this move does not confuse or disorient his opponent, Diomedes: Athena has removed the mist (*akhlun*) from his eyes that prevents mortals from recognizing gods (5.127–8), and Diomedes presses his attack even in the knowledge that Apollo is protecting Aeneas (5.432–5). Earlier Hephaestus saves Idaeus from Diomedes by shrouding him in darkness (*nukti kalupsas*, *Iliad* 5.23). Diomedes expresses no frustration at this turn of events perhaps because he has already killed Idaeus's brother, Phegeus, (5.18–19) and can seize their horses as spoils (5.25–6). I turn to the four other instances.

Aphrodite covers Paris in a thick mist and whisks him away before Menelaus can kill him (*Iliad* 3.381). When the narrative returns to Menelaus, he is looking in vain for Paris as he stalks through the crowd of Trojans and Achaeans "like a wild beast" (*thēri eoikōs*, 3.449). This phrase describes a fearful and stunned Ajax in retreat (*Iliad* 11.544–7). Antilochus stops trying to despoil Melanippus of his armor upon seeing Hector heading his way: he retreats "like (*eoikōs*) a beast (*thēri*) that has done a bad thing" (*Iliad* 15.582–90). *Homeric Hymn* 20 (to Hephaestus) reports that men lived in the mountains like beasts (*ēute thēres*, 4) before Hephaestus and Athena gave them the skills necessary to thrive. Applied to mortals, the simile appears when someone fails to achieve a goal, a position no one typically enjoys.

Apollo envelopes Hector in a thick mist, protecting him from Achilles's onslaught (*Iliad* 20.443–5). After four failed attempts to strike Hector, Achilles "shouts terribly" (*deina d' homoklēsas*, 20.448). In the two other appearances of this phrase, Apollo shouts at a warrior who repeatedly and unsuccessfully attempts something (*Iliad* 5.439, 16.706). "Shouting terribly" seems to be the tone one adopts when telling someone, "Stop it now!" Achilles exhibits a similar exasperation. More indicative of Achilles's frustration is his declaration, "Again now (*au nun*), dog, you fled death" (*Iliad* 20.449). Achilles's words (and the whole speech they introduce) recur in the mouth of Diomedes at *Iliad* 11.362. To find the frustration evident in this assertion (cf. Beck 2018: 154), one should note that exasperation or despair marks uses of *au nun* or *nun au*. Upon learning of Achilles's rejection of Agamemon's offer in *Iliad* 9, Diomedes states, "He [Achilles] is as it stands a haughty one; now again (*nun au*) you have increased his haughtiness still more" (*Iliad* 9.699-700). When Hera asks Sleep to lull Zeus to sleep, he replies, "Now again (*nun au*) you command me to perform this other impossible task" (*Iliad* 14.262). Alcimedon chastises Automedon after observing Automedon's inability to drive Patroclus's chariot and fight from it at the same time. In response, Automedon notes Patroclus's incomparable skill as a horseman and adds, "Now in turn (*nun au*) death and fate reach him" (*Iliad* 17.478; cf. 17.672, 22.436). In his supplication of Achilles, Lycaon laments, "Now again (*nun au*) destructive fate put me in your hands" (*Iliad* 21.82-3). Telemachus decries the second evil he is facing, the gluttony of the suitors: "and now in turn (*nun d' au*) an even greater one, which indeed soon will destroy completely my whole house" (*Odyssey* 2.48-9). Penelope weeps as she speaks of the loss of Odysseus and anticipates the loss of Telemachus: "Now in turn (*nun au*) the storm winds snatched away my beloved child" (*Odyssey* 4.727; cf. 4.817, 14.174). Calypso rebukes the gods for their persistent resentment: "And so again now (*au nun*), gods, you begrudge me for having a mortal man nearby" (*Odyssey* 5.129).

Apollo shrouds Agenor in a mist and removes him from the fray in order to save him from Achilles (*Iliad* 21.596-8). Apollo then assume Agenor's likeness and lures Achilles away from the Trojans who flee into the city. When Apollo discloses this ruse to Achilles, the narrator captures Achilles's exasperation by labeling him "greatly vexed" (*meg' okhthēsas*, *Iliad* 22.14), and Achilles goes on to make plain his disappointment himself: "You misled me, far-shooter, most destructive of all the gods.... But now you deprived me of great glory.... I would pay you back, if the power were in me to do so" (22.15, 18, 20).

Poseidon covers Achilles's eyes with a mist (*akhlun*), extracts Achilles's spear from Aeneas's shield and lays it at Achilles's feet, tosses Aeneas to another part of the battlefield, and removes the mist (*akhlun*) from Achilles's eyes (*Iliad* 20.318-42). The narrator notes Achilles's vexation (*okhthēsas*) once Poseidon removes the mist and Achilles sees his spear but no Aeneas (20.343).

One should view Nestor's report of Poseidon's defense of the Moliones from the perspective offered by these four passages and should assign a high degree of frustration to the young warrior. We find here another chance for Patroclus to experience emotional identification with the Nestor of the tale. This cue joins with the other cues for emotional identification as well as with the cues for cognitive and motivational identification.

I repeat *mutandis mutatis* my final point about Agamemnon's speech to Diomedes. Several components of Nestor's tale enable Patroclus to identify with the young Nestor. By encouraging this response, Nestor increases the likelihood of persuading Patroclus.

### 3.4. Conclusion

Numerous attributes of Homeric poetry lay the groundwork for recipients to identify with the characters. Recipients can take epithets to signal an overlap between their own attitudes and the attitudes of a character and to point up a character's virtue. The poet provides basic, but sufficient, information that allows us to construct mental images of what the characters look like and of the physical settings in which the characters operate. The poetry scores well enough in external realism and especially high in narrative realism. Characters' membership in a group informs their characterization. The characters talk and act in front of audiences: they are put on stage. The prevalence of what narratologists call transference enhances the prospect of experiencing cognitive identification with a character. The characters themselves identify with one another, thereby providing a model for the audience to follow. Finally, the poet works with familiar characters whom the audience is already invested in and cares about.

Homeric characters aim to get their addressees to identify with the protagonist of their tales. Putting to work the tools provided by the research presented in Chapter 2, we have seen how Agamemnon in *Iliad* 4 and Nestor in *Iliad* 11 fashion various cues toward that end. That internal narrators strive for this goal suggests that the poet will seek to get external audiences to identify with his characters. Taken together, this chapter's findings prepare for the next chapter's additional seven close readings wherein I consider how the external audience can identify with specific characters.

# 4
# Identification with Mortals and Gods

## 4.1. Overview

This chapter explores how external audiences might identify with the characters in several episodes in the *Iliad*, looking first to mortal characters (4.2) and then to divinities (4.3). I distinguish between identification with mortals and identification with immortals because the latter may not seem as obvious a possibility as the former. Section 4.4 highlights factors that block a recipient's ability to identify with a character. Section 4.5 rounds out the chapter and Part I by considering the politics of identification.

## 4.2. Identification with Mortals

I examine four episodes: Agamemnon's display of martial excellence (his *aristeia*) in *Iliad* 11 (4.2.1); Andromache's reaction to the news of Hector's death in *Iliad* 22 (4.2.2); the funeral games for Patroclus in *Iliad* 23 (4.2.3); and Priam's decision to ransom Hector's corpse in *Iliad* 24 (4.2.4).

### 4.2.1. Agamemnon in *Iliad* 11

Richard Rutherford asks why the *Iliad* poet devotes so much narrative time to describing warriors killing: "When a hero launches upon an *aristeia*, the audience is surely meant to sympathize with his energy and to relish the excitement of the battlefield, to enjoy the cruel wit of the taunts directed at his opponents; the analogies drawn with the modern western or war film are not unreasonable" (2013: 63). Viewing a warrior's *aristeia* from the angle provided by the concept of identification offers the chance to explore these words, "sympathize...relish... enjoy." Agamemnon's *aristeia* in *Iliad* 11 can serve as a test case. Modern readers may be primed to detest Agamemnon (cf. R. Friedrich 2019: 190–2; A. Porter 2019), but one of the most famous ancient exegetes of Homeric poetry, Aristarchus, thought him a great hero, worthy of respect (Schironi 2018: 717–18). With that salutary shift in perspective in mind, I suggest that the *Iliad* poet gives recipients the opportunity to identify with Agamemnon in *Iliad* 11.

An essential criterion for identification—time spent with a character—has been met: Agamemnon has already passed significant amounts of time in the narrative spotlight. Unfolding over the course of *Iliad* 11.16–45, Agamemnon's arming scene also prepares us to identify with him.

A granular investigation of the arming scene's component parts can trace simultaneously both how the distinctive features of the scene draw our attention to Agamemnon (cf. A. Porter 2019: 153) and the way the scene encourages us to visualize Agamemnon. James Armstrong notes the "extraordinary expansion" of the basic arming template, its "sumptuous" handling here (1958: 344, 345; cf. Fenik 1968: 79; Tsagalis 2012: 413; R. Friedrich 2019: 199; Kretler 2020: 67 n. 53). His framing proves more illuminating than labeling the scene "highly traditional" (A. Porter 2019: 153).

Agamemnon's greaves are typical, "fitted with silver ankle-pieces" (*Iliad* 11.18) like Paris's (*Iliad* 3.331), Patroclus's (*Iliad* 16.132), and Achilles's (*Iliad* 19.370) (Hainsworth 1993: 217 at 17–19). His corselet (*thōrēx*), with forty-two decorative rings—listed as an increasing tricolon: ten of cyanus, twelve of gold, and twenty of tin—and with three decorative snakes on either side (*Iliad* 11.19–28), stands apart. Paris's (*Iliad* 3.332) and Achilles's (*Iliad* 19.371) corselets lack any notable decoration, although Achilles's is said to be "more radiant than the gleam of fire" (*Iliad* 18.610). Patroclus's corselet is "elaborate and decorated with stars" (*poikilon astrepoenta*, *Iliad* 16.134). In the Hesiodic *Shield of Heracles*, Heracles's corselet is "beautiful, golden, richly worked (*poludaidalon*)" (125 Most 2007). Corselets mentioned outside of arming scenes can be "richly worked" (*poludaidalos*, e.g., *Iliad* 3.358, 4.136) or "elaborate" (*daidaleos*, *Iliad* 8.195). Achilles observes that Asteropaeus's corselet has "an overlay of bright tin set in circles" (*Iliad* 23.560). None of these, even Patroclus's, would seem to compare to Agamemnon's corselet. At the very least, the poet only details the decorations on Agamemnon's corselet.

Agamemnon's sword has studs (*hēloi*) of gold (*Iliad* 11.29), the only sword so decorated in extant archaic Greek hexameter poetry: a scepter has golden studs (*Iliad* 1.246), as does Nestor's cup (*Iliad* 11.633). Other swords have silver studs (e.g., *Iliad* 2.45, 14.405; *Odyssey* 8.406), or a silver hilt (*Iliad* 1.220; *Odyssey* 8.403–4); they can have dark thongs at the hilt to enhance the grip (*Iliad* 15.713; Hesiod *Shield of Heracles* 221). Agamemnon's sword with golden studs may take us far from the typical warrior: to Apollo and his epithet "of the golden sword" (*khrusaoros*, e.g., *Iliad* 5.509; *Homeric Hymn to Apollo* 123)—an epithet assigned to Demeter too (*Homeric Hymn to Demeter* 4 West 2003a)—or to Chrysaor, the child of Medusa, who gets his name from wielding a golden sword (*aor khruseion*, Hesiod *Theogony* 283).

Agamemnon's scabbard (*kouleon*) is silver (*Iliad* 11.30–1), again the only such item found among the eleven occurrences of the noun in archaic Greek hexameter poetry. Euryalus gifts Odysseus a scabbard of "fresh-sawn ivory" (*Odyssey* 8.404).

Apart from these two instances, a scabbard is only ever elsewhere said to be "great" (*mega*, *Iliad* 3.272 = 19.253). The straps (*aortēressin*) of Agamemnon's scabbard are gold (*Iliad* 11.31). Only here are we specifically informed that a scabbard has straps (cf. *Odyssey* 11.609), and gold ones at that.

The description of the decoration on Agamemnon's shield requires five verses: bronze circles, white bosses of tin, a boss of cyanus, and three terrifying figures—a Gorgon, Terror, and Flight (*Iliad* 11.33-7). Two other shields merit lengthier descriptions, Achilles's in *Iliad* 18 and Heracles's in the *Shield of Heracles*. Setting aside Achilles's and Heracles's shields as things apart so as not to skew the search for comparanda, one comes to the description of Ajax's shield: the poet also spends five verses on Ajax's shield, noting that it has seven layers of ox hide under a layer of bronze (*Iliad* 7.219-23). But the description of Ajax's shield brings us to a crucial point of difference between Agamemnon's shield and other shields (apart from Achilles's and Heracles's): the poet does not elsewhere describe the decorations on shields. The narrator does not tell us how the top layer of Ajax's shield is decorated, or even if it is decorated (cf. *Iliad* 13.803-4). We are left to wonder if Nestor's famous shield (*Iliad* 8.192-3) is decorated. At one point the narrator refers to it as one piece of Nestor's "wrought armor" (*entea poikil'*, *Iliad* 10.75-6), which presumably means the shield has decorations in bronze: elsewhere we hear of "armor wrought/inlaid with bronze" (*teukhea poikila khalkōi*, e.g., 6.504). Still other shields might be decorated in a distinctive fashion: Pandarus thinks he can determine that Diomedes is the one wreaking havoc among the Trojans on account of his shield and helmet (*Iliad* 5.182). The poet, however, does not tell us about these decorations.

Agamemnon's silver shield strap (*argureos telamōn*, *Iliad* 11.38) finds a parallel in Achilles's silver shield strap (18.480; cf. 18.598). Its decoration finds a parallel in Odysseus's report on the terrifying decorations on Heracles's golden strap for his sword (*khruseos...telamōn*, *Odyssey* 11.609-14). One could picture the bears, boars, and lion on Heracles's strap but not really the "battles and fights and scenes of murder and man-slaying" (11.612). By contrast, one can imagine the three-headed snake on Agamemnon's strap (Hainsworth 1993: 222 at 40).

With its two crest-holders and four bosses (*Iliad* 11.41; van Wees 1994: 151 n. 73), Agamemnon's helmet finds its partner in Athena's helmet (5.743). Only these two helmets have these adornments. Other helmets also have the horse-hair plume (*hippourin...lophos*, *Iliad* 11.42), such as those of Paris (*Iliad* 3.337), Hector (6.469), Teucer (15.481), Patroclus (16.138), and Odysseus (*Odyssey* 22.124).

Lastly, Agamemnon picks up two spears (*Iliad* 11.43). Like Paris (*Iliad* 3.17-18) and Patroclus (16.139), he is armed to the teeth with a sword and two spears. Not all warriors go into battle thus: Meriones takes one spear from Idomeneus's hut (*Iliad* 13.295). Achilles arms with a sword and a spear (*Iliad* 19.372, 387). Asteropaeus has two spears (*Iliad* 21.145), but evidently no sword, which is why he tries to make use of the spear that Achilles hurled at him (21.174–5). After he runs out of arrows with which to take aim at the suitors in *Odyssey* 22, Odysseus picks up two spears, but no sword (22.125). To decapitate Leodes, Odysseus has to pick up a sword that the fallen suitor Agelaus dropped (22.326–8). By giving Agamemnon two spears, the poet rounds out his maximalist presentation: Agamemnon could not possibly wear or hold anything else.

The rapid juxtaposition of different materials becomes a leitmotif of this description and a neat emblem of the visual magnificence of the armed Agamemnon: the corselet has cyanus, gold, and tin; the silver scabbard has golden straps (the juxtaposition of *argureon, khruseoisin* (*Iliad* 11.30) stands out especially); the shield has bronze, tin, and cyanus; the shield strap has silver and cyanus. The Hesiodic *Shield of Heracles* makes explicit this equation between a variety of materials and an arresting sight: Heracles's shield, decorated with gypsum, white ivory, electrum, gold, and cyanus, is "a marvel to see" (*thauma idesthai*) (140–3). The sentence with which the description of the armed Agamemnon closes also emphasizes the striking visual tableau: the gleam from the armor of the fully armed Agamemnon goes up to the sky (*Iliad* 11.44–5). Finally, the epithet applied to Mycenae in verse 46's "the king of Mycenae rich in gold (*polukhrusoio*)" reaffirms this emphasis on spectacle. Gold gleams: the golden studs in Agamemnon's sword gleam (*pamphainon, Iliad* 11.30); the gold on Heracles's shield gleams (*phaeinōi / lampomenon*, Hesiod *Shield of Heracles* 142–3); Athena's golden armor gleams (*pamphanoōnta*, Homeric Hymn to Athena 28.6). Moreover, in other hexameter poems apart from the Homeric epics, Aphrodite receives the epithet *polukhrusos* (Hesiod *Theogony* 980; *Works and Days* 521; *Shield of Heracles* 8, 47; *Homeric Hymn to Aphrodite* 1, 9 West 2003a). The Homeric epics speak of Aphrodite as *khruseē* "golden" (*Iliad* 6x; *Odyssey* 5x). Aphrodite merits these epithets because of how she dresses, "adorned with gold" (*khrusōi kosmētheisa, Homeric Hymn to Aphrodite* 65; cf. 89)—that is, because of how she looks.

This rehearsal prompts two conclusions. First, distinctive features abound in Agamemnon's panoply. His sword and scabbard, for example, stand out for the materials used in their construction. Only one other helmet, Athena's, resembles his own. More abstractly, the narrative presentation has distinctive features: only here do we learn about the elaborate decoration on a corselet; only here (if we pass over Achilles's and Heracles's shields) do we learn about the elaborate decoration on a shield. The distinctiveness of Agamemnon's war gear and the distinctiveness of the presentation of that war gear draw our attention to the character. The peculiarities of the arming scene prime us to wonder about what will happen to Agamemnon as the episode unwinds. This analysis, then, builds on ancient commentators' interest in how arming scenes capture our attention (Nünlist 2009: 138).

Second, the poet gives us a lot to see and advertises that fact: he thereby encourages and enables us to construct an image of what the character looks like. One can compare how Plutarch's description of Alexander's weapons and armor (*Life of Alexander* 32.8–12) "prompt[s] the reader to visualize the scene" (Grethlein 2013: 94). As I noted earlier (section 3.2, p. 54), the *Iliad* poet and the *Odyssey* poet do not go in for detailed descriptions of their characters' physiques, but they will dilate on what a character is wearing and holding. The arming scene may not specify Agamemnon's physical attributes, but it gives us a sense of how the armed Agamemnon appeared (cf. Minchin 2001: 117). Even if one grants the difficulty in envisioning precisely the decoration on the corselet and the shield (Hainsworth 1993: 218 at 24–8, 220 at 32–9)—and I think those sorts of positivistic complaints arise only upon deliberate reflection, not when one reads or hears the poetry as a leisure activity—the point remains that we have ample opportunity to craft an image of Agamemnon. I recall the importance of physical description—that is, ultimately, the opportunity to envision a character—to identification.

The arming scene as a whole also prepares us to identify with Agamemnon in one other way. Verse 16—"and he himself put on the gleaming bronze"—makes us assign Agamemnon to that large class of individuals who arm: it prompts us to think of him as a warrior. Yet, as the poet embarks on a full-scale arming scene, we reassign Agamemnon to that small group of distinguished fighters who receive a lengthy arming scene: Paris (see *Iliad* 6.521–2; Arnaud 2019: 111), Patroclus, and Achilles in the *Iliad* to whom we can reasonably add those characters of the poems of the Epic Cycle who have an *aristeia* that presumably included an arming scene (Sammons 2017: 166)—namely, Telephus, the king of the Mysians, in the *Cypria*; the Amazon princess Penthesileia and the Ethiopian king Memnon in the *Aethiopis*; and Telephus's son Eurypylus in the *Little Iliad* (Sammons 2017: 163–5). Agamemnon's arming scene makes us think of Agamemnon not simply as a warrior but as one capable of performing notable feats on the battlefield (cf. Myers 2019: 152). This classification has an impact. María-Ángeles Martínez examines a passage in Jeff Lindsay's novel *Darkly Dreaming Dexter* wherein the crime scene analyst and serial killer, Dexter, describes the uniform he wears to work (2018: 103). Martínez shows how the focus on the uniform of a crime scene investigator can complicate our evaluation of the character: we may want to dislike Dexter because he is a serial killer, but our positive associations with "law-abiding policemen" make us more sympathetic. Just so, placing Agamemnon in the category of those capable of performing notable feats on the battlefield may induce recipients who have come to question Agamemnon's leadership—"incompetence" (A. Porter 2019: 51); "thoughtless[ness], impetuousness, and despotic leadership style"; "given to thoughtless, foolish, and rash words and actions...a penchant for arrogance, imperiousness, irreverence, and insult...inept and unconvincing in his relations with others" (101); "a weak character" (128)—or even grown to dislike him (cf. Burgess 2015: 47) to soften their attitudes. They concentrate less on their gripes with the character and anticipate rather his demonstration of martial skill. That Agamemnon elsewhere appears as a good fighter (A. Porter 2019: 160–1) eases this shift in perspective. Here I suggest is one reason for an arming scene at this moment, a moment that may not self-evidently call for it, as Magdalene Stoevesandt opines (2004: 74–5). The scene puts us in a state of mind in which thoughts that might block our identifying with Agamemnon are less prevalent.

Instead of sticking with Agamemnon, however, the poet turns to assembling the other fighters, both Trojan and Achaean. Only in verse 91 does Agamemnon return to the spotlight. This perceptible departure from the individual who will be the focus of the fighting to come also occurs after Patroclus's arming scene and Achilles's arming scene; it does not transpire after Paris's arming scene at *Iliad* 3.328–38. Patroclus arms at *Iliad* 16.130–9, at which point the poet turns to Automedon, who yokes the horses to Patroclus's chariot, and then to Achilles, who musters his Myrmidons and afterward retires to his tent to pray to Zeus. We have to wait until verse 257 for Patroclus's return to the spotlight. Achilles arms at *Iliad* 19.364–91. Achilles's conversation with his horse Xanthus follows (19.401–23), but *Iliad* 20 takes us among the gods and only gets back to Achilles in verse 158. Bernard Fenik notes of all three instances, "The arming takes place just before the battle in which the arming warrior will enjoy his aristeia" (1968: 79). The phrase "just before" occludes the effect of setting the character aside for a moment. In each case, this species of epic retardation (Reichel 1990; Morrison 1992: 36; Rengakos 1999: 311–20; Rutherford 2013: 51; Scodel 2021: 65) augments our interest in the ostensible protagonist of the fighting to come. He remains on our minds while we wait for the poet to bring him back into the foreground. Again, Fenik reviews the typical nature of what intervenes between Agamemnon's arming scene and his return to the spotlight (1968: 79–82) and between Patroclus's arming scene and his return to the spotlight (191). But even if the tradition-oriented recipient expects the poet to proceed in a typical fashion before a battle scene that features an *aristeia*, that factor does not diminish the anticipation the recipient feels at the prospect of the armed *aristeuōn*'s return to the spotlight. In sum, verses 16–90 prime us in various ways to identify with Agamemnon.

Soon after Agamemnon regains the narrative spotlight in verse 91, potential triggers for identification appear. Verse 101 gives Agamemnon a goal: "but he went on (*bē rh'*) intending to slay (*exenarixōn*) Isus and Antiphus." The finite verb form and particle *bē rh'* means to move with a goal in mind (e.g., *Iliad* 2.17, 5.848, 17.212; *Odyssey* 6.2; cf. Kelly 2007: 235); the future participle *exenarixōn* implies a goal and may even here mean "intending to despoil." Other verses in the episode also highlight Agamemnon's goals. Verses 181–2 indicate that he wants to drive the Trojans back to their city walls, if not into Troy: "But when he was on the point of being about to (*takh' emellen* (with West 1998)) come beneath the city and the steep wall..." (cf. *Iliad* 10.365, 23.773; *Odyssey* 4.514). Verse 217 states that Agamemnon "wanted (*ethelen*) to fight far in front of all." In each case an opportunity for motivational identification arises.

Cues for emotional identification emerge too. Agamemnon kills Isus and Antiphus, recognizing them as he despoils them of their armor (*Iliad* 11.110-12):

σπερχόμενος δ' ἀπὸ τοῖιν ἐσύλα τεύχεα καλά,
γινώσκων· καὶ γάρ σφε πάρος παρὰ νηυσὶ θοῇσιν
εἶδεν, ὅτ' ἐξ Ἴδης ἄγαγεν πόδας ὠκὺς Ἀχιλλεύς.

Hastening he stripped the lovely armor from the pair,
recognizing them: for in fact he had seen them before by the swift ships,
when swift-footed Achilles led them from Ida.

On the battlefield, victors usually give no indication of recognizing their victims (e.g., *Iliad* 16.745) or recognizing whom they are despoiling (e.g., *Iliad* 11.100, 13.619), but moments in which a warrior succeeds in taking spoils from opponents whom he recognizes are not infrequent. Diomedes plots with Sthenelus to capture Aeneas's horses (*Iliad* 5.260-73), and they manage to do so (5.319-27). Odysseus points out Rhesus to Diomedes who then kills the Thracian king (*Iliad* 10.477, 493-5), and the pair make off with Rhesus's horses (10.498-501), having been alerted to their value by Dolon (10.435-41). Hector knows that he has killed Patroclus (*Iliad* 16.724, 830) and that the armor he has stripped from Patroclus belongs to Achilles (*Iliad* 17.186-7). Hector expresses the wish to win Nestor's shield and Diomedes's corselet (*Iliad* 8.191-7), but Hera begrudges him the chance (8.198). Seizing spoils from victims they recognize pleases warriors: Diomedes speaks of the excellent glory (*kleos esthlon*) that Sthenelus and he will acquire if they take Aeneas's horses (*Iliad* 5.273); Hector imagines that the Achaeans would be so despondent over the loss of Nestor and Diomedes that they would depart from Troy (*Iliad* 8.196-7); Odysseus explains how Diomedes and he acquired Rhesus's horses and "rejoices" (*kagkhaloōn*) as he takes them into the Achaean camp (*Iliad* 10.564-5); Euphorbus wants the excellent glory (*kleos esthlon*) that will come from stripping Patroclus of his armor (*Iliad* 17.13-16). Acquiring these spoils pleases warriors because the acquisition of spoils increases a warrior's status (Ready 2007: 3, 13), and holding a position of status (*Odyssey* 13.265-6, 14.211-45 (esp. *tetarpomenos* at 244)) and having one's status acknowledged (*Iliad* 23.647-9) are eliciting conditions for happiness in the Homeric world as they are elsewhere (see section 2.5, p. 49).

Recipients might intuit Agamemnon's pleasure at stripping Isus and Antiphus of their armor, and recipients might feel happy right along with him. An opportunity for emotional identification arises. What is more, the foregrounding of Agamemnon's perspective in these verses enhances the possibility for emotional identification. The participle *sperkhomenos* shows us that he feels the urgency of the moment and wants to act quickly (cf. *Iliad* 23.870, 24.322; *Odyssey* 15.60). With the participle *ginōskōn*, the poet tells us one of the things going through

Agamemnon's mind at this point: he stripped them in part because he recognized them. The sentence introduced by *kai gar* (at least up to the *hote* in verse 112) perhaps recounts Agamemnon's memory at this moment of seeing (*eiden*) Isus and Antiphus before.

Some lines later, Agamemnon rejects the pleas for mercy from Peisander and Hippolochus, sons of Antimachus. From the victims' perspective, his words are "pitiless" (*ameilikton*, *Iliad* 11.137), but we should also consider how the poet takes us inside Agamemnon's head with this speech. Agamemnon recalls Antimachus's proposal that the Trojans kill Menelaus when he came on an embassy to Troy. Agamemnon deems this proposal, even though the Trojans did not carry it out, an "unseemly...outrage" for which his sons will suffer retaliatory vengeance (*aeikea tisete lōbēn*, *Iliad* 11.142). He presumably labels Antimachus's proposal thus not only because it violates the customary treatment of *xenoi* (guests) and *philoi* (friends)—Antenor hosted them in Troy as *xenoi* and *philoi* (*exeinissa...philēsa*, *Iliad* 3.205-7), and the first rule of *xenia* is that one does not kill one's visitors (cf. Rinon 2007: 319-20 on Polyphemus in *Odyssey* 9)—but also because he feels protective of his brother. One of Agamemnon's perennial anxieties is that Menelaus's death will lead to the failure of the Achaean expedition (cf. Sammons 2009b; Stelow 2020: 65-6). Agamemnon's concern for Menelaus's fate emerges when one contrasts his version of the story of the embassy with that found in Apollodorus. Agamemnon makes it seem as if only Menelaus, and not his fellow emissary, Odysseus, was threatened with death. Apollodorus reports that the Trojans wanted to kill both Menelaus and Odysseus (*toutous*) during this embassy (*Cypria* argumentum 10 West 2003b). One can read more into this phrase, however: the following analysis of the diction of 11.142 suggests that a recipient can deduce Agamemnon's emotional state when he utters the verse and when he kills the pair.

Witnessing another or others suffer something unseemly (*aeikēs*) can prompt an emotional reaction. Patroclus groans deeply (*baru stenakhōn*, *Iliad* 16.20) as he tells Achilles of the Achaeans' pain (*akhos*, 16.22) and goes on to chastise Achilles as pitiless (*nēlees*) for failing to ward off the "unseemly (*aeikea*) destruction" from his compatriots (16.32-3). Zeus groans (*stenakheskh'*) upon seeing Heracles engaged in unseemly (*aeikes*) work (*Iliad* 19.132-3). Andromache includes in her emotionally laden lament over Hector a vision of Astyanax performing unseemly labor (*erga aeikea*) as a slave (*Iliad* 24.733). The disguised Odysseus says he would rather die than witness a litany of unseemly (*aeikea*) deeds that includes the mistreatment of strangers and slave women (*Odyssey* 16.105-9; cf. 20.315-19). When he uses this adjective to characterize the outrage suffered by Menelaus, Agamemnon telegraphs his emotional reaction upon recalling the event (and presumably at the time of the event itself).

Turning to the noun *lōbē* ("outrage"), one notes that to suffer an outrage is to experience pain (*akhos*) and, more precisely, that which pains one's heart (*thumalgea*) (*Iliad* 9.387; *Odyssey* 18.347–9 (= 20.285–7), 24.326). To suffer an outrage is to experience wrath. Achilles declares Agamemnon's seizure of Briseis an outrage (*Iliad* 9.387); both the noun *mēnis* ("wrath") and the verb *mēniō* ("to feel wrath toward") label Achilles's anger at this seizure (e.g., *Iliad* 1.422, 9.517, 12.10, 18.257, 19.35). In these instances, the victim of the outrage experiences these emotions (cf. Scodel 2008: 85–6). In another passage, Achilles labels Hector's slaying of Patroclus an outrage (*lōbēn*, *Iliad* 19.208). Achilles's distress at the death of Patroclus needs no rehearsal: he even expresses the wish to eat Hector raw (*Iliad* 22.346–7). Keeping all these passages in mind, it would seem obtuse to take Agamemnon as meaning simply that Menelaus suffered an outrage that caused him, Menelaus, anguish, and that that outrage had no effect on Agamemnon. Rather, by labeling Antimachus's proposal an outrage (*lōbē*)—as opposed to *kaka* (cf. *Iliad* 3.351) or *huperbasiē* (cf. *Odyssey* 3.206) or *ergon* (cf. *Odyssey* 15.236)— Agamemnon clarifies not just his take on the proposal but also the emotions he has when he remembers the episode (and, again, presumably had at the time of the event).

We come to *tisete* ("you will pay back"). Characters desire to exact payback. Menelaus is "especially eager (*malista...hieto*) in his heart to avenge (*tisasthai*) his efforts and groans on behalf of Helen" (*Iliad* 2.589–90). Telemachus wishes that the gods would grant him the strength to punish (*tisasthai*) the suitors (*Odyssey* 3.205–7). And characters are pleased when the chance arises to exact payback. Menelaus delights (*ekharē*) at the opportunity to punish (*tisasthai*) Paris (*Iliad* 3.27–8) and laments (*ōimōxen*) when he thinks Zeus has stymied his effort (3.364–8). Odysseus "delighted in (*khairen*) the spoken omen and in the thunder of Zeus: for he thought he would punish (*tisasthai*) the sinners" (*Odyssey* 20.120–1; cf. 17.539–47). Gaea urges her children to take vengeance on Ouranus for his transgression (*teisaimetha lōbēn*) and rejoices (*gēthēsen*) when Cronus volunteers (Hesiod *Theogony* 165, 173). One can impute a similar feeling to Agamemnon when he realizes he has the sons of Antimachus at his mercy.

Lastly, the actual exacting of payback can trigger a surge of delight that compels one to celebrate in various ways. Menelaus vaunts in triumph (*eukhomenos*) over a victim, another Peisander, casting his death as payback for the outrage (*lōbēs... lōbēsasthe*) committed by the Trojans when they took Helen and treasure from his house (*Iliad* 13.619–23). Achilles declares Hector's killing Patroclus an outrage requiring vengeance (*tisaimetha lōbēn*, *Iliad* 19.208). After he kills Hector, he invites the Achaeans to join him in singing a victory song (*aeidontes paiēona*), one that he may even compose himself on the spot (*Iliad* 22.391–4; cf. Ready 2019a: 30). Athena laughs (*gelasse*) after knocking Ares to the ground and declares, "Thus you would pay back (*exapotinois*) your mother's Furies" (*Iliad* 21.408, 412). Having expressed the wish that Melanthius pay for his transgressions (*huperbasias apotisēi*, *Odyssey* 22.168), Eumaeus taunts (*epikertomeōn*, 22.194) the trussed-up goatherd as he hangs from the ceiling. When Odysseus stops Eurycleia from vocally expressing her happiness at the sight of the dead suitors—whose outrages he has spoken of previously as demanding vengeance (*tisaiato lōbēn*, *Odyssey* 20.169-71; cf. *apotisomai*, 13.386)—he acknowledges how one might react upon taking vengeance: one rejoices (*khaire*); one wants to shout out in victory (*ololuze*); one wants to boast (*eukhetaasthai*) (*Odyssey* 22.411-12). A recipient can assign the sentiments expressed in these passages to Agamemnon as he kills Peisander and Hippolochus.

The text, then, cues us to impute a range of emotions to Agamemnon over the course of his encounter with Peisander and Hippolochus. In turn, the recipient can join Agamemnon in feeling any of this range of emotions.

Verse 154 too provides an opportunity for emotional identification: αἰὲν ἀποκτείνων ἕπετ' Ἀργείοισι κελεύων ("killing always he followed, giving orders to/exhorting the Argives"). In scenes of battle, the adverb *aei*—sometimes accompanied by words for killing and shouting—appears in contexts in which a warrior achieves his goal to the extent that he reaches peak performance on the battlefield. Diomedes "was always (*aiei*) eager" to kill Aeneas in spite of Apollo's defense of the Trojan (*Iliad* 5.434); that verse presages Diomedes's attacking Aeneas "like a god" (5.438). Hector drives the Achaeans in flight "always killing the last one" (αἰὲν ἀποκτείνων τὸν ὀπίστατον, *Iliad* 8.342). In the midst of his *aristeia*, Idomeneus "was always (*aiei*) eager either to envelop someone of the Trojans in black night or himself to fall while warding off ruin for the Achaeans" (*Iliad* 13.424-6). Ajax's defense of the Achaean ships finds him "with his spear always (*aiei*) warding off Trojans" (*Iliad* 15.730-1) and "always shouting (*aiei...booōn*) terribly" (15.732). In addition, the participle *keleuōn* ("ordering/exhorting") in verse 154—with its implication that the Achaeans heed him—points up Agamemnon's leadership at this moment. To give orders or to exhort (and to be heeded implicitly or explicitly) indicates that one performs a vital component of leadership. Sarpedon chastises Hector, "You stand here and do not even give orders (*keleueis*) to the rest of the host to stand fast and defend their wives" (*Iliad* 5.485-6). Later, Hector gives orders (*keleuōn*) "now among the foremost...and now among the hindmost" (*Iliad* 11.64-5) and exhorts (*keleuse*, *Iliad* 15.545) his kinsmen, above all Melanippus who heeds the prince (*hespeto*, 15.559). Patroclus exhorts (*keleuōn*, *Iliad* 16.372) the Achaeans as they drive the Trojans from the ships. Ajax orders (*keleuōn*, *Iliad* 17.356) the Achaeans to defend Patroclus's corpse. In sum, verse 154 depicts Agamemnon succeeding on the battlefield as fighter and leader. Verse 165 ("and the son of Atreus followed (*hepeto*) eagerly giving orders to/exhorting (*keleuōn*) the Danaans"), verse 168 (Agamemnon "shouting followed always" (*keklēgōs hepet' aiei*): compare *Iliad* 13.754-7 wherein *keklēgōs* indicates "ordering"), and verses 177-8 ("he followed (*ephepe*)...always killing the last one (αἰὲν ἀποκτείνων τὸν ὀπίστατον)") make the same point about Agamemnon's success as warrior and commander.

Warriors revel in their success on the battlefield. I add the following to the passages I mentioned in the earlier discussions of the feelings engendered when taking spoils and when exacting revenge. Ajax delights in (*khairō*) the prospect of defeating Hector (*Iliad* 7.191–2) and delights in (*kekhareōta*) what he takes to be his victory in their duel (7.312). Achilles delights (*khaire*, *Iliad* 22.224) after Athena predicts that together they will kill Hector (22.216–18). Odysseus delights (*khaire*) after defeating the suitors' relatives in combat (*Odyssey* 24.545; cf. Ready 2019b). Success on the battlefield even makes one's family happy: Hector imagines Andromache delighting in (*khareiē*) her son Astyanax's kills (*Iliad* 6.481; cf. 17.38–40, 17.208; *Odyssey* 24.513–15; Kozak 2017: 166–7). Agamemnon's exultation comes implied in verse 154. Recipients can feel happy right along with Agamemnon as he achieves, however temporarily, his goal.

Two further opportunities for emotional identification arise in this episode, but in each case an opportunity to co-experience a negative emotion. When Coön wounds Agamemnon, Agamemnon "shivered" (*rhigēsen*, *Iliad* 11.254). This shivering is a physical manifestation of fear (cf. Cairns 2013: 91–2). Priam shivers (*rhigēsen*) upon learning of the impending duel between Menelaus and Paris (*Iliad* 3.259): as he says later, he cannot "bear to watch with my eyes my dear son fighting Menelaus, dear to Ares" (3.306–7); fear for his son provokes his initial shiver, not the prospect of having to make an oath-sacrifice (*pace* Cairns 2017: 60–1), an activity nowhere else in the Homeric epics said to produce a shiver (cf. esp. *Iliad* 19.191, 19.250–68). Menelaus shivers (*rhigēsen*) upon seeing blood flow from the arrow wound he sustains (*Iliad* 4.150); he calms down once he determines that the wound is not that bad (4.151–2). Penelope says, "my heart in my dear chest continually shivered (*errigei*) in fear that (*mē*) someone might beguile me with words" (*Odyssey* 23.215–16). Agamemnon experiences a momentary bout of fear when he is wounded. Recipients can feel a jolt of fear for the king too.

Agamemnon persists for a time, but eventually he cannot endure the pain. He mounts his chariot "for he was vexed in his heart" (*ēkhtheto gar kēr*, *Iliad* 11.274). A wound can vex one (*Iliad* 5.354, 5.361), but the statement in verse 274 means that Agamemnon is vexed, not from, or not solely from, his wound but because he can no longer achieve his goal of defending the ships: he can only urge his fellow Achaeans to do so because "counselor Zeus does not allow me to fight all day against Trojans" (*Iliad* 11.275–9). Diomedes is vexed in his heart (*ēkhtheto gar kēr*) because the wound he suffers at the hands of Paris compels him to leave the field (*Iliad* 11.400), and Poseidon is vexed (*ēkhtheto*) that Zeus frustrates his goal of Achaean victory (*Iliad* 13.352–3). Recipients can join in Agamemnon's vexation at his inability to accomplish his desired goal.

In this examination of Agamemnon's *aristeia*, we have encountered other characters too—namely, his opponents and eventual victims. Do recipients identify with Agamemnon's foes? I take up the question of identification with these sorts of minor characters in section 4.4.

## 4.2.2. Andromache in *Iliad* 22

The poet provides ample opportunity for the recipient to identify with Andromache over the course of *Iliad* 22.437–515 (cf. section 2.2, pp. 19–20). Critics talk about the "pathos" of these verses or our feeling "sympathy" or "pity" for Andromache (Segal 1971: 47; N. Richardson 1993: 154, 155 at 442–6, 157 at 468–72; Nagy 2009: 579–80; Allen-Hornblower 2016: 41), but coming at it from the perspective of identification will provide a still greater appreciation of the workings of this famous scene. My analysis has more in common with Rachel Lesser's suggestion that the portrayal of Andromache in *Iliad* 22 "invite[s] our empathy" and "encourage[s] us to feel with the heroine" (2022: 219; cf. 125, 128 on Andromache in *Iliad* 6).

Typical details abound in the scene (cf. Hainsworth 1993: 154–63). Andromache weaves, like other elite women, such as Helen and Penelope. She rushes (*diessuto*) to the wall of Troy in a frenzied state "like a possessed person (*mainadi*)" (*Iliad* 22.460-1), just as a maid tells Hector that she hastened (*epeigomenē*) to the wall of Troy "like a raving woman (*mainomenēi*)" (*Iliad* 6.388-9). Her lament (*Iliad* 22.477-514) cleaves to the generic parameters for such a speech act (Tsagalis 2004, esp. 129–33). To these typical details that suggest the narrative realism of the passage, one can add the details in the passage that have struck readers as realistic and so point to the external realism of the passage. A scholion comments on verse 463 wherein the narrator notes that Andromache looked around once she got to the wall: "Well done is the bit about her not learning from others; but it is the mark of a troubled spirit to want to see things for oneself" (bT scholion at *Iliad* 22.463; N. Richardson 1993: 156 at 463). Details in Andromache's lament prompt a similar assessment. Marilyn Arthur understands Andromache's failure to consider that a royal relative would take care of Astyanax "a product of psychologically realistic despair" (1981: 37). Nicholas Richardson finds a "realistic visual detail" in Andromache's depiction of the fatherless Astyanax begging for food: "the child is trying desperately to attract the attention of these indifferent grown-ups" (1993: 161 at 493). He also cites the bT scholion at verses 512–13 wherein Andromache pledges to burn Hector's clothes (1993: 162 at 510–14): "these are pathos-inducing and true to life (*biōtika*): for they destroy their clothes along with the dead" (bT scholion at *Iliad* 22.512-13). Taken together, these details render the perceived realism (comprising narrative and external realism) of the passage quite high and thereby increase the likelihood of the recipient identifying with Andromache.

The poet provides some details about the physical setting: in the inner part (*mukhōi*) of the house, Andromache weaves on a loom (*Iliad* 22.440); she rushes from the hall (*megaroio*) to the tower (*purgon*) and the wall (*teikhei*) (22.460-3). References to a character doing things to objects in a place and moving through and between places make those places more vivid and thereby enhance the recipient's feeling of being in that place with the character (Grethlein and Huitink 2017; section 6.2). Other details provide some sense of Andromache's physical appearance. The report that she weaves (*huphaine*, *Iliad* 22.440) and holds a *kerkis* (22.448) would have given ancient audiences a clear sense of what she was doing with her body: whereas modern scholarship continues to debate the precise bodily movements of the ancient Greek weaver and the exact nature of her tools (cf. Rahmstorf 2015: 13), ancient recipients would have had no such trouble. Still, we can imagine that Andromache stands[1] and that she puts her *kerkis* (pin beater) to any number of uses: "one function of the pin beater is to beat the weft into place. Another is to even out the warp threads by strumming across them. A third likely use is to pick the shed, especially in pattern weaving" (S. Edmunds 2012: section 46, italics removed; cf. Spantidaki 2016: 52, 99–100; Fanfani 2017: 422). When Andromache faints, the narrator spends three verses on her elaborate headdress, reviewing its four distinct items (*Iliad* 22.468–70), "a headband,...a cap...some kind of woven or plaited binding...shawl or headscarf" (N. Richardson 1993: 157 at 469–70). These specifications of setting and appearance help the recipient to identify with Andromache.

The poet gives us access to Andromache's point of view from the start: she did not know (*ou...pepusto*) anything about Hector's situation (*Iliad* 22.437); the purpose clause at 22.443–4 that explains why Andromache has ordered her maids to prepare a bath for Hector—"in order that there might be a warm bath for Hector when he returned from battle"—represents her thoughts (de Jong 2004: 118, 269 n. 39); she did not know (*oud' enoēsen*) that Athena had seen to his demise (22.445); she hears (*ēkouse*) cries and lamentation from the wall (22.447); she casts her gaze about (*paptēnas'*) and then sees (*enoēsen*) Achilles dragging Hector behind his chariot (22.463–4); the adverb *akēdestōs* ("ruthlessly"), to which I return momentarily, reflects her take on Achilles's action (22.465; Allan, de Jong, and de Jonge 2017: 42). And, of course, the poet provides access to Andromache's mind when she speaks, as she does for most of the passage. To repeat, recipients frequently identify with the character whose perspective dominates the telling.

The beginning of the scene not only foregrounds Andromache's perspective. Recipients may also be prompted to identify with Andromache because they assign her a high score for virtue. The identifying term "the wife of Hector" (*alochos... / Hektoros*, *Iliad* 22.437–8) leads the recipient to evaluate her performance in that role (cf. Segal 1971: 37). Andromache weaves in the inner chamber of the house (*mukhōi*, *Iliad* 22.440), the place where women properly do their work (Canevaro 2018: 65). Furthermore, she does not just weave but weaves a

---

[1] *Iliad* 1.31; *Odyssey* 7.105–6; Forbes 1964: 205; Hainsworth 1990: 328 at 106; N. Richardson 1993: 253 at 759–64; Roller and Roller 1994: 15–18; S. Edmunds 2012: section 16; Spantidaki 2016: 52–3; *pace* Wace 1948: 55.

twofold (*diplaka*) tapestry with an intricate floral (*throna poikil'*) decoration (*Iliad* 22.440-1; cf. van Wees 2005: 9; Nagy 2010: 273-6). This technically ambitious project highlights her skill as a weaver, highlights, that is, her expertise in a field in which Homeric women and Homeric wives are supposed to seek expertise.[2] In addition, the design Andromache chooses may reaffirm her devotion to her husband: starting from the idea that *throna* are "love charms," Gregory Nagy writes, "Andromache is passing the time by pattern-weaving a sequence of *throna*, 'flowers' that have the power of love charms. The sequence of *throna* tells its own story: it is a story of love, a love story in the making" (2009: 276). Homeric men, of course, prize their wives' devotion: poets, Agamemnon declares, will sing songs in praise of Penelope, the emblem of wifely fidelity (*Odyssey* 24.197-8). Even if one wishes to restrict the significance of her decoration to proof of her skill, one can still say that her choice of decoration does not run the risks posed by the decoration on the other twofold tapestry in the Homeric poems (cf. Canevaro 2018: 65; Arnaud 2019: 133-4)—namely, Helen's twofold tapestry that, with its depiction of the trials (*aethlous*) suffered (*epaskhon*) by the Trojans and Achaeans for her sake (*hethen heinek'*) (*Iliad* 3.125-8), gives the (uncharitable?) recipient the opportunity to blame Helen for the toils she portrays on the tapestry.[3] Andromache's dedication to her gender's duties also appears in the narrator's next item: she orders her maids to prepare a bath for Hector (*Iliad* 22.443-4), the preparation and ministration of a bath for a living individual being women's, both servile and elite, work (Lateiner 2011). Over these verses, Andromache emerges as an emblem of female and wifely virtue, as that concept was understood in Homeric epic and in Greek culture writ large (cf. Adkins 1960: 36-7; Canevaro 2018: 67).

At the same time, these initial lines advertise Andromache's goal. She aims to run a thriving household: her weaving (*huphaine*, *Iliad* 22.440) signals her participation in the household economy (cf. Nosch 2014: 97-8); her ordering (*kekleto*, 22.442) her maids signals her control over her slaves; her preparation of the bath (22.443-4) signals her attention to her husband. The poet then uses this final detail about a bath to pivot to declaring Andromache ignorant of Hector's death: Athena, the narrator says, subdued Hector "far from baths" (*tēle loetrōn*, *Iliad* 22.445). By linking that declaration of Hector's death to the rehearsal of Andromache's goal, the poet draws attention to the imminent frustration of Andromache's goal of maintaining her household. For, as Andromache herself states in her subsequent lament, Hector's death presages the dissolution of his household (esp. *Iliad* 22.489). We cannot adopt Andromache's goal and hope she

---

[2] Cf. *Iliad* 23.704-5; *Odyssey* 15.105, 15.517, 21.350-2; Arthur 1981: 28; Pantelia 1993: 493; Karanika 2014: 25, 45, 87; Canevaro 2018: 62, 64.

[3] Cf. Blondell 2013: 66-7, 87-8; Arnaud 2019: 129-32; L. Edmunds 2019: 39, 147; Alcaeus fragment 42.3 Campbell: *ek sethen* "from you" (with, e.g., W. Allan 2010: 13; Lesser 2021: 137-8); Aeschylus *Agamemnon* 1456-7 West 1990: *mia / ... olesas'* "alone destroying."

fulfills it because we know she will not. Motivational identification is not at issue here. Rather, I would suggest speaking of emotional identification using the subject of motivational identification—goals. That is, the poet immediately gives us in this scene the opportunity for a sort of proleptic emotional identification with Andromache whereby we can feel sadness that Andromache will fail to achieve her goal, a sadness that Andromache will herself soon express.

To be sure, the poet emphasizes the state of Andromache's ignorance in describing her as preparing a bath for Hector for "when he returned from battle" (*Iliad* 22.444)—the phrase only appears in reference to warriors who die in battle (Segal 1971: 41; N. Richardson 1993: 155 at 442–4; Grethlein 2007b: 30)—and in the very next verse labeling her *nēpiē* (22.445)—an adjective routinely used to stress a character's ignorance (Ready 2011: 181). The recipient does not share Andromache's ignorance (cf. Grethlein 2007b: 28). There is no epistemic identification here. Nevertheless, as the passage progresses, other opportunities arise for emotional identification. The poet makes explicit Andromache's emotional state: the narrator says that, upon seeing Hector, Andromache is "distraught to the point of death" (*atuzomenēn apolesthai*, *Iliad* 22.474; trans. N. Richardson 1993: 157 at 474); she speaks her personal lament *amblēdēn gooōsa* (22.476): one could translate "with deep sobs" (Tsagalis 2004: 57), "she started wailing," or "lifting up [her voice] in wailing" (González 2013: 387). Other potential triggers for emotional identification are less explicit: descriptions of Andromache's actions and physical state require attention because physical actions signal emotional states or, if one prefers, emotional states go along with physical actions (see section 3.3.2, pp. 76–7; cf. Lesser 2022: 219).

Verses 447–8 report, "She heard shrieking and lamentation from the wall; and her limbs were whirled around (*elelikhthē*), and the pin beater fell (*ekpese*) [from her hand] to the ground." The most apposite parallels for the use of the verb *elelizō* appear at *Odyssey* 12.416 and 14.306: a ship is hit by Zeus's thunderbolt and whirled around (*elelikhthē*). The fatally wounded drop things—a corpse (*Iliad* 4.493), a fire brand (*Iliad* 15.421), a drinking cup (*Odyssey* 22.17)—as do those in danger of physical harm—Teucer drops his bow when he is hit by a boulder and knocked to his knees (*Iliad* 8.329); the disguised Odysseus drops his staff when he is faced with the threat of a mauling (*aeikelion... algos*, "an unseemly grief") by Eumaeus's dogs (*Odyssey* 14.31–2) (cf. Segal 1971: 43–4). These parallels reveal the extent of Andromache's physical incapacitation. Of course, no one has assaulted Andromache physically; she has suffered a psychic blow: hearing the shrieking and lamentation causes profound mental anguish that manifests itself physically.

Her subsequent speech makes clear what she is feeling. Like the narrator, she uses physical symptoms as markers of psychic distress. Highlighting her anxiety, she describes her heart as leaping into her mouth (*Iliad* 22.452). The image is reminiscent of Agamemnon's own profession of anxiety—"terribly do I fear for (*perideidia*) the Danaans, and my *ētor* [pulse, thought, mind?] is not steadfast, but I am tossed to and fro, and my heart leaps outside of my chest" (*Iliad* 10.93–5)—or Idomeneus's description of the anxious coward preparing for an ambush—"his heart pounds (*patassei*) violently in his chest as he thinks about death" (*Iliad* 13.282–3) (see Clarke 1999: 104–5).

With her claim that her knees are frozen, that she can hardly move (*gouna / pēgnutai*, *Iliad* 22.453–4), she highlights her despair. For her image evokes another expression for immobility, the formula λύτο γούνατα καὶ φίλον ἦτορ ("knees and heart went slack"). That formula elsewhere describes five times a character who despairs of the hope of living (*Iliad* 21.114; *Odyssey* 5.297, 5.406, 22.68, 22.147) and one time Penelope, as she despairs over Telemachus's survival (*Odyssey* 4.703).[4] When Metaneira collapses (*gounat' elunto*) after Demeter's epiphany (*Homeric Hymn to Demeter* 282), one can attribute it to despair over the possibility of appeasing the goddess (cf. *deimati pallomenai*, "shaking with fear," 293–4). In Euripides's *Heracles*, the eponymous hero, now in his right mind after having killed his wife and children in a fit of madness, claims that he is unable to stand up, that his limbs are stiff (ἄρθρα πέπηγέ μου, 1395). The line emphasizes his despair, right before he finds a glimmer of hope in his friendship with Theseus (cf. Halleran 2004: 297).

The narrator then reiterates just how distraught Andromache is by comparing her to one out of her mind (*mainadi isē*, *Iliad* 22.460; Segal 1971: 47–8) and noting that her heart was beating furiously (*pallomenē kradiēn*, *Iliad* 22.461). Picking up on the image of the leaping heart in verse 452, the latter phrase reaffirms her fearful anxiety. With verse 465's *akēdestōs*, one finds another cue for emotional identification. The adverb means something like "without regard for funeral rites" and, as I noted earlier (p. 95), represents Andromache's judgment on Achilles's actions. Both in the world of the Homeric epics and in the world of its ancient recipients, women do not just participate in funerals (e.g., *Iliad* 11.395, 21.123–4; *Odyssey* 3.260–1) but use them to accomplish important work on behalf of (or even to influence) their family or the broader community (Alexiou 2002; Hame 2008; Frisone 2011). When in her subsequent lament, Andromache claims that worms will eat Hector after the dogs have had their fill (*Iliad* 22.508–9), she implies that Hector will not receive a proper funeral. One can conduct a funeral in the world of the Homeric epics without a body (*Odyssey* 2.220–3), but the more typical claim in the poems is that leaving a corpse for animals to mutilate prevents

---

[4] On two other occasions, the phrase describes a reaction to unexpected news: Penelope and Laertes each go limp upon being presented with proofs of Odysseus's identity (*Odyssey* 23.205, 24.345). This resonance would not be apposite in Andromache's case because, as she goes on to say, she has long imagined Hector's manliness (*agēnoriēs*) and might (*menos*) leading him to his death (*Iliad* 22.454–9). The phrase also describes Aphrodite's reaction to being struck by Athena (*Iliad* 21.425): in this case, the formula functions like the frequent assertions that a warrior has loosened another mortal's limbs—that is, that he has killed him (e.g., *gounat' elusen*, *Iliad* 5.176).

a proper funeral and burial in a tomb (Ready 2011: 238–9; cf. Sophocles *Ajax* 1062–5). The adverb in verse 465 allows one already at that point to impute to Andromache that thought and the emotions that go along with the prospect of being denied the chance to contribute to such a significant event. Those emotions would presumably be similar to Hecuba's when she considers the prospect of not having the chance to bury Hector (*Iliad* 22.86–9): the queen wails and cries (*odureto dakru kheousa*, 22.79).

Finally, what of Andromache tossing her elaborate headdress far off (*tēle... bale*, *Iliad* 22.468)? (The following analysis depends on reading *bale* in verse 468 with Martin West (2000), not *khee* ("fell") with Helmut van Thiel (2010).) Charles Segal takes the gesture to point up Andromache's despair: Hector's death signals her social death because she will no longer reap the rewards of being Hector's wife; hence she tosses aside the emblem of her "social position in a highly formalized society" (1971: 38; cf. 50). Similarly, Hecuba's tossing her veil far off (*erripse kaluptrēn / tēlose*, *Iliad* 22.406–7) as she cries upon seeing Achilles abuse the dead Hector signals a mother's "fall from womanly happiness and fulfillment" (Segal 1971: 50; cf. Canevaro 2018: 93, 114). Lilah Grace Canevaro draws attention as well to Andromache's throwing off her *krēdemnon* ("veil") in particular (2018: 240). That word also describes the towers of Troy (*Iliad* 16.100). Her gesture signals not only her understanding of her own fate but also her realization that Troy itself will soon fall.

This overdetermined passage prompts additional readings. With verse 468 τῆλε δ' ἀπὸ κρατὸς βάλε δέσματα σιγαλόεντα, one can compare Apollo's move when he begins his disarming of Patroclus: τοῦ δ' ἀπὸ μὲν κρατὸς κυνέην βάλε Φοῖβος Ἀπόλλων ("Phoebus Apollo threw the helmet from his head," *Iliad* 16.793; Segal 1971: 49). Following Leonard Muellner (1996: 10–18), we can understand Apollo's anger (*mēnis*) at Patroclus for transgressing the boundary between god and men to motivate the god's action here (cf. *Iliad* 16.698–711). Circle back as well to Hecuba's tossing her veil far off when she sees Hector dragged behind Achilles's chariot (*Iliad* 22.406–7). While her lament immediately following this gesture stresses her despair at Hector's death (*Iliad* 22.431–6), her grief at some point mingles with rage: she declares to Priam that only the opportunity to eat Achilles's liver would provide adequate recompense (*antita erga*) for Hector's killing (*Iliad* 24.212–14; cf. D. Wilson 2002: 32–3, 174). Perhaps anger underlies Andromache's action as well. With that possibility in mind, I look to two other elucidating parallels.

Full of anger (*kholoio*, *Iliad* 1.224), Achilles throws (*bale*, 1.245) the scepter to the ground. Agamemnon's disabling of the heroic economy, wherein warriors fight in exchange for the spoils of war (Ready 2007: 17–18), has angered Achilles (D. Wilson 2002: 86, 103; cf. Gill 2002: 139–41). Declaring of the suitors, "But now you throw upon me troubles that can't be handled (*aprēktous odunas*)" (*Odyssey* 2.79), full of anger (*khōmenos*, 2.80), and bursting into tears (2.81), Telemachus throws (*bale*, 2.80) the scepter to the ground. The suitors' destruction of his household economy (*Odyssey* 2.48–9), as well as his inability to re-coup his losses by demanding recompense (2.76–8), has angered Telemachus. Both Achilles and Telemachus have assumed and hoped that the relevant economies would operate in a certain way but have found that not to be true. Perhaps Andromache is angry, not in this case about the breakdown of an economy but about the futility of the transaction between Hector and Eëtion in yet another economy, the marriage market. The narrator foregrounds this transaction in the description of Andromache's headdress: "which golden Aphrodite gave her on that day when Hector of the gleaming helmet led her from the house of Eëtion, after he brought a massive bride price (*muria hedna*)" (*Iliad* 22.470–2; cf. Canevaro 2018: 93). Ultimately, no one ended up with what they hoped for from this deal. Andromache's husband is dead, and she understands that her household faces imminent destruction (*Iliad* 22.488–9, 24.725–38); Achilles killed Eëtion, destroyed his household and his town, and took the Cilicians' goods, including presumably those given by Hector as a bride price (*Iliad* 6.414–28, 23.826–9). In her anger at the way in which Hector and Eëtion's exchange seems in the end to have amounted to nothing, Andromache hurls to the ground the emblem of that exchange. Another opportunity among several emerges for audience members to experience emotional identification with Andromache.

Pathos, sympathy, pity—these words capture something of how recipients respond to this scene. But approaching it with a view to how recipients can identify with Andromache does greater justice to the range, nature, and intensity of our responses to Andromache's penultimate appearance in the *Iliad*.

### 4.2.3. The Funeral Games in *Iliad* 23

Achilles organizes eight events in the funeral games for Patroclus—chariot race, boxing, wrestling, footrace, duel with spears, shot put, archery, and javelin (cf. Kelly 2017: 91). At several points, the poet shows that the internal spectators have their favorites. Nestor wants Antilochus to put in a good showing in the chariot race (*Iliad* 23.314, 345), and Apollo and Athena intervene to help their chosen contestant (*Iliad* 23.383–400, 23.405–6, 23.768–74, 23.863–5, 23.872–3). Sthenelus wastes no time (*oude matēsen*) in eagerly collecting (*essumenōs labe*) the prizes Diomedes wins for placing first in the chariot race (*Iliad* 23.510–11), and, presumably having attended to their leader's obvious success in the shot put (*Iliad* 23.847), Polypoetes's companions carry off his prizes: Sthenelus and Polypoetes's companions are to be thought of as rooting for the eventual winner. Diomedes hopes Euryalus will win the boxing match (*Iliad* 23.682). The Achaeans cheer on Odysseus in the footrace (*Iliad* 23.766–7) and make clear their favoritism by laughing at Oïlean Ajax after he falls in a pile of dung (*Iliad* 23.784). These moments encourage the external audience to pick favorites too. Here is another example of how "the Homeric poet uses the vision and response of those who watch the action unfolding within the poem as a way of shaping the audience's vision and experience of that action" (Allen-Hornblower 2016: 23; cf. Myers 2019: 2, 24, 66, 125, 155).

Even without this guidance, recipients will still be inclined to pick favorites and take sides. After all, we readily take sides: "This quality—and it is a quality, if a peculiar one, that seems to be rare in non-human animals—can hardly be overestimated. It is, surely, part of our development as social creatures. Humans are uniquely focused on side-taking and on the judgment of their fellow humans" (Breithaupt 2019: 97). And we readily take sides when watching sports: "Our societies have built many institutions and rituals around the central human activity of side-taking. Some of these are designed to be enjoyable. In sports, for example, side-taking not only simplifies and focuses our experience, it makes the game fun" (103).

These observations prompt a close reading of the funeral games with the question of motivational identification in mind. The poet alternates between, on the one hand, encouraging motivational identification—encouraging us to root for one of the competitors in an event to win—and, on the other hand, not so explicitly encouraging, or complicating the possibility for, motivational identification. This alternation is itself useful because recipients appreciate and even require breaks from vigorous side-taking (Breithaupt 2019: 92–3, 167–70; cf. J. Eder 2006: 69). An ancillary benefit of this query, then, is that it will further illuminate the structural principles at work in the poet's presentation of the funeral games (Hinckley 1986: 221; Stanley 1993: 221–32; W. Scott 1997; Tsagalis 2012: 109; Kelly 2017: 106–7).

Nestor thinks Antilochus can pass (*parexelasēistha*, *Iliad* 23.344) his competitors in the chariot race if he deploys his cunning (*mētis*) (23.313–18) and his understanding of what brings profit (*kerdea*, 23.322) and if he keeps his wits about him and pays attention (*phroneōn pephulagmenos*, 23.343). He should display these attributes in two ways: he should not let the need to keep control of his horses from the start—that is, regulate their speed—escape his notice (*lēthei*) and, more important, he should not make an unnecessarily wide turn at the turning post (*Iliad* 23.319–25). Scholarship devoted to the subsequent account of the chariot race tends to focus on a few related questions: how does Nestor's speech relate to what happens in the chariot race? does Antilochus follow Nestor's advice? does Antilochus play fair? where in fact does the main action of the race take place: at the turn or on the return leg? These are worthy questions, and I deploy some of this work in what follows, but my focus differs. Scholarship's clinical explorations of these questions have illuminated the episode and its themes, but they have also obscured a more probable response to this scene: the recipient's motivational identification with Antilochus.

Nestor's injunctions prime the recipient to attend to Antilochus especially among the race's competitors and to anticipate his putting to use his mental acumen in order to overtake his competitors. Yet, after recording that Antilochus draws what we would call the pole position (*Iliad* 23.353-4), the poet turns to the other characters: the competitors take their places from left to right at the starting line (23.354-8); Achilles shows them the turning point and assigns Phoenix the task of officiating the race (23.358-61); the race begins, and the poet, after noting the exertions of all the competitors and their horses (23.362-75), relates what happened to Eumelus and Diomedes due to Apollo's and Athena's interventions (23.375-400). Only at this point, after forty-eight verses—including the additional note that Menelaus was now in second place and pursing Diomedes (*Iliad* 23.401)—does the poet get back to Antilochus. With this delay, the poet stimulates our curiosity about when or even if Antilochus will be able to pass anyone. This forty-eight-verse delay for the purpose of building suspense finds a parallel later in the same episode: the dispute between the spectating Idomeneus and Oïlean Ajax interrupts the account of the chariot race proper (*Iliad* 23.448-98). We have to wait fifty-one verses before learning the outcome of the event (cf. Scodel 2021: 60-1).

When the narrative spotlight finally returns to Antilochus, he exhorts his horses in a lengthy speech that closes with the following statement: ταῦτα δ' ἐγὼν αὐτὸς τεχνήσομαι ἠδὲ νοήσω / στεινωπῷ ἐν ὁδῷ παραδύμεναι, οὐδέ με λήσει ("I myself will contrive and think over these things, to pass in the narrow road, and it will not escape my notice," *Iliad* 23.415-16). We have been wondering when or if Antilochus will implement his father's advice of deploying his *mētis* to pass someone. With their language of mental dexterity echoing Nestor's words (Gagarin 1983: 36 n. 11; Dunkle 1987: 6; Frame 2009: 152-3), these verses indicate that we have reached that point. At this juncture, recipients may experience motivational identification with Antilochus. For it is an easy jump from wondering when or if Antilochus will follow his father's advice and pass someone to— now that we have finally arrived at the moment in which he says he will make his move—hoping that he does so successfully. Of course, if we are prone to root for the underdog, Nestor's representation of Antilochus as the underdog—his horses are the slowest (*Iliad* 23.309-11)—has perhaps already primed us to experience motivational identification with him now (Scodel 2021: 60). The other trigger to identification at this moment is the simple fact that Antilochus speaks. We have not heard from any of the characters in their own words since Nestor finished giving Antilochus instruction fifty-four verses previous. By switching to character speech after some time away from it, the poet forefronts Antilochus's perspective.

How long does this motivational identification persist? Does it persist up through Antilochus's passing Menelaus? I think it can. In order to pass Menelaus, Antilochus moves off the track (*Iliad* 23.423-4). Menelaus, fearful of a crash when Antilochus returns to the track, slows down, and Antilochus shoots ahead (*Iliad* 23.433–7). Scholarly opinions diverge on the validity of Antilochus's tactics (Kelly 2017: 99 n. 36). Some critics fret over Antilochus's cutting off Menelaus: "it seems that Antilochus did not pass Menelaus all that fairly" (Roisman 1988: 117); "dangerous and unfair tactics" (N. Richardson 1993: 218 at 418–24); "dubious tactics" (Alden 2000: 107); "dangerous tactic" (Frame 2009: 153); "reckless" (Grethlein and Huitink 2017: 78); "an unfair and angry competitor" (Bierl 2019: 60). One who evaluates Antilochus's driving in this way will be hard pressed to root for him.

But this reaction stems from reading back into this portion of the scene what happens later (cf. Gagarin 1983: 35). Because Menelaus immediately condemns Antilochus's move and declares that Antilochus will not "carry off a prize without an oath" (*Iliad* 23.438–41); because, as the prizes are being awarded, Menelaus insists that Antilochus swear an oath that he did not win through trickery (*dolōi*) (23.581–5); and because Antilochus declines to swear the oath and hands over the mare he won to Menelaus (23.586–95)—for these three reasons, Antilochus's tactics seem dubious, dangerous, and unfair. By contrast, Michael Gagarin, arguing that Antilochus passes Menelaus at the turning post, not on the return lap (cf. Forte 2019), contends that Antilochus uses legitimate tactics "in a daring maneuver" (1983, quotation from 38): "from Menelaus' point of view Antilochus cheated, but the more objective view is that he used skill to compensate for his slower horses" (39; cf. Scodel 2008: 47, 103; Forte 2019: 123 ("crafty technique")). Whether Gagarin rightly (so Forte 2019) or wrongly (see Forte 2019: 120 n. 2) focuses on the turning post, his argument has the salutary effect of keeping us from reading backward and suggests another possible response to Antilochus's actions.

Identifying with Antilochus, we root for him to best Menelaus and we dismiss Menelaus's rebukes (*Iliad* 23.425–8, 23.438–41). One might disagree with Menelaus's assertion that Antilochus acts senselessly or without due regard for the consequences (*aphradeōs*, *Iliad* 23.426). Antilochus's maneuver might be risky, but he executes it deliberately (cf. Purves 2019: 78). More to the point, once we have adopted Antilochus's goal and taken his side, the criticism from Menelaus may strengthen our support for Antilochus. Far from making us reevaluate our choice of whom to root for, criticism of our favored side tends to reinforce our initial side-taking (Breithaupt 2019: 101, 107, 112).

Even if recipients find Antilochus's tactics questionable or worse, their experience of motivational identification can offset that judgment. We readily overlook or rationalize away characters' doing bad things when we root for them (cf. Vaage 2016: 45–7, 58; Breithaupt 2019: 101). In particular, the phenomenon known as the actor/observer bias (Oatley 2012: 28–9) becomes relevant (as do the findings of attribution theory more generally (Palmer 2011, esp. 278; Budelmann et al. 2017: 242–3; Scodel 2018, esp. 2–3; De Temmerman and Emde Boas 2018: 16)). Whereas Menelaus claims that Antilochus's maneuver reveals a flaw in his character—"no other of mortals is more destructive than you;... not rightly do we Achaeans label you wise" (*Iliad* 23.439-40)—we might see his maneuver as a necessary response to the circumstances in which he found himself: Antilochus had to cut Menelaus off at that point. Here one finds an example of what Keith Oatley says happens when we identify with a character: we characterize their actions as responses to their immediate situation, not as evidence of deep-seated attributes (2012: 29; cf. Knox 2021: 153). This supposition gains empirical support from Felix Budelmann et al.'s finding that identifying with a character goes hand in hand with attributing that character's or another character's misfortunes to other people, not to his own traits (2017: 242-4, 248 n. 40). (Note too Jacqueline Thompson et al.'s finding that transported (immersed) readers attribute a protagonist's misfortunes to other people, not to the protagonist's character traits (2018: 212). Given its connection with immersion, one surmises that identification prompts a similar evaluation.)

In the description of the boxing match, opportunities for motivational identification are less apparent. After Achilles solicits entrants, Epeius rises (*Iliad* 23.664-5). Recipients' openness to identifying with him will depend initially on how familiar they are with him given that we need to spend time with a character before we can identify with them. We have not encountered Epeius yet in the *Iliad*, but connoisseurs among the tradition-oriented audience may recall that he makes a poor showing in the shot put event wherein his efforts provoke mocking laughter among the Achaeans (*Iliad* 23.839-40; Scanlon 2018: 7). If we assume that this Epeius is the same Epeius who builds the wooden horse with which the Achaeans take Troy (cf. West 2013: 193; Langella 2018; Scanlon 2018: 7-8), tradition-oriented audience members may or may not recall that he goes on to make this important contribution to the Achaeans' success (*Odyssey* 8.492-3, 11.523; Proclus *Little Iliad* argumentum 14 Bernabé). The poet does not remind us of that fact in this passage (Dunkle 1987: 11; Scanlon 2018: 8). Another factor affecting an initial propensity to identify with Epeius is that, based on our extant evidence, only here does he emerge as a skilled boxer. His unanticipated entry into the contest may hinder identification as recipients are not familiar with seeing him in such a role.

As for opportunities for motivational identification based on Epeius's portrayal in this scene itself, I turn to his speech. He notes that, whereas he may not be the best in martial combat, he excels in boxing and that no one can be good at everything (*Iliad* 23.667-75). Recipients may join the *Odyssey*'s Odysseus in endorsing that latter point (*Odyssey* 8.167-8; cf. Scanlon 2018: 13-14). If so, here is an opportunity for recipients to judge the character to hold attitudes similar to their own—he makes "a claim with which the audience could sympathize, namely that not all men can do all things well" (Scanlon 2018: 10)—and similarity in attitude is a predictor of identification. Conversely, one may follow Plutarch's assessment of these verses (*On Praising Oneself Inoffensively, Moralia*

544a de Lacy and Einarson). When Epeius says he falls short in battle (*makhēs epideuomai*, *Iliad* 23.670), he implies that he is cowardly and unmanly (*deilias kai anadrias*, 544a): the relevant parallel here comes in Glaucus's clarifying his assertion that Hector falls short in battle (μάχης ἄρα πολλὸν ἐδεύεο) with the claim that Hector is a "runner," or "a coward" (*phuxēlin*, *Iliad* 17.142–3). Epeius's admission clashes with his claim of athletic prowess—can a successful boxer really be cowardly?—and this failure of rhetoric renders him "perhaps ridiculous" (*isōs geloios*, 544a). One will be less apt to identify with a character one thinks ridiculous (cf. N. Richardson 1993: 242 at 665).

Epeius's next statement further complicates our response: "utterly will I smash his skin and crush his bones. And let his attendants remain here in a group, who will carry him out subdued by my hands" (*Iliad* 23.673–5). Odysseus claims that he will bloody Irus's chest and mouth (*Odyssey* 18.21–2), and Irus responds that he will knock Odysseus's teeth out (18.28–9). These threats pale in comparison to the one Epeius issues: he implies that he may kill his opponent (cf. Bierl 2019: 67). First, the three other occurrences of the phrase "crush his bones" (here, *oste' araxō*, *Iliad* 23.673) refer to a fatal blow: Ajax strikes Epicles with a rock, crushing his skull (*oste' araxe*, *Iliad* 12.384); as the swimming Odysseus tries to make it to the shore of Scheria, "his skin would have been stripped off there, and his bones would have been crushed together (*oste' arakhthē*)," had not Athena helped him (*Odyssey* 5.426–7); the broken mast fatally strikes Odysseus's steersman in the head and crushes his skull (*oste' araxe*, *Odyssey* 12.412). Epeius could have used the verb *thlaō*, which, although one time it signals a fatal blow (*Iliad* 12.384), on two other occasions implies a devastating but not fatal blow: Diomedes disables Aeneas by hitting him in the hip with a rock (*thlasse*, *Iliad* 5.307); in their boxing match, Odysseus disables Irus: ὀστέα δ' εἴσω / ἔθλασεν ("he smashed the bones within," *Odyssey* 18.96–7). Second, the noun *kēdemōn* ("attendant") occurs in the Homeric epics one other time—in reference to the mourners who attend to Patroclus's funeral (N. Richardson 1993: 186 at 163)—and Epeius's verb form *exoisousin* ("will carry him out") hints at a "funeral procession" (N. Richardson 1993: 243 at 674–5). Third, Epeius's phrase ἐμῆς ὑπὸ χερσὶ δαμέντα ("subdued by my hands") parallels Menelaus's prayer to Zeus that the god "subdue [Paris] by my hands" (ἐμῆς ὑπὸ χερσὶ δάμασσον, *Iliad* 3.352), Diomedes's decision to subdue Dolon (ἐμῆς ὑπὸ χερσὶ δαμείς, *Iliad* 10.452), and the dying Patroclus's prediction that Hector will be "subdued by the hands of Achilles" (*khersi damenta Akhilēos*, *Iliad* 16.854): both Menelaus and Diomedes mean that they will kill their opponent; Patroclus means Achilles will kill Hector.

Recipients can respond in different ways to Epeius's boast. If we take him seriously, we can arrive at diametrically opposed views of the propriety of his goal. On the one hand, when the suitors, having set up a boxing match between the beggar Irus and the disguised Odysseus, say, "In truth, soon Irus, as Un-Irus (*Airos*), will have an evil he has brought upon himself (*epispaston kakon*)"

(*Odyssey* 18.73), they imply that Irus might die (cf. *Odyssey* 24.462). For his part, Odysseus contemplates killing Irus with his fists (*Odyssey* 18.91). Per a story related in a D scholion to *Iliad* 23.660 (van Thiel), Apollo squares off against the arrogant boxer Phorbas and kills him (*sustas...apekteinen*). In general, spectators in the ancient world would not have been surprised to see a boxer die from his injuries (Cornell 2002: 31). On the other hand, Antinous seems to assume that Odysseus will not kill Irus: his threat to send Irus, should he lose the fight, to Echetus so that Echetus can mutilate him rests on Irus's being alive to suffer the torture (*Odyssey* 18.83–7). Moreover, the setting for Epeius's boxing match may matter: judging from the fact that the Achaeans break up the duel with weapons between Ajax and Diomedes because they fear for Ajax's safety (*Iliad* 23.822–3), one should not aim to kill one's opponent in a boxing match during funeral games. In short, Epeius's goal of killing his opponent will either strike the recipient as okay or not okay.

Or perhaps Epeius's language is that of the boastful, hyperbolically inclined prize fighter (Redfield 1975: 207; N. Richardson 1993: 243 at 673; Kyle 2015: 60). We are not to take him literally: he just threatens to "kill" his opponent, not actually to take his life. That hyperbole, however restrained, abounds in the Homeric epics (Scodel 2008: 52; J. Porter 2015: 190–2; Horrell 2017; Schironi 2018: 163) suggests there is nothing wrong with hyperbole per se. Recipients who find his phrasing amusing may be prone to take his side. Yet speakers can be rebuked for having engaged in hyperbolic trash talking. Sarpedon chastises (*neikesen*, *Iliad* 5.471) Hector for claiming that he could defend Troy alone, "without men and allies, by yourself, with your sisters' husbands and brothers" (5.473–4). Agamemnon chastises the Achaeans for boasting that each of them individually could stand up to one hundred or two hundred Trojans (*Iliad* 8.229–34). The work attributed to Plutarch that I cited a moment ago concerns how to engage in "self-praise" (*epipainein*) in an "inoffensive" manner (*anepiphthanōs*) (*On Praising Oneself Inoffensively*, *Moralia* 539a–547f)—no easy feat (cf. Spatharas 2019: 159–88). Recipients whom Epeius's boasting puts off will be less inclined to endorse his goal. From the variety of possible responses to Epeius's words, one concludes that it is not clear whether we are encouraged to experience motivational identification with Epeius and that, if we are encouraged to do so, it is not clear how vigorously the text pushes us in the direction.

Nor does the poet provide opportunities to identify with Euryalus, Epeius's opponent—however familiar one may have been with Euryalus from accounts of the Epigonoi's sack of Thebes (Tsagalis 2012: 118 n. 63, 222; Cingano 2015: 249). Consider the simple matter of narrative attention over the course of verses 677 to 684. The narrator states that Euryalus stood up and then turns to describe his father's feats at the funeral games for Oedipus. Next, we learn that Diomedes serves as Euryalus's second, and we watch him prepare his cousin for the match; we even get a glimpse inside Diomedes's head: "he really wanted victory for him"

(*Iliad* 23.682). At verse 685, the fight begins: "the two having girded themselves stepped into the middle of the place of assembly." During the verses ostensibly intended to introduce Euryalus, he shares the spotlight with his father and then with Diomedes. One will be hard pressed to identify with a character obscured in this fashion. That the narrator moves from describing how Euryalus "alone" (*oios*, *Iliad* 23.677) accepts Epeius's challenge to foregrounding first his father, Mecisteus, and then Diomedes emphasizes the obscuring of Euryalus: he is far from alone in these verses. The same effect arises from the deviation from the typical pattern wherein all are silent and then one person speaks. The formula that appears after Epeius's speech—"and then all became quiet in silence" (οἳ δ' ἄρα πάντες ἀκὴν ἐγένοντο σιωπῇ, *Iliad* 23.676)—occurs nine other times in the *Iliad* and six times in the *Odyssey*. It is always followed by one character coming forward to give a speech (cf. Kelly 2007: 85–8; A. Porter 2011) and stepping into the spotlight. When Euryalus stands up in verse 677, we expect him to give a speech. That the pattern is not adhered to—Euryalus does not give a speech (cf. A. Porter 2011: 503)—highlights the obscuring of Euryalus.

I do not see any obvious cues that encourage one to identify with Odysseus or Ajax in the wrestling match, with Ajax or Diomedes in the duel with spears, or with any of the four contestants in the shot put (Polypoetes, Leonteus, Ajax, and Epeius). Achilles's decision to award each wrestler "equal prizes" (*Iliad* 23.736), his offering a set of armor to be divided equally (*xunēia*) by the contestants in the duel with spears as well as his extending an invitation to both to a feast (23.809–10), the Achaeans' ordering Ajax and Diomedes to "stop [competing] and take equal prizes (*aethlia is'*)" (23.823)—these three moments mirror the poet's disinterested portrayal of those two contests. In the shotput contest, the poet focuses for ten verses on the history and value of the item to be putted and won as a prize—the only prize on offer—the mass of iron taken from Eëtion (*Iliad* 23.826–35), uses three verses to name the contestants (23.836–8), and then relates the unfolding of the contest over eleven verses (23.839–49). N. Richardson rightly assesses the relative importance of these three units: "the interest lies first in the history of the prize ... ; second in the information about its value ... ; and finally in the contestants" (1993: 262–3).

Still, we should view the wrestling match, the duel with spears, and the shot put contest from the perspective of Homeric characters' plurimediality discussed in section 3.2. Having heard stories about Odysseus and stories about Ajax, having seen depictions of Odysseus and of Ajax in other media, such as vase paintings, one might have developed an attachment to one or the other and might choose sides in the wrestling match in accordance with that attachment. The variables—Odysseus, Ajax, wrestling—could bring one story to mind. Menelaus refers to Odysseus's defeating Philomeleides in a wrestling match (*Odyssey* 4.341–4). Recipients familiar with such a story might root for Odysseus to win again. It is perhaps more likely that pitting Odysseus against Ajax recalls the contest between

Odysseus and Ajax over Achilles's armor (N. Richardson 1993: 246; Grethlein 2007a: 162–3; Bierl 2019: 68). Knowledge of that scene might reinforce partisan responses to the match. Knowing that Ajax will lose the contest over the armor, go temporarily mad, and commit suicide (Finglass 2011: 27–36), one might want him to win here. Or knowing that Odysseus wins the contest on the readily disputed point that he is a better warrior (scholion at *Odyssey* 11.547 Dindorf; Pindar *Nemean* 8.26–30; Sophocles *Ajax* 1273–87, 1339–41; Gantz 1996: 629–30; cf. Blundell 1989: 88, 100), one might root for Odysseus to reveal his superiority as a wrestler on the grounds that wrestling is a good proxy for warring: both require strength and skill (Dunkle 1987: 13–15; Hawhee 2005: 37–8; Ready 2011: 130–2). Again, the other competitor in the duel with spears, Diomedes, is, like Ajax, a prominent figure in archaic Greek tale telling in a number of media. Recipients may have a favorite of the two that they root for. For their part, the two Lapith leaders (*Iliad* 2.738–47) who compete in the shot put, Polypoetes and Leonteus, make a fine showing of defending the Achaean wall (*Iliad* 12.127–94); Eustathius reports versions of the story of the Wooden Horse in which Leonteus was one of the twelve Achaeans who hid out in it (vol. 1, p. 432 Stallbaum). Some recipients may be predisposed to favor these characters too.

By contrast, the description of the footrace encourages recipients to identify with one particular competitor. Three enter the event—Oïlean Ajax, Odysseus, and Antilochus—but from the start the race becomes a contest between Oïlean Ajax and Odysseus. With the simile that runs from verses 760 to 763, the narrative spotlight rests on Odysseus. The simile describes how close Odysseus stays to Oïlean Ajax and points up his tactics: he drafts, running right behind his opponent such that his own feet land in Oïlean Ajax's footprints before the dust has settled (Ready 2011: 158). Highlighting Odysseus's skillful running, these verses provide access to Odysseus's mind: they show us what he is trying to do. Having foregrounded Odysseus's perspective, the poet then notes that the spectators were rooting for Odysseus: "and all the Achaeans shouted out to him as he strove for victory, and they gave him encouragement as he exerted himself greatly" (*Iliad* 23.766–7). The prioritizing of Odysseus's perspective, coupled with the detail that the Achaeans want him to win, can propel the recipient to experience motivational identification with Odysseus.

Teucer and Meriones compete in the archery event. Achilles tasks them with hitting a bird tied to a string attached to the mast of a ship: first prize for hitting the dove; second prize for hitting the string (*Iliad* 23.852–8). Teucer shoots first, but, because "he did not promise to sacrifice to the lord [Apollo] a splendid hecatomb of first-born lambs" (*Iliad* 23.863–4), Apollo, begrudging (*megēre*) him victory, sees to it that he only hits the string (23.865–7). The narrator makes plain that not offering a hecatomb at this moment—when an archer aims to make a successful shot (N. Richardson 1993: 268 at 863–4)—qualifies as a misstep. If we follow the bT scholion here—"this urges one toward piety (*eusebeian*)" (bT scholion at *Iliad* 23.685)—we take the misstep to be a failure to make a required display of piety. Recipients will not be inclined right away at least to identify with a character whom they are told acts without a required display of piety. Moreover, in the one other moment in the Homeric epics' narrator-texts in which a god begrudges a mortal's success, Poseidon begrudges Adamas's killing Antilochus (*Iliad* 13.563). It seems unlikely that we are to experience motivational identification with Adamas at this moment, and this parallel suggests that we are not to identify with Teucer when he is begrudged by Apollo.

The bird starts to fly away; the string drifts to the ground; the Achaeans shout (*Iliad* 23.868–9). These two verses shift our attention away from Teucer and prepare for a shift of attention to Meriones. Meriones then moves into the spotlight, and we immediately get a glimpse into his mind: "in haste (*sperkhomenos*)" he snatches the bow from Teucer (*Iliad* 23.870–1). The participle reflects his assessment of the need to act quickly (see section 4.2.1, p. 89). The following detail—"and in fact he had been holding an arrow for a long time (*palai*), while he [Teucer] was aiming" (*Iliad* 23.871)—also foregrounds Meriones's perspective because it makes us see Teucer's shot from his point of view: he had to wait his turn for what must have seemed like a long time (*palai*). In favor of taking *palai* as reflecting Meriones's experience of time is that *palai* elsewhere refers to situations or states that have been the way they are for what most would label an extended period of time: for instance, Sarpedon has been fated to die for a long time (*palai*, *Iliad* 16.441); maids make use of "dry firewood, dry for a long time, exceedingly dry" (ξύλα κάγκανα... / αὖα πάλαι, περίκηλα, *Odyssey* 18.308–9). Only from the perspective of an impatient Meriones himself could he be said to have been holding the arrow *palai*, for a long time. (Taking the comment to reflect Meriones's point of view also helps explain the ostensibly awkward shift in subject in the clause "while he [Teucer] was aiming" (N. Richardson 1993: 268 at 870–1). From Meriones's perspective, to say "while he was aiming" means "while Teucer was aiming.") If this reading does not convince, one should nevertheless grant that the detail in verse 871 forefronts Meriones's presence in the scene. The poet does not simply switch to Meriones after he finishes with Teucer. The detail makes us revise our mental image of Teucer's shot: Meriones is now a presence at that moment too, waiting to compete; he jostles for attention in our mind's eye with Teucer. In any case, Meriones focalizes verse 874: "High up, beneath the clouds he saw (*eide*) the fluttering dove." To repeat, recipients identify more easily with a character from whose perspective the narrative unfolds.

The narrator's report on Meriones's vow to Apollo invites motivational identification with Meriones. Repeating nearly exactly verses 863–4, verses 872–3 state, "immediately he promised to the far-shooting lord Apollo to sacrifice a splendid hecatomb of first-born lambs." If we merely contrast Teucer's failure to demonstrate piety with Meriones's display of piety and leave it at that, we neglect a likely outcome of this repetition. Stressing Meriones's piety by contrasting it with

Teucer's failure to show piety, the poet encourages recipients appreciative of displays of the virtue of piety to root for Meriones to achieve his goal.

The javelin throw is supposed to be the final event of the games, but Achilles decides that the two competitors who have put themselves forward, Agamemnon and Meriones, should not compete: everyone knows that Agamemnon is the best in this event; he should take the first prize and Meriones, the second (*Iliad* 23.890–4). When Achilles short-circuits the whole event, he denies internal spectators and external recipients the chance to experience motivational identification with either of the competitors. Precluding this response both highlights by way of contrast the importance of motivational identification to several of the other contests and signals that the games, regularly a site for the experience of motivational identification, have come to a close. The brevity of the episode (Stanley 1993: 230; M. L. West 2011: 399) has a point.

### 4.2.4. Priam in *Iliad* 24

The poet provides a striking visual image: the grieving Priam wrapped in a cloak (ἐντυπὰς ἐν χλαίνῃ κεκαλυμμένος, *Iliad* 24.163) and covered in the filth (*kopros*) that he picks up with his own hands and mashes onto his head and neck (κεφαλῇ τε καὶ αὐχένι) as he grovels on the ground (24.163–5). Recipients could easily imagine the wrapped-up and grieving Priam. Several literary and material artifacts testify to the frequency of the veiled and grieving mourner (Cairns 2009, esp. 48, 49; 2011; Muellner 2012, esp. 209). To cite some examples from archaic Greek epic: the *Odyssey* describes a grieving (*gooio*) Telemachus holding up his cloak in front of his eyes (4.113–16) and a grieving (*goaasken*) Odysseus covering (*kalupsamenos*) his head with his cloak (8.83–92) (Muellner 2012: 207–9). Sorrowful (*tetiēmenē*) over the abduction of her daughter, Demeter sits veiled (*prokatesketo khersi kaluptrēn*) (*Homeric Hymn to Demeter* 197–8). By depicting Priam's adoption of a recognizable pose, the poet gives recipients a sense of what the character looks like at this moment. Moreover, not just the references to specific body parts—his head and neck—but also the reference to those body parts being covered in filth prompts one to envision the grieving king. I recall that descriptions of what a character looks like aid identification.

Just as Priam does what Telemachus and Odysseus do, so too his befouling himself with dirt and rolling on the ground in grief find parallels (N. Richardson 1993: 150 at 414). Achilles grieves at the news of Patroclus's death: "and taking in both hands the dark dust (*konin*), he poured it over his head (*kephalēs*) and defiled his seemly face (*prosōpon*): and on his fragrant tunic the black ashes fell. And he himself great in his greatness stretched out in the dust lay (*keito*)" (*Iliad* 18.23–7). Remembering Odysseus, Laertes grieves and "taking in both hands the dark dust (*konin*) he poured it over his gray head (*kephalēs*)" (*Odyssey* 24.316–17). That

Priam's manner of grieving overlaps with Achilles's and Laertes's enhances the narrative realism of the passage. Again, I recall that recipients who deem a narrative realistic are more apt to identify with the characters.

Motivational identification with Priam may occur. Priam last appeared in *Iliad* 22, already rolling around in the dirt (*kulindomenos kata kopron*, 22.414). Even at that point, Priam expresses the wish to go himself to Achilles and retrieve Hector's corpse (*Iliad* 22.416–20). So eager (*memaōta*) is he to set out that his people must literally restrain him: they "held him back with difficulty" (*mogis ekhon*, *Iliad* 22.412–13). Priam has to put off embarking on the steps necessary to achieve his goal, but the foregrounding of his goal at this juncture presages the attention lavished on the goal in *Iliad* 24.

At *Iliad* 24.171–87, Iris relays Zeus's command to Priam: he is to go to Achilles's tent and bring a ransom to pay for the return of Hector's body. Priam gets to work, ordering his sons to prepare the required wagon and descending to the storeroom to assemble the ransom (*Iliad* 24.189–92). He seems to have eagerly embraced the goal of ransoming Hector himself, but he then asks Hecuba for her opinion, "But come now and tell me, how does it [this plan] seem to your mind?," before, in keeping with his earlier haste to get the process started, declaring his own intense desire to set out for Achilles's tent: "for terribly (*ainōs*) my spirit and heart urge me myself to go there to the ships to the wide camp of Achaeans" (*Iliad* 24.197–9). This back and forth on Priam's part suggests that he experiences a moment of doubt as to the viability of the undertaking and either genuinely wants Hecuba's input or merely wants her to endorse his own wishes. Priam's words make clear the challenging nature of his goal and his hesitation or even anxiety over embarking on the trip in the hopes of achieving that goal. For her part, Hecuba suggests that Priam seeks the impossible: his mission is suicidal because Achilles, once he has Priam in his grasp, will kill him (*Iliad* 24.201–9). Better to adopt the far more circumscribed goal of lamenting Hector "at a distance, sitting in the hall" (*Iliad* 24.209–10). Her answer to Priam's query keeps the matter of Priam's goal and its difficulty foremost in the audience's mind. In response, Priam again insists on his eagerness to set off: "Do not try to restrain me when I wish to go" (*Iliad* 24.218). At this point, Priam has firmly decided upon his goal and he goes on to explain why: the injunction to ransom Hector came from the gods, not from any human source (*Iliad* 24.220–4). The narrator then echoes Priam's desire to see this project through to a successful conclusion—that he includes in the ransom a cup from Thrace reflects his determination: "because he was exceedingly eager (*peri d' ēthele*) in his heart to ransom his dear son" (*Iliad* 24.236–7).

This stretch of verse focuses attention on Priam's goal—his trepidation about taking on this task, the difficulty posed by the task, the reason for embarking on the task, and his resolve to accomplish the task. The narrative time devoted to the matter gives the recipient the chance to ponder the goal, and that concentration on Priam's goal along with the posing of alternatives that suggest the difficulty of the goal—Priam himself allows for the possibility that Achilles will kill him (*Iliad* 24.224-7), as Hecuba suggests—can make the recipient more apt to hope that Priam succeeds. The recipient can experience motivational identification with Priam.

I cite as well Fritz Breithaupt's discussion of the decisive moment as a trigger to empathy: we are prone to empathize "when someone has to make a decision, has to act, has to choose" (2018: 55). In *Iliad* 24, Priam confronts a decisive moment and selects a course of action. Per Breithaupt's model, that scenario prompts us to empathize with him. I note again the overlap between Breithaupt's understanding of empathy and the models of identification I deploy here (see section 2.2, p. 24). To translate from one model to the other: that we find Priam at a decisive moment cues us to identify with him.

After Hecuba attempts to dissuade Priam, the perspective of the Trojan king becomes primary. Priam delivers the next three speeches in the poem: the poet quotes his ten-line response to Hecuba (*Iliad* 24.218–27) and then his eight-line rebuke of the Trojans (24.239–46) and his twelve-line rebuke of his children (24.253–64). The most speeches a character in the Homeric epics utters before someone else speaks is three. Menelaus gives three consecutive and uninterrupted speeches over the course of *Iliad* 17.666–714. By limiting who speaks solely to Priam over the course of these lines, the poet seems to tell the tale from Priam's perspective. The concentration on Priam appears as well in the verses that describe Priam assembling the ransom (and I am talking about the initial assembling of the ransom: his sons later put it on the wagon (*Iliad* 24.275-6)). He does so seemingly single-handedly: he opens (*aneōigen*) the chests in the storeroom, he takes out (*exele*) various textiles, he weighs and carries out (*stēsas epheren*) ten talents of gold and collects tripods, cauldrons, and a cup from Thrace (*Iliad* 24.228–35). Contrast this sole effort with the way a group assembles the goods that Agamemnon gives Achilles. Agamemnon tells Achilles, "The attendants will take the goods from my ship and bring them" (*Iliad* 19.143-4). A moment later, Odysseus leads a large contingent—the sons of Nestor, Meges, Thoas, Meriones, Lycomedes, and Melanippus—in gathering the goods (*Iliad* 19.237–48), which "they put (*thesan*) in the middle of the meeting place" (19.249). But the passage in *Iliad* 24 does not just focus on Priam: he turns out to be the focalizer. Zooming in on the cup from Thrace, the narrator concludes with the following note: "not even this (*tou*) [cup] did the old man spare (*pheisat'*) in his halls because he was exceedingly eager in his heart (περὶ δ' ἤθελε θυμῷ) to ransom his dear son" (*Iliad* 24.235–7). These verses remind us, if reminding is needed, that we are to view the previous description of Priam's assembling of the ransom from Priam's point of view: it is so lavish because he spares nothing in his desperation to ransom Hector (cf. Tsagalis 2012: 395). In sum, from *Iliad* 24.218 to 264, Priam's perspective dominates. Once again, we are more apt to identify with the character from whose perspective the story is told.

Beyond motivational identification, one might experience cognitive identification (per, again, Cohen and Tal-Or, "the adoption of a character's view of things and his/her interpretation of events" (2017: 134)) and emotional identification with Priam. For instance, one might agree with his claim that the other Trojans should not add to Priam's distress by performing their own lamentations next to him: "Is there not now even for you lamentation at home, that you come here to trouble me? Do you think it insignificant that Zeus son of Cronus gave me pains, to lose my best son?" (*Iliad* 24.239–42). And one might agree that the other Trojans "will be much easier for the Achaeans to kill because that one [Hector] is now dead" (*Iliad* 24.243–4), given the clear link between Hector's death and the sack of Troy (e.g., *Iliad* 22.410–11). One might also share the exasperation he expresses toward his own children: "Will you not prepare (οὐκ ἂν δή... ἐφοπλίσσαιτε) a wagon for me most quickly?" (*Iliad* 24.263). The potential optative construction here indicates annoyance or even contempt (cf. N. Richardson 1993: 301 at 263). Despite his having already issued this command some verses previous at *Iliad* 24.189–90, apparently no one had fulfilled his order.

These verses also bring out how the passage provides an opportunity to take sides. One might be inclined to take sides with Priam against those he rebukes and so to identify with him. At the same time, once we identify with Priam—say, once we adopt his goal—the opportunity to take sides strengthens that sense of identification: compare my earlier discussion of Menelaus's rebuke of Antilochus (section 4.2.3, p. 103).

## 4.3. Identification with Gods

The Homeric gods regularly stand as foils to mortal men. Only the Muses can provide mortal poets access to the heroic past (*Iliad* 2.484–6). Mortal men risk their lives on the battlefield in the hopes of gaining status (*timē*) and renown (*kleos*); as Sarpedon shrewdly observes, their immortality excludes gods from this economy (*Iliad* 12.310–28). Gods do not have the same physical limitations as mortals do: they can travel from one place to another as rapidly as a mortal's thoughts move from one topic to another (*Iliad* 15.79–83). Those are just a few of the ways in which the epics articulate profound differences between men and gods, and scholarship has brought out the extent to which the poets thematize that gulf (e.g., Griffin 1980; Benardete 2005: e.g., 15). On top of that, it has been observed that the gods "rarely draw much sympathy" (Myers 2019: 62). We might reflexively anticipate, then, that the mortal audiences of epic identify more readily with the mortal characters and less with the divine figures.

This intuition is, I think, wrong. Lillian Doherty is on the right track when she sees a possibility for "a certain degree of identification" between human recipient and immortal character (1995: 128), but I would not hedge as she does. In the first place, the *Iliad*'s gods and the external audience find their perspectives on the storyworld in "partial alignment": they both have some sense of what will happen, and they both stand apart from the action and are therefore "capable of a detached appreciation that is unavailable to mortal characters" (Myers 2019: 6 (citing Elmer 2013: 151), cf. 107). This overlap encourages the recipient's cognitive identification with immortals. Moreover, to borrow from Longinus (*On the Sublime* 9.7) (who borrowed the sentiment from earlier writers (J. Porter 2016: 140–1)), the Homeric poets and other tale tellers made men out of gods (cf. E. Vermeule 1979: 110, 123–4; Myers 2019: 4–5). Like men, the gods regularly do not get what they want. Demeter fails to immortalize Demophoon (*Homeric Hymn to Demeter*). Laomedon cheated Poseidon and Apollo of the payments he promised them for their service: Poseidon built a wall around Troy; Apollo tended his cattle (*Iliad* 21.441–57). Hera dupes Zeus in *Iliad* 14—she seduces him, and he falls into a post-coital slumber—and as a result the Achaeans push back the Trojans, contravening Zeus's plan. Zeus cannot save his son Sarpedon from death (*Iliad* 16.431–61; cf. Johnston 2018: 165). Ares's son Ascalaphus dies unbeknownst to Ares (*Iliad* 13.521–5); he learns about the death in *Iliad* 15 and prepares to ignore Zeus's ban on the gods' entering the fight, but he gives up after Athena warns him of the consequences (15.110–42). Poseidon has to acquiesce to Odysseus's making it back to Ithaca and grows angry upon seeing the Phaeacians escort him home so quickly with more treasure than he took from Troy (*Odyssey* 13.125–38). In short, it is often an open question as to whether a god will get everything they want, and it is easier to experience motivational identification with them in such circumstances.

Furthermore, recipients did not just come across gods when hearing or reading Homeric poetry. They interacted with divinities all the time in different spaces and in different media (cf. Martin 2016: 76). I return to Sarah Iles Johnston's discussion of "plurimediality" and the "accretive characters" of Greek myth and cult (2018: 156–61), reviewed in section 3.2 (p. 60) (and evoked in section 4.2.3, p. 107), and repeat what I wrote *mutatis mutandis*. There I was concerned with mortal characters, but now we should add that ancient Greeks fashioned their understanding of a particular divinity over time from their various encounters with portrayals of the divinity (if not encounters with the divinity) in various contexts, be it as a statue, in a painting, or as a character in a tale. (Along with actual cultic practice, literature and art contributed to an individual's sense of a divinity (e.g., W. Allan 2004: 130; Mastronarde 2010: 161).) Manufacturing this understanding required "cognitive and emotional energy" (Johnston 2018: 158) especially because the portrayal of the divinity changed depending on the context of the portrayal (cf. Feeney 1991: 45–8). Putting time and effort into this assemblage led one to care about the assemblage, to care about the divinity; but one also cared about the assemblage, about the divinity, because it was one's own construction. With its abundance of familiar divinities, Homeric epic capitalized on this phenomenon: it gave audience members characters they cared about. Moreover, it had to be the case that individuals, although they may have had a general understanding of a large number of divinities, had invested more energy in creating a vision of some as opposed to other divinities and as a result had favorites. If so, they might be more apt to identify with a particular divinity when hearing about that divinity's exploits. Again, Homeric epic, with its abundance of familiar divinities, provided something for everyone on this front.

With these thoughts in mind, I step away from the Homeric epics for a moment and consider a poem with a divine protagonist, the *Homeric Hymn to Demeter* (4.3.1). I have noted that recipients are frequently prone to identify with protagonists: if we want to test out the idea of identifying with a god, the Homeric hymns with their divine protagonists offer a good starting point. This preparation will enable us to come back to the Homeric epics with a clearer sense of what is possible in terms of audience's connections to divine characters (4.3.2 and 4.3.3).

### 4.3.1. The *Homeric Hymn to Demeter*

I propose to build on Nicholas Richardson's passing comment: "In terms of sympathy, the poet encourages us to identify with the female characters, especially Demeter and Kore in the portrayal of their suffering, and Metaneira in her anxiety and subsequently her grief for her son" (2011: 47). Richardon errs in conflating sympathy with identification, and, as we will see, I do not see textual cues that prompt the recipient to identify with Metaneira. Still, I applaud Richardson's willingness to acknowledge one of the ways in which recipients likely respond to texts—by identifying with the characters.

Recipients start the poem with more knowledge than Demeter: they know that Hades has seized Persephone and carried her off to the underworld; Demeter does not. This difference in knowledge may keep recipients from an initial identification with Demeter, despite the opportunity for emotional identification in the narrator's report that "a sharp pain (*akhos*) seized her heart" and that she tears her veil (40–1) when she hears her daughter's cries. One may feel sympathy for, but not identify with, Demeter. Instead, prompted by the narrator's comment—"not was anyone of gods or mortals willing to tell her the truth, nor did any of the birds come to her as a true messenger" (44–6)—recipients may wait to see how and when Demeter will learn what transpired: "the revelation of her daughter's fate to Demeter" constitutes "the second movement of the hymn's first section" (Clay 2006: 216; cf. 221).

The recipient's stance may, however, change. Helios fills Demeter in: Zeus gave Persephone to Hades to be his wife (77–9). Helios suggests that Demeter cease her lamentation and set aside her anger (*kholon*): Hades, the powerful ruler of the underworld, is not "an unsuitable son-in-law" (82–7). He fails to convince

Demeter: she is pained to a still greater degree than before—her *akhos* is now "harsher and crueler (*ainoteron kai kunteron*)"—and she is angry (*khōsamenē*) at Zeus (90–1). Recipients have a choice at this point because here is an opportunity to take sides. They can accept Zeus's right to give Persephone to Hades, and they can agree with Helios's analysis. Or they can take Demeter's side. The text perhaps nudges them in the latter direction when it provides them with a model for taking Demeter's side in the character of Hecate. Hecate seeks out Demeter to report that Persephone was abducted (52–8): the verb *ēnteto* suggests an active search (cf. *Iliad* 8.412, 16.788, 22.203). She also goes with Demeter (*sun autēi*) to consult Helios (60–3): the plural verb forms "they went" (*hikonto*) and "they stood" (*stan*) highlight their joint action. Recipients have the chance, then, to adopt Demeter's perspective on the abduction and to experience cognitive identification with her.

Demeter has caught up to the recipients in terms of their knowledge of what happened to Persephone. There now emerges a discrepancy in knowledge between Demeter and external recipients, on the one hand, and the members of Celeus's household, on the other hand. The recipients know that Demeter has disguised herself as an old nurse; the members of Celeus's household do not. The poem foregrounds this disjunction: the daughters of Celeus "did not recognize" the disguised Demeter (111); when Demeter enters the house, her head touches the roof, and she radiates a divine light (188–9), but her mortal hosts do not acknowledge that she is a divinity and do not even seem to suspect her true nature (Clay 2006: 232; *pace* H. Foley 1999: 44–5); Metaneira speculates on the high status of Demeter's mortal parents (212–15) and attempts to console Demeter by reminding her that "we men"—a category in which she includes Demeter—"endure" (*tetlamen anthrōpoi*, 217) what the gods allot, a truism already offered to Demeter by Callidice, the eldest daughter (147–8). This connection on the level of storyworld knowledge between Demeter and external recipients—perhaps all the stronger in light of the earlier difference in knowledge at the start of the poem—encourages recipients to continue experiencing cognitive identification with Demeter. In particular, recipients may share Demeter's judgment of Metaneira's bumbling intrusion into the nighttime procedure by which Demeter works to render Demophoon ageless and immortal. Demeter, "angered exceedingly terribly" (255), declares, "Ignorant humans and witless to recognize a portion either of good when it is coming or of evil. For you are incurably deluded by your folly (*aphradiēisin*... *aasthēs*)" (256–8). The narrator has already previewed this assessment, stressing Metaneira's folly (*aphradiēisin*, 243) and delusion (*aasthē*, 246). This overlap between narrator (an authoritative voice) and character further cues the audience to evaluate Metaneira's action from Demeter's point of view.

The joyous reunion between Demeter and Persephone (385–90) appears a spot for recipients to experience emotional identification with the pair. Lacunae abound in this section, but the readings in Martin West's text seem suitable (2003a). First, the poet describes each one seeing the other and then sprinting full tilt toward the other: Demeter tears down the mountain like a maenad (385–6); Persephone leaps off the chariot to run (*alto theein*) to her mother (387–9). Compare the use of the more restrained verb *kiō* ("go") in reference to Penelope as she moves to embrace Odysseus (*Odyssey* 23.207). That Demeter's and Persephone's initial stillness gives way to movement underscores those movements by way of contrast: Demeter waits (*mimnen*, 384), presumably seated (see *hēstai* at 356), in her temple; Persephone stands on a chariot from which she has to dismount (*prolipousa... alto*, 388–9). The scene of two family members running toward one another after a long or unexpected separation is timeless. I will forgo my usual pedantic search for parallels in archaic Greek poetry and state what I take to be obvious: emotions of joy course through Demeter and Persephone (cf. H. Foley 1999: 58). Second, the poet describes them hugging (*amphikhutheisa... ekhousēi*, 389–90), and "happy tears" (Clay 2006: 254) or at least displays of affection come implied. When Odysseus discloses his identity, Telemachus embraces (*amphikhutheis*) his father and cries (*dakrua leibōn*) (*Odyssey* 16.214). Odysseus's slave women embrace him (*amphekheonto*), greet him, kiss him, and shower him with affection (*agapazomenai*) (*Odyssey* 22.498–9; cf. 21.223–4). A crying Penelope "threw her arms around his neck" and kissed (*ekus'*) Odysseus (*Odyssey* 23.207–8). Third, after Persephone provides an account of what she endured, the poet does not leave it to us to intuit their emotions and makes explicit their delight: "so they then all day long, at one in their minds, greatly warmed each other's hearts with embraces, and assuaged their sorrows, giving each other joy and receiving it" (*Odyssey* 23.434–7). All these passages can cue emotional identification.

If one experiences cognitive and emotional identification with Demeter, might one experience motivational identification with her? Demeter roams presumably without any real sense of where she should go for only a few verses: the disjunction between the narrated (or story) time of nine days and the narrative (or discourse) time of five lines emphasizes the rapidity with which the poet handles this stretch of *aporia*. Rather, Demeter's active planning provides a structure for much of the poem (even if the poem does not clearly explain the reasons for her actions (H. Foley 1999: 48, 101; N. Richardson 2011: 56–7)). Demeter has two plans. Her first plan—to make Demophoon immortal—aims squarely at Zeus and fails (Clay 2006: 226, 229, 236–7, 240, 246; Slatkin 1991: 98). Her second plan—to compel Zeus to release Persephone from the underworld by causing mortals' crops to fail (see verses 304 and 333)—aims at all the immortals and succeeds in part (Clay 2006: 247, 250; H. Foley 1999: 93–4): Persephone will spend two-thirds of the year with Demeter and one-third in the underworld (398–400). To the extent that the poem portrays Demeter as an active agent with goals, it provides opportunities for recipients to experience motivational identification with her.

If one roots for her first plan to succeed, one roots for a challenge to the way Zeus has organized the cosmos and therefore a challenge to Zeus. In Zeus's world, only gods are immortal, not men, and Demeter seeks to confound that distinction by immortalizing Demophoon: "In Eleusis, she attempts to obstruct Zeus's plan by making a mortal divine. Had the project been successful, it would have thrown Zeus's authority to rule open to question and led to a blurring of the boundaries defining gods and mortals" (Clay 2006: 263; cf. 226; H. Foley 1999: 114–15). Some recipients might revel in the chance to root for the subversive Demeter that the hymn offers here. Other recipients may balk at hoping Demeter achieves her first goal. Still, even these recipients may be inclined to root for her when she embarks on her second plan.

I close my examination of this hymn with a bit of speculation that will allow me to gesture toward the several important interpretations of the hymn that situate it in a specific historical and religious context. The hymn ends by recounting Demeter's founding of a cult in her honor at Eleusis (473–82), the entire poem moving methodically toward this conclusion (H. Foley 1999: 84). Scholars continue to debate the hymn's connections with actual cults, some linking elements of the hymn to cultic practices at the Eleusinian Mysteries and others to components of a festival known as the Thesmophoria (N. Richardson 2011: 49–53). The hymn might have resonated with recipients who participated in these rites in Demeter's honor (cf. H. Foley 1999: e.g., 50), and that resonance might have primed such individuals to identify with the character Demeter.

This section has detailed the possibilities for cognitive, emotional, and motivational identification with the goddess Demeter in her long eponymous Homeric hymn. It thereby encourages investigations of the sort undertaken in the next two sections into the possibilities for identification with divinities in the Homeric epics.

### 4.3.2. Hera in *Iliad* 14

Lesser mentions in passing the possibility of recipients' identifying with Hera in *Iliad* 1 (2022: 67). I explore the goddess's turn in the spotlight in *Iliad* 14.

Hera prepares to seduce Zeus. The poet takes us into Hera's mind and stays there for thirteen verses: she looked on (*eiseide*) the battlefield (*Iliad* 14.153); she recognized (*egnō*) Poseidon as he urged on the Achaeans (14.154); she delighted (*khaire*) in his actions (14.156); she saw (*eiseide*) Zeus sitting on Ida (14.158); he was hateful (*stugeros*) to her heart (*hoi…thumōi*) (14.158); she debated (*mermērixe*) how she might distract Zeus from the events on the battlefield (14.159–60); she resolved upon a plan (*boulē*) (14.161), and verses 162–5 detail that plan to seduce Zeus. This stretch of verse forefronts Hera's perspective, a typical trigger for identification, in three different modes, detailing what she sees (the battlefield, Poseidon, Zeus), what she feels (delight, hatred), and what she thinks about (deceiving Zeus). She even thinks about what Zeus may think when he sees her in her seductive attire: she wants him to desire her (*himeiraito*, *Iliad* 14.163).

Building on Richard Janko's comment—"The poet outlines Here's plan to ensure that we can *enjoy* its execution" (1992: 173 at 159–61, my emphasis)—I note that verses 161–5 also assign her a goal, the first required step in offering recipients the chance to experience motivational identification. These verses bring out the difficulty of Hera's goal: she aims to deceive the mind (*noon*, *Iliad* 14.160) of Zeus, but Zeus possesses a cunning mind (*phresi peukalimēisi*, 14.165). The complexities of her task will become more apparent as the episode unfolds and she takes several intermediate steps in pursuit of her overarching goal: getting dressed up, tricking Aphrodite, and cajoling Sleep. Again, a difficult goal triggers motivational identification more easily than a simple task. Observe too that the goal involves her tricking Zeus, so it gives the recipient the opportunity to take sides, another prompt to identification. Indeed, the episode starts with a reminder of which side Hera is on: she delights in Poseidon's actions because she favors the Greeks. The scene forefronts her membership in that group of pro-Greek divine partisans. Recall that if group membership represents an important component of a character's portrayal, that fact can enhance identification.

Hera remains alone in the narrative spotlight as the poet details how she gets dressed for her adventure. She cleans and anoints herself, combs and styles her hair, steps into a robe that she pins with brooches, and puts on a belt, earrings, a veil, and sandals (*Iliad* 14.170–86). All but the last item, the sandals, receive an elucidating detail: the robe has "many embroideries" (*daidala polla*, 14.179); the brooches are golden (*khruseiēis*, 14.180); the belt has "100 tassels" (*hekaton thusanois*, 14.181); each earring has "three clustering drops" (*triglēna moroenta*, 14.183); and her veil shines white (*leukon*) like the sun (14.185). As the arming scene in *Iliad* 11 enables recipients to craft a mental image of what Agamemnon looks like (section 4.2.1, pp. 86–7), recipients can construct a mental image of what Hera looks like. The physical description eases identification.

Hera then approaches Aphrodite and requests that Aphrodite give her "love and desire" so that she can put an end to a quarrel between Oceanus and Tethys (*Iliad* 14.198–210). The narrator states that Hera speaks *dolophroneousa* (*Iliad* 14.197)—she has something in mind that she does not express (cf. *Iliad* 19.106; *Odyssey* 18.51, 21.274). But unlike in those three occurrences of the participle just cited in parentheses, Hera flatly lies here. We know that she lies, and that shared knowledge nudges us to come at their conversation from Hera's point of view: like Hera, we wait to see if the lie will work. The construction of the scene encourages cognitive identification with Hera. Contrast the construction of the *Homeric Hymn to Hermes*, which also involves divine deceit. Hermes steals fifty of Apollo's cattle and drives them as far as the Alpheius river (69–141). The subsequent narrative does not prompt us to wonder if he can deflect Apollo with his lies: Maea sees right through Hermes (154) and predicts that Apollo will soon be after him (154–9); a bird omen alerts Apollo to the identity of the thief (213–14); and the first thing Apollo asks Hermes is where his cattle are (254–5). So, when Hermes falsely declares his innocence "with crafty (*kerdaleoisin*) words" (260), we do not wait to see if the lie will work: Apollo's subsequent laughter (*gelasas*, 281) and demand that Hermes lead the way to his cattle (302–3) does not surprise us. Likewise, we do not wait to see if Hermes's misleading claims to Zeus about not leading the cattle home (379) will convince Zeus: Zeus's subsequent laughter (*exegelassen*, 389) and order to Hermes to show Apollo where he hid the cattle (391–4) do not surprise us.

This moment of cognitive identification with Hera in *Iliad* 14 can morph into emotional identification. Aphrodite hands her strap over, and the narrator notes Hera's smile twice over: *meidēsen...meidēsasa* (*Iliad* 14.222–3). The repetition stresses her happiness at having pulled off this trick and achieved this intermediate goal (Lesser 2022: 164). Recipients can be happy along with her.

Having obtained what she wanted from Aphrodite, Hera immediately heads out on a journey. From verse 225 to 230, the poet details the course of her travels as she whips past Pieria, Emathia, and Thrace and comes to a stop on Lemnos. Hera thus completes a typical divine journey, marked by a mode of transport only available to a god ("the divine cross between flying and mountain-stepping") and a speed only an immortal could achieve (see de Jong 2012b: 43–8, quotation from 44). Its typicality endows the scene with narrative realism, another antecedent of identification. At the same time, just as her destination remains unclear until the end, recipients do not know why she embarks on this journey until she encounters Sleep and asks for his help. Enticing Sleep to aid her machinations against Zeus turns out to be an integral part of her plan and an unexpected one at that: verses 164–5 simply reported that Hera planned to "pour" (*kheuēi*) sleep over Zeus and did not mention the need for the god Sleep's help. We have to catch up with Hera's intentions, with what she hopes to accomplish by this journey, and this act of catching up can concentrate our attention on her goal. Furthermore, as the conversation with Sleep unfolds, we wonder if, or perhaps simply how, Hera will be able to accomplish what she considers a necessary step in her overarching plan. It is a small step from our focusing on her goal and being uncertain about her success to hoping she achieves her goal, to motivational identification, a step we might all the more readily take if we have accepted the episode's previous invitations to identify with Hera.

In contrast to her approach to Aphrodite, Hera does not lie to Sleep. She lays out her whole plan and gets him on her team. The repeated use of the dual number over verses 281–5 to describe their journey to Mt Ida emphasizes their solidarity: they act in unison. This addition of a confederate offers recipients a model to follow: like Sleep, they can take Hera's side (compare my earlier discussion of Hecate: section 4.3.1, p. 116). Or, for a recipient already fully committed to Hera's side, the addition of Sleep to the team reinforces the recipient's sense of having

### 4.3.3. Thetis in *Iliad* 18

With the portrayal of Thetis, the *Iliad* poet takes advantage of the opportunities afforded by a plurimedial and transtextual character with a rich mythological background (Slatkin 1991). Attuned to the care with which the poet crafts this character, I illustrate how she can become a candidate for identification. Before turning to *Iliad* 18, I comment first on the matter of similarity and on the matter of character virtue.

The *Iliad* poet figures Thetis first and foremost as a mother and neglects stories about her erotic allure, like that featured in Pindar *Isthmian* 8.29 wherein the lovely (*eueidea*) Thetis prompts love (*erōs*) in Zeus and Poseidon (Slatkin 1991: 31). This emphasis on Thetis as mother matters for our query. Parents will have made up some portion of the *Iliad*'s audience from the start of the performance tradition, and some of those parents may have felt themselves similar to Thetis in so far as she is a parent. Compare one critic's reaction to the verse in which Hector smiles upon seeing his son, Astyanax (*Iliad* 6.404): "the parental response is heartbreakingly familiar" (Pratt 2007: 27). One can find a similarity (here cast as familiarity) with Hector in the realm of parenthood. Yet Thetis is more than just a parent; she is a suffering parent, the only divinity routinely depicted as such in the epics (Slatkin 1991: 77; cf. Kelly 2012: 249). Although she tells Hephaestus that she suffers in part due to her forced marriage to the mortal Peleus (*Iliad* 18.432–5; Slatkin 1991: 97), she suffers primarily, like mortal parents in the audience, due to her devotion to her child. Mark Edward's comment on Thetis's declaration— "While he [Achilles] lives and looks on the light of the sun, he is pained, and I am not at all able to help him when I go to him" (*Iliad* 18.61–2)—suggests a connection on this basis: "The pathetic frustration of 62 is intensely human" (1991: 152 at 61–2). Even recipients without children can find points of contact with Thetis. She functions as "the paradigm for the image of bereavement" (Slatkin 1991: 85) and emerges as the poem's most forceful representation of "the shattering loss and sorrow that inescapably define the life of every individual" (122). Any recipient who has experienced loss and sorrow may find that the *Iliad*'s Thetis speaks to them. At bottom, Thetis's attachment to another individual defines her, and most everyone values their attachments to other people (Hogan 2011: 199–200). Perceptions of similarity with Thetis can enable identification with her.

Recipients are also apt to identify with Thetis because the poet depicts her as virtuous (cf. section 4.2.2, pp. 95–6, on Andromache). Thetis laments her son's short life (*Iliad* 1.416, 1.505, 18.95), but in the *Iliad* she does not try to prevent Achilles's death at Troy as she does in other tales (cf. Burgess 2009: 15–19). She does not even intervene on his behalf when he seems about to perish in his battle with the river Scamander: Poseidon, Athena, and Hera help him (*Iliad* 21.284–97, 304, 328–41). Contrast Aphrodite who saves her son Aeneas from danger (*Iliad* 5.314–18; Slatkin 1991: 44). Thetis does what Achilles asks and does not push back on his requests, even though she knows they will lead to his death (*Iliad* 18.95–6). Instead, Thetis tries to lessen the anguish that Achilles experiences during his short life. In *Iliad* 1, she wishes that Achilles could live "without tears and without pain" (*adakrutos kai apēmōn*), since he is fated to live only for a brief time (415–16). The hope of mitigating his suffering compels her to approach Zeus with her fateful request: she wants the Achaeans to pay Achilles back (*tisōsin*) and honor (*timēi*) him (*Iliad* 1.509–10). The same motivation drives her in *Iliad* 18. The soon-to-die Achilles's anguish upsets Thetis as well as what she deems her inability to comfort him: "but I will not welcome him back again returning home to the house of Peleus. And while he lives and looks on the light of the sun, he is pained (*akhnutai*), and I am not able to help him (*khraismēsai*) when I go to him (*iousa*)" (*Iliad* 18.59–62). "Nevertheless," she continues, "I will go (*all' eim'*) in order that I may ... hear what grief (*penthos*) has come over him" (*Iliad* 18.63–4). When she arrives at Achilles's tent, she straightaway asks him, "Why are you crying? What grief (*penthos*) has come over your heart?" (*Iliad* 18.73 = 1.362). Later, she requests Hephaestus's help for Achilles who at present "lies on the ground grieving in heart (*thumon akheuōn*)" (*Iliad* 18.461). As in *Iliad* 1, Thetis aims to help Achilles overcome his distress. This time she will help him take vengeance on Hector (*Iliad* 18.128–37). Thetis, then, tries to keep Achilles from misery and pain while he lives. She thereby adheres to the "parental ethos" (Pratt 2007) that pervades the *Iliad*: both mortal and divine parents love and care for their children. The ethos appeared in the broader epic tradition to which the *Iliad* belonged and the artistic tradition with which it interacted: for instance, both the *Aethiopis* and vase paintings depicted Eos supporting and working on behalf of her son, Memnon (Slatkin 1991: 23–7; Sammons 2017: 196–7). Thetis scores high in the category of character virtue to the extent that she is a devoted parent.

I offer one more general comment about Thetis in the *Iliad*. The horse Xanthus (*Iliad* 19.416–17) and the dying Hector (22.359–60) prophesy Achilles's death at Troy (Grethlein 2006: 263; Burgess 2009: 44–5; Currie 2016: 121, 144–5). Hera obliquely refers to his death: Achilles will suffer later (*husteron*) what fate wove for him (*Iliad* 20.127–8). The narrator notes that Achilles will not grow old in his father's armor (*Iliad* 17.197) (Burgess 2009: 44–5). Far more evocations of Achilles's death stem or come from Thetis (cf. Burgess 2009: 41–51; Kelly 2012: 249–50). Achilles first notes the brevity of the life he will lead (*minunthadion*, *Iliad* 1.352), information he presumably learned from Thetis (Burgess 2009: 47–8), just as he learned from her what he tells the emissaries in *Iliad* 9: that he can live a short and glorious life if he remains at Troy or a long life without renown if he returns home (9.410–16). Nestor speculates that Achilles refrains from battle because of a prophecy, surely about his death, that Thetis reported to him (*Iliad* 11.794–5). In her first lengthy speech in *Iliad* 1, Thetis mentions Achilles's short life (*aisa minuntha*) and labels Achilles "swift-fated" (*ōkumoros*) (1.416–18). When later in the same book she beseeches Zeus on Achilles's behalf, she speaks of Achilles as "the most swift-fated" (*ōkumorōtatos*, *Iliad* 1.505). In *Iliad* 18, she cradles Achilles's head (18.71) as one cradles the head of a dead person (Currie 2016: 119). In her lament, she bewails that she will not welcome him home (*Iliad* 18.59–60), a fact she repeats to Hephaestus when she asks the smith to make a set of armor for Achilles (18.440–1). Speaking with Achilles in *Iliad* 18, she again calls him "swift-fated" (*ōkumoros*, 18.95), an adjective she deploys still again when addressing Hephaestus (*ōkumorōi*, 18.458). After Thetis reports Achilles's situation to Hephaestus, including that he will die at Troy, Hephaestus expresses the wish that he could save Achilles from that death (*Iliad* 18.464–5). Fearing that the river Skamander will overwhelm him, Achilles recalls that Thetis told him he would fall to Apollo's arrows (*Iliad* 21.277–8; cf. 17.407–8, 21.110–13 (with Burgess 2009: 44)). With the foresight available to the dead, Patroclus declares that Achilles will die at Troy (*Iliad* 23.80–1) but then notes that Thetis gave Achilles a golden amphora to house Achilles's and Patroclus's bones together (23.91–2; cf. *Odyssey* 24.73–7). In *Iliad* 24, Iris finds Thetis "lamenting the fate of her son" (24.83–6), Thetis dons the dark cloak of a mourner (24.93–4), and Thetis reminds Achilles that "death and fate" are coming for him (24.131–2). It is Thetis who generates the most references to the death of Achilles.

To highlight the *Iliad*'s implicit anticipations of and allusions to Achilles's death (Burgess 2009: chs. 5 and 6) is to follow Thetis's lead and in essence to see the events at Troy through her eyes: "the *Iliad* allows an extended envisioning of the death of Achilles," so Jonathan Burgess (2009: 97), adopting, I suggest, a Thetis-like position on the poem. For a recipient who has not heard the *Iliad* before to "expect that it will narrate his [Achilles's] death too" (Grethlein 2006: 264, my translation) is to venture a guess informed especially by Thetis. Thetis seeps into our consciousness and affects our approach to and experience of the poem. We are more apt to identify with her when the opportunity arises.

One could reconfigure the component parts of this argument. The poem regularly alludes to Achilles's death, and Thetis is a consistent source of this anticipation. When in *Iliad* 18, Thetis laments Achilles as if he were already dead, we do not object. Counter arguments forestalled, we are more apt to feel for and with Thetis.

I come to *Iliad* 18 and start with the eleven-line list of Nereids at 18.39–49. Adrian Kelly notes a typical Neoanalytical response to the Nereids' presence in this scene: "the chorus of Nereids appears a trifle otiose" (2012: 224) and reflects the origins of this passage in the lament over a dead Achilles (as related in *Odyssey*

24.47–62). To counter this idea, Kelly argues that Thetis's presentation of what he labels a "prospective lament" explains the Nereids' appearance: a group usually surrounds the lamenter in such scenes (250–3). Continuing in this vein, I see reasons behind and work being done by the narrator's list of Nereids.

*Iliad* 18 begins with Achilles's soliloquy about the possibility of Patroclus's death (18.5–14). A crying Antilochus arrives to confirm this intuition (18.16–21). Racked with grief (*akheos*), Achilles pours dirt on himself, falls to the ground, and tears his hair (18.22–7). The female slaves cry out in anguish (*thumon akēkhemenai*), run out of the tent, and beat their breasts in a typical gesture of lament (18.28–31). Continuing to weep, Antilochus holds Achilles's hands "for he feared (*deidie*) that he [Achilles] might cut his throat with a knife" (18.32–4). Achilles "groaned terribly, and his queenly mother heard (*akouse*) him" (18.35); Thetis too wails aloud (*kōkusen*, 18.37). At this point, the Nereids gather around Thetis, and the narrator lists thirty-three of their names. Only after this list concludes does Thetis begin her formal lament (18.51–64).

Verses 5 to 37 take us into the minds of all the characters: Achilles and Antilochus most obviously, but the female slaves and Thetis as well. Antilochus's fear that Achilles may kill himself in his sorrow represents an especially memorable dive into a character's mind. The construction of verse 35 brings out this concentration on the characters' minds: the narrator moves from the mind of Achilles in the Achaean camp in the first hemistich of verse 35—"and he groaned terribly"—to the mind of Thetis in the depths of the sea in the second half of the verse—"and his queenly mother heard him." Mid-verse switches in location are rare but do occur: the *Iliad*'s narrator switches from Achilles's tent to the town of Chryse (1.430); the *Odyssey*'s narrator switches from Athena entering Erechtheus's palace in Athens to Odysseus coming to Alcinous's palace (7.81), from the Phaeacians dropping off Odysseus on Ithaca to Poseidon conversing with Zeus on Olympus (13.125), from the Phaeacians standing around an altar on Scheria to Odysseus waking up on Ithaca (13.187), and from the suitors preparing a feast in Odysseus's palace to Odysseus and Eumaeus in Eumaeus's hut (17.182). *Iliad* 18.35 stands apart from these instances of mid-verse switches in location because it takes us from the mind of a character in one place to the mind of another character in another place.

The list of Nereids provides a break from this engagement with the characters' thoughts. Above all, it gives us time to move away from contemplating Achilles's reaction to the news of Patroclus's death and Antilochus's reaction to Achilles's display of grief. This pause allows us to re-engage with another character's mind once Thetis begins her formal lament. One factor that makes this break feel like a break is the shift the list introduces in the pacing of the narrative. At the start of the book, narrative time (the amount of time allotted to relating an event in the storyworld) and narrated time (the amount of time it takes an event to unfold in the storyworld) seem to coincide. With the list of Nereids, narrative time (the amount of time it takes to go through the list) seems to exceed narrated time (the amount of time it takes for the Nereids to assemble).

The list of Nereids also emphasizes the audience Thetis has for her lament: she becomes the center of this group's attention and thereby draws our attention. Thrust into the spotlight, Thetis becomes a prime candidate for identification. Finally, I note again the factor of group membership and its relevance to identification. As both other early Greek epics and representations on vases do (Kelly 2012: 225–6, 254 n. 87), the lengthy list reminds one of the group to which Thetis belongs. Other components of the passage function in the same way: the Nereids accompany her lament (*Iliad* 18.50–1) and go with her to Troy (18.65–6). And the passage stresses that she heads up this group: she leads the lament (*exērkhe*, *Iliad* 18.51); once she has finished talking to Achilles, she orders them to go back (*dute*) to the sea and report back (*agoreusat'*) to Nereus (18.138–42).

Thetis's lament offers a cue for cognitive identification. She makes plain the following: that Achilles was a great fighter "conspicuous (*exokhon*) among the heroes" (*Iliad* 18.56) does not make up for his death at Troy. Thetis has "pains" (*kēdea*) and labels herself "miserable" (*deilē*) and "one who suffers because bearing the best of men" (*dusaristotokeia*) (*Iliad* 18.53–4) because she will not "welcome him again returning home to the house of Peleus" (18.59–60). With these verses, Thetis renders the same judgment on the heroic project as other relatives of dead warriors.

Warriors pursue renown (*kleos*) that will attach to them both while they live and after they die (*Iliad* 5.273, 7.91, 17.16, 17.232, 18.121; *Odyssey* 5.311, 9.264). A warrior's tomb serves as a mechanism for perpetuating his *kleos* (*Odyssey* 4.584), and, according to a repeated couplet in the *Odyssey*, a warrior's tomb can also serve as a mechanism for passing on a warrior's glory to his son (*Odyssey* 1.239–40 = 14.369–70 ≈ 24.32–3). One implication of this transfer of glory is that the son takes solace in the glory his father achieved with feats on the battlefield. For her part, Hecuba reveals her pride in the dead Hector's earlier determination in battle: Achilles killed Hector, she says, "when he was not being a coward, but standing in front of the Trojans and deep-girdled Trojan woman, taking thought neither of flight nor withdrawal" (*Iliad* 24.214–16). This statement is the sort that Hector imagines when he wishes, "May I not perish without a struggle or without glory (*akleiōs*) but doing something for those in the future to hear of" (*Iliad* 22.304–5).

But often relatives do not find any consolation in a dead warrior's glory (cf. Murnaghan 1999: 204, 215; Perkell 2008: 94–6, 107). Andromache declares that there will be not "another source of comfort (*thalpōrē*)" for her when Hector dies, "only pains (*akhe'*)" (*Iliad* 6.411–12). Hector agrees: he imagines someone praising him after his death, claiming that he excelled in battle (*aristeueske makhesthai*), and this praise causing Andromache "fresh grief (*algos*)" at the thought of having lost such a husband (*Iliad* 6.460–2; Slatkin 2007: 29–31).

Later, in her lament over the dead Hector, Andromache declares herself left with "grievous pains" (*leleipsetai algea lugra*, *Iliad* 24.742; Murnaghan 1999: 216). Hecuba contrasts how she boasted (*eukhōlē*) of Hector's exploits while he lived with the misery that awaits her now that he is dead: "What will my life be as I suffer terrible things (*aina pathousa*)?" (*Iliad* 22.431–6; Murnaghan 1999: 214–15). Penelope feels only "unforgettable sorrow" (*penthos alaston*) and longing (*potheō*) when she thinks about Odysseus "whose fame (*kleos*) is widespread" (*Odyssey* 1.342–4) and whom she assumes is dead (4.724 = 4.814, 19.257–8). Thetis's assessment dovetails with that of other bereft relatives. Her verses provide an opportunity for cognitive identification: one can see the heroic project in the same way as Thetis sees it.

Thetis's appeal to Hephaestus offers another chance for cognitive identification. Thetis reviews some of the main events of the preceding days: Agamemnon took Achilles's war prize Briseis; Achilles "vexed over her was wearing away his mind"; the Trojans drove back the Achaeans to the ships; the elders supplicated Achilles, offering him many gifts; he rebuffed their offer but armed Patroclus in his own armor and sent Patroclus into battle along with a large host; they fought "all day around the Scaean gate," and they would have taken the city, if Apollo had not killed Patroclus and "granted the ability to win to Hector" (*Iliad* 18.444–56). Laura Slatkin writes, "Thetis prefaces her request of Hephaistos with a summary of the *Iliad* up to that juncture; the *Iliad* recapitulates itself here from Thetis's viewpoint, so that it represents itself as a mother's narrative about her son" (1991: 46). I focus on the equation between "a summary of the *Iliad* up to that juncture" and "the *Iliad* recapitulates itself here from Thetis's viewpoint." Thetis reviews what has happened to Achilles. She reduces the story so far to one about a handful of characters and their interactions with one character in particular, Achilles. Her narrative omits all the other characters who have populated the tale since Achilles's withdrawal. That she refers to Achilles solely by way of pronouns (cf. de Jong 2004: 217) but uses proper names to identify the other relevant players brings out her concentration on Achilles. Slatkin rightly labels this portion of her speech a recapitulation from Thetis's point of view, one focused on her son. But Slatkin's conflation of that recapitulation with "a summary of the *Iliad*" testifies to the slippage we can make as we hear this partial rehearsal. (Compare Mark Edwards's comment, "448–52 do not necessarily imply anything other than the story of our *Il*." (1991: 198 at 444–56) or Kelly's reference to "Thetis's mini-*Iliad*, told to Hephaistos" (2018: 352).) We adopt Thetis's point of view and allow that she presents a (fair) summary of the *Iliad*, that everything we have heard up to this point can be condensed in this fashion. Some recipients may pick apart her recapitulation—Achilles did not respond to the embassy by sending out Patroclus; Patroclus did not spend all day fighting by the Scaean gate (Scodel 1999: 63)—but many others will not. They will see the previous events from her perspective.

## 4.4. Limits to Identification

We may find ourselves identifying now with one character, now with another. Martha Nussbaum posits that the reader of Charles Dickens's *Hard Times* "identified first with Louisa and then with Stephen Blackpool" (1995: 87). M. Smith uses a close reading of Alfred Hitchcock's *The Man Who Knew Too Much* to argue for "plural identification" with more than one character (1995: 93). Breithaupt suggests that in *Odyssey* 22, "our empathetic identification oscillates between" Odysseus and the suitors (2019: 224; cf. Kozak 2017: e.g., 22, 39–40, 43, 53, 169, 232). Nonetheless, no text can ask us to identify with every character or even to identify with one character for an excessive amount of time (cf. Keen 2007: 96). Just as we cannot empathize continuously and require a range of unconscious and conscious empathy filters or blocks to keep us from empathizing continuously (Breithaupt 2019: 81–8), so we cannot identify with character after character or with one character continuously (see section 2.2, pp. 25–6). Inspired by Jenefer Robinson's argument that a text's formal devices enable us "to deal with" the emotions it generates, especially in response to its "pessimistic message" or "disturbing material" (2005: 195–228, quotations from 212, 227), we can trace how breaks from and impediments to identification are built into the Homeric epics.

As the episodes examined in this chapter show, triggers for identification appear sporadically throughout a scene. The text does not bombard us with such cues as a scene unfolds. If we focus on the numerous scenes of fighting with this thought in mind, we note how frequently we encounter characters we have never met. We are not apt to identify with a character whom we have just met, time and familiarity with a character being a prerequisite for identification. For example, after Agamemnon kills Iphidamas, we meet Iphidamas's brother, Coön: "And when Coön conspicuous among men perceived him, [Coön,] the eldest child of Antenor, then a great sorrow (*penthos*) enveloped his eyes on account of his fallen brother" (*Iliad* 11.248–50). Because we have not previously spent any time with Coön (and he is unlikely to be a traditional character with an existence outside the *Iliad*; cf. Burgess 2001: 86–7), the description of Coön's sorrow probably does not trigger emotional identification with him.

Some discrete segments do not cue identification. The proleptic description of how Apollo, Poseidon, and Zeus destroy the Achaean wall after the war ends (*Iliad* 12.9–35) occurs between the scene in which Patroclus attends to the wounded Eurypylus (11.809–12.2) and the one in which Hector tries to lead his men across the trench in front of the wall (12.40–59). Its placement offers a break from identification with the mortals toiling at Troy. For however thematically or metapoetically significant (Myers 2019: 137–8; Ready 2019a: 70), the vignette about the wall takes us away from the mortal characters. Indeed, in pointing up the ultimate futility and triviality of human endeavor when contrasted with immortal action and when considered under the aspect of eternity, it distances us from the mortals' perspectives and concerns (cf. Caracciolo 2014: 150). At the same time, in stressing the gulf between men and gods, the verses do not encourage its mortal audience to identify with the immortal Poseidon and Apollo. The episode describing the scenes depicted on Achilles's shield in *Iliad* 18 provides one of the lengthier respites from identifying with the poem's characters. One is unlikely, for instance, to take sides with either of the disputants "over the recompense for a slain man" (*Iliad* 18.498–9) or with the attackers or defenders of the besieged city (18.509–40) (Giuliani 2013: 23–4, 68). Might an audience member "identify with the ploughmen" described on the shield at *Iliad* 18.541–9 because the poet depicts "what it is like to be a ploughman in all its perceptual and emotional aspects" (Allan, de Jong, and de Jonge 2017: 40)? I think not. First, identification typically finds us identifying with one character or one character at a time, not a group of characters. Second, the "all" overstates the access provided to the ploughmen's perspective. Third, the authors again overlook the necessity of our spending time with a character before we can identify with them (section 2.2, pp. 19–20).

In the analysis of the funeral games in *Iliad* 23 (section 4.2.3), I spoke not of breaks from identification but of how the poet impedes our experiencing motivational identification with a character. Elsewhere too the poet inhibits our identification with characters, especially minor or secondary characters. Carl Plantinga draws attention to "distanced narratives" that do not encourage a connection with any of the characters (2018: 194; cf. 142, 202), but I build here on discussions of how texts can impede identification with specific characters: for instance, John Peradotto declares that Odysseus's hapless helmsman, Elpenor, is not "designed to win our sympathies" (2002: 5); Nussbaum finds that Bitzer in *Hard Times* "repels our sympathy and our identification" (1995: 30); Rita Felski writes of the narrator in Gayl Jones's 1976 novel *Eva's Man*, "Eva's words repel any potential surges of empathy or identification" (2008: 128); Vaage suggests of the character of the protagonist's wife in *Breaking Bad*, "we are not invited to feel with Skyler, but rather to see her as an annoying obstacle to everything fun" (2016: 165; cf. Holladay and Click 2019); and Eric Douglass considers why we are directed away from identifying with certain characters in the Gospel of Mark (2018: 141–3).

Return to those numerous minor characters, like Coön, who fall in battle. I noted that we are unlikely to identify with a character whom we have just met, but these scenes also frequently contain obstacles to identification. The *Iliad* poet often gives some background information on these doomed warriors. Whereas scholarship tends to focus on the pathos induced at such moments (Ready 2020: 304), I take a different tack. Sometimes this background information interferes with identification because it does not provide any access or any real access to the character's views and attitudes, emotions, or goals and plans. This lack of access is especially noticeable when the poet focuses more on a character's family member than on the character himself, as happens in the case of Laogonus: "Then in turn Meriones slew an armed man of the Trojans, Laogonus, a bold son of Onetor, [Onetor] who was a priest of Idaean Zeus and was honored like a god by the people" (*Iliad* 16.603–5; see Ready 2020: 302–3). Similarly, the background information the poet provides can prompt questions that increase our distance from the character. Consider a portion of the presentation on Iphidamas, who falls to Agamemnon (*Iliad* 11.227–30):

> Married he went away from the bride chamber, after the report of the coming Achaeans,
> with twelve curved ships that followed him.
> These balanced ships he had left behind in Percote,
> and he had gone on foot to Ilium.

Why did he leave behind his ships at Percote? Was it not possible to sail to Troy itself? Paris sailed from and to Troy on the trip in which he absconded with Helen from Sparta (*Iliad* 3.46–9, 3.443–5, 5.62–4, 7.389–90; Proclus *Cypria* argumentum 9–20). How did the other Thracians mentioned in the catalogue of Trojans get to Troy (*Iliad* 2.844–5)? Does any other Trojan ally sail to Troy? (How do Memnon and his Ethiopian contingent actually get to Troy (*Aethiopis* argumentum 2 West 2003b)?) Was there a marina popular with Trojan allies in Percote? Some of these questions reveal our inability to get inside Iphidamas's mind because we have so little to go on. Others of these questions prompt us to think about other characters. Taken together, these questions lead us away from Iphidamas himself. The poet can also short circuit efforts to connect with a character by failing to explain his seemingly strange actions. For instance, Nastes falls victim to Achilles: "he decked out in gold came to the battle like a girl, fool, and it did not keep off grievous death from him" (*Iliad* 2.872–3). We may be tempted to guess at what Nastes was thinking, but the poet provides no hints at all (cf. Scodel 2014: 65–74). When denied any way to get into the mind of a character who does something unorthodox, we are unlikely to try very hard. The poet does not allow us to account for the character's behavior and thereby impedes identification (cf. Breithaupt 2019: 128).

Descriptions of the fatal wounds minor characters suffer can interfere with identification (cf. Lovatt 2013: 293–7). Take Idomeneus's slaying of Alcathous. Idomeneus pierces his breastplate, and Alcathous "fell with a thud, and the spear shook in his heart, which by beating made even the butt of the spear shake" (*Iliad* 13.442–4). This image of a still beating heart causing a spear that protrudes from it to shake has no parallel in the epics: the closest one gets is the spear that shakes while fixed in Aretus's belly (*Iliad* 17.523–4), but there the spear's own dissipating momentum makes it shake (W.-H. Friedrich 2003: 14). Recipients may pause to consider whether the atypical passage at *Iliad* 13.442–4 adheres to the conditions for narrative realism. And recipients may pause to consider whether the passage adheres to the conditions for external realism: if so, they will find themselves in the company of Wolf-Hartmut Friedrich (2003: 14–15) and Kenneth Saunders (2003: 140–1). Either way, a recipient wrapped up in trying to determine whether the verses are realistic will be hard pressed to identify with either the victorious character or the victimized character. The *Iliad* abounds in passages of this sort, as Friedrich's and Saunders's explorations make clear. In most cases, the wound is singular (cf. Fenik 1968: 62) and so may prompt one to pause over its degree of narrative realism; in all cases, the recipient may pause to join Friedrich and Saunders in deliberating over its degree of external realism. This pause to ponder the tale's realism inhibits identification. All that said, there may be components of these scenes that enhance immersion. I will return in section 6.3 (pp. 179–81) to the possibility that descriptions of wounds can trigger motor resonance in recipients.

A recipient need not continually expend the emotional and cognitive resources required for identification. The breaks and impediments discussed so far provide respites and the opportunity to recharge for the next moment of identification. Another impediment to identification, however, does not allow us to catch our breath: hatred will block identification.

The study of modern anti-fandom demonstrates the ubiquity of hatred as a response to characters (Gray 2005; Holladay and Click 2019), but ancient authors use the same language. Gorgias defends Helen by claiming that we should pity her and direct our hatred (*misēsai*) toward Paris (7.49; cf. Munteanu 2012: 37–8), and the scholiastic commentary on the epics also gets us thinking about hatred as a reaction to Homeric characters. Agamemnon dissuades Menelaus from sparing Adrastus on the grounds that all the Trojans should die, even those still in utero (*Iliad* 6.55–60). A bT scholion comments, "The words are hateful (*misēta*) [that is, they make one hate the speaker] and not suitable for a kingly figure: for they show a brutality of character, and the hearer, being human, hates (*misei*) the excessively harsh and inhuman." Indeed, tragedians, the scholion continues, do not show actions of this sort on stage lest "they become hated along with (*summisēthōsi*) the things being done." Yet, the scholion adds, Agamemnon does not cause offense (*epakhthēs*) here: because the Trojans have proven themselves violators of an oath—the one made in *Iliad* 3—he is "angry on behalf of the gods" (bT scholion at *Iliad* 6.58–9b). The comment suggests that one might hate Agamemnon at this moment or, conversely, justify his words to Menelaus: the narrator (perhaps reporting Menelaus's assessment via embedded focalization (Scodel 2008: 83–4)) labels them "fitting" (*aisima*, *Iliad* 6.62; cf. Pagani 2018: 79–81; A. Porter 2019: 155). If one does feel hatred toward Agamemnon at this moment, one will not identify with him.

The *Odyssey* provides more characters to hate than the *Iliad*. Telemachus urges Penelope's suitors to "avoid the wrath of the gods lest they turn against you, angered (*agassamenoi*) at your evil deeds" (*Odyssey* 2.66–7). A scholion to verse 67 glosses *agassamenoi* with *misēsantes*, "hating" (2.67g), and indeed one might come to hate the most prominent among Penelope's suitors, Antinoos and Eurymachus. One might follow a scholiast in hating Polyphemus: a scholion to *Odyssey* 9.276— wherein Polyphemus declares that the Cyclopes do not take thought for the Olympian gods "because we are far stronger"—reports, "with these words the poet rouses the listener in order that we may hate (*misēsōmen*) the Cyclops for his impiety and delight in his being punished." I doubt the goatherd Melanthius has many fans either: in his first appearance in the poem, he insults the disguised Odysseus and the swineherd Eumaeus "in an excessive and shameful manner" (*Odyssey* 17.216), tries to kick Odysseus (17.233–4), and prays for Telemachus's death (17.251–3).

Hating a character takes energy, probably just as much as identifying with a character does (cf. Heath 1987: 208). For many recipients, the effort will be worth it because antipathy offers its own pleasures (M. Smith 1999: 224; Woodruff 2008: 106, 148; Plantinga 2009: 31–2; Vaage 2016: 103), from reveling in the negative emotions antipathy prompts to enjoying sharing one's hatred with one's fellow recipients to delighting in the antagonist's come-uppance. If hating a character does not provide mental respite, it does get us doing something other than identifying and thereby does make a return to identification easier.

Discussions of modern anti-fandom address the extent to which anti-fandom challenges or reinforces structures of power (Holladay and Click 2019; Jane 2019; Phillips 2019). In the last section of this chapter, I explore the politics of identification.

## 4.5. The Politics of Identification

Lionel Knights had no patience for critics and readers who identify with characters: their failure to exercise the appropriate level of detachment compelled them to make the fatal mistake of treating characters as if they were real people (1933; see Moi 2019: 33–47). Identification is not seen only to hamper literary analysis, however: it has perhaps more significant deleterious political effects. Victorian-era critics cautioned that female readers' propensity to identify with literary characters divorced them from reality, inflated their sense of "self-importance," prompted excessive "self-involvement," and led them to "act upon their own initiative" (Knox 2021: 8–14). One influenced by early and mid-twentieth-century luminaries such as Walter Benjamin and Theodor Adorno would declare that identification with characters in narratives produced for the masses (and immersion in those narratives) makes for apathetic drones (Davis 2007: 155–6; Plantinga 2018: 118–19; Knox 2021: 13). Rita Felski succinctly reviews the problem that identifying with characters poses from Lacanian and Althusserian perspectives (2008: 28):

The work of fiction...seeks to lull readers into a misapprehension of their existence as unified, autonomous individuals. Storytelling and the aesthetics of realism are deeply implicated in this process of misrecognition because identifying with characters is a key mechanism through which we are drawn into believing in the essential reality of persons.

In truth, the self is fragmented, empty, and unknowable, and to think of oneself as a discrete subject is "to accede to one's own subjection."[5] For feminist theorists of the second half of the twentieth century, identification does real harm in reifying identities by teaching people to act in specific ways—women should behave like this; men should behave like that—and by lulling women into acquiescence to and even complicity with an oppressive patriarchy (Davis 2007: 46, 65).

In her essential book on the *Odyssey*, Lillian Doherty works in this vein, problematizing the reader's, especially the female reader's, experience of identification. When offering readers a chance to identify with a character higher up the social ladder than they themselves occupy, a text "may resign the reader to her or his own place in the social hierarchy by making the hierarchy itself appear more 'natural' or acceptable" (1995: 26 n. 39; cf. 181). At the same time, identification with the paramount *basileus* Odysseus engenders a pernicious quietism among readers of relative privilege: "There is thus a danger that in identifying with Odysseus, critics and other relatively privileged readers may ignore their own privilege and be reconciled to a status quo in which they share, if only vicariously, in the exercise of power" (29). The female reader may identify with female characters who somehow stand in opposition to Odysseus but then end up compelled by the thrust of the tale "to participate in the denigration of a figure whose subject position she *can* share by one whose position she *cannot*, qua female, share"; female readers, that is, end up identifying against themselves (27, emphasis in original; cf. 41, 177, 181). If the female reader takes the bait laid out by Odysseus and identifies with the Phaeacian queen Arete or with the Ithacan queen Penelope, "she runs the risk of ignoring the link between this honor and an insidious class privilege that isolates her from other groups of women" (29; cf. 119, 159). Likewise, when female audience members identify with female characters who help Odysseus on his journey, they end up "isolated from one another, and their desires are ultimately subordinated to those of the hero" (124). Doherty proposes to "identify patterns in the *Odyssey*'s depiction of audiences and narrators that can seduce female readers (as for many years they seduced me) into identifying with 'good' female characters like Penelope while ignoring the silencing of other female voices" (63). We need to be aware of "the danger that admiration may blind us to the work's implications" (120) and, per the

---

[5] Felski 2008: 27; cf. Felski 2020a; 2020b: 81; Davis 2007: 44; Plantinga 2009: 20; 2018: 102, 229; Knox 2021: 13.

book's final sentence, to be "on guard against the Siren songs of the Homeric text itself" (193).

Many of us trained at the turn of the twenty-first century will find familiar, even comforting, this quintessentially paranoid reading in which the critic uncovers the hidden workings of power. The critique that follows is not meant to discount that sort of reading and its utility for Homerists. Nor do I deny the possibility of a palpable unease among recipients who identify with the characters, either during or after that experience of identification. My goal is to demonstrate that there are additional ways to think about identification.

One might query the strict binaries that underlie Doherty's analysis. In general, when we talk these days about identity, we think with more permeable categories and in terms of more complex intersectionalities: it is not just male/female or rich/poor, and one's identity cannot be reduced to a solitary term, like male, female, rich, or poor (cf. Davis 2007: 42–50). Identity encompasses a range of components, so it becomes both harder and less useful to generalize about, for instance, "female" recipients and to privilege one component of a notional recipient's identity as the factor that determines their response to a narrative.

More specifically, Doherty contends that the poem invites female audience members to identify with Odysseus (1995: 177), but for the most part, when Doherty points to the characters with whom female audience members can identify, she points to female characters (e.g., 121, 127, 138, 144, 192; cf. 179–80). Doherty thereby replicates the arguments she sees embedded in the *Odyssey* itself. Doherty finds that the *Odyssey* presents a vision of what different audience members favor (1995: 103):

> A woman will be interested in accounts of famous women, while a man, though willing to hear and even to praise such accounts, can also be expected to request accounts of famous men.... A female listener will appreciate attention to the point of view of female characters.... Genealogical poetry focusing on "heroines" will please a female audience, while a male audience can be expected to request material from the Iliadic repertoire.

To posit that female recipients identify first and foremost, perhaps solely, with female characters, as Doherty does, is to endorse the text's own propositions. But, as the literature on identification reviewed in section 2.3 stresses—and I now add that interventions in literary and film studies subsequent to Doherty's make much the same point[6]—demographic similarity and self-concepts do not determine with which characters we identify. Other Homerists also give too much weight to demographic similarity when it comes to identification: in the *Odyssey*, "the

---

[6] Davis 2007: 5–6, 32; Felski 2008: 43–4, 46; 2020b: p. xiii, 83, 98, 103–4; Plantinga 2009: 110–11; Lesser 2022: 216; cf. Hogan 2011: 248–9.

faithful slave [e.g., Eumaeus] offered free but nonelite listeners an opportunity for identification" (Thalmann 1998: 298); in the *Iliad*, Thersites and Epeius are "both ordinary men with whom the peasantry of Homer's audience could identify" (Scanlon 2018: 10).

Also lacking in subtlety is the claim that identification with characters leads inevitably to our colluding with those in charge and even participating in our own oppression. Plato may have thought that sympathizing and identifying with characters means "the reader or viewer internalizes an entire value system, adopting a whole set of ideas about what constitutes a good person and a good life" (Nightingale 2006: 42), and then acts in accordance with that set of ideas after the narrative experience ends. But Plato and Doherty overstate the danger of identification. Michael Slater et al. write, "The temporary excursion into the experience of alternative social and personal identities does not mean that the audience member necessarily internalizes the values and perspectives of that identity and carries them into the post-viewing world" (2014: 448). Patrick Hogan observes, "It is not clear that an experience of identification while reading will necessarily lead a test subject to report that he or she would be likely to do the same thing as the character" (2018: 127). Plantinga gives an example of this nuanced reaction when reviewing a critical component of Murray Smith's discussion (1995) of our engagement with characters (2018: 196; cf. Kozak 2017: 18 (quoted in section 2.2, pp. 29–30)):

> Spectators will allow their usual moral suppositions to become flexible during the viewing of a screen story, such that they may accept a story's moral "system" for the purposes of pleasure and entertainment, even when that system conflicts with their moral beliefs outside the movie theater. Thus a spectator may delight in the vengeful pleasures of the beating and killing of the murderer Scorpio by Harry Callahan in *Dirty Harry* (1972), when said viewer would be disinclined to relish such actions outside the movie theater.

Critics, then, rightly stress the partial nature of our attachment to characters. Rita Felski doubts that identification requires us to "swallow the ideologies represented by that persona *wholesale*" (2008: 34, my emphasis). Elsewhere, Felski concentrates on "allegiance"—"a felt sense of affinity or attachment" (2008: 34) wherein "we find ourselves siding with a character and what we take that character to stand for" (2020b: 96; cf. Plantinga 2009: 108). Taking allegiance as one of her "strands of identification," Felski notes that it "can, of course, be partial, qualified, or ambivalent" (2020b: 96; cf. 113). Kimberly Chabot Davis reports, "Identification is often ambivalent and partial.... I saw many instances of ambivalence in which people both identified and disidentified with the same character" (2007: 48; cf. 67, 80, 139). Katalin Bálint and Ed Tan's "qualitative interview study" (2019: 212) also turns up "oscillations of attachment and detachment with the protagonist":

"character engagement seems to involve dynamic degrees of connectedness across the experience" (223).[7]

Doherty's analysis ignores this important nuance in suggesting that, because identification compels us to acquiesce to suppression and repression in literary texts, we are more prone to acquiesce to suppression and repression in the real world. In truth, I can root for a character to achieve their goals and be happy right along with them when they do, but those responses do not mean that I agree to live in a world structured according to what makes that character happy. I can be happy that they achieved their goal in their world, but that reaction does not mean that I want to live in their world or that, endorsing the practices and power structures in their world, I want to import them into mine. I can want the serial killer to succeed in killing other serial killers (the premise of the novel *Darkly Dreaming Dexter* and its spin-off television show, *Dexter*) but not want to live in a world in which vigilantes mete out justice (Vaage 2016: 23–4, 26; cf. 97–8, 115). I can be chagrinned right along with Achilles that Agamemnon seizes Briseis without endorsing her being a captive slave, required to provide sex on demand (*Iliad* 1.185, 23.176). I might root for either Ajax or Odysseus in the wrestling match during the funeral games for Patroclus. That motivational identification does not mean that I would hold a contest in which one of the prizes is a female slave, valued at four oxen (*Iliad* 23.702–5). A notional fifth-century Athenian might identify with the Achaean *basileis* but, not wanting to be subject to such big men himself, jealously guard his right to serve on juries and participate in the assembly. A Greek hoplite might identify with Patroclus as he confronts Sarpedon but consider such duels an extremely silly way to fight. Recipients can identify with the Homeric elite's female characters without endorsing the systems on which their elite status depends in the storyworld. Recipients can identify with the female characters who help Odysseus without exporting to their own world the isolation and subjugation implied, per Doherty, in such identifications. Identification only takes the recipient so far. To adapt Charles Altieri's formulation (regarding Gustave Flaubert's assessment of the fictional world he creates in *Madame Bovary*), one can care about characters in a storyworld while also finding that world "almost unbearably ridiculous" (2003: 128).

A related difficulty in Doherty's portrayal of identification as politically suspect is that it glosses over the differences in kinds of identification, which range from physical to motivational identification. Felski rightly insists on these distinctions: "One can identify with a character's perceptions, emotions, motivations, beliefs, self-understanding, physical characteristics, experiences, or situation, for example—none of which necessarily implies the others" (2020b: 82; cf. Gaut 1999: 205–6; Caracciolo 2016: 41, 47). For instance, in Arthur Conan Doyle's

---

[7] Cf. Gaut 1999: 208; Plantinga 2009: 89, 105, 156; 2018: 124; Vaage 2016: 55, 93; Levett 2018: 38.

stories about Sherlock Holmes, recipients might experience cognitive identification with Watson because access to the storyworld comes courtesy of his perspective and might experience other forms of identification with Holmes (Felski 2020b: 109). Felski further observes that storytelling "techniques of focalization, point of view, or narrative structure" can make us align with a character—see the storyworld from their perspective and perhaps experience perceptual identification—but they do not guarantee our allegiance (2008: 34): we might not side with the character and root for their success (cf. section 2.2, p. 18). Pondering a notional female viewer's reaction to Alfred Hitchcock's *Rear Window*, Plantinga suggests that she may at times want James Stewart's Jeffries to achieve his goals but still think him "an arrogant cad" (2009: 110): one might experience motivational identification but distinctly not experience cognitive identification. As a consequence of the diversity in forms of identification, we can be said to experience identification without endorsing every one of that character's ideas, or attitudes, or goals. I can experience emotional identification with Agamemnon in *Iliad* 11 without supporting his autocratic tendencies.

Another batch of literature on identification goes on the offensive, proclaiming its positive effects. One applauds the possibility that identifying with literary characters leads to demonstrable progressive change, and Davis argues for this equation: identification, especially across demographic boundaries, "disrupts stasis and leads a reader or viewer to new ground, to consider change in his or her own attitudes, relationships, politics, and self-constructions," and such changes "encourage left-leaning political engagement and sympathy for subordinate groups" (2007: 6–7; cf. 23, 29, 47, 66, 80, 99, 132–4, 139, 152, 176). Even if narratives alone do not generate activism, they can sustain it (30, 54, 176). Yet that ideal outcome cannot be the sole metric by which we determine the value of identification (Felski 2020b: 118–19). Felski suggests the following upside: "Identifying...does not simply entrench a prior self but may enrich, expand, or amend it. Perhaps we glimpse aspects of ourselves in a character, but in a way that causes us to revise our sense of who we are"; "as I recognize myself in another, I may also see something new in myself, and I may be startled or discomfited by what I see" (2020b: 83, 101; cf. Jollimore and Barrios 2004: 38; Slater and Cohen 2016: 121–2, 127; Consoli 2018: 94). Davis provides a clarifying example in her study of how recipients identify with the characters in Manuel Puig's *Kiss of the Spider Woman* (be it the novel or its adaptations as a movie and musical): they "loosen their own self-conceptions" and engage in "self-criticism" (2007: 139). To interact with a narrative in this way is to follow in the footsteps of the Victorian-era readers studied by Marisa Knox for whom identification enables "understanding and constructing" the self (2021: 6). What of women identifying with male characters? When Doherty critiques how the *Odyssey* gets female recipients to identify with Odysseus—"This may lead in turn to their 'identifying against' the autonomous female figures who oppose him, or who threaten to usurp his primacy" (1995: 177)—she joins other feminist critics in seeing real problems in what happens when female recipients identify with male protagonists (Davis 2007: 50). Davis counters, "Women viewers identifying with male characters could be read as a progressive rather than a regressive political development, a reflection of a growing anti-essentialist feminist sensibility and a rejection of female stereotypes" (2007: 50). One should explore "the potentially subversive effects of a loosening of the boundaries of the self through cross-gender identification." (Davis defends cross-racial identification in her 2014 book (e.g., 110).) These considerations show us why it matters that demographics do not determine identification. That we can identify with characters who are not demographically similar means that we have more opportunities over the course of a given narrative to experience identification's positive outcomes. In particular, these writers highlight the introspection afforded by identification.

Yet a challenge emerges for those who criticize identification and those who defend it: we need to be honest about the degree to which identification has lasting effects and about our current state of ignorance on the matter. I return to a point made in section 3.3 (pp. 64–5): research into narrative impact finds that "highly transporting narratives have the potential to alter beliefs, attitudes, and behaviors" (Fitzgerald and Green 2017: 62) and that identification with characters makes an important contribution to this equation or brings about similar changes. For instance, "identifying with a narrative character who espouses the opposite beliefs from the reader regarding an intense political conflict can lead to a tempering of attitudes" (Slater and Cohen 2016: 121, citing Cohen, Tal-Or, and Mazor-Tregerman 2015). Researchers draw their conclusions by testing participants right after exposure to a narrative. They can show short-term effects. This immediate impact is why it made sense to think in section 3.4 about how paradigm tellers in the Homeric poems try to get their listeners to identify with a character in the paradigm. The big question becomes, how long does the impact last? I have not seen any longitudinal studies that query the durability of the changes wrought by identification. There are a few longitudinal studies that look at the durability of the changes wrought by transportation. Transported recipients were "more likely to report attempts to quit smoking at a two-week follow up"; over a two-week period, transported recipients came to believe even more firmly in false information gleaned from a narrative (Fitzgerald and Green 2017: 60–1). Transported fiction readers revealed greater empathy after a one-week interval (Bal and Veltkamp 2013). Conversely, over the course of a year the effect of reading Michael Pollan's *The Omnivore's Dilemma* wore off (Fitzgerald and Green 2017: 60). Still, a 2012 review of studies on narrative impact concludes by calling for additional investigations into "how attitudes and behaviour can be changed on a long-term basis" (Sanford and Emmott 2012: 264), and a 2020 paper ends, "in order to empirically support possible long-term effects of narratives on the self, longitudinal designs are needed" (Krause and Appel 2020: 56), suggesting the relative paucity of such investigations. If we take these studies of transportation (or lack thereof) as our guide, we should refrain from declaring identification to have enduring effects. I would draw a similar lesson from the current aporia in video game studies. Video game players identify with their avatars (van Vught and Schott 2017; Allen and Anderson 2019; Ferchaud et al. 2020). Does playing violent video games and experiencing some form(s) of identification while doing so have the lasting impact of making you more aggressive? A 2018 meta-analysis concludes, "Playing violent video games is associated with greater levels of overt physical aggression over time, after accounting for prior aggression. These findings support the general claim that violent video game play is associated with increases in physical aggression over time" (Prescott, Sargent, and Hull 2018: 9887). Another study published in 2018 states precisely the opposite (Kühn et al. 2019: 1232):

> An extensive game intervention over the course of 2 months did not reveal any specific changes in aggression, empathy, interpersonal competencies, impulsivity-related constructs, depressivity, anxiety or executive control functions; neither in comparison to an active control group that played a non-violent video game nor to a passive control group. We observed no effects when comparing a baseline and a post-training assessment, nor when focussing on more long-term effects between baseline and a follow-up interval 2 months after the participants stopped training.

Observing this schism should make us skeptical at present about assumptions regarding the durability of the effects of identification with literary characters.

Scholarship gives us a third option beyond blaming or praising identification. Two unrelated studies highlight the appeal of identification. Fritz Breithaupt writes, "The longing for intensity, presence, and aesthetic clarity becomes the motor of identification; inhabiting the glowing skin is the reward" (2019: 216). Suffice it to say that one could unpack each word and phrase at length. The first two, "intensity" and "presence," invoke the work of Altieri (2003: 187–94; cf. Liebert 2017: 115–16) and Hans Gumbrecht (2004). By "aesthetic clarity," Breithaupt refers to the fact that we find other people easy to read and other people's situations easier to address than our own (2019: 12–16, 18, 226). By "glowing skin," he refers to "when an experience is heightened by the awareness of being observed" (224). If we identify with a character who is the center of attention—perhaps one even seen by other characters—we feel that we too are in the spotlight. Recipients seek out all four experiences.

Another appealing feature of identification is that it allows for "temporary expansion of the boundaries of the self" (Slater et al. 2014; cf. Slater and Cohen 2016: 122–4). We spend almost all of our time constructing and maintaining our self-concept, our understanding of who we are, given that a self is actually a plurality of numerous selves, at times mutually exclusive and at odds with one another, and given that we have to defend that self against criticisms and inevitable failures. This work exhausts us and brings us up against our limitations: we cannot successfully be all of our selves simultaneously; we cannot even be all of our selves simultaneously. At some point, we wish to pause this endeavor. Identification with characters in a narrative—characters with their own jobs and lives, their own personalities and goals—helps us to do just that: "we are momentarily relieved of the task of maintenance of our personal and social identity. We are no longer confined to the roles, unrealized potentials, or limitations of that identity. We have temporarily expanded the boundaries of the personal and social self" (Slater et al. 2014: 444, italics removed). Identification, therefore, offers "a most convenient means to address a subtle yet fundamental threat to a subjective sense of well-being: the inherent limitations of being a single, limited human being" (Slater and Cohen 2016: 123). The proponents of this model are "agnostic as to whether the experience of expansion of self is beneficial, destructive, or neutral in its effects on the person in the long term" (124).

Doherty's 1995 book has generated my discussion so far. To drive home the point that still today classical studies writ large will benefit from renewed attention to how it talks about the politics of identification, I juxtapose the thoughts on identification presented so far with Victoria Wohl's 2015 analysis of Euripides's *Alcestis*. Wohl does not speak of identification, but she could have (11, 15, 17):

> How can we not be sad, seeing Admetus's grief? Likewise, how could we not share his joy at the end, when he finally takes his revived wife by the hand?... We are rooting for Alcestis's return and the happy ending: we wept to see Alcestis die, we will rejoice to see her return.... We are asked to be loyal friends to this lucky king, to feel (as the chorus do) for his misfortune and to cheer at its reversal.

To translate into the terms of this project, spectators experience emotional and motivational identification.

For Wohl, to engage in this way is to experience "mere emotional catharsis" and "simple fun, an escapist fantasy or emotional joyride" (12). Note the denigration of identification signaled by this diction. What is more, these sentiments are "hard to resist" (11); "almost despite ourselves...we succumb" to them (12) because the play's "formal elements conspire to make that emotional trajectory compelling" (15); the play "forces us into an emotional position" (16) and offers "a reward for our acquiescence" (17). Note the suspicions voiced about identification: it cannot be good to succumb, to be subject to forces that conspire and compel and force, to acquiesce. Framing recipient engagement (what I am glossing as identification) in these ways allows Wohl to get to the real business of her reading, unmasking the ideological operation embedded in the play. We "join in Admetus's celebration at the end. But what exactly are we celebrating?" (15). We are celebrating the ability of elites to get around the rules the rest of us abide by, even the seeming necessity of death (13–16), and accordingly we take on that ultimate Marxist bête noire: "false consciousness" (17; see Plantinga 2009: 190, 199–200). There follow "political consequences" and "political implications" (Wohl 2015: 16, 17). Spectators carry these ideas with them after the play is over: as they "acquiesce in its romance of elite prerogative," they leave the theater ready to accede to aristocratic power and privilege (17; cf. 65–6). At other points in her discussion, however, Wohl grants audience members an awareness of this anti-democratic position: it produces "political discomfort" (16). From here, Wohl can envision a dichotomous response. Either the play's "extravagance of pathos" (11)—again, what I would link to identification—governs our response or we question the play's vision of elite exceptionalism: one "comes away from the play [either] with a warm glow of love regained and prosatyric jubilation at the reversal from bad fortune to good, or with a vague sense of unease—or a more acute sense of class *ressentiment*—at the licensed transgression by which that reversal is achieved" (18).

Three points can be made. First, Wohl ventures, "Maybe after suffering along with their grief, we should just enjoy the reunion of husband and wife, and not worry about the larger metaphysical or political implications of that happy ending achieved in breach of an ostensibly universal law" (16–17), but the rhetorical thrust of her presentation implies that do so is naïve, especially for the critic bent on a suspicious demystification (cf. 121). Such a critic will not stop to ask what benefits might accrue from identification with the characters or what precisely makes identification appealing.

Second, Wohl finds that we celebrate "the fact that the universality of death holds for the rest of us, but not for the elites" and "the fact that a good aristocrat has been rewarded for, essentially, being a good aristocrat" (15). She adds, "If we leave the theater feeling grateful to that aristocratic hero for whom wrestling Death is all in a day's work... we might also come to feel that he and his friends deserve whatever good luck happens to come their way" (17). The absence of proper names and the use of the plural number (elites, friends) in these formulations merit attention. In this reading, to celebrate the successes of Admetus and Heracles is actually not to celebrate those characters' successes but to celebrate and endorse class hierarchies and ideological claims about aristocratic privilege. The occlusion of the characters' names in the quoted sentences emblematizes and perhaps even enables this extrapolation and the further extrapolation reviewed two paragraphs earlier that spectators take these ideas with them when they exit the theater and apply them to aristocrats in their actual world. Yet, as I discussed previously in this section (pp. 134–6), I can root for and revel in a character's success (that is, I can experience motivational identification with them) without endorsing (celebrating) the system within which they operate and without desiring to implement that system in my world.

Third, Wohl's discussion problematically cleaves identification from interrogation. Yes, our tendency to find fault with a narrative (to counterargue) decreases when we are immersed in a narrative and identify with its characters (see Conclusion, p. 248). Nevertheless, getting wrapped up in a narrative can make recipients engage in self-reflection (Koopman and Hakemulder 2015, esp. 92–6; cf. Vaage 2016: 107, 117), and, even if we can remain in thrall to a narrative's mystifications for some period of time, it must be equally true that we can eventually reflect on those mystifications in a dispassionate manner and that we are more likely to do so with respect to narratives that initially grabbed us. This movement is evident in Paul Woodruff's evolving response to William Shakespeare's *Henry V*: he used to react with "pride and excitement," "swept up in the mood of Henry's heroism," "enthralled and inspired" (2008: 208); now "forty years later" he finds that "the play represents the defeat of France by an irresponsible boy-king, an event that is stirring, exciting, terrible all at once. The appropriate response [to the play] is complex and disturbing" (208–9). Margrethe Bruun Vaage's intense engagement with the male anti-hero protagonists in television shows, self-reflexively explored throughout her study, gives her the time and ability to see a disconcerting subtext: his wife, rooted in her markedly feminine domestic sphere, keeps the male hero from living life to the fullest (2016: 154, 174). Investigating Spike Lee's film *BlacKkKlansman*, Plantinga connects our "allegiance for" the protagonist and our propensity to "root for him" with our engaging in "reflective thought" and "questioning" about the persistence of racism (2019, quotations from 165–6). I invoke too Jenefer Robinson's defense of the proposition that one's emotional response to a literary work enables one to understand and interpret the work (2005: 105–35, 192). To the extent that identification gets us to engage with a tale, it does not just prompt subsequent revelations about, say, the relationship between the tale's parts (cf. M. Smith 2017: 196); it can also ultimately prompt questioning and critique (cf. Gaut 1999: 216; Plantinga 2019: 153, 165–6). Such interrogations are not simply the province of those who never succumb to the allure of a narrative. Better is Wohl's statement in her book's concluding chapter: tragedy "heightens our feelings and, in this way, exposes them to intellectual examination" (2015: 136).

Wohl's incisive readings prompt a final reflection. In her analysis of Euripides's *Orestes*, Wohl stresses the audience's initial propensity to root for Orestes and Electra as they seek help from Menelaus and Tyndareus (120–2); furthermore, they "would have understood, perhaps even shared, the protagonists' desperation" (126). But when Orestes, Electra, and Pylades try to kill Helen and her daughter Hermione and find themselves squaring off against Menelaus and his army, our "sympathy...becomes much harder to sustain" (127)—or better, the play "set[s] our sympathies against themselves." To rephrase, we can experience motivational, cognitive, even emotional identification with the protagonists, only to find that attachment severely tested, even severed. I pointed out earlier that identification comes and goes (sections 2.2, pp. 25–6, and 4.4, p. 127). Now we can add that recipients not only do not experience identification at certain points but also actively disidentify, rejecting a character's interpretation of events or not wanting them to achieve their goals. The emotions and judgments that attend those moments of disidentification become all the stronger and the more vigorous for our having identified with the character previously—a point neatly articulated by those in film and television studies (cf. Grau 2010: 57–8; Vaage 2016: 25–6, 53, 57, 83, 109–10). If part of the pleasure of watching a play or movie or reading a novel comes from the intensity of the experience (e.g., Altieri 2003: 187; cf. Vaage 2016: 101–2), then not just identification (cf. Liebert 2017: 118) but the movement from identification to disidentification enhances the pleasure of engagement with narratives. We find another appealing feature of identification.

## 4.6. Conclusion

I draw one main lesson from Part I's discussion of identification. Homeric poetry—although really countless narratives (cf. Plantinga 2018: 40), but let us stick with Homeric poetry—does not encourage in recipients a disinterested response to how the characters felt or what they thought or what they wanted to do. The epics provide cues for identification with its characters.

One wonders how recipients' identification with the *Iliad*'s characters affects their response to the narrator and so to the poet given the slippage in the Homeric context between the narrator and poet (e.g., Porphyry *Homeric Questions on the Iliad* at 6.275 MacPhail; see de Jong 2004: 4; Ready 2011: 152 n. 6; cf. Grethlein 2021b). Patrick Hogan speculates on what makes us consider a narrator reliable (2018: 161):

> Trust and distrust are affected by a wide range of factors, including what other emotion systems are active at the time. For example, research indicates that increasing oxytocin levels increases proneness to trust.... Since oxytocin is linked with attachment feelings, we might conjecture that the cultivation of attachment feelings in a literary work will foster trust of the narrator.

In so far as identification with characters generates feelings of attachment (cf. Bopp et al. 2019), one might position identification with characters as in turn generating confidence in the narrator. One could yoke this claim to the continued scholarly interest in how the Homeric poet establishes his authority (beyond, for instance, invoking the Muse), exemplified in Adrian Kelly's examination of how the poet inspires trust by juxtaposing his accounts of events with his characters' accounts of the same events (2018; cf. Kozak 2017 (see under "diegetic re-telling" in their index)).

The primary goal of Part I has been to defend the following claim: to the extent that identification contributes to immersion, identification with Homeric characters will prompt immersion in the epic's storyworld. Hoorn and Konijn, however, have challenged the importance of identification to the "appreciation" of a fictional character (2003: 255). Nor is identification the whole story when it comes to immersion. Our investigation of immersion has properly started with identification, but there is much more to consider.

# PART II
# IMMERSION AND THE *ILIAD*

# 5
# Ancients and Moderns on Immersion

## 5.1. Overview

Part I's discussion of identification prepares us to address immersion. As I remarked in section 2.1 (p. 15), identification and immersion are "empirically correlated" (Oliver et al. 2019: 188), and the literature on identification overlaps and intersects with that on immersion. Furthermore, we will find some opportunities to supplement and build on Part I's presentation in the following chapters. To ease us into the topic of immersion, section 5.2 explores ancient precedents for such a study. This review will also help assuage fears readers may have that it is anachronistic to talk about immersion in the context of ancient responses to literature, just as section 2.4 aimed to do in the case of identification with characters. Section 5.3 provides some preliminary orientation regarding research into immersion in fields outside classical studies.

## 5.2. Ancient Precedents for a Study of Immersion

Ancient authors spoke in two ways about what happens when a narrative captures recipients' attention and imagination. Aristotle urges rhetoricians to "make misfortune appear near [to the audience], making it before their eyes" (ἐγγὺς γὰρ ποιοῦσι φαίνεσθαι τὸ κακὸν πρὸ ὀμμάτων ποιοῦντες, *Art of Rhetoric* 1386a33–4). His injunction anticipates the praise lavished on Homer by Pseudo-Plutarch—"his poems resemble things seen more than things heard" (ὁρωμένοις μᾶλλον ἢ ἀκουομένοις ἔοικε τὰ ποιήματα, *Essay on the Life and Poetry of Homer* 217 Keaney and Lamberton)—and by numerous scholia (Pagani 2018: 72–5; cf. Myers 2019: 23): for instance, when Eurypylus lops off Hypsenor's hand, a scholion comments, "He [the poet] brought to be sure the incident into view (*hup' opsin*)" (scholion bT at *Iliad* 5.82; Nünlist 2009: 198 with n. 12). Still other ancient critics, such as Dionysius of Halicarnassus (*On Lysias* 7.1–2) and Lucian (*How to Write History* 51), praised other writers who made listeners, readers, or spectators seem to see before them the portrayed events (Grethlein 2013: 17–18; Sheppard 2014: 24; Allan, de Jong, and de Jonge 2017: 36–7; O'Connell 2017b: 124–5). Conversely, Polybius reproaches the historian Phylarchus for his efforts to induce pity for the Mantineans by "aiming to bring the terrible things [suffered by the Mantineans] before our eyes (*pro ophthalmōn*)" (*The Histories* 2.56.8 Büttner-Wobst) when in fact the Mantineans deserved their fate (Grethlein 2013: 246; 2021a: 111–12).

Per this model, the events come, as it were, to the recipient. For Mark Payne, this movement is an essential component of Callimachus's so-called mimetic hymns: "they project their world outward, into the world of the reader" (2007: 55). For Jonas Grethlein, this movement contributes to Thucydides's, Xenophon's, Plutarch's, and Tacitus's projects: he gives the subtitle "Making the Past Present" to the section of his book in which he discusses these four writers (2013). Homerists have leaned heavily on this idea. Andrew Ford refers to "a sense that the past is somehow present before us" (1992: 49). Egbert Bakker avers, "The past is...drawn into the present through the nonfictional activity of the performer" (2005: 102). Erwin Cook writes of the Homeric poet, "he is bringing his own poetic universe into the here and now"; "the ancient heroes appear vividly before us" (2018: 124). George Gazis notes that the poet "is able to re-enact the spectacle of the Trojan War in front of his audience's eyes" (2018: 9). Katherine Kretler interrogates "the person of the performer as a portal through which forces are made present" (2020: 30).

Longinus makes a similar claim when defining *phantasia* ("mental image"): "under the sway of enthusiasm and passion you seem to see the things which you are talking about and put it before the eyes of your hearers (ὑπ' ὄψιν τιθῇς τοῖς ἀκούουσιν)" (*On the Sublime* 15.1).[1] But Longinus also reverses directions—the recipient goes to the events, as it were—in his discussion of second-person address (Allan, de Jong, and de Jonge 2017: 37; de Jonge 2020: 165–6; Halliwell 2021: 375 at 4–5, 12–13). Second-person address can "make the hearer seem to turn about in the middle (*en mesois*) of the dangers" (*On the Sublime* 26.1). When Herodotus uses that form of address, "he takes your soul and leads (*agei*) it through (*dia*) the places, making hearing into sight" (26.2). "All the passages of this sort," Longinus concludes, "put the hearer amidst (*ep'*) the things being done themselves" (26.2). A Homeric scholion bears comparison (Nünlist 2009: 155): when the poet describes Hera's journey from Mt Olympus to Lemnos, "the mind (*dianoia*) of the readers, travelling together with (*sumparatheousa*) the naming of the places, enters into an imaginative and visual perception of the places (ἐν φαντασίᾳ καὶ ὄψει τῶν τόπων)" (bT scholion at *Iliad* 14.226–7; trans. Nünlist).

We can detect the beginning of this idea that the recipient goes to the events in a passage from Hesiod's *Theogony*. Hesiod praises the Muse-inspired poet who sings about the glorious deeds of earlier generations and about the gods of Olympus. This poet can make even those recently saddened and distressed forget their cares and woes: the gifts of the gods "turn aside" (*paretrape*) (*Theogony* 98–103 Most). The verb "turn aside" lacks an expressed object. The object could

---

[1] Cf. Manieri 1998: 52–3; Otto 2009: 92–3; Munteanu 2012: 101–2; Grethlein 2021a: 240; Halliwell 2021: 298 at 7.

be the cares and woes of the previous verses (so Most's translation (2006)). Stephen Halliwell thinks it is "the mind" of the listener (2011: 16; cf. Ford 1992: 53; Liebert 2017: 47). If the gifts of the gods turn aside the mind of the listener, to where do they direct it? Halliwell answers, "Into other worlds—the distant human past and the divine society on Olympus" (2011: 17).

A fragment from a fourth-century BCE playwright, Timocles, intrigues too (Athenaeus *Scholars at Dinner* 223c Olson):

> παραψυχὰς οὖν φροντίδων ἀνεύρετο
> ταύτας· ὁ γὰρ νοῦς τῶν ἰδίων λήθην λαβὼν
> πρὸς ἀλλοτρίῳ τε ψυχαγωγηθεὶς πάθει,
> μεθ᾽ ἡδονῆς ἀπῆλθε παιδευθεὶς ἅμα.
> τοὺς γὰρ τραγῳδοὺς πρῶτον, εἰ βούλει, σκόπει
> ὡς ὠφελοῦσι πάντας.
>
> He [man] therefore invented these ways of turning his mind from his thoughts: for the mind, seizing upon a forgetting of its own things and enchanted by another's suffering, goes away pleased and having learned something at the same time. For consider, if you will, first tragedies, how they benefit all.

Contemplating others' troubles helps one deal with one's own. Tragedies especially present scenes of such suffering that one's own woes pale in comparison (cf. Grethlein 2021a: 15). How literally are we to take the idea of movement implied in the prefix *para* in *parapsukhas* or the idea of leading embedded in *psukhagōgētheis*? For Halliwell, the noun indicates "a turning aside...of the mind" (2011: 8), and the participle connotes "the experience of being taken outside oneself" (312). Dana Munteanu translates πρὸς ἀλλοτρίῳ τε ψυχαγωγηθεὶς πάθει as "being mesmerized by the *pathos* of another" but then paraphrases it as "by being transported into the emotion of another" (2012: 134; cf. Grethlein 2021a: 99, 109–10).

Plato clarifies the matter in his *Ion*. Socrates asks the rhapsode Ion about his experience as a performer of Homeric poetry: "are you of sound mind or do you become outside (*exō*) of yourself and does your soul think that it is alongside (*para*) the affairs that you sing about in your possessed state, [the affairs] either being in Ithaca or in Troy or however the verses have it?" (535b7–c3). Ion agrees that he finds himself transported to the world he depicts in song (535c4–5). Socrates and Ion then note that Ion also brings about the transportation of his audience (535d8–e3):

> Socrates: Do you know then that you do these same things (*tauta tauta*) even to the majority of the spectators?
>
> Ion: And indeed I know it well: for I see them on each occasion from above from the stage crying and looking about fearfully and being amazed at the things being said.

Like Ion, audience members are transported to the storyworld,[2] and Ion's following observation suggests they seek this effect: "For I must pay attention to them zealously: because if I make them cry, I myself will laugh when I get money, but if I make them laugh, I myself will cry when I lose money" (535e3–6). Socrates, of course, banishes Homeric poetry from the *Republic*'s fantastical Callipolis but makes allowances for non-mimetic poetry, such as hymns and encomia (607a4), precisely because it does not offer "compelling stories whose worlds are not continuous with our own" and "does not transport the audience into an illusory world, but rather engages them in their own" (Liebert 2017: 197). To be transported in this fashion means to have one's soul "dragged about" (to use Plato's subsequent words in the *Ion*: *helkei tēn phukhēn*, 536a2). That Plato uses the movement of the soul as shorthand for transportation into the world of the story suggests that Halliwell is on the right track: Hesiod and Timocles intimate the recipient's heading to the world of the story.

Socrates's suggestion, and Ion's agreement, that the performer is transported into the storyworld finds a parallel in Longinus's injunction that an author writes best when so transported (cf. de Jonge 2020: 162–3; Grethlein 2021b: 221). Praising verses from Euripides's *Phaethon*, Longinus asks rhetorically, "Would you not say that the soul of the poet mounts the chariot too (*sunepibainei*) [with Phaethon] and sharing his danger (*sugkinduneuousa*) takes wing along with (*sunepterōtai*) the horses? For it would never have formed images of this sort, if it had not been carried along, running alongside (*isodromousa*) those celestial actions" (*On the Sublime* 15.4). The underlined prefixes stress the poet's position in the storyworld close to the characters.[3] Aristotle may also provide a parallel in his *Poetics* (1455a22–9):

> One [the poet] must put together the plots and work out the accompanying language while putting the things being done before one's eyes as much as possible. For by seeing in this fashion most vividly, as if being present among the things being done themselves (ὥσπερ παρ' αὐτοῖς γιγνόμενος τοῖς πραττομένοις), he would find that which is fitting and least of all would the unsuitable things escape his notice. Proof of this is the censure that befell Carcinus. For Amphiaraus was coming out of the shrine, which would escape the notice of one who was not seeing it from the vantage point of a spectator, but on the stage everything fell apart because the spectators were unable to tolerate it.

---

[2] Cf. M. Power 2006: 37–8; Liebert 2010: 198–201; Halliwell 2011: 170–3; Graziosi 2013: 33–4; Sheppard 2014: 21–2; de Jonge 2020: 149, 155; Grethlein 2021a: 85–6; Giordano 2022: 187–8.

[3] Cf. Ooms and de Jonge 2013: 106; J. Porter 2016: 157–8; Webb 2016: 218; de Jonge 2020: 163; Huitink 2020: 198; Halliwell 2021: 305 at 40–2.

The phrase "as if being present among the things being done themselves" (ὥσπερ παρ' αὐτοῖς γιγνόμενος τοῖς πραττομένοις) could mean that the poet should place himself "in the middle of the fictional incidents" (Munteanu 2012: 89; cf. 99). The transported playwright writes best. The phrase could also mean that the poet should transport himself into the storyworld as it will be depicted on stage and think in advance about what the spectators will see (Gill 1984: 152; Tarán and Gutas 2012: 273 at 1455a22–26, 1455a27–29; Sheppard 2014: 23; Halliwell 2017: 122).

At the same time, the rhapsode Ion's words quoted a moment ago—"I see them on each occasion from above from the stage crying and looking about fearfully and being amazed at the things being said" (535e1–3)—highlight an important restriction. Despite being transported, he remains sufficiently aware of his real-world surroundings to keep tabs on his audience. Ion does not in fact suffer from the delusion that he is "in Ithaca or in Troy," and he carefully monitors his audience's emotional reactions to his performance (Murray 1996: 123 at e4–6; Rijksbaron 2007: 184 at 535d6–7; Grethlein 2021a: 91). Ion's subsequent observation, also quoted a moment ago, reinforces this idea: "For I must pay attention to them zealously: because if I make them cry, I myself will laugh when I get money, but if I make them laugh, I myself will cry when I lose money" (535e3–6).[4] This explanation illustrates as well that audience members, despite their transportation into the storyworld, remain aware of their real-world surroundings: they are able to reward the rhapsode for a good performance because they remain aware of his being the agent of their immersion during the performance (cf. Plotz 2018: 27). Longinus offers similar caveats regarding the immersed audience several centuries later (de Jonge 2020: 154–5, 162), while in his *Imagines* Philostratus the Elder makes the same point by having his exegete seem to move in and out of the world of the paintings he describes at will (Newby 2009; Grethlein 2017a: 18–24). Fifth-century Athenian dramatists already pondered in a self-reflexive fashion the spectators' awareness of the distinction between storyworld and real world (Lada 1993: 120–2; cf. Grethlein 2021a: 39–42), and, when Gorgias says of the spectator of tragedy that "the one who is deceived is wiser than the one who is not deceived" (fragment B 23 Diels-Kranz), he too highlights the spectator's awareness of the distinction (Grethlein 2021a: 18–20, 38, 100).

Ancient authors worked with two propositions, then: that the events come to the recipients and that the recipients feel themselves going to the events (cf. Bakker 2005: 160, 167). Still, the direction in which recipients or events go perhaps matters less than the nature of the recipient's engagement—an intense one—with the narrated events. Aristotle's account of the tragedian Carcinus's

---

[4] Cf. Munteanu 2009: 133; Liebert 2010: 201; Sheppard 2014: 22; Grethlein 2021a: 91; 2021b: 221–2.

error—Amphiaraus was supposedly returning to the stage from a shrine but entered from the wrong direction and thereby broke the dramatic illusion (cf. Hutton 1982: 99)—brings out the spectator's desire for an intense engagement with the storyworld: they map the fictional world onto the real world of the theatrical space (cf. Weiss 2020; 2023, esp. ch. 1) and do not appreciate inconsistencies that confound their mapping. Prioritizing this point, Aristotle unsurprisingly conflates the two propositions in the preceding sentences of that passage (*Poetics* 1455a22–6):

> One [the poet] must put together the plots and work out the accompanying language while putting the things being done before one's eyes (*pro ommatōn*) as much as possible. For by seeing in this fashion most vividly, as if being present among the things being done themselves (ὥσπερ παρ' αὐτοῖς γιγνόμενος τοῖς πραττομένοις), he would find that which is fitting and least of all would the unsuitable things escape his notice.

The phrase "before one's eyes" suggests that the events come to the poet. The phrase "as if being present among the things being done themselves" suggests that the poet goes to the events (be they in the storyworld or in the storyworld as depicted on stage). One phrase glosses the other. The fifth-century CE Neoplatonist Proclus also conflates these ideas in his commentary on Plato's *Republic*. On the one hand, Homer and Plato each "represents (*paristēsin*) those whomever he imitates as all but present (*parontas*) and speaking their thoughts and living" (*Commentary on the Republic of Plato* K163.24–6)—the action comes to us; on the other hand, "we do not seem to be apart from (*apeinai*) the events," or, more loosely, "we feel we are actually present at the events" (K164.5–6; trans. Lamberton)—we go to the action. Compare Ford's and Jenny Strauss Clay's interweaving of the language of presence with the language of movement. Archaic Greek epic poetry "claims to transport us to an *au delà*, not a beyond buried in the vault of recollection but a place as present as our own, though elsewhere" (Ford 1992: 55). On the one hand, "the [*Iliad*] poet seems to convey his audience to another place and another time" (Clay 2011: 17) and "leaving our everyday world behind, we enter one grander than ours" (18); on the other hand, "it would not be quite accurate to say that his audience is transported.... The poet brings the deeds of the heroes enacted in a distant time and faraway places into the immediate present and imagined proximity of his audience" (17; cf. 20, 26).

Ancient critics took the additional step of recommending how authors might get recipients to see events and characters before their eyes or feel themselves in the world of the tale. I select three studies of ancient terminology, each devoted to different words. Ruth Webb analyzes discussions of the terms *enargeia* (let us translate, "vividness") and *phantasia* in the work of scholars like Quintilian, Dionysius of Halicarnassus, and Longinus (cf. Bussels 2013: 57–77; O'Connell

2017a: 226–32). To begin with, "the inclusion of details" contributes to *enargeia*.[5] Details can be "attendant circumstances" (Webb 2009: 92; cf. Zanker 1981: 297–300; Plett 2012: 8) as well as "the visual appearance of persons, places and actions" (Webb 2009: 92). René Nünlist points to two illuminating comments on such details in the Homeric scholia. A bT scholion at *Iliad* 16.762-3 observes, "He [sc. Homer] described the dragging of the body [sc. of Cebriones] most graphically (*enargestata*) by adding the limbs which they [sc. Hector and Patroclus] were holding and pulling in opposite directions" (trans. Nünlist 2009: 196). Nünlist interprets: "This note makes it explicit that the descriptive details (here: Cebriones' limbs) contribute to or even bring about ἐνάργεια" (196). According to a bT scholion at *Iliad* 4.154, the verse's details about Agamemnon's holding Menelaus's hand and his companions' groaning enhance the passage's *enargeia* (Nünlist 2009: 197; cf. Manieri 1998: 180-1). Orators in particular must also aim for "probability and verisimilitude" (Webb 2009: 102–3). They have to stay "close to the world" (102): "a narrative needs to conform to an audience's expectations of what is likely or probable and to their experience of the world if it is to be believed" (103; cf. 109–10, 122; Otto 2009: 120; Plett 2012: 9; Spatharas 2019: 89–94). At the same time, orators should give audience members breaks from the intense experience of engagement with past or future events: one must interweave argumentative portions that lay out the facts (Webb 2009: 99).

Steven Ooms and Casper de Jonge's article on the term *enagōnios* discusses techniques that critics—such as Longinus, Demetrius, and anonymous scholiasts—find contributing to the audience's "active involvement and engagement" (2013: 98): the historical present tense (98–9, 104; cf. Sheppard 2014: 24, 34; de Jonge 2020: 167; Huitink 2020: 206); second-person addresses (Ooms and de Jonge 2013: 103–4; cf. Sheppard 2014: 34); and suspense—not anticipating the outcome but only divulging information gradually (Ooms and de Jonge 2013: 105–7; cf. Manieri 1998: 135–6; Otto 2009: 128).

Grethlein argues that the word *apatē* can mean or point toward "aesthetic illusion" (2021a), one of the other terms scholars use for immersion. Tracking uses of the word *apatē*, he directs attention to the *Life of Aeschylus*'s discussion of what makes for an engaging presentation (43–4): "reversals and twists" (*peripeteias kai plokas*, 5 Herington) in the plot and "gnomic statements or scenes that evoke pity (γνῶμαι δὲ ἢ συμπάθειαι) or any other of the things able to lead one to tears" (7). In his *On Literary Composition*, Dionysius of Halicarnassus connects *apatē* with what he labels "the refined style of composition" (*glaphura...sunthesis*, 23 Usher 1985), a style wherein the individual words and clauses go together seamlessly

---

[5] Webb 2009: 91; cf. Manieri 1998: 133–4; Nünlist 2009: 195–6; Otto 2009: 128; Plett 2012: 13; Sheppard 2014: 35; O'Connell 2017a: 235–6.

(Kim 2014: 372). To generate aesthetic illusion (*to apatēlon*) this style deploys "figures of speech" that are "delicate and appealing" (σχήμασί... τοῖς τρυφεροῖς τε καὶ κολακικοῖς) as opposed to those that exhibit "a certain solemnity or weight or intensity" (σεμνότης τις ἢ βάρος ἢ τόνος, 23; Grethlein 2021a: 117). In his *On the Style of Demosthenes*, Dionysius suggests that *kōtillein kai ligainein*—"hypnotic or striking phonetic effects" (trans. Usher 1974), "a seductive and sweet voice" (trans. Kim 2014: 379)—contribute(s) to aesthetic illusion (*apatēs*, 44 Usher 1974) and then aligns the refined style as a whole (*tais glaphurais*) with "charm and pleasure and aesthetic illusion and similar things" (τὴν χάριν καὶ τὴν ἡδονὴν καὶ τὴν ἀπάτην καὶ τὰ παραπλήσια τούτοις, 45; cf. Grethlein 2021a: 118).

Ion was on to something when he observed that his hair stands on end and his heart leaps (cf. Lucian *The Lover of Lies or the Doubter* 22 with Grethlein 2021a: 172). Engagement with stories reveals itself in changes to the electrical characteristics of recipients' skin, in changes to their heart rates, and in their facial expressions (cf. Sanford and Emmott 2012: 227; Sukalla et al. 2016; van Krieken, Hoeken, and Sanders 2017: 11–12). Likewise, the degree to which ancient critics anticipate modern investigations into what engenders narrative immersion impresses (cf. de Jonge 2020: 151, 166, 170–1). We will encounter these items—details, realism, variation, suspense, plotting, sound—in the following section and following chapters.

## 5.3. Modern Studies of Immersion

In the previous section's review of ancient testimony, I spoke of transportation and immersion. Modern scholarship in a range of fields, from (cognitive) literary studies to media studies, uses both terms to describe the phenomenon wherein recipients of a narrative get wrapped up in that narrative. As I recorded in section 1.2 (p. 2), they deploy a number of other terms as well, such as absorption, aesthetic illusion, enchantment, engagement, engrossment, entanglement, and involvement.[6] Whatever label they attach to the phenomenon, researchers stress, as Plato's Ion makes sure to do, that immersion (or absorption, aesthetic illusion, enchantment, engagement, engrossment, entanglement, involvement, and transportation) does not mean delusion; the immersed recipient of a narrative does not suffer from the delusion that the storyworld—or "the non-actual possible world" per possible worlds theory (Ryan 2013: 131)—is the real world—or the actual

---

[6] See Felski 2008: 54; Tal-Or and Cohen 2010: 405; Mousley 2011: 12–14; Wolf 2013: 19–20; 2014: section 2.1; Kuijpers et al. 2014; Reinhard 2016: 222; Allan, de Jong, and de Jonge 2017: 47 n. 1; Bilandzic and Busselle 2017: 24; Grethlein 2017a: 4, 18–19, 110; 2021a: 3; Kuiken and Douglas 2017: 217; Oliver et al. 2017: 255; Meineck 2018: 168; R. Allan 2019a: 60, 73 n. 3; Budelmann and Emde Boas 2020: 60.

world per possible worlds theory—in which the recipient exists.[7] The immersed recipient is, rather, "semi-detached" from their surroundings (Plotz 2018; cf. Felski 2020b: 10).

For some features of the phenomenon that ancient and modern critics unpack, then, the precise label does not really matter. Terminology does come to matter when one starts to break the phenomenon down into component parts, and it is here that differences begin to emerge in what modern researchers think is at stake.

Some determine the specifics of their models via introspection. In *Narrative as Virtual Reality 2: Revisiting Immersion and Interactivity in Literature and Electronic Media* (2015a), Marie-Laure Ryan investigates spatial, spatio-temporal, temporal, and emotional immersion. Spatial immersion gives recipients the impression of being in the place in which the tale occurs. Spatio-temporal immersion adds the factor of time: it gives recipients the impression of being in the place in which the tale occurs at the same time as narrated events occur in that place. As I reviewed in section 1.3 (p. 9), temporally immersed recipients attend to a character's past, present, and future: they focus on the relationships between events in the character's past to their present circumstances and between events in their present to possible outcomes in the future (Ryan 2015a: 99–106). Suspense is one mechanism for generating temporal immersion. Emotional immersion comprises three experiences: we assess the characters and experience emotions as a result (such as "like and dislike"); we feel for the characters ("sad/happy," or "pity, grief, and relief"); and we experience our own emotions, "such as fear, horror, disgust, and sexual arousal" (Ryan 2015a: 108).

Other researchers seek to verify their models empirically. Helena Bilandzic and Rick Busselle review three different approaches. In that of Melanie Green and Timothy Brock, one speaks of "transportation" and divides the concept into three components: "attentional focus," wherein attention "is withdrawn from the actual world and redirected to the story"; "emotional reaction to characters and events"; and "imagery," or "the generation of mental images from descriptions contained in the text" (Bilandzic and Busselle 2017: 14–15). In summarizing the components of this model, Kaitlin Fitzgerald and Green highlight "emotional involvement in the story, cognitive attention to the story, feelings of suspense, lack of awareness of surroundings, and mental imagery" (2017: 50).

Bilandzic and Busselle speak of "narrative engagement" and "four distinct but related dimensions" of narrative engagement: to "attentional focus" and "emotional engagement," familiar from Green and Brock's model of transportation, they

---

[7] Felski 2008: 74–5; Barker 2009: 83–4; Plantinga 2009: 64; 2018: 31, 109, 121, 150; Wolf 2013: 14–19, 22–3, 52; Ryan 2015a: 68–9; Cohen and Tal-Or 2017: 134; Grethlein 2017a: 7, 14, 24, 26, 43, 51; 2021a: 3, 20, 281; Kuiken and Douglas 2017: 233; Tan et al. 2017: 98; R. Allan 2019a: 62; 2019b: 133; 2022a: 81; cf. Nussbaum 1995: 8, 75; M. Smith 1995: 42–4; Bakker 2005: 102–3.

add "narrative understanding"—"readers or viewers follow the plot, understand motivations and actions of characters"—and "narrative presence"—"the impression that a reader or viewer is present in the narrative rather than the actual world" (2017: 15).

Moniek Kuijpers et al. have fashioned a "story world absorption scale," the components of which are "attention, emotional engagement, mental imagery, and transportation" (Bilandzic and Busselle 2017: 15; cf. Kuijpers et al. 2017: 34). Like Bilandzic and Busselle's model, this model has four components (Bilandzic and Busselle 2017: 15). Three of its components overlap with the three components of Green and Brock's model. Unlike Green and Brock's model wherein transportation is the umbrella term, in Kuijper et al.'s model transportation is another component of storyworld absorption (15).

Still other researchers have developed additional models. Investigating "absorption," Peter Dixon and Marisa Bortolussi look to "transportation, evoked realism, and emotional reactions" as well as "personal memories" (2017: 200; cf. Bortolussi and Dixon 2015). Combining a cognitivist approach with a phenomenological approach, Don Kuiken and Shaun Douglas find "three different forms of absorption (integrative comprehension, expressive enactment, and reactive engagement)" (2017: 218). Arthur Jacobs and Jana Lüdtke focus on "mental simulation, cognitive and affective empathy, situation model building, and meaning-making by the reader" as the components of "immersion" (2017: 70).

Here too (cf. section 2.2, p. 21) the surveys these researchers generate for their participants to fill out clarify how they define the components of their models and what they mean by, for example, evoked realism or expressive enactment. Kuijper et al. use the following items to fashion their story world absorption scale (2014: 98). The category of attention includes:

> When I was reading the story I was focused on what happened in the story.
> I was reading in such a concentrated manner that I had forgotten the world around me.

The category of emotional engagement includes:

> I felt how the main character was feeling.
> I felt sympathy for the main character.

The category of mental imagery includes:

> When I was reading the story, I could see the situations happening in the story being played out before my eyes.
> I could imagine what the world in which the story took place looked like.

Dixon and Bortolussi's survey contains the following items under the category of transportation (2017: 206):

> After finishing the story, I wished there was another one that continued where this one left off.
> I felt as if I was experiencing the events of the story world personally.

It includes the following items under the category of evoked realism (205):

> I easily imagined all of the things going through people's heads in the story.
> The situations seemed very real.

In seeking to determine "expressive enactment," Kuiken and Douglas's survey asks subjects to rate the following statements (2017: 230):

> Remembering experiences in my own life helped me to sense what the character was going through.
> I could almost feel what it would be like to move or change position in relation to the things (objects, characters) in the story world.
> For a moment I felt like I "was" the character described there.

In seeking to determine "reactive engagement," their questionnaire asks subjects to rate the following statements:

> I identified with someone other than the character described in that part of the story.
> I felt close enough to the situation to think I understood it better than the character did.
> I thought about how this part of the story might have unfolded differently.

By breaking down immersion (the umbrella term I will deploy from now on) into components such as these, researchers can explore the interactions between components. For instance, Dixon and Bortolussi contend that "evoked realism" and "personal memories" prompt "emotional responses" that in turn generate a sense of "transportation" (2017: 208–9). They conclude, "transportation was a function of emotion, and not, as typically claimed, the other way around" (209). They can also "identify hierarchies" among the components (Bilandzic and Busselle 2017: 16): for example, when it comes to the four components of Bilandzic and Busselle's model, "understanding and attentional focus may be necessary (yet not sufficient) conditions for narrative presence and emotional engagement" (2017: 16). Finally, they can pair components of a narrative with components of immersion. For instance, as Bilandzic and

Busselle observe, "a strong visual form in film or a 3D-presentation may facilitate a sense of narrative presence rather than emotional engagement; or, a character-driven story may stimulate emotional engagement rather than narrative presence" (2017: 16).

## 5.4. Conclusion

A quick survey finds ancient poets, commentators, and scholars interested in what we call immersion—what exactly it entails, be it the movement of the characters and their actions into the world of the audience or the movement of the audience into the world of the characters and their actions, and how to bring it about. This overlap between ancient and modern interests grants us permission, if such permission is deemed necessary, to continue exploring immersion in ancient literature using modern tools.

An introductory survey of modern approaches illustrates the several components of immersion and shows that discussions of immersion progress by looking to those components. So too will discussion of immersion in Homeric studies. The articles by Allan, de Jong, and de Jonge (2017) and R. Allan (esp. 2019b; 2020; 2022a) do just that, and I follow their example in subsequent chapters. I adhere to Ryan's template in exploring spatial and spatio-temporal immersion in Chapter 6 and emotional immersion in Chapter 7. Chapter 8 addresses other contributors to immersion, from the depiction of characters' inner lives to the formal features of the poetry. Chapter 9 focuses especially on the factor of oral performance and on how immersed recipients respond to narratives.

# 6
# Spatial and Spatio-Temporal Immersion

## 6.1. Overview

Researchers illuminate the components of immersion, but it is up to us to see triggers for those components of immersion in whichever media we study. Introspection abounds in that endeavor (cf. Huitink 2020: 191). Where appropriate, I tether the introspection that follows to prior scholarship in Homeric studies. For Homerists have frequently discussed immersive features without labeling them as such. This chapter explores several phenomena under the capacious categories of spatial immersion (6.2) and spatio-temporal immersion (6.3).

## 6.2. Spatial Immersion

Homerists have thought a good deal about space and/in the epics. Elizabeth Minchin argues that the *Iliad* poet relies on spatial memory to compose his long song: he associates specific settings with certain speeches and/or certain actions (2008a). Alex Purves brings out the implications of the *Iliad*'s plot being in Aristotle's judgment *eusynoptic*, able to be taken in at a glance, and the *Odyssey*'s adoption of the hodological perspective of the traveler (2010). Jenny Strauss Clay demonstrates the methodical way the *Iliad* poet handles the poem's spaces and the actions therein (2011): this consistency aids the poet as he composes—like Minchin, she highlights the "mutual reinforcement of the spatial and the verbal" (110)—and the audience in comprehending and envisioning the tale. Christos Tsagalis explores the imbrication of the *Iliad*'s spaces in its plot, themes, and worldview (2012). In addressing the topic of spatial immersion, one necessarily builds on these important precedents. Indeed, Clay contends that the poet depicts the battlefield "in such a coherent and vivid fashion that we can mentally transport ourselves to the Trojan plain" (2011: 51). Minchin provides additional and still more precise guidance in a 2021 article. Both our propensity to flesh out settings from the barest of details and the descriptions of human action enable us to visualize the so-called city at peace on Achilles's shield in *Iliad* 18. In visualizing the scene, "we move along the streets... we make our way through a notional three-dimensional space" (2021a: 480).

*Immersion, Identification, and the* Iliad. Jonathan L. Ready, Oxford University Press. © Jonathan L. Ready 2023.
DOI: 10.1093/oso/9780192870971.003.0006

To experience spatial immersion means to create a mental simulation of the physical space of the storyworld and to feel oneself in the places in which the story unfolds. One so immersed might declare, "I could imagine what the world in which the story took place looked like" (Kuijpers et al. 2014: 98), or "I could see (in my mind's eye) the same setting (or environment) that was 'there' for a character to see" (Kuiken and Douglas 2017: 230), or "I could almost feel what it would be like to move or change position in relation to the things (objects, characters) in the story world" (230).

The details of a text enable this experience. Elaine Auyoung reminds us: "Fragmentary details serve as cues or building blocks for creating implied fictional worlds" (2015: 582).[1] This filling out mimics how our perceptual capacities operate in real life: our "reliance on immediately available sensory information" joins with our "ability to retrieve stored knowledge about the world" (583). For instance, in the case of *Iliad* 6's description of the city of Troy (to which I return momentarily) keywords—portico, courtyard, inner chamber, temple, door, house, pleasant, threshold, highest point—activate stores of cultural knowledge that enable recipients to create mental images of the buildings (or at least portions thereof) and the topography of Troy. We do not, for instance, require an exhaustive description of Hecuba's storeroom or of Athena's temple to imagine it. The pleasant odor of the former, designated by *kēōenta* (*Iliad* 6.288; see Graziosi and Haubold 2010: 159 at 288), and the detail about a prized peplos's placement below some others (*neiatos*, 6.295) contribute especially to the imageability of the former, and the reference to its door (*thuras*, 6.298) to the imageability of the latter. Compare Minchin's assessment of the effect of keywords, such as "in the doorways to the courtyard" (*epi prothuroisin*, *Iliad* 18.496), in the description of the city at peace on Achilles's shield: "my memory store... provides rough paving in the street and stone facades for the houses" (2021a: 481).

Textual details furnish the starting point for other investigations of spatial immersion. Kobie van Krieken, Hans Hoeken, and José Sanders examine the contributions "grammatical choices, verb tense, and deictic elements" make to what they call "spatiotemporal identification" (2017). Rutger Allan, Irene de Jong, and Casper de Jonge start their discussion of spatial immersion in Homeric epic by considering epithets like "swift-footed" or "well-walled" (2017: 39). Rutger Allan urges attention to the "prepositions and adverbial phrases... that specify the spatial dimensions of the events" (2019b: 141; see also 2020: 22; cf. Webb 2020: 164). I continue this sort of granular analysis, exploring the *Iliad*'s settings, its moveable objects and its people, its treatment of changes of scene, and its myriad place names.

---

[1] Cf. Auyoung 2010; Edwards 1987: 85; S. Richardson 1990: 51; Ryan, Foote, and Azaryahu 2016: 19; Allan, de Jong, and de Jonge 2017: 48 n. 9; Oatley and Djikic 2018: 166; Minchin 2021a: 477.

Marie-Laure Ryan considers the immersive impact of describing a setting from the vantage point of a "moving body," be it an extradiegetic or intradiegetic figure (2015a: 87; cf. Ryan, Foote, and Azaryahu 2016: 30). We can focus on how the poet links, on the one hand, references to the movements of characters to, on the other hand, the buildings and city wall of Troy and the *Iliad*'s other settings (cf. Clay 2011: 38, 42) and on the contribution this practice makes to spatial immersion.

I look to *Iliad* 6 first (cf. Clay 2011: 39–41). Hector arrives (*hikanen*) at the Scaean gate and the oak tree (*pulas kai phēgon*) (6.237) where the women of Troy run (*theon*) to meet him to inquire about their menfolk (6.238–40). Next Hector arrives (*hikane*) at Priam's "exceedingly beautiful house (*domon*)" (6.242), and the poet notes one of its features that corresponds to Hector's entering from outside— the porticos (*aithousēisi*) (6.243). From here, the poet leaves Hector for a moment to detail the other arresting feature of this complex—its fifty rooms (*thalamoi*) for Priam's sons and their wives and fifty rooms (*thalamoi*) for Priam's daughters and their husbands (6.243–50). Just as Hector's arrival precedes the description of the palace, Hecuba's arrival at the palace (Graziosi and Haubold 2010: 149 at 252) follows it: "there (*entha*) his bountiful mother came (*ēluthe*) opposite him" (6.251). In response to Hector's enjoining her to try to appease Athena in her temple, Hecuba straightaway enters the palace (*molousa poti megar'*, 6.286) and then heads "into the fragrant storeroom" (ἐς θάλαμον κατεβήσετο κηώεντα, 6.288). Having gathered a peplos to dedicate to Athena, Hecuba departs (*bē d' ienai*) in the company of the old women of Troy who hasten along with her (*metesseuonto*, 6.296). This group arrives (*hikanon*) at the temple (*nēon*) of Athena on the acropolis (6.297), and Theano opens the temple doors (*thuras ōixe*, 6.298) to the group. We soon rejoin Hector who heads to Paris's palace (Ἕκτωρ δὲ πρὸς δώματ' Ἀλεξάνδροιο βεβήκει, 6.313). His arrival prompts a four-line digression on the history of the palace's construction—Paris built it with the best carpenters in Troy—its layout—an innermost chamber, an encompassing building, an outer courtyard (θάλαμον καὶ δῶμα καὶ αὐλήν)—and its proximity to Priam's palace and Hector's house at the city's most elevated spot (*akrēi*) (6.314–17). Hector enters (*eisēlthe*, 6.318) and finds Paris and Helen in the innermost chamber (*en thalamōi*, 6.321). After conversing with them, he departs for (*apebē*) and quickly (*aipsa*) arrives at (*ikane*) his own "pleasant house" (*domous eu naietaontas*) (6.369–70), a swift transition that brings out the proximity of the royals' homes. He fails to find Andromache inside (*en megaroisin*, 6.371) and, before heading out, stops on the threshold (ἔστη ἐπ' οὐδὸν ἰών, 6.375) to ask after his wife's whereabouts. Having learned from a maid that Andromache has gone to the wall of the city, Hector hastens away from his house (*apessuto dōmatos*, 6.390) and retraces his steps "along the same path" (6.391). He arrives (*hikane*) back where he started at the Scaean gate (*pulas*) (6.392–3). He is about to pass through it to head out to the plain when a running (*theousa*) Andromache meets him (6.393–4). When their conversation ends, Andromache departs homeward (*oikonde bebēkei*, 6.495) and quickly arrives (*aipsa...hikane*) at her "pleasant house" (*domous eu naietaontas*) (6.497). She encounters her maids within (*endothi*, 6.498). The narrator then turns to Paris, reporting that he "did not delay in his lofty house (*en hupsēloisi domoisin*)" (6.503) and detailing his rapid descent "from the highest point of the city (*akrēs*), Pergamus" (6.512).

That Hector retraces his steps suggests a main artery that runs from the gates to Priam's palace to Paris's house and then to Hector's house. But mental map making of the storyworld "through the simulation of characters' movements has its limits, because the visualizations produced by readers focus on individual scenes, and they do not easily coalesce into a global vision of narrative space" (Ryan 2015a: 92; cf. Ryan, Foote, and Azaryahu 2016: 75–100). As Jenny Strauss Clay observes, *Iliad* 6 allows us to "construct a general sketch of Troy's geography.... We cannot, however, draw a map of Ilium with any precision" (2011: 41). That said, the addition of a moving figure contributes to imageability: as an enactive approach to literary texts teaches (e.g., Grethlein and Huitink 2017, esp. 72; Huitink 2019: 183; 2020, esp. 200; Minchin 2021a: 478, 480, 483), mentally simulating a character's "volitional movements" (Kuzmičová 2012: 28) as they go in, out, and around a building or space helps one to imagine (and perhaps even feel oneself next to or in) that building or space. Just as this connection explains why in Lysias's *Against Eratosthenes* the speaker is able "to define the space of the crime through the movements of the characters" (Webb 2020: 166) and thereby fashions for recipients "a sense of being physically present within the scene" (167), the purposeful movements of the characters in *Iliad* 6 sharpen a recipient's mental images of the setting and thereby make their spatial immersion more likely.

What is more, the movements of the characters enhance our perception of the built environment's stability and solidity. I refer here to Elaine Scarry's discussion of how by endowing the people, places, and objects of a narrative with "solidity" authors bring about the following: those people, places, and objects come very near to possessing in our imaginations the "vivacity" and "vitality" of actually perceived entities (1995). A solid is something that "can bear our weight or impede our actual movement" (14). This imagined solidity emerges when one object (especially but not necessarily a transparent one) passes in front of or along or comes into contact with another object (especially one that is stationary): a painting slides down a wall, a shadow glides across a wall, a character puts a ring on their finger, a character holds a book. From this perspective, the repeated to-ing and fro-ing of the characters in *Iliad* 6 imparts a solidity and therefore vivacity and vitality to the structures that the characters approach, enter, and exit. These attributes enhance the possibility of a recipient's spatial immersion in the scenes that take place in the city of Troy.

The wall around the city acquires a marked degree of solidity too. The narrator's report that the Trojan elders sit on the tower (*hēnt' epi purgōi*) and watch as Helen comes along the tower (*epi purgon iousan*) point to the wall's solidity

(*Iliad* 3.153–4) (cf. Purves 2015: 91 on the preposition *epi* in *Iliad* 20.226). Andromache observes the Achaeans' attempts to find near the fig tree a weakness in the wall that encircles Troy: "three times their best came and probed it (*elthontes epeirēsanth'*) in that spot" (6.435). Her acknowledgment of the wall's weak point presumes that a city wall should be solid everywhere, but more conducive to imparting solidity to the city wall is our imagining the Achaeans coming up to and, in effect, poking around the unyielding wall. When Patroclus "three times tried to climb up the angle of the towering wall" (τρὶς μὲν ἐπ' ἀγκῶνος βῆ τείχεος ὑψηλοῖο, *Iliad* 16.702), the character's movement up the unmoving wall brings out the wall's solidity. Compare the way in which the wall of Achilles's tent gains solidity when the narrator says in *Iliad* 9, "He [Achilles] sat down (*hizen*) across from godlike Odysseus against the opposite wall (*toikhou*)" (9.218-19) and in *Iliad* 24, "He sat down (*hezeto*) on the intricately wrought couch, from where he had stood up (*anestē*), along the opposite wall (*toikhou*)" (24.597-8). The image of Achilles's body going down or up and down in front of the wall imparts solidity to the wall.

One can approach still other elements of the *Iliad*'s setting in the same way, noting the links between movement and solidity. I concentrate on the ground. The beach gains solidity because the priest Chryses walks along it (*bē…para, Iliad* 1.34) and because the Achaeans draw up their ship on it (*ep' ēpeiroio erussan*) when they come back from returning Chryseis to her father (*Iliad* 1.485). The Achaean meeting place gains solidity because speakers rise from a seated position when they wish to speak and sit back down on the ground when they finish talking (e.g., *Iliad* 1.58 (*anistamenos*), 1.68 (*hezeto*); 1.68 (*anestē*), 1.101 (*hezeto*)). When Achilles throws the scepter to the ground (*gaiēi, Iliad* 1.245) before he sits down (*hezeto*) after speaking (1.246), both actions bring out the solid nature of the ground. The battlefield gains solidity when a warrior leaps to the ground (*khamaze*) from his chariot (e.g., *Iliad* 3.29); the force of the impact even makes Diomedes's armor clash (*Iliad* 4.419-20). The battlefield also gains solidity when fatally wounded warriors fall on it (see Purves 2019: 40–1): Simoesios "fell to the ground in the dust" (ἐν κονίῃσι χαμαὶ πέσεν, *Iliad* 4.482); Thoön "fell down in the dust" (*en koniēisi / kappesen, Iliad* 13.548-9). The same effect arises when Deiphobos, struck in the arm by Meriones, drops Ascalaphos's helmet, and the narrator reports on the sound of the collision between helmet and ground: "on the ground falling it rang out" (*khamai bombēse pesousa, Iliad* 13.530). It gains solidity when, as the Achaeans march out to battle, the earth groans (*stenakhizeto gaia/erkhomenōn, Iliad* 2.784-5) and when the earth flows red with blood (*Iliad* 4.451, 8.65, 15.715, 20.494): the ground is not porous enough to absorb the liquid right away, and instead the flow of the liquid brings out the relative impermeability of the ground. The bank of the river Scamander gains solidity when Asteropaeus struggles in vain to free Achilles's spear from the earth (*Iliad* 21.174-8). The course (*dromos, Iliad* 23.758) for the foot race gains solidity when Odysseus lands on Oilean Ajax's footprints (*ikhnia tupte podessi*, 23.764). This link pertains to more than contact with the ground. When the Trojans flee Agamemnon, they speed "past the tomb (*par'...sēma*) of ancient Ilus, son of Dardanus, over the middle of the plain, past the wild fig tree (*par' erineon*)" (*Iliad* 11.166-7). The movement of the characters "past" (*para*) the tomb and the tree endow them with solidity.

I repeat the operative equation: The described movements impart solidity to some component of the setting. The solidity of the setting endows it with vivacy and vitality. The vivacity and vitality trigger a recipient's spatial immersion. I connect this analysis to an insightful discussion by Luuk Huitink. He examines *Iliad* 4.105-8, an account of how Pandarus shot an ibex with an arrow as it descended from a rock and fashioned a bow from its horns. Huitink brings out in two ways "how the rendition of bodily movement has a positive effect on visualization and on 'presence'" (2020: 201). He notes first how the passage "creates a sense of spatial vividness": "the passage makes manifest a spatial situation by emphasizing patterns of movement and orientation as they occur around the rock" (200). He then reflects on how the passage brings out "the solidity of the rock": "its solidity is apparent from the evident force which is needed for the ibex to launch itself off it and from the fatal blow when it crashes into it" (201). Huitink also comments on a quotation by Quintilian of a passage in which Cicero describes the end of a banquet (208-9; cf. 2019: 179-80, 182-3):

> The focus is first on the guests' exits and entrances..., which is likely to evoke a sense of the presence of walls and doors more vividly than an elaborate description of them could. The subsequent focus on the floor...gives the internal observer whose perception the reader simulates a solid surface virtually to stand on, which probably increases the sense of "presence".

Huitink uses these analyses to argue for an enactive approach to Homeric vividness (2020: 192), an approach to which I will return in the next section (6.3), but I note here his linking of both movement and solidity to "spatial vividness" and "presence," or what I am calling spatial immersion.

The *Iliad*'s movable objects and people require discussion from this perspective as well. Building on Roland Barthes's *l'effet de reél*, Ryan considers the impact of "concrete details" that "appear randomly chosen and deprived of symbolic or plot-functional importance" (2015a: 91). Such items are the opposite of Anton Chekhov's pistol on the wall that must eventually be fired (see Oatley 2012: 137; Grethlein 2017a: 59). These details function as a "place-constructing device" and enhance "the reader's sense of being there" (Ryan 2015a: 91). R. Allan finds an example in Lysias's *Against Eratosthenes* when Euphiletus and his men pick up torches from the nearest shop (24-6). The presence of the torches "is completely irrelevant to the legal case he wishes to make" (2022b: 295). One will be hard pressed to find an object in the Homeric poems to which critics have not imputed a symbolic or plot-functional importance (cf. Purves 2015: 82; Canevaro 2018: 40). I might nominate the spread of bar snacks that Hecamede lays out in Nestor's tent (*Iliad* 11.630–1). Instead of adding to this list, however, I yoke Ryan's mention of the way objects contribute to spatial immersion to Scarry's discussion of the solidity, and therefore vivacity and vitality, of objects and people in a storyworld.

Again, Scarry elucidates the effect of bringing two items into contact with one another. Her reading of a passage from Thomas Hardy's *Tess of the d'Urbervilles* can serve as an illustration (1995: 16):

> When Angel Clare deserts Tess to farm in Brazil, Tess places a ribboned ring next to her heart, then on her finger, in order to make Angel sensorially present, "to fortify herself in the sensation" of her connection to him (*Tess*, 312). We are instructed to brush our mental image of the ring against our mental image of Tess's breast and hand, and this light brush of image upon image inside the mind helps materialize both woman and ring in our imaginations.

Rings do not appear in the *Iliad*, but one can easily find analogous moments. Agamemnon "drew a sacrificial knife in his hand" (*erussamenos kheiressi makhairan*, *Iliad* 3.271 = 19.252). Diomedes "took a stone in his hand" (*khermadion labe kheiri*, *Iliad* 5.302 = 8.321 = 20.285). Hector sees Paris "handling his curved bow" (*agkula tox' haphaōnta*, *Iliad* 6.322). Hector "held his eleven-cubit spear in his hand" (*kheiri / egkhos ekh'*, *Iliad* 6.318–19 = 8.493–4). Nestor alone can easily lift (*aeirein*) his drinking cup when it is full (*Iliad* 11.636–7). Achilles "held his shield (*sakos*) away from himself in his stout hand (*kheiri*)" (*Iliad* 20.261). I list other passages in the *Iliad* wherein objects and people "materialize"—gain solidity and therefore vivacity and vitality—by coming into contact with another entity. Preparing the ship to return Chryseis to her father, Agamemnon picks out twenty men to serve as rowers, puts (*bēse*) a hecatomb in it, and makes Chryseis sit in (*heisen*) it too (*Iliad* 1.310–11); Odysseus mounts (*ebē*) the ship as leader of the expedition (1.311). Holding all these people and animals, the ship acquires solidity. When the warriors lean against their shields in a moment of respite from battle (*aspisi keklimenoi*, *Iliad* 3.135), the shields acquire solidity. A chariot materializes as it carries sacrificed lambs, Priam, and Antenor (*Iliad* 3.310–12). When Ajax "went back and forth on (*epōikheto*) the decks of the ships striding greatly" (*Iliad* 15.676), the decks' solidity emerges. Characters too can endow an object with solidity when they talk about it. Achilles speaks of the scepter he holds during the assembly in *Iliad* 1, imagining its initial creation from a tree: "the bronze stripped it of its leaves and bark" (1.237). The movement of the knife along the contours of the wood and the resistance of the leaves and bark implied by the need for the knife impart a solidity to both knife and wood. Scarry suggests that we believe an entity to be solid if a character asserts it to be solid (1995: 14–15).

Accordingly, Achilles's spear materializes in our mind when the arming Patroclus does not take it, "heavy, great, sturdy" (*brithu mega stibaron*), because he knows that he cannot wield (*pallein*) it (*Iliad* 16.141–2).

When a warrior dons his battle armor—from Paris (*Iliad* 3.328–38) to Diomedes and Odysseus (10.254–72) to Achilles (19.367–83)—he becomes more concrete. The narrator reports that Hector's shield struck against (*tupte*) his ankles and neck (*Iliad* 6.117–18) and later, "He [Ajax] grew tired in his left shoulder because he was always holding his gleaming shield steady" (16.106–7). Like Hardy's Tess, Hector's body and then Ajax's body become more real and substantial through this juxtaposition with a metal object—in this case, his shield (and, as Alex Purves notes, Ajax's shield itself acquires a weightiness, but one that realistically varies over time: it becomes heavier the longer Ajax has to hold it up (2015: 82; cf. Melissa Mueller 2016: 139–40)). The sweat that runs down (*ereen*) Ajax's body (*Iliad* 16.109–10) further concretizes the character; so too does the sweat that runs (*rheen*) down Eurypylus's head and shoulders (*Iliad* 11.811–12). Just as the aforementioned blood that flows on the ground brings out the solidity of the ground (see p. 163), blood stains the wounded Menelaus's "thighs and shapely lower legs and beautiful ankles beneath (*hupenerthe*)" (*Iliad* 4.146–7), and the progressive flow of the blood down his legs solidifies Menelaus's body. The same effect arises when waves slap against Diomedes and Odysseus and wash off the sweat from their bodies (κῦμα θαλάσσης ἱδρῶ πολλὸν / νίψεν ἀπὸ χρωτὸς, *Iliad* 10.574–5). The substance of a living mortal's body contrasts with the immateriality of a soul (*psukhē*). Achilles cannot grasp (*elabe*) Patroclus's soul, and it departs underground "like smoke (*kapnos*)" (*Iliad* 23.100–1; cf. *Odyssey* 11.204–22). Achilles materializes at this moment to the same degree that Patroclus's soul dematerializes.

For ancient audiences, and perhaps for modern ones as well, familiarity with the *Iliad*'s objects would also endow them with solidity. Spears, swords, axes, arrows, greaves, breastplates, helmets, cups, textiles, spits on which to roast meat, shuttles, and pin beaters—the appearance of objects such as these could trigger "sensual" and "tactile memories" (Barker 2009: 45–6). An adjective, such as "sharp" (e.g., *oxei*, *Iliad* 4.490), "stout" (e.g., *alkima*, *Iliad* 11.43), "smoothed" (e.g., *euxestōi*, *Iliad* 13.613), or "curved on each side" (e.g., *amphiguoisi*, *Iliad* 15.711), might jog one's memory by pointing up the care required to handle these items or highlighting their texture, but, even absent such a descriptor, ancient audience members would remember what it felt like to use these objects. Recalling their texture or weight in their hands or on other parts of their bodies, recipients would assign a marked degree of solidity to these storyworld objects.

The *Iliad* acknowledges the impermanence of objects (Canevaro 2018: 200–1; Ready 2019a: 34) and fixates on the fragmentation of the human body, so easily pierced, broken, or severed (W.-H. Friedrich 2003; E. Vermeule 1979: 96–9; van der Plas 2020; cf. Lather 2020: 284). Even so, the *Iliad*'s objects and people acquire a noticeable solidity. The storyworld becomes populated with solid objects and people just as solid objects populate our world. This feature of the storyworld, its apparent "ontological solidity" (Auyoung 2015: 583), makes it easier to imagine being in its spaces and places.

Another component of the *Iliad* that contributes to spatial immersion is the paucity of, to use the language of film making, cross-cuts, "a camera change to an entirely new visual scene" (Gerrig and Bezdek 2013: 107). Irene de Jong and René Nünlist highlight the poet's "general reluctance to introduce abrupt changes of scene. The unmitigated clash of two unrelated scenes is comparatively rare: smooth transitions from one scene to the next are the general rule" (2004: 73; cf. Peradotto 1990: 81; S. Richardson 1990: 117–18; Graziosi 2013: 21, 31). For instance, when the poet switches settings, he may travel alongside a character who goes between them (S. Richardson 1990: 54, 110–11; Edwards 2002: 53–4; de Jong and Nünlist 2004: 73). He frequently continues the tale by having a newly activated character in one place observe what has occurred in the place where we just were (S. Richardson 1990: 111–12; Edwards 2002: 54; de Jong and Nünlist 2004: 74; Lovatt 2013: 39–42). When he shifts from one part of the battlefield to another (e.g., *Iliad* 12.195–9), he uses the imperfect tense: "this form indicates that an action is conceived as continuing in the background while the poet focuses his attention on another part of the battlefield" (Clay 2011: 64; cf. 76, 93; de Jong 2007: 31). At least for a little while, we retain in our mind the scene (and its setting) that we have left behind. Even when the poet jumps from one setting to another—from, for instance, the Trojan camp to the Achaean camp or from Troy to the battlefield—he implements the shift in a manner that is neither "disruptive" nor "harsh" (S. Richardson 1990: 116, 118; cf. de Jong and Nünlist 2004: 74). Mark Edwards articulates the scholarly consensus: "Smoothly and almost uninterruptedly, action follows upon action, with continuity, not division, being always the poet's aim" (2002: 52; cf. Kozak 2017: e.g., 15, 112, 122, 136, 152–3, 213 on "continuity"). He even avers, "It is now clear that in actuality *there are no narrative breaks within the* Iliad *and the* Odyssey. Each is a seamless whole" (Edwards 2002: 58, emphasis in original).

Building on research into audience involvement in film, Richard Gerrig and Matthew Bezdek suggest that the absence of cross-cuts enhances "transportation" in movie audiences (2013: 107). Ed Tan et al. note how film editors aim for "smooth transitions of views of story world events across adjacent shots" and even try to obscure the transitions between shots (2017: 108–9, quotation from 108). In this way, they can generate a "fluency of experience" that "seems to ensure the feeling of being in the story world" (109). We can surmise that the *Iliad* poet's handling of changes of scene increases the probability of spatial immersion. Put simply, recipients do not feel as if they change place very often or do not find their attention drawn to the fact of a change of scene, and that sense of continuity enhances spatial immersion.

This section's final topic—place names—will see us pivot from discussing spatial immersion to discussing an essential antecedent to immersion writ large. Ryan comments on a reader's incidental response to the narrative's setting. She cites an example of a reader who claimed to be hooked by a reference to lilacs in a text: that put him in mind of his childhood home and prompted his spatial immersion in the narrative (2015a: 86–7; cf. Hogan 2018: 134). This sort of response is deeply personal, and one cannot predict which objects in a text will trigger a recipient's memories in such a manner; one cannot even predict which objects in a text will trigger one's own memories. The important point here is that spatial immersion does not require personal familiarity with the precise place in which the narrative unfolds. It is good to keep this point in mind as we consider the way place names contribute to (spatial) immersion.

Ryan contends that those who know the place where a narrative is set from personal experience will find such a setting most conducive to immersion because one can more easily imagine a place one has been (2015a: 89). Jans Eder, however, suggests that a story set in a place (and time) similar to the recipient's makes for "more automatic and less vivid reception" (2006: 72). Next on Ryan's list come the names of famous places that "we have heard of and dreamed about but never visited": because they can serve "as catalysts of desire," such names enable spatial immersion (2015a: 89–90; cf. LeVen 2014: 217–18). Ryan also argues for the immersive potential of "obscure real place names that stand for an entire category of nondescript provincial towns" (2015a: 91) and invented names that correspond to what we think a place in a certain part of the world would be named (91).

The *Iliad* unfolds in a place of which most recipients probably did not have first-hand experience: Troy (cf. Minchin 2008a: 26). Still, Troy was presumably well known as the setting of various tales—those whose performance traditions took place alongside the performance traditions of the Iliad and the Odyssey and written versions of which have come down to us as the Trojan-War portion of the Epic Cycle. Mt Olympus, the gods' abode, surely qualified as famous. Both sites may have served as "catalysts of desire" and thereby eased spatial immersion. I focus, however, on the contribution to immersion that the numerous references to places beyond Troy and Mt Olympus make. I ask after the way in which these place names aid the poet's efforts at world building, that essential prerequisite for immersing recipients.

One should pause over the abundance of place names in the poem and the diverse parts of the poem in which they appear (cf. Tsagalis 2012: e.g., 158–60). The audience regularly learns a character's place of origin right when or shortly after that character first appears. Agamemnon refers to his home in Argos (*Iliad* 1.30), and Achilles to his home in Phthia (*Iliad* 1.155). The narrator recalls that Nestor comes from Pylos (*Iliad* 1.252). The priest Chryses and his daughter Chryseis come from the town of Chryse (*Iliad* 1.431). I need not mention the plethora of points of origin detailed in the Catalogue of Ships and the catalogue of

Trojans in *Iliad* 2 (Sammons 2010: 136; Clay 2011: 117; Graziosi 2013: 30). The vignettes that accompany minor characters upon their deaths frequently refer to their homelands. Diomedes and Odysseus kill the two sons of Merops from Percote (*Iliad* 11.329). Aeneas kills Medon who lived in Phylace (*Iliad* 15.335). Ajax kills Hippothoös who came from Larisa (*Iliad* 17.301). Apisaon from Paeonia falls to Lycomedes (*Iliad* 17.350). That Locrian Ajax does not come from a specific town (Kramer-Hajos 2012: 91–2) serves as a rule proving exception: the omission or silence reminds us of just how often we learn of a character's place of origin. Characters situate anecdotes about the past in a place. Achilles speaks of the Achaeans' sack of Cilician Thebes (*Iliad* 1.366). Agamemnon recalls Tydeus's exploits in Thebes (*Iliad* 4.378) and the Argive army's encampment by the Asopus river (4.383). Glaucus begins and ends his account of his genealogy with the city of Ephyre (*Iliad* 6.152, 210) and also mentions Lycia (6.168) and the Aleian plain (6.201). Nestor places his defeat of Ereuthalion "beneath the walls of Pheia" (*Iliad* 7.135). His cattle rustling occurs in Elis (*Iliad* 11.673) and the subsequent battle by the city of Thryoessa (11.711). In that latter anecdote, he also mentions Arene (11.723) and Buprasium (11.756). Phoenix sets the story of Meleager in the city of Calydon (*Iliad* 9.530). Agamemnon sets the tale of Heracles's birth in Thebes (*Iliad* 19.99). Achilles places the petrified Niobe on Mt Sipylus (*Iliad* 24.615).

These place names aid the poet's efforts at creating a storyworld. Building such a world is a necessary step in creating an immersive narrative (Ryan 2019: 81) and is not solely the task of fiction writers (e.g., Alejandro Aranda 2016: 419–20; Ryan 2019: 62): whether we think about Homeric poetry as fiction or not is irrelevant (cf. section 1.2, p. 2). To repeat (cf. section 1.2, p. 1), storyworlds are "totalities that encompass space, time, and individuated existents that undergo transformations as the result of events" (Ryan 2019: 63). One can consider how the *Iliad*'s place names endow its storyworld with attributes of space and time.

Many of the *Iliad*'s place names would have been well known: Tsagalis can reasonably speak of "significant" or "important Greek place-names" (2012: 161). In some cases it seems that the poet chose to have a character come from a well-known place: he makes Patroclus originally from Opous perhaps because of its "prominence from the Early Iron Age onwards" (Kramer-Hajos 2012: 101). Of course, many real-world place names in the *Iliad* were not well known, but the sheer abundance of real-world place names increases the chance that some audience members would have heard of them. At the same time, if a place name was not well known, an epithet might at least make it sound real or familiar (cf. Dué 2019: 125–6). Idomeneus kills Phaestus from "deep-soiled" (*eribōlakos*) Tarne (*Iliad* 5.44). Tarne only occurs here, but the epithet *eribōlakos* endows Tarne with a sense of reality or familiarity because it occurs fifteen times in the *Iliad* and one time in the *Odyssey* in reference to other places, including Troy (e.g., *Iliad* 3.74). Obscurity marks many other place names. Margaretha Kramer-Hajos stresses the number of "unknown places in the Lokrian entry" in the Catalogue of

Ships (2012: 92): Calliarus, Bessa, Scarphe, Augeiai, Tarphe, and Thronion (*Iliad* 2.527–35). She means unknown to us today, but her implication seems also to be that they would have been "obscure" (93) and "unknown" (94) already to a later Greek audience. Other places mentioned in the Catalogue were "prominent exclusively in the Late Bronze Age" (91 n. 26), meaning that an Iron Age audience might not know anything about them or have even heard of them. Nevertheless, even these place names had the right ring to them: they sounded, I submit, in keeping with Ryan's idea about invented names, as place names should sound in the Greek world. Audiences would take for granted that they were real, imputing the same degree of reality to them as they imputed to place names they had heard.

Audiences would have been familiar with famous and not-so-famous real-world place names and would have assumed the reality of still other place names. As a result, each time they heard a place name that they took to refer to a real place, they would do what readers do today—namely, think that the *Iliad*'s storyworld "encompasses all of real-world geography" (Ryan 2019: 77). This conception of the storyworld would go a long way toward endowing it with a spatial dimension and joins with other elements that buttress this aspect of the poem's storyworld.

I note two of those elements. First, the "vertical axis" that runs from the depths of the ocean through the realm of mortals to Mt Olympus brings out the "vastness of the topography" (J. Porter 2015: 196–7; cf. Minchin 2008a: 25; Tsagalis 2012: 140–1). Second, the poet refers to the far-off geographic limits of the storyworld occupied by previous generations of gods—Iapetus and Cronus inhabit Tartarus at "the lowest boundaries (*ta neiata peirath'*) of the earth and the sea" (*Iliad* 8.478–81); Oceanus and Thetys live at "the boundaries (*peirata*) of the earth that nourishes many" (*Iliad* 14.200–1 = 14.301–2) (see Bergren 1975: 22–8)—and to the distant Ethiopians (*Iliad* 1.423, 23.206; cf. *Odyssey* 1.22–3): these references suggest that the storyworld "offers an inexhaustible space of discovery" (Ryan 2013: 143). This extension comes to the fore when contrasted with the more delimited space of the narrative's action in and around Troy, a space the gods can view all at once from their elevated perches (Purves 2010: 33, 58; Clay 2011: 3).

The poem's place names also provide opportunities to endow its world with temporality—that is, with a past and future. I refer the reader to Tsagalis's detailed exploration of this subject and his concluding remarks (2012: 257, my emphasis):

> Place-names are transformed from mere locations on a map into thematized spaces by means of which each hero's epic-mythical agenda is channeled into the *Iliad*. Phthia, Argos, Pylos, and Boeotian Thebes on the one hand, and the Troad and Lycia on the other are not just places linked to key figures of the plot. To a large extent, they constitute an integral part of the personalities of Achilles, Agamemnon, Nestor, Diomedes-Sthenelos, Hektor, Sarpedon, and Glaukos

respectively. Being embedded in typical dichotomies of κλέος and νόστος and praise and blame, geography is turned into space that represents each hero's "epic home," *the notional center around which his past, present, and future constantly evolve.*

I report here some representative passages that show how place names—beyond affirming the spatial dimensions of the storyworld—regularly accompany references either to states of affairs or events in the past that obtained or happened before the beginning of the *Iliad*'s own story or to future events that will transpire after the *Iliad*'s story ends. The poet does not just mention places but tells us or alludes to something that occurred in those places or something about life there. One could say that place names function as hooks on which the poet hangs references to the past and the future: the place names have a generative force (cf. Minchin 2008a, esp. 17, 27; Ready 2019a: 162). Or, following Ryan, one could say that setting a reference to a state of affairs or event in a specific, named place can make for a more vivid evocation of that state of affairs or event and so for a more vivid evocation of the past or future. Either way, the place names help impart a past and a future to the *Iliad*'s world.

Achilles declares of the Trojans, "For not yet ever did they drive away (*ēlasan*) my cattle or even horses, and not even ever in Phthia, deep-soiled and nurturer of men, did they destroy (*edēlēsant'*) the harvest, since much lies in between, shadowy mountains and echoing sea" (*Iliad* 1.154-7). He both stresses the physical distance between Troy and Phthia and alludes to a past in Phthia marked by a particular sort of interaction with others (or lack thereof) (cf. Tsagalis 2012: 172-3; cf. 234). Lemnos features in Hephaestus's tale of how at one point in the past (*ēdē...allot'* ("previously...at another time")) Zeus threw him from Olympus and he landed on Lemnos (*Iliad* 1.590-3; see Purves 2006). It is also the setting for Agamemnon's recollection of an Achaean feast in which the warriors boasted that they could each kill one hundred or two hundred Trojans (*Iliad* 8.229-34; see Kozak 2017: 85). In response to Agamemnon's recounting of Tydeus's feats among the Cadmeians, Sthenelus reminds him of his own generation's past heroics, "We even took (*heilomen*) the seat of seven-gated Thebes" (*Iliad* 4.406). The sole mention of Cyprus in the *Iliad* comes when the narrator details how Agamemnon obtained his corselet: because word of the Achaean expedition had reached Cyprus, its ruler, Cinyras, gave the corselet to Agamemnon as a guest gift (*Iliad* 11.19-23). The narrator reports that Othryoneus came from Cabesus and explains why: he had promised to expel the Achaeans from Troy in return for Cassandra's hand in marriage (*Iliad* 13.363-9). The narrator recounts Cheiron's giving Peleus a spear "from (*ek*) the peak of Pelion" (*Iliad* 16.143-4) (and so likely, per *Cypria* fragment 3 Bernabé (*eis to Pēlion*), giving it to him on Mt Pelion too during his wedding to Thetis). The narrator explains why Lycaon falls into Achilles's hands a second time: Achilles took him to Lemnos to sell as a slave; a certain Eëtion bought him and sent him to Arisbe on the Hellespont; from there Lykaon returned home (to Troy) (*Iliad* 20.40-4; see Kozak 2017: 193). The Catalogue of Ships in *Iliad* 2 provides numerous other examples. For instance, when the narrator tells us, "Of those who were holding (*eikhon*) Tricca and craggy Ithome and were holding (*ekhon*) Oechalia, city of Oechalian Eurytus, the leaders were in turn the two sons of Asclepius, good doctors, Podaleirius and Machaon" (*Iliad* 2.729-32), the imperfect verb forms indicate an enduring state of affairs in the past that persists into the present time of the war: these people have lived in these places for some time. The pleonastic phrasing "Oechalia, city of Oechalian Eurytus" can prompt one to recall stories about this king of an earlier generation: namely, his fateful challenge of Apollo to an archery contest (*Odyssey* 8.223-8) or Heracles's sack of Oechalia and decimation of Eurytus's children (Gantz 1996: 434-7, 457-8). All these passages join with myriad others to provide the *Iliad*'s storyworld with a past:[2] Antenor recollects hosting Menelaus and Odysseus when they came as emissaries to Troy (*Iliad* 3.205-24); the narrator describes the washing stations at which the Trojan women did their laundry "in the earlier time of peace before the sons of the Achaeans came" (22.156).

Place names also co-occur with reference to future events outside the *Iliad*'s own timeframe. The one reference to Aulis (*Iliad* 2.303) outside of the Catalogue of Ships (2.496) comes when Odysseus recollects in detail Calchas's prophecy: we go back into the past, but the prophecy itself—that the war will last for ten years—takes us into the future, and Odysseus subsequently urges the Achaeans to remain at Troy "until (*eis ho*) we take the great city of Priam" (2.332). The narrator describes Philoctetes "on holy Lemnos" and foresees his recall to Troy: "there he lay vexed: but soon (*takha*) the Achaeans by their ships were about to remember the lord Philoctetes" (*Iliad* 2.722-5). Hector anticipates Andromache's service as a slave in Greece after the Achaeans take Troy: "and being in Argos (*Argei*) you will weave at the loom of another woman and will carry water from Middle Spring (*Messēidos*) or Upper Spring (*Hupereiēs*)" (*Iliad* 6.456-7; see Kirk 1990: 221 at 456-7). In lamenting Patroclus, Achilles refers to Neoptolemus's growing up (*trephetai*) on the island of Scyrus (*Iliad* 19.326, 332): this mention can remind the audience of how, after Achilles's death, Odysseus will retrieve Achilles's son from Scyrus and bring him to fight at Troy (*Odyssey* 11.509; Proclus *Little Iliad* argumentum 10-11). These passages accompany the many others that refer to a future beyond the events of the *Iliad*, from the singular references to the destruction of the Achaean wall (*Iliad* 12.3-35; J. Porter 2011; Garcia 2013: 104-10) and the survival of Aeneas (*Iliad* 20.307-8; Marks 2010; Kozak 2017: 190) to the

---

[2] Cf. Grethlein 2006; de Jong 2007: 20-3; Turkeltaub 2010; C. Mackie 2013: 3-8; Kozak 2017: e.g., 8, 27, 29, 66, 83, 188-9, 211; Zanker 2019: 66.

numerous references to the death of Achilles (Burgess 2009) and the sack of Troy (Garcia 2013: 120–9; C. Mackie 2013: 8–13).

Kramer-Hajos points to "the impression of historical accuracy" with which the Catalogue of Ships endows the *Iliad* (2012: 93). I would inflect an interpretation of the myriad place names in the Catalogue and throughout the poem a bit differently: they enable the building of a storyworld, a storyworld in which to immerse recipients.

## 6.3. Spatio-Temporal Immersion

Introducing the category of spatio-temporal immersion, Ryan writes, "One of the most variable parameters of narrative art is the imaginative distance between the position of narrator and addressee and the time and place of the narrated events. Spatio-temporal immersion takes place when this distance is reduced to near zero" (2015a: 93). She then suggests that "the sense of presence" is greatest when readers feel themselves "actively in the scene" (95). She sees this factor at work in, for instance, Flaubert's description of Emma Bovary: "her poor hands picked at the sheets in the ghastly and poignant way of the dying, who seem impatient to cover themselves with their shrouds." Ryan suggests, "When the reader reaches this point she is no longer a passive observer but emulates (or simulates) Emma's gesture from a first-person enactive perspective. Some readers may unconsciously stretch their fingers and try to bring a sheet over their face when reading this passage." We come upon one manifestation of a phenomenon that Peter Dixon and Marisa Bortolussi query when measuring a participant's transportation into a narrative: "I felt as if I was experiencing the events of the story world personally" (2017: 206).

Researchers speak here of motor resonance—"the automatic activation of the human motor system during action perception" (Huitink 2020: 193)—and note that motor resonance occurs not only when we watch someone do something but also when we imagine or read about someone doing something.[3] Because motor resonance "is immediate and pre-reflective," a text that generates such a response "*seems* vivid" (Cave 2016: 81, emphasis in original). Motor resonance makes a critical contribution to an immersive experience: indeed, "descriptions that draw on cognitive effects are likely to be more powerfully immersive for the reader than those that don't."[4]

---

[3] Speer et al. 2009: 989; Gallese and Wojciehowski 2011; Sanford and Emmott 2012: 141–50, 159; Kuzmičová 2013: 114; Cave 2016: 29; Grethlein 2017a: 36–7, 51; 2021a: 16–18, 228; Kuiken and Douglas 2017: 229; Douglass 2018: 108–9; cf. van Krieken, Hoeken, and Sanders 2017 on "embodied identification."
[4] Cave 2016: 81; cf. Kuzmičová 2013: 116; Grethlein and Huitink 2017: e.g., 77; Huitink 2019: 183; Minchin 2021a: 479; Grethlein 2021a: 18.

Motor resonance kicks in even when we watch or hear or read about someone doing something that we have not done ourselves because we still have some familiarity with the fundamental components of their actions. A spectator who rarely exercises can experience motor resonance while watching a professional basketball player or a professional figure skater (Esrock 2018: 190–1). Moviegoers feel a chase scene in their bodies even if they have not pursued a criminal or run for their lives lately or ever (Barker 2009: 108–9). I have never been kicked in the ribs by an attacker, but I can join Rita Felski in "flinching with Bond as he receives a hard kick in the ribs from Goldfinger" (2020b: 110). Considering a scene from one of the Harry Potter novels, Antony Sanford and Catherine Emmott posit that motor resonance arises not because readers will have flown on broomsticks but because the passage deploys "strong action descriptions (*swung his right leg*), and indications of forces required to make movements (*kicked off hard from the ground*)" (2012: 156, emphasis in original). Terence Cave sees a possibility for motor resonance in the description of Nemours in Madame de Lafayette's *La Princesse de Clèves* as he steps over a seat: "They will experience it even if they have never themselves stepped over an antique item of French furniture, since our muscles know in advance what it feels like to step over an obstacle" (2016: 117). Huitink works with the same assumption when, citing a scholion on the description of Capaneus in Euripides's *Phaethon* as he climbs a ladder in the battle for Thebes, he sees the possibility for motor resonance in Euripides's verses: "the scholiast may have virtually projected himself in the position of Capaneus in an act of bodily *mimesis*, having a 'felt' understanding of what it means slowly to move upwards with a shield above one's head" (2020: 203). Now, one, some neuroscientists study specialized activities and the differences in motor resonance between experts, interested non-experts (fans), and novices; and, two, other literature looks at how differences and similarities between actor and observer can affect motor resonance (Makris and Cazzato 2020; cf. Olsen 2017: 153–4). I do not think it necessary to go down that rabbit hole because, regarding issue one, the discussion that follows concerns common actions and because it is not possible to track issue two when it comes to the reception of Homeric epic.

Investigators take different positions on whether motor resonance rises to a noticeable level (cf. Grethlein and Huitink 2017: 72 n. 34). I pick out some of those who argue for a felt experience (cf. Huitink 2019: 179). Moniek Kuijpers and David Miall find that recipients "experience the bodily sensations...described in the story as if they were their own" (2011: 172). As an example of "a level of muscular activity that is not only amenable to self-report, but draws instant attention of the reader to itself," Anežka Kuzmičová proposes, "although in reading '[Pooh] stood on a chair, and took down a very large jar of honey from the top shelf',...the reader never maintains the belief that she has moved herself, she can still experience the coming into being of Winnie-the-Pooh's clumsy power grip as the bear is getting hold of the jar" (2012: 32; cf. 2013: 115). Sanford and

Emmott consider which sorts of passages are liable to produce some degree of felt motor resonance and nominate the aforementioned scene from a Harry Potter novel in which Harry flies on a broomstick (2012: 155–60). Cave looks for "a bodily gesture that attentive readers will experience as a motor reflex" (2016: 117) and finds an illustrative example in Joseph Conrad's *Lord Jim*: "Everyone can imagine Jim's leap: you feel it in your bones, in your muscles" (124; cf. 134). Marco Caracciolo posits "full-fledged bodily feelings that are felt not only through but *in* the reader's own body" (2018: 13, emphasis in original) and "conscious feelings of participating in storyworlds and engaging with characters' bodies" (27; cf. Kukkonen and Caracciolo 2014: 265). Note again that words as well as sights trigger these responses: it is not just watching, for instance, the mountain climber in the movie *127 Hours* as he extracts himself from the boulder under which he is partially trapped that triggers felt motor resonance (M. Smith 2017: 100–1). For Cave, these sensations are one reason why we read (2016: 120).

Many passages in the Homeric epics seem capable of prompting motor resonance that rises to the level of felt experience. Scholarship in classical studies offers precedents for this claim. Huitink's analysis of some passages from the *Iliad* points in this direction: he speaks of our having "an experiential, felt understanding of the force of the ibex's jump [*Iliad* 4.105–8]" (2020: 201); "when the perspective next shifts to Eumelos, who is aware of the horses breathing down his neck [*Iliad* 23.375–81], a vivid 'echo' of this familiar sensation based on their own experiential background may be triggered in attentive readers (as well as, fleetingly, an urge to look behind themselves)" (202–3). Likewise, the Watchman's declaration in Aeschylus's *Agamemnon* that he lies on the roof "resting on the elbows (*agkathen*), like a dog" (3) "would have activated the sensorimotor regions of the brain in the spectator.... Many of them would have felt a twinge of unease, shifted their position, and felt a degree of sensory empathy to his discomfort.... We feel his discomfort" (Meineck 2018: 193–4). The "sensorimotor verbs" used to describe the Sophoclean Ajax's slaughter of livestock "primarily act on the audience's bodies, inviting them to experience what it 'feels like' to perform this violent action" (Angelopoulou 2020: 56). The reader of the imperial-era Aretaeus might find their own body moving in unexpected ways when confronted with descriptions of bodies misshapen and contorted by illness (Gleason 2020). A reperformance of Pindar's *Paean* 6 at a symposium could trigger in audiences "somatic memories," or an "embodied remembrance," of watching and performing in a chorus (Olsen 2020: 336–7), and, with their "figures of chorality and scenes of music making," Euripides's later choral odes could produce an "embodied involvement" on the part of theatergoers trained in and familiar with choral dance (Weiss 2018a: 236–8; cf. Frost 2002: 260, cited by Barker 2009: 75–6). Indeed, the diversity of archaic- and classical-era Greek texts that explicitly posit an experience of felt motor resonance among spectators of choral dance (Olsen 2017, speaking of "kinesthetic empathy") gives yet further impetus to this sort of inquiry as does Heliodorus's depiction of Charicleia moving her feet as she watches Theagenes's footrace from the sideline (*Ethiopian Story of Theagenes and Charicleia* 4.3.3): "a textbook illustration of an embodied response" (Grethlein 2017a: 115–17, quotation from 117). I now consider some examples from the *Iliad* that pertain to movements likely familiar to recipients and likely capable of provoking felt motor resonance.

Characters give objects to someone else: Diomedes gives Odysseus the spoils he stripped from Dolon (*en kheiressi'...tithei*, *Iliad* 10.529); Achilles gives Antilochus half a talent of gold (*en khersi tithei*, *Iliad* 23.797). Characters put things down: Thetis puts down new armor in front of Achilles (*kata...ethēke*, *Iliad* 19.12); Achilles puts down the armor of Sarpedon as a prize for the duel with spears in Patroclus's funeral games (*kata.../ thēk'...kata*, 23.798–9; cf. 23.700, 23.851). Recipients will know what it feels like to give something to someone or to put something down. Warriors grab things with their hands: Diomedes grabbed a rock (*labe kheiri*, *Iliad* 5.302 = 8.321 = 20.285); Hector grabbed the scepter (*en khersi...labe*, *Iliad* 10.328); Automedon grabbed a whip (*kheiri labōn*, *Iliad* 19.396). Warriors push: Achilles pushed (*ōse*) his sword back into his scabbard (*Iliad* 1.220); Pelagon pushed (*ōse*) the spear out of Sarpedon's thigh (5.694); Menelaus pushed (*ōsato*) Adrastus away (6.62). Grabbing something or pushing something that requires a push will be familiar sensations. Warriors throw their spears—Paris hurls (*proïei*) his spear at Menelaus (*Iliad* 3.346; see also, e.g., 5.15, 5.290, 7.249)—and, more specifically, warriors balance and then hurl their spears: "He [Menelaus] spoke and balancing it he let fly (*ampepalōn proïei*) his spear that casts a long shadow" (*Iliad* 3.355; see also 5.280, 7.244, 11.349, 17.516, 20.438, 22.273, 22.289). A recipient need not have thrown a spear in battle to experience motor resonance. One is likely familiar with getting ready to throw something and then throwing it, with winding up and then letting it go. A warrior regularly extracts his spear from a victim by holding the body down with his foot: "and he [Ajax] stepping on him with his foot (*lax prosbas*) drew the bronze spear from the corpse" (*Iliad* 5.620–1; see also 6.64–5, 16.503–4, 16.862–3; cf. 13.618–19). Recipients may not have performed this maneuver themselves, but they probably understand the need to use a foot to generate sufficient leverage when pulling one thing out of another.

One could extend this list by citing singular events, such as the moment when Oilean Ajax slips and falls (*olisthe*) in the footrace in *Iliad* 23 (23.774), but I move on to the observation that, befitting their interest in routine moments from daily life, similes can prompt motor resonance. We deflect flies as does the mother in the simile at *Iliad* 4.130–1 (*eergēi*). We have destroyed sandcastles as does the child in the simile at *Iliad* 15.362–4 (*sunekheue*). The precise movements of the skilled weaver in the simile at *Iliad* 23.760–3 would be familiar to weavers in the audience. The simile at *Iliad* 23.431–3 comparing the distance traversed by Antilochus's and Menelaus's horses to the distance a man hurls a discus "triggers a strong resonance in the recipient" (Grethlein and Huitink 2017: 79). In fact, because similes comprise both a vehicle portion and a tenor, the "as" portion and the relevant part of the narrative proper, respectively (Ready 2011: 4; 2018: 24–5, 72), they frequently provide an opportunity for a specific motor resonance twice (or even three times) over in repeating key terms. Athena's deflecting (*eergen*) Pandarus's arrow prompts the comparison to the mother's deflecting flies (*eergēi*) (*Iliad* 4.130–1). Idomeneus stands fast (*emen*' and *menen*) against the approaching Aeneas just as a boar stands fast (*menei*) against a cordon of hunters (*Iliad* 13.471–6). Antilochus springs at (*eporouse* and *epi… thor*') the fallen Melanippus as a dog darts at (*epi… aixēi*) a wounded fawn (*Iliad* 15.579–82). Having speared Thestor through the mouth, Patroclus drags (*helke*) him out of his chariot just as a fisherman (we supply the main verb for the vehicle portion of the simile: "drags") a fish. The simile's resumptive clause returns us to the narrative proper: "so he dragged (*heilk*') him from the chariot" (*Iliad* 16.406–9). As the Trojans and Achaeans tug (*heilkeon*) here and there Patroclus's corpse, they resemble men tugging a hide to stretch it out (*tanuein…tanuousi…helkontōn, tanutai*) (*Iliad* 17.389–95; see Edwards 1991: 31). Motor resonance, then, can arise in response to actions in the *Iliad*'s story and to actions described on the level of the discourse in similes' vehicle portions (see Ready 2011: 95).

A comparable engagement with inanimate objects seems likely. As I noted earlier (p. 175), Huitink finds a cue for motor resonance in the jump of an ibex, and it is only one more step to motor resonance triggered by an object. Moreover, as I mentioned in section 2.2 (p. 18), Ellen Esrock argues that the reader can "inhabit inanimate objects and other unnatural positions within the narrative" (2019: 284). Before I look at specific passages, I review features of the Homeric depiction of objects that prepare a recipient for this experience.

First, metaphor grants objects human capabilities (Canevaro 2018: 24; Grethlein 2020: 468–9). Arrows leap from bows (*oistoi / thrōiskon*, *Iliad* 15.314–15), just as Hector leaps from his chariot (*thore*, *Iliad* 8.320). Odysseus's bow sings (*aeise*, *Odyssey* 21.411), just as the Ithacan bard Phemius sings to the suitors (*aeide*, *Odyssey* 1.325–6). Second, similes compare people to objects (Scully 1990: 58–9; Canevaro 2018: 233–4, 254–5). Poseidon renders Alcathous unable to move: in his paralyzed state, Alcathous resembles a pillar (*stēlēn*, *Iliad* 13.437). Ajax strikes Hector with a stone and the Trojan spins around "like a top (*strombon*)" (*Iliad* 14.413). The Achaeans form up in battle "like a wall" (*purgēdon*, *Iliad* 15.618). As they wrestle, Odysseus and Ajax resemble rafters (*ameibontes*) fitted together by a carpenter (*Iliad* 23.711–13). When Athena beautifies Odysseus, she resembles a craftsman who gilds silver with gold (*Odyssey* 6.232–5, 23.159–62). Whether similes involve some degree of blending (Dancygier and Sweetser 2014: 145; R. Allan 2020: 25 n. 44) or tenor and vehicle remain "conceptually separate and distinct" (Cruse 2008: 140), we interpret the simile by tracing overlaps and commonalities. We relax the distinction between man and object and ask in what ways the two are alike.

Third, the gods have or live among objects that act of their own accord, and the Phaeacians possess ships that know how to get places by themselves. Ordinary mortals do not interact with such objects (Grethlein 2020: 468), but one telling passage suggests that they do enliven the figures depicted on objects. The disguised Odysseus describes the brooch ostensibly worn by the real Odysseus: the deer on Odysseus's brooch "eager (*memaōs*) to escape was struggling (*ēspaire*) with its feet" (*Odyssey* 19.231; cf. Canevaro 2018: 105). Furthermore, when Hephaestus crafts the various scenes on Achilles's new shield, the narrator describes the movements of the people and animals in those scenes (Purves 2010: 46; Canevaro 2018: 224). Among mortals, only Achilles seems capable of viewing the scenes on the shield (*Iliad* 19.12–19), but there is no implication that the figures on the shield move only in Hephaestus's workshop: one imagines that Achilles finds the figures on the shield come alive as he gazes on them (*leussōn*, 19.19; cf. Cullhed 2014: 194). To the extent that objects exhibit animation, the boundary between animate human and inanimate object attenuates.

Fourth, Homeric characters have intimate connections with objects. One can speak of an entangled object. An entangled object has a history, a "relationship to past and present owners...a biography" (Whitley 2013: 399; cf. Canevaro 2018: 125): examples include Achilles's armor that Hector strips from Patroclus and Odysseus's boar tusk helmet (Whitley 2013: 399–400). That objects have biographies renders them human-like to the extent that mortal characters (and audience members) are defined by others and define themselves in part by their biographies. Or one can stress characters' entanglement with objects. From this perspective, "the dichotomy of active subject vs passive object breaks down and is replaced by an entanglement of humans with things that precedes and even contributes to the constitution of the subject" (Grethlein 2020: 475). Grethlein charts Odysseus's entanglements with his bow, his bed, and his orchard in the *Odyssey*: their appearances in scenes in which Odysseus reveals himself and is recognized by others show that "a person is defined not so much in itself and as a subject in opposition to objects but rather in and through his interaction with things" (2020: 9; cf. Zeitlin 2018: 66). These entanglements weaken or even breach the barrier between man and object.

Fifth, scholars progress from entanglement to the agency of objects. Homerists grant Homeric objects varying degrees of agency (see Whitley 2013; Purves 2015; Canevaro 2018: 18–21; Grethlein 2020): the objects have as much agency as humans; objects have "secondary agency": humans endow objects with agency; or, the most conservative option, objects have agency if we set aside questions of intention and intended use and understand agency as prompting a change of some kind. To the extent that objects have agency, however we understand the term agency, they become human-like because we think of agency as an attribute of humans.

Sixth and finally, in keeping with research suggesting that we can register something that happens to an external object as if it happens to our own bodies (M. Smith 2017: 75–6), Homeric scholarship attends to the blending of man and object. Ajax and his armor function as the paradigmatic example of how "it is difficult to extricate the man from the object" (Canevaro 2018: 23–5, 54, 97, 132, quotation from 23). Odysseus tells Eumaeus of his escape from a ship moored off Ithaca (*Odyssey* 14.339–59). His swim to shore "recalls a ship's oars cutting through water," and "he becomes both man and material" (Canevaro 2018: 141).

Against this backdrop, one can reimagine audience response to the movements of objects. We will find the following. Objects and characters can perform the same actions. These equivalences remind us, if reminding is needed, that recipients too can perform those actions. Accordingly, recipients can experience motor resonance in response to an object's actions, especially because they are listening to or reading poetry in which the boundary between man and object routinely blurs.

Objects fall (*ekpiptō*) to the ground, including a sword (*Iliad* 3.363), a bow (*Iliad* 8.329, 15.465), a torch (*Iliad* 15.421), arrows (*Iliad* 21.492), and a *kerkis* (*Iliad* 22.448). Fatally wounded warriors fall (*ekpiptō*) to the ground (see Purves 2019: 40–1), including Mydon and Asius (*Iliad* 5.585 = 13.399; see also 11.179). Arrows leap (*thrōskon*, *Iliad* 15.313–14; see also 16.773); the same verb applies several times to warriors (e.g., *Iliad* 8.252, 8.320; see Kokolakis 1981: 107). The arrow with which Pandarus strikes Menelaus leaps from his bow (*alto*, *Iliad* 4.125); warriors routinely leap to the ground from their chariots (e.g., *alto* at *Iliad* 3.29), and one can add that Hector leaps against Achilles (*oimēse*, *Iliad* 22.140) just as Odysseus leaps against the suitors' relatives (*oimēsen*, *Odyssey* 24.538; see Purves 2019: 93). A spear flies from a hand (*apo kheiros orousen*, *Iliad* 13.505 = 16.615) just as men jump from chariots (*apo pantes orousan*, *Iliad* 12.83). Patroclus's helmet rolls on the ground (*kulindomenē*, *Iliad* 16.794); Priam rolls on the ground in his grief (*kulindomenos*, *Iliad* 22.414, 24.640) as does Menelaus (*kulindomenos*, *Odyssey* 4.541; cf. *Odyssey* 10.499).

I focus, however, on moments in which one object encounters another entity (besides the ground). When describing a warrior in combat, the poet frequently traces the path of his weapon (cf. de Jong and Nünlist 2004: 78). These are not simply clinical descriptions (e.g., Arnaud 2019: 39–42): they offer further opportunity for a felt experience; they may even be there to trigger such an experience. Again, I list passages in which objects do things and parallel passages in which characters do those same things.

- Weapons pass through armor and body parts: Menelaus's spear "went through" Paris's shield (*dia...ēlthe*, *Iliad* 3.357 = 7.252 = 11.435); Tlepolemus's spear point "sped through" Sarpedon's thigh (*diessuto*, *Iliad* 5.661; cf. 15.542); Deïphobus's spear "held its way through" Ascalaphus's shoulder (*di'...eskhen*, *Iliad* 13.519–20 = 14.451–2). The Achaeans go through the trench in front of their camp (*dia... ebēsan, Iliad* 8.343 = 15.1). Nestor hastens through the trench too (*diessuto, Iliad* 10.194; cf. 22.460, *Odyssey* 4.37). After killing Dolon, Odysseus and Diomedes go through "the armor and black blood" (*batēn... dia, Iliad* 10.469). Odysseus is the first of many fighters to go through the front ranks (*bē... dia, Iliad* 4.495). An undetected Odysseus goes among the Phaeacians (*erkhomenon... dia spheas, Odyssey* 7.40). The verb *peraō* describes the course of a weapon— for instance, Odysseus's spearhead "drove through (*perēsen*) the other temple" (*Iliad* 4.502; see also 4.460, 5.291, 6.10)—and the movements of characters—for instance, the Trojans were "eager to cross (*perēsemenai*)" the Achaean trench (*Iliad* 12.200).

- Hector's helmet checks Diomedes's spear (*erukake, Iliad* 11.352; cf. 20.268 = 21.165; 21.594). The simple verb *erukō* and the compound *aperukō* regularly describe characters' actions: the narrator reports that "no one could hold him [Hector] back (*erukakoi*)" (*Iliad* 12.465); Thoas urges his fellow Achaeans to see if they can stop Hector (*eruxomen, Iliad* 15.297); Idaeus holds still horses and mules (*erukōn, Iliad* 24.470); Menelaus wishes that Athena would "keep away" the enemies' spears (*aperukoi, Iliad* 17.562); Odysseus tells the beggar Irus to keep away the pigs and dogs (*aperukōn, Odyssey* 18.105).
- Ajax's spear strikes Archelochus in the neck (*ebalen, Iliad* 14.465; cf. 5.17). Characters typically strike one another with weapons (e.g., *Iliad* 3.347 (*balen*)), but they can use their fists too: Epeius strikes Euryalus (*kopse, Iliad* 23.690); Odysseus and Irus strike one another (*ēlase... elassen, Odyssey* 18.95-6).
- Peiros hits Diores with a rock, and the rock "crushed" (*apēloiēsen*) the bones in his leg (*Iliad* 4.522). The uncompounded verb describes Althaea's smiting the earth with her hand (*aloia, Iliad* 9.568).
- The rock with which Diomedes hits Aeneas in the hip joint "pushed away (*ōse d' apo*) the skin" (*Iliad* 5.308), and Hector's spear "pushed out" Coeranus's teeth (*ek.../ ōse, Iliad* 17.617-18). As I noted earlier (p. 176), Achilles's pushes his sword into his scabbard (*ōse, Iliad* 1.220); Pelagon pushes a spear out of Sarpedon's thigh (*ek... ōse, Iliad* 5.694); and Menelaus pushes away Adrastus (*apo hethen ōsato, Iliad* 6.62).
- Iphidamas cannot get his spear through Agamemnon's war belt: "the spear point met (*antomenē*) the silver and was bent like lead" (*Iliad* 11.237). The verb *antomai* describes warriors meeting one another in battle (*antesth', Iliad* 15.698).
- The tip of Polypoites's spear breaks apart Damasus's skull (*rhēx', Iliad* 12.185; cf. 16.310, 20.399). Epeius boasts that he will "break apart the skin" of his opponent in a boxing match (*rhēxō, Iliad* 23.673). The Trojans aim to break apart the Achaean wall (e.g., *rhēgnusthai, Iliad* 12.257).
- The tip of Thrasymedes's spear smashes the bones of Maris's upper arm (*araxe, Iliad* 16.324). Again, Epeius's boast provides the parallel: "I will smash his bones together" (σύν τ᾽ ὀστέ᾽ ἀράξω, *Iliad* 23.673).

- Aeneas's spear shakes when it lands in the ground (*kradainomenē*, *Iliad* 13.504 = 16.614), and Hector's spear shakes in Aretus's mid-section (*kradainomenon*, *Iliad* 17.524). Characters shake spears (*kradaōn*, *Iliad* 7.213, 13.583, 20.423; *Odyssey* 19.438). A spear stuck in the ground can quiver (*pelemikhthē*, *Iliad* 16.612, 17.528), and the same verb can bring out the stumbling of a retreating warrior (*pelemikhthē*, *Iliad* 4.535 = 5.626 = 13.148).
- Teucer's arrow "fell upon" Cleitus's neck (*empesen*, *Iliad* 15.451; cf. 4.217). Achilles urges Patroclus to "fall upon" the Trojans (*empes'*, *Iliad* 16.81).
- Peneleos's sword "entered into" Lyco's neck (*eisō edu*, *Iliad* 16.340; cf. 21.117–18). When Ajax protects Teucer, the narrator claims that Teucer "would go to (*dusken / eis*) Ajax; and he would hide him with his shining shield" (*Iliad* 8.271–2). One can "go into" one's armor (*es teukhea dunte*, *Odyssey* 22.201, 24.498; cf. *Iliad* 10.254, 10.272) or enter the house of Hades (δῦναι δόμον Ἄιδος εἴσω, *Iliad* 3.322; see also 7.131, 11.262).
- Patroclus hurls a stone at Cebriones: it "dashed together (*sunelen*) both brows" (*Iliad* 16.740). The verb describes Odysseus's gathering up the cloak and fleeces he slept on (*sunelōn*, *Odyssey* 20.95).
- Rocks "struck" against shields (*estuphelixan*, *Iliad* 16.774). Andromache imagines someone beating Astyanax out of a feast (*estuphelixe*, *Iliad* 22.496; cf. *Odyssey* 17.234).

In all these cases, recipients can experience motor resonance in response to the object's action.

The actions of the object in this list can make the recipient feel something, but the fragmentation of the victim's body that the object causes can also trigger motor resonance. Consider Xavier Aldana Reyes's discussion of "somatic empathy" and "sensation mimicry" among viewers of horror films (2016: 167–78). Viewers feel in their own bodies the meticulously depicted mutilation and destruction of the on-screen body, even if they know nothing about the character other than that they are under threat. One point of watching horror movies is to have this visceral physical engagement with the victim's body (166, 176, 184). Recipients have the same experience as they encounter the fragmentation of the *Iliad*'s bodies. As close-ups depict skin ripping and teeth and bones shattering, recipients feel it in their own bodies. This response does not require any sort of prior knowledge of or connection to the character: broken victims, such as Coeranus or Maris mentioned in the preceding list, are often new to the tale. I also follow Aldana Reyes in suggesting that, like viewers of horror, many of the *Iliad*'s recipients desire the physical stimulation these scenes offer. At the very least, that an object's action can register somatically and that what happens to the patient, the one the object meets, can register somatically—that I can feel as if I am smashing and/or being smashed—explains in part why the *Iliad*'s scenes of bodily destruction merit labels like "unforgettable" and "popular" (E. Vermeule 1979: 97–8).

To sum up, when we join descriptions of objects in action together with the descriptions of characters in action, we find an abundance of opportunities for recipients to experience felt motor resonance. This phenomenon enables their spatio-temporal immersion in the storyworld. If one is skeptical of the notion of felt motor resonance, one should still recognize the immersive effect generated by motor resonance (even if it is not felt): it makes our experience of the *Iliad* more vivid (again, e.g., Cave 2016: 81; Grethlein and Huitink 2017; Minchin 2021a).

Ryan also proposes that spatio-temporal immersion occurs when recipients see and hear what a character sees and hears (cf. Brosch 2017: 263–5). She comments on a passage from James Joyce's "Eveline" in which the title character looks out the window (2015a: 95):

> The reader does not watch a narrator watching Eveline watch the street through the window but, by virtue of the transitivity of the representation of mental processes, directly perceive Eveline's perception. Through identification with the body of Eveline, the reader gains a solid foothold on the scene, as well as a sensory interface to the textual world.

Classicists may wish to speak in this context of internal (embedded) focalization. Rutger Allan provides a detailed analysis of the immersive effects of having Hermes serve as focalizer when he arrives at Calypso's cave in *Odyssey* 5.58–76 (2019a: 70–3; cf. Haller 2007: 89–99). Ruth Webb notes the impact of the "restricted focalization" in Lysias's *Against Eratosthenes* when Euphiletus relates how he and his helpers "saw" (*eidomen*, 24) the adulterer, Eratosthenes: it prompts "the listener to visualize and place themselves in the speaker's place at the moment in question" (2020: 162–3, quotation from 162; cf. 2016: 213). Analyzing the *paedagogus*'s (false) report in Sophocles's *Electra* of how Orestes died in a crash during a chariot race, Jonas Grethlein points to the speaker's depiction of the final moments of the crash through the "lens" of the race's spectators: "the internal spectators...give the recipients an anthropocentric point of reference vis-à-vis the objects located in space and thereby help to draw them into the narrated action" (2021a: 59–60; cf. 2013: 34–6, 41–2, 54–64, 123, 302). Similarly, although not speaking explicitly of internal focalization, Peter O'Connell studies how orators place "internal audiences" in the scenes they describe in order to "encourage the jurors...to imagine sharing the experience of these internal audiences and to imitate their emotions and reactions": this merging of perspectives, a "shared spectatorship," turns the jurors into witnesses of the described scene (2017b: 141–57, quotations from 143, 167; cf. Spatharas 2019: 105).

I pause here for a moment to return to an issue raised in section 2.2 (pp. 27–8): we need to clarify what exactly we think happens during moments of internal (embedded) focalization of this sort. R. Allan writes, "We are invited to identify with Hermes' amazement and to view the scene through his eyes, to smell with his nose, and to hear with his ears.... We are observing the scene through the sensory channels of a viewer present at the scene" (2019a: 70). These sentences chime with Ryan's assessment that the passage from "Eveline" offers an example of the "fusion of the virtual body of the narrator and reader with the fictionally real body of a member of the textual world" (2015a: 95). Both assertions run some risks. It is one thing to say that the narrator presents the scene from Hermes's point of view, telling us what Hermes sees, smells, and hears. It is another thing to speak, as R. Allan and Ryan do, in terms of what I called strict perceptual identification in section 2.2, to say that we see and hear through Hermes's eyes and ears. I would hesitate to equate focalization with strict perceptual identification. Tilmann Köppe and Tobias Klauk warn against precisely this conflation (2013: para. 47; cf. Sanford and Emmott 2012: 165–7; Caracciolo 2014: 119, 128):

> It is very tempting, from an interpreter's point of view, to claim that an internally focalized passage of text makes people see things from the character's point of view. The details are tricky here once one starts to take statements like this one literally. Suppose some passage of text is internally focalized in that it represents the character's visual perspective on some scenery. Should we say, then, that this is how readers (mentally) "see" it? That the answer to this question is far from clear stems from the fact that there are many things a reader could be rightfully said to do when reading the passage: she could imagine that the focal character sees the scenery; she could imagine that she sees the scenery; she could (visually) imagine the scenery; and she could imagine visual properties of the scenery.

Benjamin Haller's summary of what happens in *Odyssey* 5 avoids these difficulties: the presentation allows "the reader to experience Hermes taking in the sights and smells of Calypso's island. The poet allows us to see the palace of Calypso as Hermes does" (2007: 92). The character serves as our guide. R. Allan moves to firmer ground when he writes that "the text encourages the listener to position him/herself within the described scene and experience it as if actually present" (2019a: 73). This positioning and experience does not require strict perceptual identification.

This distinction matters because one may intuitively but erroneously think that strict perceptual identification provides the easiest and quickest path to immersion in the storyworld. A film can restrict our vision to what a character sees through a point of view shot, but that access does not necessarily mean we know what the character thinks or feels (M. Smith 1995: 156–61, 221; cf. 83–4; Gaut 1999: 208–9) and so only gives us a small point of entry into the storyworld. Researchers of video games have also done useful work on this issue. First-person player games in which players see only what the character they play sees can generate feelings of "spatial presence" in the world of the game (van Vught and

Schott 2017: 165), but so too can third-person games in which one sees the character one is playing, and some even argue that third-person games do a better job than first-person games of moving the player into the storyworld and generating spatio-temporal immersion (160, 172).

With that clarification in mind, I turn to the impact of internal (embedded) focalization. Spatio-temporal immersion is more apt to occur when the text gives us a character who sees, hears, smells, touches, or tastes as opposed to when the text tells us what is to be seen, heard, smelled, touched, or tasted. In the former scenario, we assume that the character has a body and that the storyworld is populated by characters with bodies. Since we have bodies, we can imagine ourselves in that world too. (If the characters' bodies resemble ours, all the better, but that is not a necessary condition). Such is the effect of the "solid foothold" that Ryan says Eveline provides us. Moreover, we experience our own world through our senses. When the narrator presents a scene through a character's senses, we are given an opportunity—a clearly marked opportunity to boot—to do what the character does and experience the storyworld through our senses. Such an experience enables our entry into the storyworld. If a character sees someone walking down the street, we too can imagine seeing that someone walking down the street in the world of the story (cf. Bonifazi and Elmer 2016: section 2) and accordingly feel ourselves in that world. This outcome is what Ryan's "sensory interface to the textual world" produces. In short, it is not so much the presence of sights, sounds, and sensations that take us into the storyworld but the presence of an internal focalizer that does the trick. Analyzing a fragment of the fifth-century BCE poet Melanippides (*Poetae Melici Graeci* 757 Page), Pauline LeVen points to its "sensual vividness" as the feature that "draws us into the Danaids' world": "sight, in the description of the groves with the sun piercing through the branches...and the sacred tears of incense..., smell for the fragrant dates..., and touch for the tender cinnamon" (2014: 226–7). What needs to be stressed is that the Danaids seek out (*mateusai*) the incense, dates, and cinnamon: that they see, smell, and touch them provides the foothold and sensory interface that give us access to and draw us into their world.

At this point, one can better register the immersive potential of the myriad instances of internal (embedded) focalization in the Homeric epics that involve a character's seeing. This effect is not reserved for tour-de-force moments, such as Hermes's arrival on Ogygia. The *Iliad* includes several of what de Jong calls "find-passages" (2004: 107). A character arrives somewhere, and the following verses describe what they see. For instance, Hector finds Paris (*ton d' heur'*) in his bedroom, tending to his armor and bow, and sees Helen there as well, sitting with her slave women and directing their weaving (*Iliad* 6.321-4; see de Jong 2004: 108). These sorts of passages do more than "describe the setting or background for the ensuing scene...evoke an atmosphere...or...characterize a character" (de Jong 2004: 109–10). Looking at the passage from the perspective delineated here, one notes how the cue in *heur'* ("he found") provides a foothold and an interface that aids our immersion in the storyworld.

The same effect arises from the verses that de Jong classifies as "perception-passages" (2004: 102–7, quotation from 107). In several of these passages, the poet activates a character by having him see another who has been in focus in the previous verses (cf. section 6.2, p. 167). The narrator describes Paris as he steps out to challenge the Achaeans: he sports a panther skin cloak and carries a bow, a sword, and two spears (*Iliad* 3.16–20). Then the narrator notes, "Warlike Menelaus saw (*enoēsen*) him [Paris] as he [Paris] came out in front of the crowd, striding greatly" (*Iliad* 3.21–2). Verses 16–20 can prompt us to imagine Paris. Yet, in having Menelaus see Paris, verses 21–2 makes this imagining easier. The narrator describes the disemboweling of Polydorus (*Iliad* 20.413–18) and then notes, "But Hector, when he saw (*enoēse*) his brother Polydorus holding his intestines in his hands, slumping to the ground…" (20.419–20; see also 3.30–1, 5.95–6, 11.284, 11.575–6, 11.581–2, 15.422–3). Again, one can envision the narrator's description of Polydorus's death. Yet, in having Hector see Polydorus in such a state, verses 419–20 make this imagining easier. These couplets work toward this end because the second verse looks back to the character previously in focus—to Paris emerging from the crowd, to Polydorus crumpled on the ground. We get the chance to see that character again, this time with the "solid foothold" and "sensory interface" provided by the perceiving character. Contrast some other moments in which the narrator introduces a new character when they perceive a character already on stage. For instance, the narrator describes Nestor's ferrying Machaon out of the battle (*Iliad* 11.597–8) and states, "But him [Nestor] swift-footed brilliant Achilles saw (*enoēsen*)" (*Iliad* 11.599). The narrator does not then append another verse that returns us to Nestor (cf. *Iliad* 11.248, 17.483, 21.418).

Moments of internal (embedded) focalization that pertain to hearing function in the same ways. The Homeric narrator neglects the smells of the battlefield (E. Vermeule 1979: 99) but does stress the cacophony as sounds emanate from both weapons and warriors (Gurd 2016: 27–32; Minchin 2018: 52; Pitts 2019: 17–24). The Lapiths' armor resounds (*kompei*) as weapons strike it (*Iliad* 12.151). When Alcmaon falls in battle, his armor rings out upon impact with the ground (*brakhe*, *Iliad* 12.396). Aeneas's shield "rang out" (*lake*) as Achilles's spear passed through it (*Iliad* 20.277). Cleitus's horses pull an empty chariot, making it rattle (*kroteontes*, *Iliad* 15.453; cf. Janko 1992: 364 at 377–9). Asius's men attack "crying out shrilly" (*oxea keklēgontes*, *Iliad* 12.125). The Achaeans and Trojans join battle with "a great yell" (*megaloi alalētōi*, *Iliad* 14.393) and "shouting terribly" (*deinon ausantōn*, *Iliad* 14.401; cf.13.833–7). The Trojans flee Achilles "with a great din" (*megaloi patagōi*, *Iliad* 21.9).

The poet does not just bring out the sounds of battle. He includes characters' hearing these sounds. Hector "watched for the whistle of arrows and the thud of spears" (σκέπτετ' ὀιστῶν τε ῥοῖζον καὶ δοῦπον ἀκόντων, *Iliad* 16.361; see Janko

1992: 362 at 358–63). Menestheus does not bother to shout for reinforcements because he recognizes the futility of doing so: "for (*gar*) the din (*ktupos*) was so great, and the noise (*autē*) went up to heaven" (*Iliad* 12.338). Nestor, drinking in his tent, perceives the noise (*iakhē*) of battle in his tent (*Iliad* 14.1; see Clay 2011: 78). The gods "fell upon one another with a great din (*megalōi patagōi*), and the wide earth rang out (*brakhe*), and round about the great heaven pealed as with a trumpet (*salpigxen*)": Zeus, the narrator then states, "heard (*aie*) from his seat on Olympus" (*Iliad* 21.387–9). Odysseus shouts (*ēusen*) three times, and Menelaus hears him shouting (*aien iakhontos*) each time (*Iliad* 11.462–3). Hector advances "crying out shrilly" (*oxea keklēgōs*), and "shouting out sharply he did not escape the notice of the son of Atreus [Menelaus]" (οὐδ' υἱὸν λάθεν Ἀτρέος ὀξὺ βοήσας) (*Iliad* 17.87–9). The Trojans "took thought of ill-sounding flight" (*phoboio / duskeladou mnēsanto, Iliad* 16.356–7), the verse implying that they hear the sounds of their own retreat. Just like those involving sight, instances of internal (embedded) focalization that involve hearing provide recipients with a foothold in and interface with the storyworld (cf. Tsagalis 2012: 107). An illustrative parallel emerges when the Chorus reports the sounds made by the Argive army in Aeschylus's *Seven against Thebes* (Visvardi 2015: 149–50; Weiss 2018b: 171–4): here again it is not the mere report of the sounds but the positioning of the Chorus as the sensory conduit—"I see (*dedorka*) the noise" (103 West); "I hear (*kluō*) the rattle of chariots" (151; cf. *akousasa* (203–4), *kluousa* (239), *akouō* (245))—that enables spectators to imagine vividly the siege (just as Eteocles worries that the Chorus's descriptions will terrify their fellow Thebans (237–8, 246, 250, 262; Visvardi 2015: 152–5)).

Another attribute of the find- and perception-passages as well as several passages that involve a character's hearing is relevant to our inquiry: they specify an angle from which to imagine a or the character(s). The vantage point from which the *Iliad*'s recipients "watch the action" is "usually unspecified" (S. Richardson 1990: 112). One may at times feel like a disembodied observer floating around in the storyworld. The find-, perception-, and hearing passages encourage us to imagine the scene from the vantage point of a character, and the grounding effected by that overlap can in turn encourage our spatio-temporal immersion.

Finally, these passages of internal (embedded) focalization involving sight and sound can be juxtaposed with passages in which the characters themselves talk of their sensory experiences of taste and touch. The taste of food seems of little concern in the Homeric epics (Hitch 2018: 23–9, 43), but Achilles speaks of "tasting" a spear (*Iliad* 20.258 (*geusometh'*), 21.60–1 (*geusetai*)) and the goatherd Melanthius of "tasting" a fist (*Odyssey* 20.181 (*geusasthai*); Hitch 2018: 35, 44). Occasionally, a character comments on what something feels like. Menelaus tells Agamemnon that the wound from the "sharp" (*oxu*) arrow is not fatal (*Iliad* 4.185; cf. 20.437). Achilles urges Phoenix to sleep in his hut in a "soft" (*malakēi*) bed (*Iliad* 9.618). Polydamas labels the doors of the Trojan gates "smoothed" (*euxestoi*, *Iliad* 18.276). Now that he is dead, the Achaeans say, Hector is "softer" (*malakōteros*, *Iliad* 22.373): it is easier to push a spear into him (22.371). These references to taste and touch provide the recipient with the foothold and interface that enables entry into the storyworld.

Sometimes it is not a named character in the storyworld whose perspective triggers a recipient's spatio-temporal immersion. Other turns of phrase can prompt the same response (cf. section 2.2, p. 17). At an early stage in Diomedes's *aristeia*, the narrator notes, "but you could not discern (*gnoiēs*) on which side he fought, whether he joined with the Trojans or with the Achaeans" (*Iliad* 5.85–6). De Jong discusses this passage along with the four others in the *Iliad*'s narrator text that refer to a "you" (2004: 54–5; cf. Clay 2011: 23–4; Myers 2019: 102–5). She suggests that these passages addressed to the external primary narratee-focalizee (and so to the historical recipient) "turn him temporarily into an eyewitness" (de Jong 2004: 55) and cites Longinus's judgment that second-person address can "make the hearer seem to turn about in the middle (*en mesois*) of the dangers" (*On the Sublime* 26.1). Following María-Ángeles Martínez's investigation of "you" in modern novels written in English (2018: 62–3), I would make explicit that we are dealing in these five *Iliad* passages with yet another opportunity for spatio-temporal immersion: the second-person form can cue and enable that brand of entry into the storyworld.

De Jong also investigates two passages in the *Iliad*'s narrator text that refer to a generic man (*anēr*) (2004: 57–9; cf. Clay 2011: 24–5; Myers 2019: 103–7): a man whom Athena led safely by the hand through the melee "no longer would... make light" of it (*ouketi...anēr onosaito*, *Iliad* 4.539–42); "a man would not have recognized" the fallen Sarpedon (*oude...anēr.../ egnō*, *Iliad* 16.638–9). In her analysis of these two passages (and other related ones), de Jong introduces the idea that all these passages (both those with second-person address and those with a generic man) model an emotional response for the audience. In particular, the description of Athena leading a man through the battle encourages the recipient "to identify himself with him and to share his feelings of awe... about the intensity and fierceness of the battle" (2004: 59; cf. Allan, de Jong, and de Jonge 2017: 42–3). Identification is not the most productive frame in this case (see section 2.2, p. 18). Better is de Jong's concluding statement that *Iliad* 4.539–42 invites the recipient "to 'visit' the actual battlefield" (2004: 59). I look again to Martínez, this time to her investigation of the pronoun "one," which she sees as capable of "anchoring readers within the exact personal and spatio-temporal parameters occupied by the focalizer inside the storyworld" (2018: 64). She gives an example from Virginia Woolf's "The Lady in the Looking Glass": "The house was empty, and *one* felt, since *one* was the only person in the drawing room, like one of those naturalists, who, covered with grass and leaves [...]" (Martínez's emphasis). The *Iliad*'s impersonal and generic *anēr* works in the same way: its inclusive force can enable a recipient's anchoring in the space and time of the storyworld.

I draw this discussion of internal (embedded) focalization and inclusive forms of address to a close by positing that their appearance in character text can induce a recipient's immersion as well. Hephaestus predicts for Thetis the reaction Achilles's new armor will provoke: "beautiful armor will be his, such as someone (*tis*) in turn of numerous men (*anthrōpōn*) will marvel at, whoever sees (*hos ken idētai*) it" (*Iliad* 18.466-7). Hephaestus does not seem to have Thetis in mind as one of these viewers: she cannot be counted among "men" (*anthrōpōn*). The "'overhearing'" recipient (Martínez 2018: 66; cf. 45) will readily fall into that category, and that recipient can take the generic *tis* as Monica Fludernik suggests readers can at times understand the generic "you": "'anyone,' therefore: 'possibly, me'" (2011: 106; cf. Martínez 2018: 68). For its part, the verb expressing the act of seeing (*idētai*) can provide a sensory purchase for the recipient. In tandem, these features can pull a recipient into the storyworld: one imagines oneself looking at Achilles's armor alongside the other characters. Juxtapose Achilles's statement in which he urges on the Achaeans: "as someone (*tis*) sees (*idētai*) Achilles among the first fighters / destroying the phalanxes of Trojans with the bronze spear / so let someone of you (*tis humeiōn*) taking thought fight with a man" (*Iliad* 19.151-3). Verses 151-2 can prompt the same response in the recipient as Hephaestus's declaration to Thetis (cf. *Odyssey* 1.228-9, 12.87-8). Verse 153, by contrast, specifies that the *tis* is a character in the story—one of the Achaeans (cf. *Iliad* 17.93, 100-1; *Odyssey* 24.491)—and excludes the recipient's glossing the *tis* as "possibly me" (cf. Keen 2007: 98; Fludernik 2011: 107-8; Sanford and Emmott 2012: 173-4).

Researchers find still other factors contributing to spatio-temporal immersion. The so-called deictic shift comes up frequently in the relevant literature: the majority of the references to time and space in an immersive text pertain to the storyworld, not the time and place of narration or the actual world of the recipient.[5] Characters' speeches contain the most noticeable references of this sort. For instance, all the instances of the pronoun *nun* ("now") in *Iliad* 1 occur in character speech: this is the now of the characters, not the now of the recipients. Likewise, character speech in the *Iliad* abounds in spatial references, such as "this man here" (e.g., *Iliad* 1.287: *hod' anēr*) or "that man there" (e.g., *Iliad* 3.411: *keinou*), that refer to the immediate environment of the characters and not the here or there of the recipients (cf. Bakker 2005: 72, 78; de Jong 2012c: 71-8; Clay 2011: 66; Allan, de Jong, and de Jonge 2017: 45). Jenny Strauss Clay rightly observes, "The direct speeches of an Achilles or an Agamemnon shift the deictic center from the present moment of the performance in which we are participating

---

[5] Wolf 2013: 11; Ryan 2015a: 96-9; Bilandzic and Busselle 2017: 18-19; Kuijpers et al. 2017: 34; R. Allan 2019a: 62-3; Grethlein 2021a: 57; cf. LeVen 2014: 197.

to the here and now of the characters: the Greek camp at Troy in the tenth year of the War" (2011: 17).

Bakker contends that deictics can nevertheless make for moments in the Homeric epics in which "the past becomes now the real thing, a reality before everyone's eyes at which the poet can point" (2005: 80; cf. Myers 2019: 35). For example, summing up the Catalogue of Ships with "these (*houtoi*) then were the leaders and princes of the Danaans" (*Iliad* 2.760), the poet speaks of the leaders "as a reality before everyone's eyes, as if he is saying: 'There you have them; those were the leaders of the Danaans'" (Bakker 2005: 80). There is no pronounced deictic shift here, or, at least, the deictic shift is less emphatic: the recipient's "these here" seems to coincide with the storyworld's "these here." What is more, the poet does refer to the present time of the performance and the audience (Clay 2011: 21–3, 62; Graziosi 2013: 16; Myers 2019: 37–8).[6] Scholars like to point to the *Iliad*'s narrator's speaking four times of "such men as are now (*nun*)" (cf. Cook 2018: 118–19) or labeling the heroes one time as "demigods" (*hēmitheōn*) who belong to a distant past (*Iliad* 12.23; Lather 2020: 280). I concentrate on another scholarly favorite: researchers frequently take similes to refer to the world and experience of the audience (cf. Edwards 1991: 35–6; Minchin 2001: 148–9; Bakker 2005: 114; Clay 2011: 65; Graziosi 2013: 19). But they also stress how similes, despite being so vivid (esp. Bakker 2005: 134, 148) as to move us out of the time and space of the narrative proper, help us visualize the characters' actions (Winkler 2007: 52–7; Clay 2011: 21, 65; Hesk 2013: 34; cf. Grethlein and Huitink 2017: 79, 82). In turn, Allan, de Jong, and de Jonge suggest that this feature of similes contributes to immersion (2017: 39–40). Peter Dixon and Marisa Bortolussi's findings (2017) provide empirical support for this intuited connection between similes and immersion. Their experiments demonstrate that evoked realism generates an emotional response and that transportation arises when one has an emotional response (208–9). (To assess the characters and their actions using terms like "real," "lifelike," or "vivid" is to ponder the degree of "evoked realism" (205).) Now, "metaphor can contribute to evoked realism by leading to a vivid and distinct impression of the story world" (212). From this perspective, similes (a species of metaphor in their model) contribute to immersion because they contribute to evoked realism.

At the same time, one can become immersed in the vignette of the simile itself (cf. Hutchinson 2017: 161). Helpful in this regard is the occasional appearance of a human observer in the simile "who directs our response to the scenes evoked" (Clay 2011: 7; cf. Kretler 2020: 87–9). A goatherd shelters his flock when he sees (*eiden*) a storm coming (*Iliad* 4.275–9). A shepherd hears (*eklue*) the crash of two

---

[6] Neither the *Iliad* nor the *Odyssey* contain explicit references to a specific time when or place where they are being (or could be) performed. For the excision of references to the precise time and place of performance during the textualization of an oral traditional work, see Ready 2019a: 145–6.

rivers meeting (*Iliad* 4.452–5). A shepherd delights (*gegēthe*) in the stars and landscape visible on a clear night (*Iliad* 8.555–9). A man loses courage when he sees (*idētai*) an oak tree struck by lightning and presumably smells the "horrible smell of sulphur" (*Iliad* 14.414–17). Building on Clay's assertion that the observer "directs our response," I return to Ryan's language to note that the observer provides the recipient with "a solid foothold on the scene, as well as a sensory interface to the textual world," in this case the mini-world of the simile, to borrow Gregory Hutchinson's phrase (2017: 160; cf. Buxton 2004: 152 on "the parallel world of the similes").

Ryan also considers the immersive power of different kinds of speech presentation: direct discourse, indirect discourse, and free indirect discourse (2015a: 96–7). On the face of it, direct discourse seems the most apt to trigger immersion (97). Beyond a clear demonstration of the deictic shift, we get (or tend to assume that we get) direct access to a character's words (cf. Sanford and Emmott 2012: 181–2), and during a character's speech narrated time equals narrative (or narrating) time (see Grethlein 2013: 36; Allan, de Jong, and de Jonge 2017: 45, 41; Grethlein and Huitink 2017: 83; R. Allan 2019a: 63, 65). To repeat (see sections 4.3.1, p. 117, and 4.3.3, p. 124), narrative (or narrating) time means the amount of time it takes to tell what happened. Narrated time means the amount of time it takes for something to happen in the storyworld. When they overlap, one speaks of "scenic narration," and "scenic narration is the most common narration type in immersive texts since it presents the events at a speed at which we also experience (observe) them in our everyday lives" (R. Allan 2019a: 65; cf. Grethlein 2013: 120; 2021a: 57; Grethlein and Huitink 2017: 73; Tyrell 2020: 122–3, 132). Ryan posits that free indirect discourse has its advantages too (cf. Keen 2007: 96–7; Sanford and Emmott 2012: 188–9). Free indirect discourse combines two perspectives (Ryan 2015a: 96):

> While the reference of the spatial and temporal shifters forces on the reader the perspective of the characters, verb tense and pronouns remain assigned from the point of view of the narrative act: "Even *now*, though she *was* over nineteen, she sometimes felt herself in danger of her father's violence."
> ("Eveline," 38, italics mine [M-LR])

As a result, free indirect discourse "maintains a constant position halfway between the narrator's and the character's spatio-temporal location" (97). That feature may make free indirect discourse more immersive than direct discourse: in direct discourse, the prevalence of "the attributing expression"—the narrator's speech introduction—means that we continually move in and out of the character's perspective (cf. Sanford and Emmott 2012: 187).

Classicists have noted the immersive effects of direct speech (R. Allan 2019a: 66; 2019b: 134; 2020: 19; cf. Bakker 2005: 94; Payne 2007: 83), and, of course, the *Iliad* and the *Odyssey* score high in this category (Allan, de Jong, and de Jonge 2017: 41, 45; cf. Bakker 1997: 167; M. Power 2006: 62; Clay 2011: 17; Beck 2012: 23–7). In analyzing the historian Thucydides's depiction of the battle of Sphacteria, R. Allan advocates for free indirect thought. After emphasizing the presence of the narrator in moments of free indirect speech (cf. Keen 2007: 97), he suggests that free indirect thought tends in the opposite direction and exhibits more immersive potential (R. Allan 2019b: 148):

> It is a deviation from the norm towards less narratorial control and towards a more immediate ("vivid") representation of a character's thoughts. It thus enhances the illusion that we are actually inside the character's mind following the character's flow of thoughts and feelings as it occurs and we are encouraged to sympathize with his or her viewpoint. Since free indirect thought involves a transfer to a point of view internal to the storyworld, often accompanied by an empathetic identification with a character, it can be employed as an effective immersive narrative technique.

Opinions differ regarding free indirect discourse in Homeric poetry. R. Allan disputes its existence (2019b: 148 n. 36). Deborah Beck devotes a chapter to free indirect speech in her 2012 book on the epics. Noting that characters use free indirect speech more than the narrators (61), Beck suggests that Phoenix thereby makes his speech in *Iliad* 9 "even more vivid and emotional" (68) and that Demodocus's song about Ares and Aphrodite thereby "becomes increasingly vivid to the audience" (75). In dialogue with Beck's contribution, Anna Bonifazi queries instances of free indirect speech in the poems as moments of viewpoint blending (2018: 242–6). She concludes, "We enjoy the new elements emerging from the blend insofar as they emerge only in the blend" (251). Building on Beck's and Bonifazi's studies, one might explore free indirect discourse in Homeric epic from the perspective of immersion. (One might also consider the applicability to the Homeric epics of Maria Kotovych et al.'s finding that free indirect speech can enhance identification (2011).)

I want, however, to return to Ryan's "attributing expressions." Egbert Bakker highlights how some speech introductions anticipate the importance of the speech to the poem's plot (1997: 167–9). Beck's 2005 monograph illuminates the thematic contributions speech introductions make. In keeping with these findings and contrary to what one might expect given Ryan's analysis, I suggest that speech introductions used by the Homeric narrators can exert an immersive force. We should not neglect them because they introduce the highly immersive moments of direct speech.

Beck provides a handy list of formulas used as speech introductions by the narrators of the *Iliad* and the *Odyssey* (2005: 286–9). When compared with modern novels, a distinctive feature of the repeated Homeric speech introductions is that they regularly involve more than a reference to the act of speaking. Hands move: the speech introduction "s/he took his hand (ἔν τ' ἄρα οἱ φῦ χειρὶ) and spoke a word and addressed him" occurs six times in the *Iliad* and four times in the *Odyssey*, and the speech introduction "s/he stroked him with her/his hand (χειρί τέ μιν κατέρεξεν) and spoke a word and addressed him" occurs four times in the *Iliad* and twice in the *Odyssey*. Speakers stand: the speech introduction "standing near (*agkou d' istamenos/ē*), s/he spoke winged words" occurs nine times in the *Iliad* and four times in the *Odyssey* (cf. *Iliad* 1.58 = 19.55); the speech introduction "he stood upright (*stē d' orthos*) and spoke a word among the Argives" occurs seven times in the *Iliad*; and the speech introduction "he stood over his head (στῆ δ' ἄρ' ὑπὲρ κεφαλῆς) and spoke a word to him" occurs twice in the *Iliad* and four times in the *Odyssey*. Twice in the *Iliad* and twice in the *Odyssey* a character "shook his head (*kinēsas de/rha karē*) and spoke to his spirit." Three times in the *Iliad* a character vaunts over a character as he despoils him of his armor: "he stripped off (*exenarixe*) his armor and boasting spoke a word." In each case, the speaker's physical movement can provoke motor resonance in the recipient.

Several of these speech introductions also specify the physical position of the characters relative to one another: to take someone by the hand or to stroke someone with one's own hand or to strip someone of their armor requires being as close to them as possible; to stand near the addressee or to stand over the addressee's head also brings one close to them. Occurring three times in the *Iliad* and twice in the *Odyssey*, the following speech introduction also emphasizes the nearness of the interlocutor: "and straightaway he called to [direct object] who was near (*eggus eonta*)." So too does the speech introduction "and thus someone would speak looking to the man next (*plēsion*) to him," which occurs three times in the *Iliad* and six times in the *Odyssey*. These clues regarding the spatio-temporal orientation of the characters aid the recipient's spatio-temporal immersion (again cf. section 6.2, p. 160), R. Allan 2019b: 141; 2020: 22; cf. Webb 2020: 164–5). Speech introductions in which a character shouts also help the recipient understand the spatio-temporal arrangement of the characters in the storyworld. Programmatic here is Agamemnon's shout at *Iliad* 8.227: "he uttered a widely heard shout, calling aloud to the Danaans" (ἤϋσεν δὲ διαπρύσιον Δαναοῖσι γεγωνώς; cf. Clay 2011: 71 n. 79). In the previous verses, the narrator has specified that Agamemnon shouts standing by Odysseus's ship "which was in the middle so that a shout could reach both ends, both to the huts of Ajax, son of Telamon, and to those of Achilles, who had drawn up their balanced ships at the furthest ends" (*Iliad* 8.222–6 = 11.5–9). The speech introduction used at 8.227 and five other times in the *Iliad* prompts the recipient to envision a speaker trying to be heard by a group of people at varying distances from him. So too do four other speech introductory formulas gathered by Beck (appearing a total of fifteen times and only in the *Iliad*) that occur when a character shouts to be heard. *Iliad* 12.335–8 plays on, and thereby affirms, this connection between shouting and spatio-temporal orientation. Menestheus catches sight of the two Ajaxes as well as Teucer nearby (*egguthen*), but "it was not possible for him to shout so as to be heard (*bōsanti gegōnein*): for the din was so great." To bring out the din, the narrator highlights the impossibility of those nearby hearing a character's shout.

Other passages that introduce character speech but do not qualify as formulas also mention the physical movements or the spatio-temporal orientation of the characters. For instance, a lamenting Priam "begged, rolling (*kulindomenos*) in the dirt, calling each man by name" (*Iliad* 22.414–15). Hera "summoning Aphrodite away from the rest of the gods (τῶν ἄλλων ἀπάνευθε θεῶν) spoke a word to her" (*Iliad* 14.188–9). These speech introductions too have the potential to trigger spatio-temporal immersion.

## 6.4. Conclusion

This chapter has explored different components of immersion under the headings of spatial and spatio-temporal immersion. Recipients use the architectural and topographical details in the text to generate a mental image of Troy, but more important are the movements of characters in and around the city. These movements not only make the city imageable but also endow the city with a solidity and therefore vivacity that in turn enables spatial immersion. That latter equation obtains as well in regard to the city wall and the poem's other settings, from the Achaean meeting place, to the ground of the battlefield, to the bank of the Scamander: each gains solidity when other entities, from people to blood, move in some way in relation to it. Just so, when the *Iliad*'s moveable objects and its characters come into contact with another entity, they acquire a solidity that endows them with vivacity. Other factors contribute to spatial immersion too. By masking changes of scenes, the poet seems to keep us in the same space. Concentrating the action in and around Troy and on Mt Olympus, the poet sets his tale in famous places that recipients may long to visit: this desire can trigger spatial immersion. The abundance of other place names in the poem help the poet impart spatial and temporal depth to his storyworld, the creation of a storyworld being a prerequisite for creating an immersive narrative.

As for spatio-temporal immersion, the poem provides countless opportunities for recipients to experience motor resonance. Both the actions of characters and the actions of objects can trigger a felt response in the recipient. In addition, numerous moments of internal (embedded) focalization provide recipients with entry into the storyworld at a sensory level, and the use of inclusive forms of address, such as second-person references to the narratee or references to a generic man (*anēr*), also grants easy access to the storyworld. Like other immersive texts, the *Iliad* offers a deictic shift that contributes to spatio-temporal immersion, but even similes, set ostensibly in the here and now of the recipient, contribute to immersion. Finally, the proliferation of direct speech by the characters makes the *Iliad* an immersive text, but the narrator's speech introductions too enhance spatio-temporal immersion as they provide cues for motor resonance and position the characters spatially in relation to one another.

# 7
# Emotional Immersion

## 7.1. Overview

Spatial immersion and spatio-temporal immersion require some degree of visualization of the storyworld. Not every reader or listener creates mental images (Otis 2015; Mackey 2019), so they are less likely to experience those forms of immersion than those recipients who do visualize the storyworld. There are, however, other kinds of immersion, and I turn to them now, starting with emotional immersion.

In Part I, I discussed emotion in the context of emotional identification with characters. But not all of a recipient's emotions intersect with those exhibited or taken to be exhibited by a character. Emotional identification does not provide the only mechanism for a recipient to react emotionally to a narrative (cf. Plantinga 2009: 106, 141, 149–56). In this chapter, I consider other ways in which we can respond emotionally and thereby be immersed. (See section 2.5 (pp. 46–7) for my thoughts on the word "emotion.")

Some researchers dispute the relevance of emotions to transportation (de Graaf and van Leeuwen 2017: 277). By contrast, as evident from the overview in section 5.3, several prominent models of immersion foreground emotions (cf. Calarco et al. 2017: 301). I single out Peter Dixon and Marisa Bortolussi's argument for an intimate connection between emotional engagement and transportation (2017). They divide absorption into four components: transportation—"the extent to which the reader felt part of the story world and removed from their physical environment" (204); evoked realism—"the sense...of appreciating the story world as if it actually existed" (201); emotional responses—"felt, often physically embodied, emotions evoked by the story" (204); and personal memories—"instances in which aspects of the story elicited episodic memories of the reader" (204). Their experimental data suggest that evoked realism and personal memories predict emotional response which in turn predicts transportation (208–9; cf. 212):

> Emotional responses can be produced by either a detailed, vivid representation of a (presumably emotional) story world situation, or by remindings of (again, presumably emotional) personal experiences.... Transportation was a function of emotional response. In other words, the extent to which readers endorsed

transportation items was predicted by the extent to which they reported emotional experiences. Importantly, in our data at least, transportation was a function of emotion, and not, as typically claimed, the other way around.

No emotional response, no transportation. (That memories stir emotions is captured in the use of the phrase "emotional memory" by, for instance, Keith Oatley (1994: 63; 2012: 36, 179–80) and Patrick Hogan (2018: 57).)

Section 7.2 looks at suspense. Section 7.3 looks at other emotions. Suspense belongs in this chapter because researchers understand suspense as an emotion. Carl Plantinga deems it one of the "global emotions" that can persist for long stretches of narrative time (2009: 68–9). Keith Oatley posits that "suspense is the emotional state of curiosity" (2012: 50). Patrick Hogan defines it as a "plot emotion" (2018: 184; cf. 155–8). Rutger Allan classifies suspense under the category of emotional involvement (2019b: 136). Richard Gerrig and Matthew Bezdek cite Anthony Ortony, Gerald Clore, and Allan Collins (1988: 131) for the argument that suspense necessitates "'a Hope emotion and a Fear emotion'" (2013: 99; cf. Nabi and Green 2015: 147; M. Smith 2017: 69; Liotsakis 2021: 3, 5; Scodel 2021: 68). In addition, suspense can come first in this discussion of emotional immersion given how readily we associate suspense with immersion (cf. R. Allan 2020: 19). Empirical investigations bolster this intuition by showing their correlation. Nurit Tal-Or and Jonathan Cohen found that increasing suspense by telling subjects a bit about a character's future (but not spoiling the story) enhances transportation (2010: 408, 411–12). Kaitlin Fitzgerald and Melanie Green include "feelings of suspense" in their list of the components of transportation (2017: 50). Arthur Jacobs and Jana Lüdtke contend that "a clear or surprising chain of events providing a good deal of 'what happens next?' suspense" increases a narrative's *"immersive potential"* (2017: 80, emphasis in original). Their experiments turned up a significant "correlation" between suspense and immersion (78, 86, quotation from 78). Katalin Bálint, Moniek Kuijpers, and Miruna Doicaru found "that felt suspense and narrative absorption are strongly corresponding experiences" (2017: 189).

## 7.2. Suspense

Suspense comes in different forms. Marie-Laure Ryan sees four types (2015a: 102–4). When we experience what-suspense, we wonder what will happen to the characters or what the characters will do. When we experience how- (or why-) suspense, we wonder how (why) a situation or condition came to be. (Some would speak of curiosity (Jacobs and Lüdtke 2017: 76–7; cf. Ryan 2015a: 101).) When we experience who-suspense, we wonder who did something that happens early on in the tale or that the author tells us happened in the past. When we experience metasuspense, we wonder "how the author is going to tie all the strands together and give the text proper narrative form" (104). Ryan's what-suspense corresponds to Anton Fuxjäger's *Ob-Spannung* (whether-suspense/tension: "whether the sought goal can be reached or not") (2002: 28, my translation), but Fuxjäger differentiates between *Wie-Spannung* (how-suspense/tension: "how a particular character tried to achieve or achieved this goal") and *Warum-Spannung* (why-suspense/tension: "why something is as it is") (2002: 35, 40, my translations). Again, Ryan's what-suspense corresponds to Raphaël Baroni's *suspense simple* and her how- (why-) suspense to Baroni's *suspense moyen*, but Baroni delves into three other forms of suspense as well: *suspense par anticipation* (the tale provides recipients with some inkling of what is to come), *suspense par contradiction* (the recipient knows what will happen but hopes it does not), and *rappel* (the recipient knows what will happen and looks forward to seeing that knowledge confirmed) (2007: 269–95; cf. Grethlein 2017a: 90–1). In discussing how- (why-) suspense, Ryan notes that "the reader may be caught in *what* suspense on the level of the individual episodes" (2015a: 103, emphasis in original). This distinction overlaps with that drawn between mini-suspense or *Detailspannung*, on the one hand, and overall-suspense or *Finalspannung*, on the other hand (Hastall 2013: 265). The literature posits further discriminations and differentiations (Hastall 2013: 265), but even this brief review suffices to demonstrate the value of specifying which kind of suspense we are talking about when we talk about suspense. It can help us interpret statements like "the inclusion of a spoiler reduced fun and suspense among the audience" (Johnson and Rosenbaum 2015: 1079): the authors speak here of what-suspense. Accordingly, we should specify which kinds of suspense might be operative for a recipient of the Homeric epics.

The scholiastic commentary on the Homeric epics points to moments of what-suspense. In response to the narrator's reporting that Hector still had not found Andromache when he arrived at the Scaean gate (*Iliad* 6.392), a bT scholion attributes the verse to the poet's desire to place "the listener in a greater state of suspense (*agōniōteros*)" (bT scholion at *Iliad* 6.392; Nünlist 2009: 141). On the first hemistich of *Iliad* 7.479—"[Zeus] thundering terribly"—a bT scholion notes, "The poet excites the listener and makes him feel suspense (*agōnian*) about what is to come (*epi tois esomenois*)" (bT scholion at *Iliad* 7.479; N. Richardson 1980: 270; Ooms and de Jonge 2013: 105–6). When Hector approaches as Nestor tries to disentangle his fatally wounded horse from his team (*Iliad* 8.87–90), a T scholion declares, "Putting the listener into a state of suspense (*en agōniai*), he brings against him even the fearsome Hector" (T scholion at *Iliad* 8.87a1). A T scholion observes, "By making the ones hurling missiles often miss at first, he puts the listener into a state of suspense (*enagōnion*)" (T scholion at *Iliad* 16.463–76b; Nünlist 2009: 141–2; Ooms and de Jonge 2013: 106; Novokhatko 2021: 48). On the counterfactual in *Iliad* 8.217—Hector "would have burned the balanced ships with blazing fire"—a bT scholion links suspense with expectation: the poet "is always accustomed to bring the dangers to their peak, and putting the hearer into a state of suspense on account of their expectation (καὶ ἐναγώνιον ποιήσας τὸν ἀκροατὴν τῇ προσδοκίᾳ), he straightaway applies the remedy" (bT scholion at *Iliad* 8.217a; Novokhatko 2021: 49). The recipient experiences what-suspense insofar as they come to expect something to happen and wait to see if it will in fact transpire.

Homerists have seen still other kinds of suspense at work in the epics. Antonios Rengakos stresses the prevalence of *Wie-Spannung* (how-suspense) in the *Iliad*, prompted especially by the gradual revelation of what is to come: we move from Achilles's vague threat to Agamemnon that he will rue his mistreatment of Achilles (*Iliad* 1.240–4) to Achilles's request to Thetis that she ask Zeus to engineer the slaughter of the Achaeans by their own ships (1.407–10) to Zeus's delineations of the events to follow (8.473–6, 11.191–4, 15.52–71) (1999: 321–2). Ruth Scodel attends to the moment in *Iliad* 4 in which Zeus sends Athena to arrange the breaking of the treaty between Greeks and Trojans—"there is no indication how she will do this" (2021: 62)—and to Priam's supplication of Achilles in *Iliad* 24—"we are in suspense about how this meeting will develop" (72). Rutger Allan suggests that we feel how-suspense about the specifics of Patroclus's death (as well as Baroni's *suspense par contradiction*: we know Patroclus will die but do not want him to) (2022a: 87). Grethlein stresses the importance of how-suspense (*die Spannung auf das wie*) to the *Odyssey* (and to Heliodorus's *Ethiopian Story of Theagenes and Charicleia* (2017a: 91–2)). This kind of suspense hangs over the entire poem: how will Odysseus get back home and how will he rid his house of the suitors (Grethlein 2017b: 44; cf. Schmitz 1994: 12; Scodel 2021: 62, 64)? It is also felt in individual episodes: Odysseus reports that Aeolus sent him and his men a favorable wind, "but not then was it about to come to fulfillment: for we perished by our own recklessness" (*Odyssey* 10.25–7). This anticipation prompts us to ask how precisely their recklessness kept them from home (Grethlein 2017b: 114). When Penelope proposes to marry the winner of the bow contest, we ask how Odysseus's triumph could possibly materialize (Grethlein 2018: 82). Noting how Nausicaa and her father raise the prospect of Odysseus's marrying her, Scodel observes that we may not feel suspense over "whether Odysseus will actually reject Nausicaa, but about how he will manage to avoid insulting her family by refusing" (2021: 62). Thomas Schmitz sees an opportunity for the audience to ask how Odysseus will defeat the suitors when at *Odyssey* 22.119 he runs out of the arrows he has been using to kill them (1994: 14; cf. Xian 2017: 23).

In addition to how-suspense, Homerists speak of what we might call when-suspense. George Duckworth finds the audience member "anxious now to know, not *what* will happen (for that he already knows), but *how* and *when* it will happen" (1933: 60, emphasis in original). Wallace Anderson points to suspense over "'how' and 'when' events are going to happen" (1953: 393) and comments on the interventions of the gods: "it is not always known just when they will step in and, when they do, which side they will take" (394). Building on previous demonstrations of how retardation increases anticipation and so suspense (Duckworth 1933: 66), James Morrison concentrates on how the poet alerts us to what is going to happen but then introduces various delays. As a result, we do not know when the event he told us would happen will actually occur, and suspense arises (cf. Reichel 1990: 143). When will the Greek defeat that Zeus promises take place, when will Achilles return to the fight, and when will Achilles slay Hector (Morrison 1992: 36, 49, 51, 83)?

Audience members new to the *Iliad* could experience what-suspense. Morrison envisions a first-time audience hearing the *Iliad* (1992: 9, 13, 14) and finds numerous moments in which the poet keeps such an audience on edge. At *Iliad* 11.195–209, Iris brings a message from Zeus, promising Hector success in battle for the whole day, but instead Diomedes drives Hector from the fight (11.349–56) (1–2). The presentation of individual contests in the funeral games for Patroclus leave us in suspense as to the eventual winners (52; cf. Scodel 2021: 59–61). Similarly, imagining a first-time encounter with the *Odyssey* (1988: 241), Uvo Hölscher concentrates on the unexpected and surprising twists and turns of the poem's plot (235–42; cf. Rengakos 1999: 332–3, 335–6).

Still, given the importance of reperformance to the tradition of Homeric performance, let us stipulate an audience that has heard the tale before. This stipulation does not mean we have an audience of connoisseurs. Many audience members might recall the overall trajectory of the plot but not the details of individual episodes (cf. Morrison 1992: 92). They could experience some degree of what-suspense. Nonetheless, previous scholarship rightly highlights the prevalence of how-suspense in the Homeric poems. We can think here of suspense regarding events audience members know will happen and events the poet declares will happen. One can speculate endlessly about the former category. A recipient might know that Achilles will not return to the battle in *Iliad* 9 but wonder how exactly he will refuse or how the emissaries will fail (cf. Scodel 2021: 66). A recipient might recall that Patroclus dies in battle but wonder how that comes to pass (cf. Allen-Hornblower 2016: 67).

For our purposes, it is easier and more constructive to explore the latter category, events the poet declares will happen. I emphasize the possibility of suspense at the level of the individual scene (cf. Duckworth 1933: 37 n. 91; Schmitz 1994: 7) and how triggers for suspense are built into the typical structures of the presentation. As I observed a moment ago (p. 197), scholia note the suspense created when, as regularly happens, a warrior misses with his initial spear cast (Nünlist 2009: 141). The poet will also tell us that a warrior threw a missile "not in vain," leaving open for a moment how he was successful in his throw, and then tell us the unlucky victim: Odysseus "did not let fly his spear in vain (*ouk halion*), but he hit Democoön, an illegitimate son of Priam" (*Iliad* 4.498–9); Antilochus "did not let fly his spear in vain (*ouk halion*), but Melanippus, the son of stout-hearted

Hicetaon, he hit" (*Iliad* 15.575–7); Patroclus "was not fruitless (*oud' haliōse*) in his cast, but he hit the charioteer of Hector" (*Iliad* 16.737; cf. Janko 1992: 403 at 737–9). Six times in the *Iliad* and one time in the *Odyssey* occurs the following statement: "balancing his spear that casts a long shadow he threw it, and he hit..." (ἀμπεπαλὼν προΐει δολιχόσκιον ἔγχος, / καὶ βάλε...; cf. Hutchinson 2017: 148). Five times the missile does not kill the target (*Iliad* 3.355–6, 5.280–1, 7.244–5, 11.349–50, 22.289–90); twice it does (*Iliad* 17.516–17 (passing through the shield); *Odyssey* 24.522–3 (passing through the helmet)). The statement may or may not presage death. When the statement appears in scenes in which we know the warrior who is hit will not die at that exact moment—such as Diomedes at *Iliad* 5.280–1—it prompts us to wonder how exactly he will avoid a fatal blow.

The poet's killing scenes frequently comprise a more elaborate typical structure: first an overview spelling out who killed whom, then an anecdote about the victim, and then further details about the act of killing (Bakker 1997: 116–18; Ready 2020). We can examine this phenomenon from the perspective of suspense, building on previous discussions of how epic regression—the telling moves in reverse chronological order—increases suspense (R. Allan 2022a: 88–9). Consider a moment in the fight over the corpse of Sarpedon (*Iliad* 16.569–80):

| | |
|---|---|
| And first the Trojans pushed back the bright-eyed Achaeans: | 569 |
| for by no means the worst among the Myrmidons was hit (*blēto*), | 570 |
| the son of great-hearted Agacles, brilliant Epeigeus, | 571 |
| who ruled Budeum with its large population | |
| formerly; but then he killed a noble kinsman | |
| and fled as a suppliant to the house of Peleus and silver-footed Thetis; | |
| they sent him to follow along with Achilles the breaker of men | |
| to Ilium of the good horses in order to fight against the Trojans. | |
| Him then, as he grabbed hold of the corpse, famous Hector hit | 577 |
| with a stone on the head: and his head was split in two completely | |
| in the heavy helmet; and he fell down face first on the corpse, | |
| and spirit-destroying death poured over him. | |

Verse 569 prompts the question, how did the Trojans push back the Myrmidons? Verse 570 provides an answer of sorts—a prominent Myrmidon fell—but prompts three questions: who fell, how did his falling come to pass—being hit is vague—and who hit him? Verse 571 answers the first of those three questions: Epeigeus was hit. But the other two queries remain. The poet increases the how- (and who-) suspense here by pausing to review Epeigeus's background. It is only when the narration of the events on the battlefield resumes at verse 577 that we get an answer to the question of how it happened that Epeigeus was killed and who killed him: Hector killed him by striking him in the head with a rock.

We can continue to distinguish between what- and how- suspense, but the categories can quickly blur, and that which triggers what-suspense in one audience member can trigger how-suspense in another. I want to address what I take to be the more pressing question that arises when we think about reperformance and suspense: why can recipients who know what will happen experience (what- and how-) suspense? My answer brings us back to identification with characters. Suspense may prompt a connection with a character (Vaage 2016: 65, 68, 77), but I will trace the opposite interaction.

In his 1933 dissertation, *Foreshadowing and Suspense in the Epics of Homer, Apollonius, and Vergil*, Duckworth reviews moments in the *Iliad* and the *Odyssey* in which we (the audience) know what will happen but the characters do not. He thinks that "the reader of the epic hopes and fears with the characters and, for the moment at least, is less conscious of his own foreknowledge" (1933: 70–1). Compare Victoria Wohl's assessment of a recipient's response as Euripides's *Ion* unfolds: "as we are drawn into Creusa's suffering, it becomes harder and harder to remember that all will be well that ends well.... The audience become as uncertain of the end as the characters themselves" (2015: 34, 36). Duckworth also explores episodes in which the following occurs: both we (the audience) and a character know what will happen, but despite this knowledge the character expresses doubt about what will transpire. Duckworth posited that, given our attachment to the character, we too have our doubts (94):

> When, however, both characters and reader know the outcome, and the characters, losing their earlier certainty of the future, repeatedly give utterance to expressions of uncertainty and despair, the reader too feels his foreknowledge shaken and rendered insecure.... As he sympathizes with the characters and vicariously shares their experiences, he becomes less certain of the inevitability of the foreshadowed events. The suspense which he feels is thus a combination of anticipation and uncertainty.

For example, we know that Odysseus will make it back home, and Teiresias told Odysseus that he would make it back to Ithaca one way or another (*Odyssey* 11.100–37). Yet when Poseidon conjures a storm that destroys Odysseus's raft, Odysseus expresses dismay at what he takes to be his imminent death far from home (*Odyssey* 5.299–312). In light of our attachment to Odysseus, Odysseus's despair rubs off on us, and we begin to worry about what will happen to him: "This intense despair, which seems inconsistent with the prophecy of Teiresias, is most effective in arousing the suspense of the reader concerning the fate of the hero" (Duckworth 1933: 95). Compare Scodel's assessment of how a recipient might respond to Priam's effort to ransom Hector in *Iliad* 24 (2021: 71).

We know that Achilles will return Hector to Priam, and Iris has told Priam as much (*Iliad* 24.173–87). Still, Priam is "terrified" and "mistrusting," and our "sympathy with Priam...seems to allow some of the character's emotions to blunt our knowledge that the ransom will be successful."

Rudolf Griesinger had noted that suspense arises when the Homeric poet puts characters "who have the sympathy of the reader" into dangerous situations (1907: 75, my translation), but Duckworth's comments do more than expand on that point. They strikingly presage by several decades the discussions in literary and film studies of the so-called paradox of suspense: we feel suspense even when we know the outcome.[1] Ryan explores this phenomenon in the context of audience responses to blockbuster movies. She gives the example of re-watching a scene from the 1995 movie titled *Apollo 13* and still asking oneself, will the astronauts' capsule successfully reenter the atmosphere or will it burn up in the process (Ryan 2015a: 104–5)? Setting aside the idea that "repeated suspense" is "a matter of self-induced amnesia or of pretended ignorance" (106; cf. Beecher 2007: 262), Ryan argues in a manner reminiscent of Duckworth that, no matter how often we re-watch a movie, our "emotional involvement" with the characters explains why "we can repeatedly experience anxiety over destinies that are already written in our memories" (2015a: 106).

Even if we posit that the *Iliad*'s audience members know pretty much everything that is going to happen, they can still experience suspense because they are attached to, involved with, invested in the characters and their fates—in other words, because they identify with them. To stick with Odysseus: audience members are likely familiar with the character of Odysseus and, more than that, used to identifying with him. We can attend to how the scene at, for instance, *Iliad* 11.401–88, wherein Odysseus finds himself in danger, capitalizes on a recipient's propensity to identify with the Ithacan king and generates suspense.

I will not launch a full-scale inquiry into the ways the scene cues identification with Odysseus. (I refer the reader to Chapter 2's analysis of identification.) One might root for Odysseus as soon as the narrator turns to him simply because he is a favored character whom one has already encountered and rooted for countless times. In addition, Odysseus's soliloquy at *Iliad* 11.404–10 can trigger identification. In this speech, he ponders whether to flee or fight although his fellow Achaeans are absent and then resolves to fight (cf. Garcia 2018: 304). The speech gives us access to his perspective on the battle; showcases his virtue: he is not one of the *kakoi* who retreat but one of those who excel in battle (*aristeuēisi makhēi eni*, 11.408–9); and also provides the chance to experience motivational identification: one can hope he succeeds in his implied goal of "striking another" as opposed to himself "being struck" (ἤ τ' ἔβλητ' ἤ τ' ἔβαλ' ἄλλον, 11.410).

---

[1] Robinson 2005: 121; Sanford and Emmott 2012: 229–31; M. Smith 2017: 69–72; cf. M. Power 2006: 78–9; Liotsakis 2021: 16–18; Novokhatko 2021: 32; Scodel 2021: 55.

It is above all the recipient's identification with Odysseus that makes what follows suspenseful. Socus wounds Odysseus. Odysseus kills Socus and then finds himself beset by the Trojans invigorated by the sight of Odysseus's blood. Odysseus calls for aid, and Menelaus tells Ajax that they had better hurry to help lest Odysseus fall to the Trojans (*Iliad* 11.465–71). Menelaus's statement primes us to worry about Odysseus. Identifying with Odysseus, we ask, will he escape this predicament? Menelaus and Ajax make their way to Odysseus where they find him surrounded by Trojans. At this point the poet moves into an extended simile in which jackals track down a wounded stag that falls dead: before they can finish eating him, a lion scares them away and eats the rest (*Iliad* 11.473–81). Interrupting the flow of the narrative, the placement of the simile works in two ways to ratchet up the suspense for the recipient who identifies with Odysseus. One: Ajax and Menelaus have arrived, but did they get there in time to help? And two: the simile prompts the question, will Odysseus suffer the fate of the deer? We have to wait to see what will happen to Odysseus. What is more, the matter is not resolved in the first lines after the simile: those verses (*Iliad* 11.482–3) actually link Odysseus with the deer (Ready 2011: 255). Only at verse 484 do we begin to get a clear answer: Odysseus defends himself ably, and Ajax scatters the Trojans.

My point is that when it comes to audiences of Homeric epic—audiences familiar to greater and lesser degrees with what will happen—suspense depends to a significant extent on identification with characters. And I stress again that when I talk about identification I have in mind the multi-faceted definitions of the concept discussed in section 2.2. We know that Odysseus will survive in *Iliad* 11, but we still paradoxically feel suspense because we identify with him.

In addition to Ryan's argument, other research on the relationship between suspense and connections to characters helps us articulate this link. Richard Gerrig contends, "A theory of suspense must include within it a theory of empathy" (1993: 80), and, while stressing that empathy cannot in all cases account for suspense (2007: 258, 272, 275–6), Donald Beecher builds on Gerrig's work in averring, "Where there is literary suspense there are characters who serve as the center of concern through empathy" (270). Keith Oatley observes, "If we are attached to the character...we might feel anxious" (2012: 53), and "if, in a story, a character whom we like is in danger, we feel anxious.... The process is one of identification and empathy" (56, citing Zillmann 1996). Discussing *paralittérature* (essentially, popular fiction), Grethlein writes, "The *suspense moyen* [how-suspense] gains force from sympathy with or even identification with the characters" (2017a: 133). Using "allegiance," his preferred term for what others would call identification, Carl Plantinga contends, "If the filmmaker can elicit strong allegiance with a protagonist, this also ensures continued interest in, and anticipation, curiosity, and suspense about, what will happen *to* the protagonist" (2018: 44, emphasis in original; cf. 51). He comments on a scene in the movie *The Silence of the Lambs:* "The stronger my concern for Clarice Starling's well-being, the greater my suspense as she confronts Buffalo Bill in his dark basement" (2009: 75). Comparable too is the connection Paul Woodruff draws between our caring about a character and our desire to see how the plot unfolds (2008: 103–5, 148–50).

Classicists also make these sorts of statements. For Vasileios Liotsakis, it is when we "empathize" with the characters, are "favourably predisposed" toward them, and "approve morally" of their behavior that we experience suspense (2021: 11–13). Scodel writes, "We certainly do not feel suspense if we do not care about the characters" (2021: 68). Rachel Lesser finds that our sense of "anticipation" increases when we "care for" a character and experience "empathy" with them (2022: 87–8). Still more useful is Nikos Miltsios's discussion of suspense in the works of Appian and Polybius. The sentence, "One basic precondition for the creation of suspense is that readers of a work identify with its protagonists" (2021: 301), would seem to articulate my thesis. Although Miltsios does not go into the specific components of identification, his presentation does suggest how one sort of identification can trigger suspense. Discussing how Polybius creates suspense in describing Apelles's conspiracy against Philip II of Macedon, Miltsios writes, "He prefers to let readers learn of how the plot unfolds at the same time as the characters, enabling them to experience the openness of the past and the concomitant suspense over the final outcome" (2021: 291; cf. 295). I would speak here of "epistemic identification" (see section 2.2, p. 22): recipients think they "believe or know the same thing about the narrative situation as the character does" (van Vught and Schott 2017: 169).

Most important is the empirical support for the connection between identification and suspense. In a 1984 study of second-, fourth-, and sixth-graders in which the second-graders heard stories and the others read them, Paul Jose and William Brewer found that the more recipients identified with the characters the more suspense they felt (cf. Thissen, Menninghaus, and Schlotz 2020: 712). Bálint, Kuijpers, and Doicaru's 2017 study reinforces this equation. They introduce a presentation of their own results by noting that "only if a reader values the outcome event of a story they will feel suspense" (cf. Grethlein 2017a: 118) and by pointing to Doicaru's 2016 findings that "outcome value" is based on "character likeability; outcome desirability/undesirability; and likelihood that an expected negative event will affect the protagonist" (2017: 180–1). When we talk about character likeability and concern for effects on the protagonist, we are quickly approaching triggers for identification. More illuminating, however, is their own experiment. They queried subjects' "emotional engagement" while watching a movie with such prompts as "I felt connected to the main character in the story" (184). I take what they call "emotional engagement" to reflect identification (cf. Tal-Or and Cohen 2010: 413). The researchers affirmed that "emotional engagement was found to be a good predictor of felt suspense in general"

(Bálint, Kuijpers, and Doicaru 2017: 191), and their experiment replicated Doicaru's 2016 findings of "significant correlations between felt suspense and emotional engagement, which were significantly higher than the correlations between suspense and other dimensions of narrative engagement (i.e., presence, focused attention, understanding)" (181). Intricate plotting can trigger suspense (Grethlein 2017a: e.g., 45, 55), but this literature illuminates how our identification with characters enables our feelings of suspense.

This proposal differs in important respects from that of Grethlein whose eminently readable analysis I quote at length (2017a: 55):

> Note however that the attention and absorption of the reader need not be mediated through a character in the narrated world. Sympathy or even identification with characters certainly help to pull the reader into the action, but they are not a necessary condition for immersion. The reader's attention may be simply directed to the further course of the action without depending on a character's perspective. She may wonder about what is going to happen next without adopting the viewpoint of a character. When for example in the *Ethiopica* the heroine, Charicleia, stands on a pyre that is about to be kindled, the reader feels suspense. This suspense, however, does not build on how she or any other character feels and assesses her future; it is immediately directed towards the outcome of the scene.

Grethlein's presentation reduces identification to perceptual/cognitive identification, finds a moment in which that perceptual/cognitive identification is considered not to be operative, declares the moment suspenseful, and concludes that the suspense does not depend on identification. I counter, one (and once again), that there are different kinds of identification and that we should not limit identification to perceptual or cognitive identification—for instance, we can experience motivational identification with Charicleia at this moment (and her death by burning is not part of her plan)—and, two, that we should not ignore our history of identification with a protagonist: our attachment develops and endures over time; because I have identified with a character in the past, I care about what happens to them at this moment and accordingly feel suspense, even if I am not experiencing any of the forms of identification at that moment other than a vague motivational identification.

The connection between suspense and identification obtains even for narratives that deploy one-dimensional characters and focus on their actions, not their inner lives. Identification does not require complexity (cf. Felski 2020b: 109–10, 119; *pace* Grethlein 2017a: 141). These sorts of stories tend to offer a protagonist whom recipients more or less automatically care about and root for because of their physical and mental (but especially physical) attributes (cf. Plantinga 2009: 103; Grethlein 2017a: 133). These characters are constructed to exploit a host of biases that recipients have acquired over the years, biases that quickly bind them to the protagonist. That numerous recipients have so-called parasocial relationships ("a lingering sense of intimacy and connection with media personalities" (Tukachinsky, Walter, and Saucier 2020: 868)) with the same character from a popular movie, television show, or novel makes this fact clear (e.g., Superman (Peretti 2017)). At the very least, one notes that the prevalence of parasocial relationships with popular characters proves that, in the real world, identification does not require complex characters. It is our identification with these straightforward, even simple characters that propels our feelings of suspense. In applying these principles to Homeric epic, even if one adhered to those mid-twentieth-century readings that insisted on the static, un-changing nature of Homeric characters (de Jong 2018a: 27–8, 40), one would not label Hector or Achilles or Odysseus one-dimensional. But other characters might nevertheless not merit the label complex, even if we allow that they do change: take, for instance, Diomedes (O'Maley 2018). Our ability to identify with the characters who seem pretty easy to get a handle on whether we spend a lot of time with them—such as Diomedes— or a bit less time with them—such as Eurypylus—allows us to feel suspense over their fate.

When we talk about suspense as bound up with our identification with the characters, we can best account for the immersive force of suspense whether we are re-experiencing a narrative, whether that narrative is Homeric or anything else. Being exposed to an event that unfolds over time may pique our interest. As Oatley notes, "In day-to-day life we're very interested in how actions turn out" (2012: 43). As I walk past a tennis court or basketball court, I routinely find myself watching to see if a player's shot will clear or find the bottom of the net. I may feel suspense, but the degree of suspense must be minimal, and I doubt I could be said to be engrossed in the spectacle. By contrast, when I watch my sister race in a swim meet, I care about her success and identify with her, the suspense is far greater, and my engrossment in the event far more likely. Likewise, we have a real need to know how stories we are told or stories we read turn out (Christensen 2020: 249–52). Still, we cannot be said to be immersed simply because we "wonder about what is going to happen next" and "desire to learn the further course of the action" (Grethlein 2017a: 55, 151). It is because we have attachments to characters who try to do some things and avoid other things—attachments that develop over time and that we signal by speaking of a "hero" (cf. Hogan 2018: 143–4)—that we can be gripped by the emotion of suspense and thus gripped find ourselves immersed.

Bálint, Kuijpers, and Doicaru provide further nuance to a discussion of the relationship between suspense and immersion. They focus on the way in which delay enhances suspense (2017: 178) and distinguish between diegetic delay and non-diegetic delay. Diegetic delays take place in or pertain to elements in the storyworld: "in written text they can be extra descriptions of the location, or the state of mind of the characters" (179). Non-diegetic delays introduce elements that do not appear in the storyworld: they tend to have a metaphorical relationship to what is happening in the storyworld (179, 184). As an example of a non-diegetic delay, Bálint, Kuijpers, and Doicaru give the insertion of "non-diegetic animated sequences into live action movies" (179). Similes, those cousins of metaphor (Aristotle *Art of Rhetoric* 1410b17–20; Ready 2004: 158–9), also constitute non-diegetic delays—similes like the one from *Iliad* 11 discussed earlier (p. 203). In their experiment, Bálint, Kuijpers, and Doicaru found "that the level of felt suspense is higher in cases of diegetic suspense compared to non-diegetic suspense" and that "scenes with non-diegetic suspense delay elicited lower levels of narrative absorption... than scenes with diegetic delay" (2017: 187).

When scholars point to the components of the presentation that create suspense in the Homeric epics, they frequently point to diegetic delays, such as lengthy speeches (Janko 1992: 77 at 246–97; cf. Austin 1966: 306; Kirstein 2022: 127, 130–1), descriptions of locations (Schmitz 1994: 14), backstories about doomed warriors (Janko 1992: 128 at 660–72), and presentations of inner thoughts (Janko 1992: 301 at 674–703 with 304 at 699–703). For example, consider the beginning of *Iliad* 2. Agamemnon tells his counselors that he wants to test the troops: "I will test them with words, which is customary, and order them to flee with their many-benched ships; but you, different ones in different spots, try to restrain them with words" (*Iliad* 2.72–5; see A. Porter 2019: 123–8). The recipient wants to learn how the soldiers will respond to this astonishing proposal and how the leaders will react to their response. But the poet spends eight lines on a description of Agamemnon's scepter (*Iliad* 2.101–8) and thirty-three lines on Agamemnon's deceptive speech to the troops (2.109–41) before describing the Achaeans' flight to the ships. Of the two forms of delay—diegetic and non-diegetic—the Homeric poets rely on the one, diegetic delay, that makes for greater suspense and that pairs most readily with narrative immersion.

At the same time, to repeat, the poet of the *Iliad* makes frequent use of similes that function as non-diegetic delays. As we just saw, "the level of felt suspense is higher in cases of diegetic suspense compared to non-diegetic suspense," and "scenes with non-diegetic suspense delay elicited lower levels of narrative absorption... than scenes with diegetic delay" (Bálint, Kuijpers, and Doicaru 2017: 187). But the details matter here. In the trio's model, narrative absorption segments into three components: "emotional engagement," "attention," and "transportation" (186). They understand attention "as a subjective experience of being fully concentrated on a narrative" (192). They measure transportation with such items as "When I was reading the story it sometimes seems as if I were in the story world too" (184). Of the three components of absorption, non-diegetic delays affected attention: "Suspense structure has no significant effect on emotional engagement... and transportation..., but it influenced attention.... Attention for non-diegetic suspense scene was lower... than for the diegetic suspense scene" (187). Their explanation for this impact on attention runs thus: "comprehending a non-diegetic insert requires a larger amount of allocated cognitive load and, at the same time, it breaks the natural flow of the events, therefore disrupting the subjective experience of attention" (192). Now, non-diegetic delays may affect attention, but they are far from snapping a recipient out of an immersed state (192):

> the disruption of the subjective experience of attention does not lead to a decreased emotional engagement or transportation, which suggests that non-diegetic suspense delay does not fully ruin the experience of narrative absorption, but rather affects the attentional component of it. It seems that the different components of narrative absorption have different levels of sensitivity to changes in suspense structure.

Back now, with these results in mind, to Homeric similes. From the perspective outlined here, the similes, as non-diegetic delays, do not make for as much suspense as diegetic delays and, at best, do not impede immersion. That latter point helps us qualify the intuitively attractive idea that when an extended simile occurs "the illusion that we are present on the scene, that there is no barrier between us and the events of the story, is broken by the reference to something within our own sphere of activity quite separate from the Trojan War" (S. Richardson 1990: 66). But to leave off there would be to occlude the extent to which the poet integrates similes into the diegesis. Recognizing that fact allows us to align similes with the diegetic delays in the epics and, building on discussions of how Homeric similes make for suspense (Ready 2012: 76 n. 101), to pinpoint how similes increase suspense.

The poet regularly includes an action in a simile that presages what will happen in the narrative proper. Pre-positioned similes (the vehicle portion comes before the tenor (see Ready 2018: 50–1)) perform this service most explicitly. An example comes in the description of men stretching an oxhide (*Iliad* 17.389–93), "which is not closely connected with the preceding account of the sweating weary warriors but introduces the following picture of the two sides tugging vainly at Patroklos' body" (Edwards 1991: 28). At other times, a simile "is so powerfully integrated into the narrative, looking both forward and backward, that its removal would be impossible" (Edwards 1991: 28; cf. Ready 2018: 52–3). For instance, a simile describes Menelaus stripping the fallen Euphorbus of his armor (*Iliad* 17.61–7): a lion killing and eating a cow connects to what came before; the herdsmen and dogs who fear to attack the lion anticipates the Trojans' fear of attacking Menelaus (see also Edwards 1991: 32). One can speak of "narration through imagery" at such moments (Lyne 1989: ch. 4) and also chart how similes often allow for "the continuation of the text" (Nimis 1987: 84–95, quotation from 93). In addition, several similes in the narrator text reflect the point of view or emotions of the characters,[2] and the poet can even craft a simile in which the vehicle portion comes from the same area of life as the narrative proper: the distance between Menelaus's and Antilochus's chariots equals the distance between a horse and the chariot it pulls (*Iliad* 23.517–23; Grethlein and Huitink 2017: 81–2; cf. Ready 2011: 195 on *Iliad* 21.281–3; Myers 2019: 189 on *Iliad* 22.21–5).

A simile technically introduces a non-diegetic delay, but its entanglement in the diegesis has two knock-on effects. First, this entanglement lessens the degree to which it strikes us as a non-diegetic delay. That it does not seem like a non-diegetic delay might mean that we treat it more along the lines of a diegetic delay and, accordingly, that it makes for as much suspense and immersion as a diegetic delay would.

Second, entangled in the surrounding narrative, a simile can increase suspense because it leads us to ask what will transpire in the narrative. Recall the *Iliad*'s final extended simile. Priam enters Achilles's tent and performs the gestures of the suppliant: "he took his knees in his hands and kissed the hands, fearsome, manslaying, which had killed many of his sons (*poleas... huias*)" (*Iliad* 24.478–9). That Priam appears to be the only suppliant in archaic- and classical-era literature who kisses the hands of the supplicated (Forte 2020: 20) draws our attention to the elaborate description of Achilles's murderous hands and to the couplet's juxtaposition of supplication with killing, in particular the killing of Priam's sons. This juxtaposition can make us fear for Priam because of what it brings to mind. It reminds us that no one has yet spared a suppliant in the *Iliad*'s story proper (A. Porter 2019: 103, 156). More specifically, it conjures Lycaon's failed supplication of Achilles during which Achilles declares that he will spare none of the Trojans, especially none of Priam's children (*paidōn*) (*Iliad* 21.103–5). The couplet also recalls Hecuba's amazement that Priam would contemplate talking with the man who has killed so many of his sons and her subsequent prediction that Achilles will dismiss Priam's supplication and instead kill him: "How are you willing to go alone to the ships of the Achaeans, to the eyes of a man who killed many of your noble sons (πολέας τε καὶ ἐσθλοὺς / υἱέας)?... He will not pity (*eleēsei*) you, nor at all will he respect (*aidesetai*) you" (*Iliad* 24.203–5, 207–8). Achilles himself attests to the fact that our fears for Priam at this moment were not misplaced when he later brings up the possibility of his killing Priam despite his status as a suppliant: "Do not then rouse my heart all the more in pains, lest I do not spare even you yourself in my huts, even though you are a suppliant, and I violate the orders of Zeus" (*Iliad* 24.568–70).

Having made us worry about Priam's fate, the poet introduces a simile: "And as when sheer folly seizes a man, who in his fatherland has killed a man and goes into the land of others, into the house of a rich man, and amazement (*thambos*) holds

---

[2] Bremer 1986; Patzer 1996: 118–30; de Jong 2004: 123–36; 2018a: 38; Edwards 1991: 33–4; Hesk 2013: 39.

those who see him" (*Iliad* 24.480–2). Nicholas Richardson deems this "the most dramatic moment in the whole of the *Iliad*" (1993: 323 at 480–4; cf. Heiden 1998: 1). I would say suspenseful: this prepositioned simile joins with verses 478–9 in leading us to ask how Achilles will respond to Priam. Will he kill him, or will he experience and act in accordance with the amazement (*thambos*) referred to in the simile, *thambos* being an emotion never felt by killers but only by spectators (and, along with the verb *thambeō*, frequently spectators of divine action) (Prier 1989: 87–9, 92–3; Kelly 2007: 115–17; Haubold 2014: 27; Ready 2018: 251)?

Ryan proposes metasuspense as her final category of suspense. Following Morrison, we find a brand of metasuspense in the *Iliad*: how will the narrator keep the tale on track? For Morrison, suspense arises in moments in which the poet does not provide the audience with any hints as to what is coming (1992: 51). In discussing what he calls suspense, Morrison focuses on the duel between Paris and Menelaus in *Iliad* 3 and on Hector's time in Troy in *Iliad* 6. Regarding the first episode, he writes (59; cf. Rengakos 1999: 317–18; Scodel 2021: 61–2):

> The narrator structures the narrative so that the audience experiences a strong degree of suspense. It knows that the duel must be terminated if the story is to continue, yet the narrator gives no indication how that will be accomplished: the duel's outcome remains a mystery. The audience must set its own previous ideas about what is likely to happen against the narrative, which at this point moves in an entirely different direction. The audience has no idea of what will happen to interrupt this digression. In a sense, it expects renewed battle and an ensuing Greek defeat, yet it does not know how the narrator will return the narrative to its former track. It can only wait to see how the narrator takes the armies from the prospect of a truce and negotiated settlement back to battle and a Trojan victory.

Consider the sentences later in his presentation: "Epic suspense follows from a lack of information. The audience is uncertain how the narrator will return to the story he has promised" (Morrison 1992: 62; cf. Rengakos 1999: 317; Scodel 2021: 64–5). And a sentence in his concluding chapter: "Homer provokes his audience and keeps it wondering how the singer will reconcile his tale with the tradition at large" (Morrison 1992: 112; cf. Schmitz 1994: 14; Scodel 2021: 63). These quotations suggest that, when Morrison talks about suspense, he is talking about a type of metasuspense. To repeat, Ryan's metasuspense emerges when the audience wonders "how the author is going to tie all the strands together and give the text proper narrative form" (2015a: 104). In Morrison's model, the audience wonders, how will Homer keep his story together, making sure it adheres to the traditional plot? The audience asks not whether but how the poet will return the story to the expected path. This intersection between Ryan's and Morrison's discussions not only helps us clarify Morrison's model. It also reminds us to provide a history for the various forms of suspense evident in modern narratives.

## 7.3. Other Emotions

A character can be said to feel a certain way, but that does not mean a recipient will feel that way (cf. Ryan 2015a: 107; cf. Plantinga 2009: 159, 167). I doubt anyone feels the wrath that Agamemnon feels at *Iliad* 1.247 (*emēnie*) after Achilles insults him. When Hector feels "stung" by Sarpedon's words (*dake*, *Iliad* 5.493), a recipient is unlikely to feel stung. Let us dig a little deeper to find out what prompts emotional engagement in recipients.

We can display "subjective reactions to characters and judgments of their behavior" (Ryan 2015a: 108). Ryan lists the following: "primarily like and dislike but also admiration, contempt, pity, amusement, Schadenfreude (when bad characters get their comeuppance), and exasperation (when good things happen to bad characters)." The important thing here is the relationship between judgment and emotion, and Lynn Kozak is a bit more precise on that front: defining "allegiance" (see section 1.3, p. 5), they note, "The audience morally judges them [the characters] and will feel either sympathy or antipathy with them in part based on those judgements" (2017: 5; cf. 20, 147). One can also invoke Christopher Gill's contention that what he calls our "special sympathetic involvement" with a character—manifested at least in part in our emotional reactions to them—"is bound up with" our ethical judgments of their motivations (2002: 97–107, quotations from 105).

As Aristotle recognized, one's emotional state can affect one's judgment (Lada 1993: 117; Konstan 2006: 33–8; Plantinga 2009: 200–1, 218; Todd et al. 2015: 375), but the equation goes the other way too (as again Aristotle recognized (Lada 1993: 116; Konstan 2006: 21, 37; Visvardi 2015: 11–12)). The movement from judgment to emotion lies at the heart of appraisal theory, one of the popular and enduring explanatory models of emotion (and I highlight Plantinga's (2009: 49–59, 223; 2018: 43, 176) and Hogan's (2011: 42–54; 2018: 54–61) independent efforts to reconcile appraisal theory with its apparent antagonist, what Hogan terms "perception theory" (42)). Per appraisal theory, "emotions are elicited and differentiated by the subjective interpretation of the personal significance of events."[3] We interpret, evaluate, assess, or judge (consciously or not) how an event affects what we care about, and then the appropriate emotion comes.

One can apply appraisal theory to explain a character's emotions (Oatley 2012: 30–1; Hogan 2018: 54–61). Or one can follow Oatley who suggests that we identify with a character when we take on their goals and concerns and that that identification leads us to appraise the events of the narrative with a view to those goals and concerns and experience emotions as the character succeeds or fails in their efforts (1994: 66; 1999a: 114). Likewise, Carl Plantinga proposes that, when we

---

[3] Scherer and Ellsworth 2009: 45; cf. Robinson 2005: 26–7; Konstan 2006: 21–5; Oatley 2012: 36; Hogan 2018: 54; Eder, Hanich, and Stadler 2019: 93, 95.

adopt a character's goals, we appraise the situations the character faces from the character's perspective and thereby feel "sympathetic emotions" of "compassion, pity, admiration, [and] happiness" (2009: 88, 69; cf. 93–5, 171). Ryan's, Kozak's, and Gill's statements suggest an additional adaptation of appraisal theory to account for the emotions a recipient feels even when not identifying with a character. Plantinga seems to be driving at that adaptation: "while a film character may experience extreme fear, the spectator may be privy to superior information and know that he or she is in no imminent danger. The spectator may experience something like mild pity and amusement at the character's fearful response" (2009: 156–7). The viewer's judgment generates the emotional response. Elsewhere, Plantinga writes, "When the spectator *has* a moral emotion in relation to a character, this means that the spectator has construed [i.e., appraised (JR)] the behavior of the character in moral terms. When viewers become angry, disgusted, compassionate, or elevated by a character, it is because they have made a moral judgment" (2018: 46, emphasis in original). Again, judgment prompts emotion. In short, as we repeatedly make judgments about a character, we experience the items in Ryan's list—and other emotions too, such as "elevation" ("the opposite of social disgust, which takes as its object the witnessing of acts of human beauty or virtue" (Plantinga 2009: 183)). Still, to the extent that our identifying with characters prompts evaluations that lead to emotions, those experiences go hand in hand with feeling (and perhaps even prepare us to feel) emotions that stem from assessments even if or when we are not identifying with characters.

Homeric epic provides recipients ample opportunities to react subjectively to and judge the characters. It trains us to do so by having its characters "evaluate themselves and others, anticipate and infer the judgments of others" (Scodel 2008: 157). Characters pronounce judgments on another's words or deeds. Thersites criticizes Achilles for failing to be sufficiently angry with Agamemnon (*Iliad* 2.241–2; Cairns 2003: 47), and the Achaeans declare Odysseus's silencing of Thersites the best thing he has yet done (*ariston, Iliad* 2.274). Menelaus rebukes his fellow Achaeans for their unwillingness to fight a duel against Hector (*Iliad* 7.96–100). After Menelaus says that he will face Hector and puts on his armor (*Iliad* 7.101–3), Agamemnon chastises Menelaus: "You are mad" (*aphraineis*, 7.109–10). The leaders of the Achaeans approve Diomedes's recommendation at the end of *Iliad* 9 to stop obsessing over the prospect of Achilles's return: "And so he spoke, and all the chiefs then indicated their approval (*epēinēsan*), since they marveled at (*agassamenoi*) the speech of Diomedes breaker of horses" (*Iliad* 9.710–11; cf. Elmer 2013: 124). Zeus deems "not in good order" (*ou kata kosmon, Iliad* 17.205) Hector's stripping of Achilles's armor from Patroclus (Kozak 2017: 166). For Hecuba, Hector was a source of pride to her (literally, "a boast" (*eukhōlē*)) and "a source of help" (*oneiar*) to all the Trojans (*Iliad* 22.433; Kozak 2017: 208). In the archery contest during the funeral games for Patroclus,

Meriones's skillful shot impresses the Achaeans: "and the people in turned gazed (*thēeunto*) and were struck with wonder (*thambēsan*)" (*Iliad* 23.881). Even a hypothetical observer at *Iliad* 4.539–42 (technically not a character in the storyworld although he does acquire the attributes of such to the extent that Pallas Athena touches him (cf. Myers 2019: 105)) assesses the warriors' efforts: "Then no longer would a man enter the fray and make light of it (*onosaito*), whoever still unwounded by the throw or unharmed by the thrust of sharp bronze should go through their midst, and Pallas Athena should lead him taking by the hand and check the onrush of missiles" (cf. de Jong 2004: 59; Myers 2019: 105).

Readily susceptible to a feeling of shame (e.g., Scodel 2008: 19–20; Yamagata 2020), characters anticipate being judged (cf. Gill 2002: 75). Menelaus first fears that he will be criticized (*nemesēsetai*) for abandoning his defense of Patroclus's corpse but then decides that no one can reasonably fault (again, *nemesēsetai*) his yielding to the divinely backed Hector (*Iliad* 17.91–101; Gill 2002: 79–80; Garcia 2018: 304). Later in his dispute with Antilochus after the chariot race in the funeral games, "Menelaus is very concerned about how the Achaeans will judge him" (Scodel 2008: 45–7, quotation from 45). Hector says that Polydamas "will be the first to put a reproach (*elegkheiēn*) on me" for failing to pull the Trojans back from battle (*Iliad* 22.100) and that an anonymous Trojan will declare, "Trusting in his own might, Hector destroyed his people" (22.107; Gill 2002: 82–5; Scodel 2008: 20; Garcia 2018: 308). Characters also judge themselves (cf. Scodel 2008: 20–1). Pandarus claims that he should have heeded his father's advice to take a horse and chariot to Troy: "it would have been much better (*polu kerdion*)" (*Iliad* 5.197–205). Hector determines that "it would have been much better (*polu kerdion*)" if he had listened to Polydamas's suggestion that the Trojans retreat (*Iliad* 22.100–3).

The narrator assesses words and deeds as well. Agamemnon "urged fitting things" (*aisima pareipōn, Iliad* 6.62, 7.121; de Jong 2004: 205). Hector "counselled badly" (*kaka mētioōnti, Iliad* 18.312): if the narrator "is not so much criticizing Hector as emphasizing the dramatic mistake...he and the Trojans make" (de Jong 2004: 138), he still passes judgment. When Patroclus fails to stick to the original plan of merely driving the Trojans from the ships and presses on, the narrator labels him "foolish" (*nēpios, Iliad* 16.684–7; Kozak 2017: 159), and, when Achilles holds his shield away from his body for fear that Aeneas's spear might penetrate it, he too shows himself to be "foolish" (*nēpios, Iliad* 20.259–66) (Edwards 1991: 4–5). As "*interpretations of events*" (de Jong 2004: 125, emphasis in original), the narrator's similes can express judgments: Paris's likeness to a lion's prey and to a man withdrawing from a snake depict him as incapable of success on the battlefield (*Iliad* 3.21–37; Ready 2011: 203–5). This last observation prompts me to sum up these paragraphs with one final permutation. Characters can speak similes that the audience can understand as responses to and judgments of the assessments that the narrator makes through similes (Ready 2011:

150–210). For instance, Paris is made to dispute the way the narrator (and Hector) depicts him as an incapable warrior (*Iliad* 3.60–3; Ready 2011: 206–9).

In our scholarly mode, we might look today with a bemused sense of superiority on Bernard Fenik's assessment of Menelaus's speech at *Iliad* 13.620–39: "a fatuous tantrum from start to finish, feeble in conception and long-winded" (1986: 42). But judge the characters we do—if perhaps not always with the deliberateness and rigor with which Peter Ahrensdorf makes his cases for and against Hector, Achilles, and Odysseus (2014)—and the frequency and rapidity with which characters and narrator issue judgments in the *Iliad* encourage our own such assessments and gives us license to judge the characters too. This modeling may not be necessary, judgments (especially quick ones) being a specialty of ours (Breithaupt 2019: 98), but it helps.

N. Richardson can find "no apparent reason" (1993: 222 at 473–81) behind the insulting speech Oilean Ajax directs at Idomeneus when the latter declares Diomedes in the lead during the chariot race in the funeral games for Patroclus. More indicative, I think, of a typical reaction is Margareta Kramer-Hajos's assessment of Oilean Ajax's speech: "during the games he managed to alienate even the most sympathetic audience by verbally abusing Idomeneus when the latter correctly thought that Diomedes had taken the lead in the chariot race (*Il.* 23.473–81). Aias could have been forgiven, had he been right; but he was not" (2012: 96). We might try to figure out why Glaucus exchanges his gold armor for Diomedes's bronze armor (*Iliad* 6.234–6; cf. Graziosi and Haubold 2010: 39; Tsagalis 2010a: 96 n. 37), but we also judge him for doing so ("foolishness" (Edwards 1991: 5); "a dupe" (Graziosi and Haubold 2010: 143 at 230–1)). Hector refuses wine offered by Hecuba when he returns to Troy (*Iliad* 6.264–8). We might try to figure out why he does so—"he is in a hurry" (Kirk 1990: 196 at 264–5)—but beyond such disinterested analysis we might judge his reasoning as well ("mit guten Gründen" (Stoevesandt 2008: 94 at 264–85)). The brilliant and varied analyses of why Achilles refuses Agamemnon's offer in *Iliad* 9 (Gill 2002: 124–54; D. Wilson 2002: 85–96; Scodel 2008: 146–9) should not obscure the fact that we judge the Myrmidon for doing so (Gill 2002: 143; Scodel 2008: 150). The river Scamander grows angry when Achilles kills Trojans within its waters (*kholōsato*, *Iliad* 21.136): we might join the god in condemning this "horrific," "transgressive," "heedless" slaughter (Holmes 2015: 38, 40, 43). Whether they approve or disapprove, recipients will judge Achilles's mistreatment of Hector's corpse. The narrator's use of the adjective "unseemly" (*aeikea*) to describe Achilles's actions (*Iliad* 22.395, 23.24) may reflect Achilles's own intentions and not the narrator's opinion (de Jong 2004: 138; Edwards 1991: 6), but the presence of the evaluative term—it cannot be reduced to the descriptive sense of "disfiguring" (*pace* de Jong 2018a: 44)—can help to trigger a recipient's own assessment (cf. Kozak 2017: 217; Scodel 2021: 71). Even if we cannot figure out exactly what Epeius does in the shotput contest that provokes laughter (Scanlon 2018: 7), we can judge him for it: "He deserved to lose this event, the heroes and the Homeric audience will have thought" (10). Hecuba's opposition to Priam's plan to recover the corpse of Hector from Achilles (*Iliad* 24.200-9) can generate a countervailing judgment in the recipient that endorses his course of action (cf. Herrero de Jáuregui on "Priam's new heroism" (2011: 61-4, quotation from 63)).

Characters do not just judge one another's actions: they give free rein to their actor/observer bias (Scodel 2008: 31 n. 24). According to this principle (see section 4.2.3, p. 103), we explain our own actions as responses to circumstances but explain others' actions as arising from attributes of their character. These explanations usually imply judgments of those attributes and of the individual possessing those attributes. I noted previously (section 4.2.3, pp. 103-4) Menelaus's claim that Antilochus's maneuver in the chariot race reveals a flawed character: "no other of mortals is more destructive than you... not rightly do we Achaeans label you wise" (*Iliad* 23.439-40). Achilles takes Agamemnon's declaration that he will seize Briseis as indicative of fundamental character flaws: "You, heavy with wine, with the eyes of a dog, and the heart of a deer" (*Iliad* 1.225; cf. Scodel 2008: 133-5). When Hera asks Zeus if he has been conniving with Thetis, Zeus retorts, "You are always suspicious" (*aiei ... oieai*, *Iliad* 1.561). Hector sees in Paris's retreat from Menelaus evidence of his brother's misplaced priorities: "the lyre and the gifts of Aphrodite, your hair and beauty" (*Iliad* 3.54-5; cf. Kozak 2017: 34). Antenor recounts an initial assessment of Odysseus when Menelaus and Odysseus came on an embassy to Troy: because Odysseus looked at the ground and did not move his scepter, "you would say that he was some sort of churl (*zakoton*) and nothing but a fool (*aphrona*)" (*Iliad* 3.220). Agamemnon thinks that Menelaus's willingness to ransom Adrastus stems from his general "concern for men" (*kēdeai outōs / andrōn*, *Iliad* 6.55-6). Andromache avers that Hector's "inherent trait" of *menos* (Kozak 2017: 65), his "impulse to fight" (Graziosi and Haubold 2010: 194 at 407-13), will kill him (*Iliad* 6.407). Diomedes attributes Achilles's refusal to return to the fight to an enduring trait: "he exhibits excessive manliness in general" (ὃ δ᾽ ἀγήνωρ ἐστὶ καὶ ἄλλως, *Iliad* 9.699; cf. Graziosi and Haubold 2003: 67; Scodel 2008: 150). Odysseus opines that cowards (*kakoi*) flee from battle while those with a disposition "to be the best in battle" (*aristeuēisi makhēi eni*) stand fast (*Iliad* 11.408-10; cf. Gill 2002: 73). Polydamas explains Hector's earlier refusal to abide by Polydamas's interpretation of an omen: "you are difficult to persuade with persuasive words" (ἀμήχανός ἐσσι παραρρητοῖσι πιθέσθαι, *Iliad* 13.726). For Polydamas, Hector's refusal in that instance stems from his innate stubbornness (or bravery (Janko 1992: 138 at 726-9)). Hector assigns Achilles's unwillingness to return his corpse to Troy to the Myrmidon's "heart ... of iron" (*sidēreos ... thumos*, *Iliad* 22.357). Oilean Ajax claims that Idomeneus misjudges who is leading the chariot race and sees the error as evidence of Idomeneus's propensity for bluster: *aiei muthois labreueai* (*Iliad* 23.478). A character can fear this kind of assessment. Diomedes expresses chagrin at the prospect of Hector's recounting how the Achaean fled before him in battle (*Iliad* 8.148–50). He envisions Hector not merely recalling an event on the battlefield but attributing Diomedes's flight to an underlying cowardice (Scodel 2008: 3). In all these cases, the speaker renders a not so implicit judgment on the addressee or referent.

Recipients can follow the model provided by the characters in pronouncing more vigorous judgments of this sort upon the characters. (Again, recipients may not require this modeling: Richard Gerrig and David Allbritton suggest that readers readily attribute a character's actions to their dispositions, not their situations (1990: 381–4; cf. Knox 2021: 153).) Glenn Most observes Patroclus's "universally acknowledged kindness and pity" (2003: 67), acknowledged, that is, by the narrator and other characters. Recipients too find Patroclus a good man (e.g., "highly sympathetic" (Edwards 1991: 3)) and may attribute his actions to his fundamental decency: for example, he "put[s] his mission for Achilles on hold because someone [Eurypylus] needed his kindness" (Kozak 2017: 175). Ajax nods to Phoenix to signal that Phoenix should address Achilles, but Odysseus jumps in and speaks first: "Odysseus' prompt intervention reminds us that he is ever-alert, ready to take the initiative should it present itself. Its interpersonal implications (Odysseus' outmanoeuvring of Aias) hint at Odysseus' quicker wits in comparison with Aias' slower, more circumspect disposition" (Minchin 2008b: 27; cf. Scodel 2008: 143). Odysseus's decision not to reveal himself straightaway to his father, Laertes, shows "that secrecy, dissimulation, and restraint are innate, not to say incorrigible, traits of Odysseus' character" (de Jong 1994: 37). We might note a "special trait of Menelaus' character, his sympathy" and see therein an explanation for his actions (Stelow 2020: 29–30, quotation from 30; cf. 71, 75, 89, 102, 114): "Menelaus is impelled by a strong sense of justice and acute sensitivity toward his fellow Achaeans" (291; cf. Kozak 2017: 212; Castiglioni 2020: 223). That Agamemnon is not "able to *regulate* his own emotions" explains his behavior in *Iliad* 1 and "his almost surly reaction (at 19.78–144) to Achilles' announcement (at 56–73) that he has decided to return to the fighting" (Minchin 2021b: 53–4, emphasis in original). Sthenelus suggests that Diomedes yield before Pandarus and Aeneas, but Diomedes refuses, claiming, "It is not in my blood (*gennaion*) to fight skulking about nor to cower" (*Iliad* 5.253–4). One might take Diomedes's readiness to fight as evidence of his heroic temperament. Hector proclaims that the Trojans will at last "take the [Achaean] ships, which came here against the will of the gods" (*Iliad* 15.720). We can evaluate his speech—his words "show his folly" (Janko 1992: 306 at 718–25)—and take it as indicative of his tendency toward misplaced optimism or "his characteristic and increasing overconfidence" (Rutherford 1982: 157): compare his prayer that his son, Astyanax, will one day rule the Trojans and excel in battle (*Iliad* 6.476–81), a prayer "far removed from what will actually happen" and "unrealistic" (Graziosi and Haubold 2010: 219 at 482–93). All these attributions imply judgments.

Plantinga rightly emphasizes how (screen) narratives prime recipients to judge the characters (2018: 35, 39, 145–6) and how recipients vigorously do so (149; cf. Nussbaum 1995: 83; Oatley 2012: 48–9; Hakemulder and van Peer 2016: 196–8), and Kozak rightly emphasizes how the *Iliad*'s recipients judge the characters (2017: 5, 8, 34–5, 52, 62, 67, 96, 98, 111, 122, 124, 145, 192; cf. Minchin 1999: 61; Scodel 2008: e.g., 11, 83, 141, 150; de Jong 2018a: 42). We continually make judgments about a character's actions and we continually assign them certain traits for which we judge them. As we judge, we experience a range of emotions, such as, to repeat, "like and dislike but also admiration, contempt, pity, amusement, Schadenfreude…, and exasperation" (Ryan 2015a: 108), emotions that endure for however long or short a time. Note the sequence in Ruth Scodel's comment on Hector's boast over the fallen Patroclus (*Iliad* 16.830–42, 859–61): "by boasting *foolishly* he makes the hearer feel more *pity* than wonder" (2008: 26, my emphasis). If we follow Gill, we might even see the *Iliad* enabling our reactions by articulating a connection between judgments and emotions: for example, in *Iliad* 9 "Ajax presents Achilles' emotional responses as deliberate, as reflecting judgements" (2002: 195; cf. 178–9, 203–4). That the *Iliad* prompts engagement of this sort represents another component of its immersive pull.

Ryan posits that immersion becomes still greater when narratives prompt recipients to experience emotions for themselves, "not for others," and assigns "fear, horror, disgust, and sexual arousal" to the former category (2015a: 108). This experience necessitates that "we imagine ourselves as directly facing the objects that inspire such reactions" (110). Ryan allows that consumers of visual media more easily feel these emotions but argues that readers of literature can too (cf. Plantinga 2009: 210).

A recipient can identify emotionally with a character who exhibits one of these reactions and feel fear, horror, disgust, and sexual arousal themselves. But in this portion of our study we are after moments in which recipients have emotional reactions without being prompted by a character's having that reaction. When Plato's Ion says that he sees his audience members *deinon emblepontes* (*Ion* 535e2–3), he could mean "looking about fearfully." In section 2.4, I saw in this phrase the possibility for identification with a character, but it may also mean that audience members grow scared on their own without any explicit prompting from a character (cf. Cairns 2017: 66).

From that perspective, consider a moment in Achilles's pursuit of Hector around the walls of Troy that one commentator labels "haunting" (de Jong 2012d: 108 at 199–201). The narrator illuminates with a simile Achilles's inability to catch Hector and Hector's inability to get away from Achilles: "And as in a dream someone is not able to catch the one who flees: neither then is one able to escape nor the other to catch up" (*Iliad* 22.199–200). The simile presents a common type of nightmare in which we can neither reach nor flee something or someone (de Jong 2012d: 109 at 199–201). Its resumptive clause at verse 201 states, "so he [Achilles] was not able to track him down while running, nor was he [Hector] able to escape" (ὣς ὁ τὸν οὐ δύνατο μάρψαι ποσίν, οὐδ᾽ ὃς ἀλύξαι). This progression could lead one to think about being in the situation described in verse 201. First, the nightmare used to illuminate verse 201 is a common one: one may think about being in the situation verse 201 describes because one has just thought about one's own experience of the nightmare that is used to illuminate verse 201. Second, verse 201 only uses pronouns (*ho*, *ton*, and *hos*), not proper names, a formulation that makes it easier to place oneself in the described situation. Moreover, verse 201 (ὣς ὁ τὸν οὐ δύνατο μάρψαι ποσίν, οὐδ᾽ ὃς ἀλύξαι) mimics in diction and structure verse 200 (οὔτ᾽ ἄρ ὁ τὸν δύναται ὑποφεύγειν οὔθ᾽ ὁ διώκειν). If verse 200's depiction of the nightmare makes one recall one's own experience of that nightmare, one may insert oneself in the situation described in verse 201 given that verse 201 takes the same form as verse 200. If this progression leads one in this direction, one may also feel a twinge of fear upon encountering verse 201: one may grow fearful at the thought of being unable to catch up or to escape; one may even transpose the feeling of fear evoked by the nightmare to the vision of being in the situation described in verse 201.

The *Iliad*'s recipients more routinely come across passages that can trigger disgust. Section 6.3 (pp. 179–81) traced how the poem's descriptions of bodies coming apart generate a felt response in recipients and how a prior connection with the shattered character is not necessary for the recipient to have that sort of response. These descriptions can also be said to prompt disgust (Lateiner 2017: 37–8), and here too disgust is not dependent on attachment to or identification with the character (cf. Aldana Reyes 2016: 52).

Four times, *entera* (intestines) spill out of bodies torn by weapons (*Iliad* 13.507–8 (*ēphus*'), 14.517 (*aphusse*), 17.314–15 (*ēphus*'), 20.418). The final instance is perhaps the most notable because it does not use the same formulaic language as the other three. Ripped apart by Achilles's spear, Polydorus holds his intestines (*entera*) in his hands (*Iliad* 20.413–18). The narrator repeats this detail when turning to Hector's response: "But when Hector saw his brother Polydorus holding his intestines (*entera*) in his hands" (20.419–20). Two other times, *kholades* (intestines) spill out (*ek*.../ *khunto*) of bodies pierced by weapons (*Iliad* 4.525–6, 21.180–1). Peneleos's spear enters Ilioneus head and forces out (*ek*... *ōse*) an eyeball (*Iliad* 14.493–5; cf. 17.741–2). Idomeneus kills Erymas with a blow to the head: "the teeth were shaken out (*ek*... *etinakhthen*)," and "through (*ana*) his mouth and nose he spurted blood as he gaped" (*Iliad* 16.345–50). When Patroclus yanks his spear out of Sarpedon's chest, Sarpedon's lungs come with it (*Iliad* 16.504). Achilles stabs Tros in his liver, and the liver comes out (*ek*... *olisthen*) of Tros's body (*Iliad* 20.469–70). Achilles decapitates Deucalion, and "the marrow gushed out from (*ekpalth*') the neckbone" (*Iliad* 20.481–3). The piercing of the human casement and the consequent appearance of what is usually kept inside, and even concealed inside, prompts disgust (cf. Plantinga 2009: 205;

Aldana Reyes 2016: 58–60, 67–8; Lateiner and Spatharas 2017: 34). Just as we react to the leaking corpse with disgust (Brockliss 2018: 27; cf. Aldana Reyes 2016: 60–1), so we react with disgust to breaches of the fatally wounded body. Perhaps a recipient's familiarity with the depiction on black- and red-figure vases of human entrails or of blood pouring from wounds (D. Saunders 2008; 2010) made it easier to imagine and feel disgust at these scenes.

Disgust can also arise at the prospect of ingesting things (cf. Felski 2008: 124; Plantinga 2009: 205; Aldana Reyes 2016: 56). Granted, the *Iliad* does not give us anything like what presumably happened in the *Thebaid* of the Epic Cycle: Tydeus ate Melanippus's brain, and, upon witnessing this act, a disgusted Athena (*musakhtheisa* (cf. Euripides *Medea* 1149; Xenophon *The Education of Cyrus* 1.3.5)) did not grant Tydeus immortality (fragment 9, line 37; cf. Lateiner and Spatharas 2017: 36–7). Still, in the *Odyssey* the suitors are said to eat meat that drips with blood (*haimophorukta*, 20.348), and, when Achilles wishes to eat Hector raw (*Iliad* 22.346–7) or Hecuba wishes to eat Achilles's liver (*Iliad* 24.212–13), recipients might also feel disgust.

When the *Iliad*'s proem speaks of the corpses of heroes as "spoils for dogs and birds" (1.4–5), it yokes together both triggers of disgust—rent human bodies and alimentary taboos. A similar conflation underlies our disgust at the image conjured at length by Achilles and Thetis: when Achilles worries "that flies entering the stout son of Menoetius through the bronze-dealt wounds may breed worms and disfigure his corpse," Thetis assures him that she "will try to ward off the savage tribes, the flies, that feed on men killed in battle" (*Iliad* 19.24–6, 30–1). The image of insects eating exposed insides evokes both kinds of disgust (cf. Harris 2018: 477–8). This passage joins the one from the *Thebaid* as a rare presentation in archaic Greek epic of what the characters themselves consider disgusting. On the battlefield warriors have no compunction about stripping blood-covered armor (*enara brotoenta*) from their opponents (e.g., *Iliad* 6.480) or feces-covered armor from their disembowed victims (e.g., 17.314–18). Even if the characters have a higher tolerance than we do, the passages examined here can prompt recipients' disgust.

Rita Felski distinguishes (primarily for heuristic purposes) between shock, in which she includes disgust, and enchantment, her preferred term for an experience that overlaps to a significant degree with what I have been calling immersion (2008: 112–13, 117). She then backtracks: "any hard-and-fast opposition between shock and enchantment implied by my argument can be effortlessly deconstructed" (133). I favor this messier reformulation. On the one hand, when the words we read or hear compel us to gag, we are deep down in the storyworld. On the other hand, one should acknowledge the "allure of disgust," recognizing its immersive potential.[4] Recipients' disgust evinces their immersion, but scenes that

---

[4] Quotation from Lateiner 2017: 32; cf. 38; Felski 2008: 134; Plantinga 2009: 212; Brockliss 2018: 31; Worman 2018: 47–8; Spatharas 2021: 67–9.

prompt disgust draw them in. Lucian's Zeus cannot forget the smell of human flesh as it burns (*Fugitives* 1): the disgust induced here in the recipient can "be interpreted as an attempt on Lucian's part to involve his readers in the world of his text and secure their attention" (Lateiner and Spatharas 2017: 34; cf. Spatharas 2021: 67–8). The chance to confront disgusting images persists as one attraction of, for instance, the horror genre (Felski 2008: 134; Aldana Reyes 2016: 55; Lateiner and Spatharas 2017: 20; cf. 35). What precisely this attraction entails remains a subject of debate (Robinson 2014; Aldana Reyes 2016: 71–2, 133–4, 196–7).

## 7.4. Conclusion

The *Iliad* immerses recipients at the emotional level. The recipient of Homeric epic can experience how-, when-, and what-suspense. Two features stand out: the way typical structures are put together can trigger how-suspense; their attachment to characters can prompt recipients with prior knowledge of what will happen to feel suspense because there is an intimate connection between identification and suspense. The *Iliad* relies primarily on diegetic delays to create suspense, but a well-placed simile, a non-diegetic component that can be enmeshed in the diegesis, can also build suspense. Recipients may also experience metasuspense when they wonder how the teller will keep the story on its proper course. In addition, the *Iliad* prompts us to feel a range of other emotions by triggering our propensity to judge people (and characters), and the poem can get us to feel emotions for ourselves, such as disgust.

For explanatory purposes, I have examined discrete emotional engagements. But Robin Nabi and Melanie Green rightly speak of "emotional flow": "the evolution of the emotional experience during exposure to a media message, which is marked by a series of emotional shifts" (2015: 143; cf. M. Smith 2017: 202). The *Iliad*'s recipients can experience an admixture of emotions (cf. Hesk 2013: 47–9; Myers 2019: 194): for instance, over the course of a battle scene, one might feel happiness at a warrior's success, admiration for a warrior's selflessness, sadness at a warrior's death, pity for a warrior's surviving relatives, and disgust at the explosion of a body. Nabi and Green contend that narratives that trigger different emotional states as they unfold produce an enhanced sense of transportation (2015; cf. Fitzgerald and Green 2017: 55), and Nizia Alam and Jiyeon So provide empirical support for this proposition (2020). From this perspective, one should speak not only of the immersive impact of feeling certain emotions but also of the immersive impact of experiencing a sequence of varied emotions.

# 8
# Content and Form

## 8.1. Overview

Immersive narratives take us into the inner lives of the characters (8.2). At the same time, narratives rank as immersive when they cue us to think about ourselves and trigger personal memories (8.3). Along those same lines—immersion is not a matter of completely forgetting oneself, and one retains some distance from the storyworld—our knowledge of the components of an author's tool kit can facilitate immersion, and we can even be immersed in the formal features of a presentation (8.4). This chapter yokes these findings from the empirical study of immersion to related ideas in Homeric studies.

## 8.2. Inner Life

Arthur Jacobs and Jana Lüdtke find that "segments classified as *action-oriented*... yielded significantly higher immersion ratings than those categorized as *inner life*" (2017: 83, emphasis in original). This finding will not surprise those of us raised on a diet of action and adventure television shows and movies. That the action sequences of the *Iliad* are absorbing simply by virtue of being action sequences—depictions of people doing things—is one of the main lessons to be drawn from Jonas Grethlein and Luuk Huitink's discussion of the chariot race in *Iliad* 23 (2017). They note the suspenseful dynamics of the scene but emphasize the immersive impact of the narrative's being "rich in bodily movements and simple actions" (82). They conclude, "Bodily motion and the description of features relevant to the action determine the texture of Homeric narrative and are key to Homer's capacity to transport listeners and readers to the battlefield of Troy" (83). Section 6.3 has expanded on this point, charting the many moments in the epic in which recipients can experience (felt) motor resonance in response to the action.

Nonetheless, Jacobs and Lüdtke acknowledge Frank Hakemulder's (2013) demonstration that depictions of characters' inner lives can induce immersion more readily than action sequences or gripping plots (2017: 88). With inner life, the researchers refer to "intentions, emotions, mental conflicts" (80). This research put some weight behind assertions like that offered by Ryan: "accessible minds are certainly a source of immersion" (2015a: 80; cf. Russo 2012: 15; R. Allan 2020: 19).

To talk of a Homeric character's inner life is to say neither that what goes on in their head is somehow different from what they might say or express in conversation with someone else nor that the essence of (Homeric) personhood resides in a coherent and discrete individual consciousness manifested in the existence of an inner life. It is simply to say that the poet gives us, the external audience, access to emotions and thoughts that are not necessarily accessible to the other characters (cf. Gill 2002: 58, 182–3, 187).

We have already had occasion to review some moments in which the *Iliad* poet gives us access to a character's mind (sections 4.2.2, 4.2.3, and 6.2). We gain that access when they speak and in moments of embedded focalization (de Jong 2004: 101–94). Monologues especially reveal their inner conflicts, as the formulaic line that introduces these speeches makes clear: "and then vexed (*okhthēsas*) he spoke to his great-hearted spirit" (e.g., *Iliad* 11.403; see Garcia 2018: 299–300; Stelow 2020: 93). As I mentioned earlier (section 7.2, pp. 208–9), mental states can serve as the tenor of a simile: Agamemnon's frequent groans of dismay as he ponders the situation of the Achaean army resembles Zeus's lightning strikes (*Iliad* 10.5–10); Nestor's indecision between two courses of action brings to mind the moment right before a gust of wind pushes waves in one direction or another (*Iliad* 14.16–21; see also 9.4–8).

In addition, we enter the character's heads when we read their minds. Mind reading means attributing mental states—attitudes, beliefs, desires, emotions, goals, and intentions—to other people, including characters in stories (B. Vermeule 2010: 34; Altmann et al. 2012: 1–2; Turner and Felisberti 2017). To judge from scholars' commentary, the audience mind reads Homeric characters all the time:

- "We may read into it his [Hector's] alarm, vexation, and guilt…" (Janko 1992: 141 at 765–87).
- "The change in the queen's [Arete's] attitude…has more point if she is responding to his otherwise unmotivated account of the famous 'heroines'— that is, if she is taking this account as an implicit complement to herself.… The first half of the Nekuia seems designed, at least in part, as a tacit compliment to her, as Demodocus' song of Ares and Aphrodite was designed as a compliment to Odysseus himself" (Doherty 1995: 67, 78; cf. 85, 99).
- "Where we are not told explicitly of a character's motivation or psychology, the narrative quite commonly invites the audience to engage in conjecture. …Hector in explaining to the army why he must enter the city (*Il.* 6.113–15) shrewdly downplays Helenos' emphasis on the need for calling together the women of Troy to sacrifice specifically to Athene and win her favour (6.86–95)" (Baragwanath 2008: 38, 45).
- "We have to assume that Achilles feels some anxiety about Agamemnon's success" (Scodel 2008: 157).

- "Odysseus *wants to repeat* the experience of the first song—wants to be exposed once more to the emotions which it made well up in him" (Halliwell 2011: 82, emphasis in original).
- "Athena, feeling resentment (probably at Apollo, though this is not specified), broke Eumelus' chariot..." (Scodel 2018: 17).
- "The narrator confirms our suspicion as to what Agamemnon had in mind" (Stelow 2020: 78).
- "Achilles' claim that one of the Greeks might have sight of Priam in his tent and tell this to Agamemnon (*Il.* 24.653–655) is to be understood as a lie that is deliberately used to terrify the Trojan king" (Xian 2020: 189; cf. 186).
- "In the young man's [Antilochus's] words and demeanour Achilles recognizes something of his own self" (Minchin 2021b: 57).[1]

Critics' attempts to divine Penelope's motivation for setting the contest of the bow are too numerous to list (Doherty 1995: 35, 142–3; Grethlein 2018: 72–6).

Three of the poet's storytelling tactics prompt us to mind read. First—and to repeat (see sections 2.2, p. 17; 6.3, p. 182; and p. 222)—the application to the epics of classic narratology's concept of focalization teaches us that every one of the characters potentially has a discrete perspective or viewpoint, perhaps more than one. The *Iliad* poet repeatedly casts his characters as focalizers. Even for minor characters the poet makes use of free indirect discourse (Beck 2012: 57–78), which "present[s] a character's inner thoughts from a third-person point of view" (B. Vermeule 2010: 75). Constantly confronted with characters' points of view, we are more prone to attempt mind reading. Second, Homeric characters regularly

---

[1] I continue this list here:
- "[Zeus] tactfully omits the death of her [Hera's] favorite, Akhilleus" (Janko 1992: 234 at 56–77).
- "So the lyre suggests something about Achilleus' state of mind now that he is in self-imposed exile from the active life. He is searching for a means to fill in time. And, for all that, the lyre—paradoxically—is a reminder of that life for which he yearns" (Minchin 1999: 59).
- "Odysseus' plea to the shade of Aias that Zeus alone is to blame for this fate may well be his sincere view of the matter..., but Aias rejects it in silent scorn" (Teffeteller 2003: 22).
- "Odysseus is angry, but that is probably precisely the response Agamemnon seeks" (Scodel 2008: 60).
- "This interpretation opens up the possibility that Agamemnon knows full well that his brother is not seriously injured" (Sammons 2009a: 171).
- "We may guess that Hecuba assumes..." (Scodel 2012: 326).
- "He [Achilles] is distressed, probably, not because..." (Scodel 2014: 71).
- "The poet implies that Achilles' resemblance to Hector strikes Priam in turn, who succumbs to the same impulse and joins Achilles in lament" (Liebert 2017: 87).
- "Odysseus feels more like a victim than a victor" (de Jong 2018a: 39; cf. Halliwell 2011: 89).
- "We understand that Odysseus has read the social context, has concluded from the young shepherd's appearance what his listener might know of the world, and has guessed at what might impress him" (Minchin 2019b: 112).
- "Helen seems first to be stricken by passion for Paris and then by fury at Aphrodite for inspiring that feeling" (Lesser 2022: 90).

make inferences about what their fellows are thinking and feeling.[2] Constantly seeing the characters engage in mind reading, we are led to engage in our own mind reading. (Just so, in preparing for the battle of Sphacteria, Thucydides's Demosthenes "imagin[es] what the Spartans would be thinking when surrounded by the Athenians" (R. Allan 2019b: 149; *History of the Peloponnesian War* 4.32.3–4). The "blend" of viewpoints may contribute to immersion (R. Allan 2019b: 149), but I highlight the instigation to mind read prompted by the character's own mind reading.) Third, I go back to a point made in section 3.3.2 (p. 76). Simply by describing his characters doing things, the poet prompts us to mind read because we do not need access to a character's thoughts to engage in mind reading. Lisa Zunshine speaks of (2003: 270):

> our evolved cognitive tendency to assume that there must be a mental stance behind each physical action and our striving to represent to ourselves that possible mental stance even when the author has left us with the absolute minimum of necessary cues for constructing such a representation.

Minchin reads Hector's gestures and movements in *Iliad* 6 (2008b: 24–5):

> Hektor's actions are eloquent: in kissing his baby he expresses the joy and the pride of fatherhood; in returning the baby to his wife, he makes it clear that he entrusts their offspring to her care (this is a family moment); and in caressing her he is expressing his tenderness and concern (this is an intimate moment).

When Hector passes Astyanax back to Andromache, "it feels as though Andromache responds to Hektor's future absence when she cries" (Kozak 2017: 67; cf. Minchin 2008b: 25). When Ajax nods to Phoenix at *Iliad* 9.223, "we have to infer that Ajax thinks Phoenix should speak" (Scodel 2014: 66; cf. Minchin 2008b: 27). Each character who performs an action can prompt the audience to mind read.[3]

---

[2] de Jong 1994: 41, 44; Baragwanath 2008: 40–1, 45–6, 48–9, 53; Scodel 2008: 79; 2012: 320; 2014: 63; 2015: 222–3; Kozak 2017: 59, 61; Grethlein 2018: 84; Minchin 2019a: 357, 365; 2021b; cf. De Temmerman and Emde Boas 2018: 17 n. 55.

[3] Grethlein critiques the application of research into "theory of mind" to literary studies (e.g., 2017a: 44–5, but see his 2021a: 60–1). He contends that many ancient texts enchant us not so much because they give us the opportunity to read character's minds. Rather, "the immersive appeal of narrative hinges on plot and time" (45; cf. 2015: 262, 274): we want to know what will happen next and we appreciate the chance narratives afford to "reflect on time" (2017a: 66; cf. section 1.3, pp. 9–10). Grethlein's arguments are salutary, reminding us that a both/and approach is necessary: immersion comes both from access to characters' minds and from, for instance, suspenseful plotting. Still, I endorse Fludernik's objections to Grethlein's analysis of Heliodorus's *Ethiopian Story of Theagenes and Charicleia* (2015: 290): "we immerse ourselves into the fictional world by means of sympathizing with characters and their minds. Those minds do not need to be rendered in detail; characters' intentions, wishes, plans, and calculations are more than sufficient to raise our interest in them.... Why indeed should we care for those two lovers and their trials unless it were for the cognitive and

Four investigations bring out how mind reading can draw in and affect the audience. Rita Felski sees the acquisition of knowledge "about the way things are" (2008: 77)—more specifically, "the hope of gaining a deeper sense of everyday experiences and the shape of social life" (83)—as one reason why people are drawn to reading and deems the mind reading so prominent in modern novels one means by which such tales imparts that lesson (89–93). Investigating mind reading in Greek tragedy, Felix Budelmann and Pat Easterling connect the "power" (2010: 292, 293, 295, 301) of the plays to their depictions of characters engaged in mind reading other characters (esp. 296) and to their capacity to prompt the audience to mind read the characters. Investigating the Second Testament, Eric Douglass situates mind reading in the category of cognitive empathy and posits a recipient's cognitive empathy as one component of their identification with characters (2018: 126–9; cf. 136). Katalin Bálint and Ed Tan find that "absorbed moments of character engagement occur when viewers and readers intensely exercise mind modelling" (2019: 214), "absorbed moments of character engagement" meaning "memorable and impactful experiences" (227) and "intensely" meaning that the modeling of what goes on in a character's head is "complex" (223) and "explicit" (227). Still more instructive for my purposes is a fifth intervention, finding that readers with a greater motivation to mind read experience a greater degree of transportation into a narrative (Carpenter, Green, and Fitzgerald 2018: 219, 221, 225). An interest in mind reading contributes to immersion.

Following in these researchers' footsteps, I observe that mind reading takes us into the characters' inner lives and thereby facilitates immersion. In providing ample opportunity to learn about and delve into the inner lives of its characters, the *Iliad* finds another way to immerse its recipients.

## 8.3. Ourselves

Felski acknowledges the suspicion with which literary criticism tends to treat the prospect of connecting "a literary work to one's own life" (2008: 26). Yet she rightly stresses the fact of readers' experiences of "recognition," of "seeing traces of myself in the pages I am reading" (23) and of being able to say, "I know myself better after reading a book" (29). To illustrate one form recognition can take, Felski recounts her experience of reading Hilary Mantel's *An Experiment of Love*:

emotional transposition (i.e., immersion) into their situation, which crucially includes their hopes, desires, fears, and disappointments?" Moreover, readers should be skeptical of Grethlein's claim that "the notion of the Theory of Mind has long lost its lustre in psychology" (2017a: 45). One can consult, by contrast, Oatley 2016, Calarco et al. 2017, Oatley and Djikic 2018, Spaulding 2018, and Wimmer et al. 2021 as well as the 2017 meta-analysis by Mumper and Gerrig in the journal *Psychology of Aesthetics, Creativity, and the Arts*.

she was "floored by the shock of the familiar" (39). This exploration of recognition is one component of Felski's attempt "to engage seriously with ordinary motives for reading" (14). They do not cite Felski's work, but Anežka Kuzmičová and Katalin Bálint devote a review article to the observation that "personal relevance is a key factor at many stages and levels of literary reading"; personal relevance means that "the information presented carries special importance with respect to the individual reader's self, knowledge, or past experiences" (2019: 430). We already saw in section 2.3 (p. 30) how a narrative's evocation of experiences and subjects important to a recipient contributes to their identification with characters. In this spirit, I review in this section how immersion is not just a matter of exposure to the inner lives of the characters as detailed in the previous section: immersion also comes about when texts bring us back to ourselves.

As I noted in section 6.2 (p. 168), Ryan begins her discussion of spatial immersion by pointing to "the coincidental resonance of the text with the reader's personal memories" (2015a: 86; cf. Kuiken, Miall, and Sikora 2004: 182–3). Subsequent research has fleshed out the link between memories and immersion. I return to Peter Dixon and Marisa Bortolussi's discussion of absorption (see sections 5.3, pp. 156–7, and 7.1, pp. 195–6). They posit personal memories as one of their four components of absorption. Here are several of the statements they had participants respond to under the category of personal memories (2017: 206):

> The story reminded me of people that I have known.
> Some of the situations made me think of things that have happened to me.
> The story reminded me of decisions I've made in the past.
> Some of the events had something in common with my experiences.
> I have memories similar to some of the things in the story.
> The events of the story were sometimes predictable from what's happened in my life.

They determine that, along with evoked realism, "remindings of (again, presumably emotional) personal experiences" produces emotional responses and that "transportation was a function of emotional response" (208). Anneke de Graaf and Lonneke van Leeuwen point to similar findings in their review of the literature on the connection between "self-referencing" and "transportation," understood as comprising "the level of attention, emotion, and imagery in response to the narrative" (2017: 282, 284). I quote their summary (284):

> Recipients can have attention for the narrative, experience emotions, and create mental images in response to the narrative, and think about themselves at the same time. Moreover, images and emotions may even be enhanced by personal memories triggered by the narrative. When a story about an ill person makes you think back to a time you were ill yourself, the emotions you felt then may carry

over to the emotions you feel for the character. The relation between transportation in this sense and self-referencing is confirmed by several studies which show the extent to which attention, emotion and imagery are focused on the narrative is positively associated to self-referencing.... This means that more transportation in the sense of a focus of attention, emotion, and imagery on the story is related to more self-referencing.

Bálint and Tan find that "absorbed moments of character engagement largely involve self-referencing of character-related information, for example, through comparison with one's own personal life experiences or with hidden parts of the self" (2019: 216). I cite too Birte Thissen, Winfried Menninghaus, and Wolff Schlotz's begrudging acknowledgment (2020: 722):

> In a less optimal reading experience, cognitive involvement (e.g., drawing a connection between the narrative and personal memories) may help to mentally reframe the reading experience in a way that allows for optimal engagement, flow, and ultimately absorbed reading with a high sense of presence, identification, and suspense.

A memory or a moment of self-referencing triggered by a text can distract one from the text (Kuzmičová and Bálint 2019: 443–5), but these discussions bring out the importance of personal connections to a narrative: immersion depends to a significant degree on our connecting the tale to our own experiences (cf. Hogan 2003: 66–8; Oatley 2012: 100–1; Fitzgerald and Green 2017: 53; Kuiken and Douglas 2017: 233–4; Tan et al. 2017: 111–12). They also remind us that immersion does not mean a complete loss of self-awareness and the inability to distinguish between the storyworld and the actual world (see section 5.3, pp. 154–5). So, to bring these initial comments full circle, while I started with Felski's defense of recognition, I dispute the opposition she draws between a reader's being "immersed ... transported, caught up, or swept away" and "another experience of reading," namely that of "self-scrutiny" (2008: 34–5).

We can find prompts in the *Iliad* that encourage recipients to see their own experiences reflected in the poem. First, the characters tell one another stories about events in the past that they intend to serve as exempla: they want their hearer to use the actions related in the story to guide their actions in the present (e.g., Grethlein 2006: 46); they want, that is, their hearer to self-reference, to use de Graaf and van Leeuwen's term. Menelaus imagines this same process at work in the future: he prays to Zeus that he, Menelaus, defeat Paris in their duel in *Iliad* 3 "in order that someone even of later born men may shudder to do bad things to a host" (3.353–4; cf. Stelow 2020: 57). A variant of this equation arises when a character directs an exemplum toward himself: he uses a story from the past to guide his action in the present. Diomedes tells the story of Lycurgus's assault on

Dionysus's nurses to justify the claim, "I would not want to fight against the blessed gods" (*Iliad* 6.141). Achilles says that Priam and he (*nōi*) should eat even in the midst of their sorrow just as the devastated Niobe did (*Iliad* 24.602–19). The frequency with which characters either ask another to draw a lesson from or themselves draw lessons from exempla model the possibility for recipients of a self-directed response to the tale (cf. M. Power 2006: 32). Second, on occasion, we see a listener connect to his own past a tale told by someone else. I look beyond the obvious example from *Odyssey* 8 wherein Odysseus cries in response to Demodocus's songs about the Trojan War (8.73–95, 499–534; M. Power 2006: 27, 30, 95; Liebert 2017: 2–7; Ready 2018: 172–3). After Agamemnon recalls the exploits of Tydeus during the war of the Seven against Thebes, Sthenelus retorts that he and the other Epigonoi, the sons of the Seven, sacked Thebes and thereby did what their father's generation could not (*Iliad* 4.404–10). Glaucus's story of Bellerophon prompts Diomedes to recall that, when he came to Troy (*iōn*), he left behind (*kateleipon*) in his house a golden cup that Bellerophon gave to his grandfather, Oeneus (*Iliad* 6.216–21). We also see Achilles determine a course of action based on (or at least link his own actions to) the actions of Meleager in the tale Phoenix relates: Achilles's declaration that he will only return to the fight after Hector sets fire to the Myrmidons' huts and ships (*Iliad* 9.650–3) stems from (or cites as a parallel) Meleager's only returning to the fight after attackers set fire to his city (*Iliad* 9.587–97; D. Wilson 2002: 107). Again, the characters in these instances can model a recipient's response to the tale. Third, I noted in section 6.3 (p. 189) the scholarly consensus that similes evoke the world and experience of the audience. We typically cast this move as a desire on the part of the poet to illuminate the thoughts and actions of the characters by referring audience members to something they may know firsthand. We can now add that to the extent that similes prompt recipients to think about their own world they may also trigger personal memories. Prompted repeatedly by similes in this fashion, recipients may find themselves more apt to recall personal memories in response to the narrative proper, not just in response to similes.

These observations prepare for the following suggestion: The range of human experience presented in the *Iliad* provides numerous opportunities for recipients to self-reference and recall personal memories. The *Iliad* gives us mortal characters experiencing bodily pain and profound psychological devastation; engaged not just in physical violence but in verbal disputes as well; alternately persuading and failing to move divinities; witnessing epiphanies and participating in funerals; feasting and having sex; and—to acknowledge that the poem can take us back and forth between the sublime and the ridiculous—day drinking and stepping in animal waste. Despite its setting in the heroic past, the *Iliad* presents an accessible and recognizable world populated by accessible and recognizable characters having accessible and recognizable experiences. It can make recipients think about themselves and their own lives.

There is another, albeit less perceptible way in which recipients contribute to their own immersion. I look to Werner Wolf's discussion of what he terms "aesthetic illusion" (2013). He builds on research into the inevitable presence of gaps in a fictional world (Eder, Jannides, and Schneider 2010: 11–12; Bernaerts et al. 2013: 3; Cave 2016: 25, 27) and on the resulting importance of recipients' mental schemata and scripts in the comprehension of literary and filmic texts.[4] Wolf attributes aesthetic illusion (what I call immersion) in part to a text's "activating content-related concepts, schemata or scripts stored in the recipients' minds mostly from previous real-life experiences but also from their enculturation" (2013: 44; cf. 25; R. Allan 2020: 18; Grethlein 2021a: 62). Immersion arises when the world in the text functions more or less as our world does (and as the storyworlds in other texts do): we assess the match based on whether what happens in the text unfolds the way our mental models say it should unfold. Recall Elizabeth Minchin's demonstration of the Homeric poet's reliance on scripts (and tracks in those scripts) to help him compose in performance (2001). The apprentice poet would have found that many of these scripts already corresponded to those he relied on in real life, and he would have learned any unfamiliar scripts in his apprenticeship. In keeping with our concern for reception, we can now observe that the poet's use of scripts known to recipients aids recipients' immersion in the narrative.

Other, frequently more self-evident components of traditional oral performance have a similar impact. Oral performers from a given tradition use the same formulae, runs of lines, type scenes, repeated passages, and story patterns (Ready 2018: 84–112). The use of shared, familiar material helps not only the poet perform but also the tradition-oriented audience comprehend what the poet presents (114). Homeric scholarship continues to bring out the nature and extent of the poet's reliance on what we should take to be material shared with his predecessors and contemporaries (Ready 2018: 191–245; cf. Jensen 2011: 201). The Homeric poet's use of this material—familiar because it is shared—helps the poet compose and the tradition-oriented audience understand. The ease with which audience members understand, an ease stemming to a great degree from familiarity, enables immersion: "familiarity and processing fluency are assumed to be major factors facilitating immersion" (Jacobs and Lüdtke 2017: 79; cf. Bilandzic and Busselle 2017: 17–18; Fitzgerald and Green 2017: 51).

One should not overstate the matter. Jacobs and Lüdtke write, "A certain amount of *unfamiliarity* and *exoticism* might also facilitate global transportation, i.e., spatial immersion, for example in novels playing in exotic places or the so-called regional crime stories about Brittany, Provence etc." (2017: 72, emphasis in

---

[4] M. Smith 1995: 30–1, 48, 53–4, 120–1, 166; Stockwell 2002: 75–89; M. Power 2006: 66–8; Bortolussi and Dixon 2015: 531; Brosch 2017: 257; De Temmerman and Emde Boas 2018: 15, 17; Lloyd 2018: 337–41; Plantinga 2018: 56.

original; cf. Ryan 2015a: 89). I noted in section 6.2 (p. 168) that most recipients will not have visited Troy and Mt Olympus, but the unfamiliar and exotic go beyond matters of geography. At any point in time in the lengthy performance tradition of Homeric epic, ancient audiences would have detected numerous differences between the heroic world and their own world: for instance, the heroes carry shields made of hide and bronze, not the wooden shield of the hoplite (Viggiano and van Wees 2013: 57–60; Lloyd 2020: 402); grant authority (frequently even power) to a single paramount *basileus* (Ready 2019b: 130–1; Crielaard 2020: 232, 234)—no democracies or oligarchies here; and subsist entirely on meat—an impractical diet in the real world of ancient Greece (Bakker 2013: 48–50)—that they wash down with wine, thus ignoring the alimentary protocols of the archaic and classical symposium (Węcowski 2020: 333). These and numerous other points of difference distinguish the storyworld from that of the typical recipient: "for Homer's audiences his heroes were part of a 'foreign country' where things were done very differently" (Whitley 2020: 266). These disjunctions make a contribution to immersion as well.

## 8.4. Formal Features

The previous section has emphasized the recipient's role in immersion and reminded us that immersion is not about a complete loss of self-awareness. We can now add that it is not even about complete immersion in the storyworld. I pivot to a review of scholarship on the impact of formal features.

Wolf asserts that attention drawn to the mediating form impedes immersion. He writes, "Aesthetic illusion can, for instance, to a certain extent include *rational reactions*, although this does characteristically *not* mean a pronounced 'technical' interest in or appreciation of...the way in which the artefact is made or structured" (2013: 7, emphasis in original). And again, "the illusion at hand does not refer *to* the representations as such as artefacts (their structure, form or make-up), but to *what is represented or created* by them" (9–10, emphasis in original). He sums up by invoking *"the principle of 'celare artem'"*—in its lengthier form *ars est celare artem* (the art is to conceal the art)—as essential to aesthetic illusion (50–1, emphasis in original; cf. Ryan 2013: 142–7). Rutger Allan follows suit: an immersive text "directs the addressee's attention to the storyworld, that is, it defocuses from the text itself as a medium....The artificiality of the text is concealed" (2020: 19).[5]

These claims seem exceptionally intuitive and have a fine pedigree. In his *How to Study Poetry* (*Moralia* 14d–37b), Plutarch contends that "contemplating the way in which a poet presents his material, young readers defy the immersive tug of

---

[5] Cf. R. Allan 2019b: 134; 2022a: 82; Robinson 2005: 137; Plantinga 2009: 36; 2018: 64–5; Vatri 2020: 217.

poetry, as their attention is directed away from the represented action" (Grethlein 2021a: 146). Focusing on form and structure keeps one from being immersed in the storyworld. Kendall Walton declares, "Gratuitously flowery or alliterative or otherwise self-conscious language may take on a life of its own, calling attention to itself at the expense of the thing described" and taking us out of the "fictional world" (1990: 276). The same binary is essential to what Carl Plantinga calls "estrangement theory": drawing viewers' attention to the medium forestalls immersion in the storyworld (and hinders the dangerous effects of such immersion) (2018: 100–7, 119–20). One might also connect the proposed dichotomy between attention to form and attention to the storyworld to Pierre Bourdieu's argument about taste and class: elites attend to form; non-elites to the storyworld (1984). But in the spirit of critiques of Walton's discussion (Altieri 2003: 112–16) and Bourdieu's model (Davis 2007: 18–19, 98, 110–17), I look to researchers who provide different ways to think about form and immersion. After all, Plutarch himself allows that one can "cling closely (*emphuetai*) to the beauty and the arrangement of the words" (ὁ δ' ἐμφύεται τῷ κάλλει καὶ τῇ κατασκευῇ τῶν ὀνομάτων, *How to Study Poetry, Moralia* 30d), *emphuetai* suggesting an intense engagement of some sort.

For Rita Felski, style makes for what she terms enchantment (2008: 63):

> While Ryan captures well the quality of one kind of aesthetic enchantment, she fails to consider the possibility of being seduced by a style, assuming that any attention to language will be purely cerebral and analytical in nature. What such an argument overlooks is the possibility of an emotional, even erotic cathexis onto the sounds and surfaces of words. Here language is not a hurdle to be vaulted over in the pursuit of pleasure, but the essential means to achieving it. We need only think of those moments when a reader, on opening a book, is drawn in by a cadence of tone, by particular inflections and verbal rhythms, by an irresistible combination of word choice and syntax.

Felski points to "the seductiveness of sound" (71), the "music and musicality of sound," and "their pertinence to any genealogy and phenomenology of enchantment" (72). She sums up (72–3):

> Enchantment is triggered not by signifieds but by signifiers, not by mimetic identifications, but by phonic forms of expressiveness and their subliminal effects.... The seductive promise of causality or coherence serves as a lure for readers...as does the use of regular meter and repetition, with their lulling, hypnotic effects.

Felski makes similar points in her discussion of identification. She contemplates identifying with "the seductive-coercive pull of his [Thomas Bernhard's] incantatory sentences" and asserts, "Identifying involves a response not only to fictional figures but also to the overall atmosphere of the text as created by its style" (2020b: 104).

Classicists note precedents for these ideas. Socrates imputes the bewitching effect of poetry (*kēlēsin*) to its being "in meter and rhythm and harmony" (ἐν μέτρῳ καὶ ῥυθμῷ καὶ ἁρμονίᾳ), which he glosses as the "colors of poetry" (τῶν τῆς μουσικῆς χρωμάτων) (Plato *Republic* 601a4–b4; see Halliwell 2011: 196; Grethlein 2021a: 82). Isocrates "speaks of poetry 'transporting the souls'... of its hearers by its sheer rhythms and verbal patterns, (even) independent of its meaning—a sort of incantatory mesmerism, it seems" (Halliwell 2011: 225). Longinus contends that a writer can transport a reader (can bring about *ekstasis*) through "the transposition of the elements of language: the sounds, words, and rhythms of the text" (de Jonge 2012: 280): "word arrangement...can cast a spell on the listeners, so that they are enchanted and carried away" (281; cf. 2020: 151). The emphasis that still other ancient critics, such as Heracleodorus and Pausimachus, placed on form is brought out by Philodemus's rejoinder: content, not simply sound, contributes integrally to good poetry (Janko 2020a: 50–64; 2020b: 131–58).

Classicists have also applied these ideas in their own readings: "Poetic texture has the power to enthrall the recipient. Rhythm or patterns of sound may detract the reader from the represented world and nonetheless spellbind the reader, intensifying her experience" (Grethlein, Huitink, and Tagliabue 2020: 10; cf. Fearn 2020: 38–9). David Fearn sees in the poetry of Stesichorus, for instance, the chance for "divergent absorbed reactions" (2020: 44), absorption in "the lyric detail of the textuality" (44) and absorption "in a gripping narrative" (47).

Proponents of empirical studies support this position. Citing Ed Tan's 1996 book, Patrick Hogan specifies what "artifact emotion" means: "If I dwell on the brilliance of the diction, the metrical nuance, the rhyme and novel use of metaphor, then I am responding with an artifact emotion" (2018: 98; cf. Plantinga 2009: 74; 2018: 109, 121; Vaage 2016: 108). Contrasting them with "fiction emotions" that we feel when "caught up in the story," Hogan adds, "Artifact emotions...are not immersive but reflective" (2018: 98; cf. 165). But this addition confuses matters because immersion is not just relevant to the storyworld (and Hogan himself goes on to question the distinction between artifact and fiction emotions (99–100; cf. Plantinga 2009: 74, 89–90; Vaage 2016: 108–9)). David Miall and Don Kuiken speak of "aesthetic feelings" that "are prompted by the formal (generic, narrative, and stylistic) features of a text" (2002: 224). Passages that generate these feelings "capture and hold" the reader's "attention" (224; cf. 227). Marisa Bortolussi and Peter Dixon contend: "The appreciation of innovative, interesting, or effective stylistic features and techniques should also make for an engaging experience" (2015: 528–9). They offer some specifics (530):

Sometimes the way a passage is written strikes the reader as so exquisite that she or he rereads it several times to savor its beauty. Other times the metaphors are so apt and ingenious as to produce admiration. Sometimes a part of a character's speech is so poetic as to be experienced as moving or inspiring. Such writing may not be a trait of works such as *The DaVinci Code*, but to exclude appreciation of the discourse is to ignore one of the important components of literary reception, and one aspect of engagement.

Attention, engagement: we are venturing toward immersion. Note, then, that Moniek Kuijpers et al. (including Tan) investigate what they term "artifact absorption" (2017). They highlight recipients' absorption in "the form or style (artifice) of a story" (33), emphasizing that one can be engaged by "the narrative's formal features" (34–5). Artifact absorption occurs when the manufacturing of the text, "the form of representation" (35) and "the craftsmanship and beauty of the formal features of a narrative" (37), enthralls us (cf. Tan et al. 2017: 113). Fittingly, this branch of research does not advocate for the *ars est celare artem* principle and instead emphasizes other factors that impede immersion. For instance, Helena Bilandzic and Rick Busselle point to breaches in perceived realism (comprising external and narrative realism: see section 2.3, p. 32) as the culprit: "Violations of external realism occur when the narrative is inconsistent with actual world experiences or expectations. Violations of narrative realism occur when the story itself is internally inconsistent, for example when a character's behavior is inconsistent with her motivations or goals" (2011: 33).[6]

The idea here goes beyond saying that we can both be immersed in the storyworld and have our attention drawn to the constructed nature of the text so that we remember that we are watching or reading (Plantinga 2009: 90–1). (It also goes

---

[6] A related question concerns the prominence of the narrator. For Allan, de Jong, and de Jonge, immersion requires that "the role of the narrator as a mediating instance in the narration should be as invisible as possible" (2017: 44; cf. Grethlein 2013: 38–9, 66, 108, 245, 299–300; 2021a: 57; Ryan 2015a: 94; Hakemulder and van Peer 2016: 195; R. Allan 2019a: 62, 63, 74 n. 11; 2019b: 138–40; 2022a: 83–4; Tyrell 2020: 70, 87–9, 102). One should tread carefully here. Switches in diegetic levels might draw attention to the act of narration, but such switches need not impede immersion (cf. Bálint, Kuijpers, and Doicaru 2017: 192). For instance, the presentation of a story within a story—a scene that might remind us that we are listening to a narrated story—can lead us to forget momentarily that the narrator of the story within the story is themself a character in a story (Grethlein 2017a: 112–13, 124, 145; cf. 2013: 140; Mahler 2013: 168–9). For its part, first-person narration necessarily calls attention to the fact that someone is telling us the tale. Yet neither Banerjee and Greene (2012) nor Chen, McGlone, and Bell (2015) found first-person narration to make for greater transportation than third-person narration, and Wimmer et al. (2021) found no difference in transportation and identification when recipients read one of three stories: one in the first-person with internal focalization; one in the third-person with internal focalization; and one in the third-person with external focalization. Other research into identification does not find that third-person narration prompts greater identification with a protagonist than first-person narration (Oatley 1999b: 445; Chen, Bell, and Taylor 2016: 913–14; 2017: 706; Cohen and Tal-Or 2017: 145; van Krieken, Hoeken, and Sanders 2017; cf. Van Lissa et al. 2016 on empathy). McCarthy shows how the reader of Horace's, Catullus's, and Propertius's first-person poems can enter the poem's storyworld even as the poem highlights the work of the poet who provides access to that world (2019: 2–3, 12, 40–2, 66).

beyond the idea that one can be immersed while looking at a statue or painting but also appreciate the technical skill required to make it (Grethlein 2017a: 194–5, 203).) Rather, one can be immersed in a narrative's form. One can distinguish between immersion in matters of form and immersion in the storyworld, as the classicists quoted on p. 232 do (cf. Jacobs and Lüdtke 2017: 89). One can also posit a connection between immersion in matters of form and immersion in the storyworld. In advocating for artifact absorption, Kuijpers et al. contend that artifact absorption and storyworld absorption "co-occur" and "overlap" (2017: 36, 39; cf. Koopman and Hakemulder 2015: 95). To formulate this link in its strongest terms would be to say that immersion in matters of form leads to immersion in the storyworld: "formal elements may ultimately help to pull the reader into the represented world" (Grethlein, Huitink, and Tagliabue 2020: 10). Consider, for example, how Dionysius of Halicarnassus analyzes Odysseus's description of Sisyphus at *Odyssey* 11.593–6 (*On Literary Composition* 20; trans. Usher 1985):

> Firstly, in the two lines in which Sisyphus rolls up the rock, except for two verbs all the remaining words in the passage are either disyllables or monosyllables. Next, the long syllables are half as numerous again as the short ones in each of the two lines. Then, all the words are so spaced as to advance in ample measures, and the gaps between them are distinctly perceptible, either because of the coincidence of vowels or the juxtaposition of semivowels or voiceless letters; and the dactylic and spondaic rhythms are the longest possible and take the longest stride.

Recipient might find themselves struck by these formal features and at the same time drawn into the scene by those formal features (cf. Purves 2020: 181–3). Keith Oatley reviews the empirical evidence for this sequence: foregrounding via "language that is especially striking" produces vividness; vividness aids the creation of mental imagery; and imagery abets transportation (2016: 621–2). But in this case too—whether we speak of co-occurrence, overlap, or causality—the point is that immersion in matters of form can stand alone: it does not merely serve the instrumental function of abetting entry into the storyworld, as a more traditional attempt to see synergies between form and content would have it.

These discussions suggest that we align our study of the formal features of archaic Greek epic with the study of immersion and allow that recipients of epic can be immersed in the poetry's form (cf. M. Power 2006: 92–4). I list here several illustrative examples of formal analysis by students of Homeric and Hesiodic poetry (earlier examples: Stanford 1967; 1976; Packard 1974). Richard Martin notes Achilles's alliteration on the letter *pi* over the course of *Iliad* 19.321–37, concluding, "The texture of speech resembles song more than oratory" (1989: 65; cf. 135). He also charts instances of alliteration, assonance, and consonance over the course of Achilles's speech at *Iliad* 9.309–90 (221). Helmut van Thiel defends retaining the aorist forms *dusato* and *bēsato* on the grounds of assonance: they echo the other vowel sounds in their verses (1991: p. vii). Paul Friedrich emphasizes the repetition of sounds in the narrator's description of the weeping Penelope (*Odyssey* 19.203-9) (2001: 237-8). Elizabeth Minchin zeroes in on "the surface features of epic song...such as rhythm, alliteration, assonance,..." (2001: 88), pointing by way of example to the list of Nereids at *Iliad* 18.43-5 and the list of Phaeacians at *Odyssey* 8.111-14. Christos Tsagalis also studies the list of Nereids, pointing out assonance and alliteration and noting verses in which the number of syllables in successive names increases (2010b: 346-7). Elsewhere, he examines the "alliteration, rhythm, enjambment, etc." in Thetis's supplication of Zeus in *Iliad* 1 (2001, quotation from 26) and illuminates the sound play in the Hesiodic *Catalogue of Women* (2017: 213):

> The *Catalogue of Women* is a treasure house of sound-play ranging from simple alliteration to vocalic, syllabic, and near-syllabic repetition in both word-initial and word-terminal position. Sound-play operates not only on verse-level but also on short-, middle-, and long-range parallel and corollary passages.

Sean Gurd tracks homoioteleuton, alliteration, assonance, and rhyme as the narrator describes Achilles's slaughter of the Trojans in the Scamander (*Iliad* 21.9-12) (2016: 29-30) and the consonance, alliteration, and assonance evident in Hesiod's description of Typhoeus (*Theogony* 820-35) (32-3).

Rhythmical arrangements attract the attention of other scholars too. Egbert Bakker points to moments in which an intonation unit—groups of words that go together—"straddles" the boundary between two verses (2005: 54-5): this arrangement becomes a noticeable way for the poet to enjamb and so connect his verses (cf. Ready 2019a: 38-9). Additional rhetorical devices prompt consideration. Rainer Friedrich comments on Diomedes's words at *Iliad* 4.415-17: "Diomedes' reflections on the profits and risks of Agamemnon...as supreme leader are shaped by a rhetorical frame of configured parallelism/antithesis/chiasm/anaphora, further enhanced by *variatio*, when the absolute particle construction of v. 417 takes the place of an εἰ-clause corresponding to that of v. 415" (2019: 128). I have elsewhere analyzed how repetition and parallelism in sound, morphology, and syntax hold together the source speech, usually by Zeus, in a messenger scene (Ready 2019a: 34-51). Much effort has also gone into illuminating the ring structures, parallelism, and narrative (often anticipatory) doublets evident in portions of and across the entirety of our *Iliad* and our *Odyssey* (see Ready 2019a: 68 for bibliography to which add, on ring composition, Kretler 2020: 115-18, 124-6, 164-5, 192-4).

Observe now that the poetry prompts one to think about its form (*pace* Bassett 1938; cf. M. Power 2006: 42). For instance, archaic Greek epic forefronts and thematizes the sounds of its storyworld (Gurd 2016: 27-38, 58-62, 99-103).

With sound brought to our attention, we note more readily the auditory component of the discourse. Similarly, verbal and structural links between passages become especially noticeable when they articulate thematic links, such as those between *Iliad* 1 and *Iliad* 24 (Whitman 1958: 259–60; Reinhardt 1961: 63–8; Macleod 1982: 32–4). One could continue to enumerate still other ways Homeric epic gets us to attend to its construction. One word or phrase regularly glosses another word or phrase: the text engages in its own exegesis and thereby draws attention to its constitution as text (Ready 2019a: 67). The *Iliad* poet's invocations of the Muses not only remind us of the performer's role as mediator (Minchin 2001: 168). The request that the Muse help him name the Achaean contingent (*Iliad* 2.484–93) can prompt us to observe how the poet puts the Catalogue of Ships together by cleaving to "a principal of geographic contiguity" with one notable divagation from the islands in the Eastern Aegean to Thessaly (Sammons 2010: 136). The *Iliad* poet three times asks whom a warrior killed first (8.273 (*prōton*), 11.218–20 (*prōtos*), 14.508–10 (*prōtos*) (asked twice of the Muse (11.218–20, 14.508–10)) and two other times whom Hector killed first and last (5.703–4 (*prōton*...*hustaton*), 11.299–300 (*prōton*...*hustaton*)) (see Minchin 2001: 173). The temporal adverbs foreground the sequence of the presentation. I sum up: Homeric poetry encourages its audiences to experience immersion in matters of form by highlighting its formal attributes.

This engagement with form is all the more immersive the more it is felt in the body. A list of names, for example, possesses a rhythm—for instance, repeated *te* and *kai* segment the list of Nereids at *Iliad* 18.39–48—and repeats sounds. One comes to register those patterns in one's body, perhaps especially as one comes to expect them and has one's expectations met. When a poet enjambs his verses by making an intonation unit straddle the boundary of the verse, an audience member can feel in their body the override of the usual pause between verses (Andrews 2005: 2; González 2013: 419): here it is perhaps the deviation from expectation that brings a physical sensation. Further attention to the fact underlying such points—that Homeric epic is hexametric poetry—would reveal additional examples. As the classicist and poet Elizabeth Young sets out, "When we read, hear, or recite lines of verse, our bodies respond, whether we like it or not: our head might nod, our fingers tap, our breath change its rhythm, our skin erupt into goose bumps, our pulse quicken or slow" (2015: 188–9; cf. 205–6; 2018: 134–5). I return in the concluding chapter to the immersive features of the poet's own embodied oral performance.

## 8.5. Conclusion

Mary Beth Oliver et al. provide yet another way to think about immersive content (2017). We like narratives that induce "hedonic fulfillment," that is, "feelings of happiness associated with positively valenced affect (e.g., joy, humor, mirth, etc.)" (254). At the same time, we like narratives that induce "eudaimonic fulfillment" by generating "feelings of *meaning, insight,* or *introspection*" (254, emphasis in original). The content that induces such feelings includes "depictions of human virtue, conflicting or not, or depictions that elicit contemplations of the vastness of the universe and the human condition" (262). "Meaningful" narratives of this sort trigger immersion, and, conversely, we label narratives meaningful as a result of being immersed in them (254–5).[7] Working from the uncontroversial assumption that the Homeric epics qualify as meaningful in Oliver et al.'s terms (e.g., Segal 1994: 227), one might include this feature in a list of their immersive properties.

This chapter has instead added four other components of immersion to the factors of spatial, spatio-temporal, and emotional immersion studied in Chapters 6 and 7. One, it is not just the *Iliad*'s action that draws us in. Exposure to the characters' minds does so as well, including when we guess at what they are thinking or feeling (mind reading). Two, the poem exercises an immersive pull when it prompts us to recall personal memories and to think about ourselves (self-reference): as with mind reading, the *Iliad* in fact models this sort of self-directed analysis. Our own understanding of the scripts the poet uses and our own familiarity with the poet's still more obvious compositional mechanisms facilitate immersion too. Three, differences persist between the storyworld and the actual world of any historical audience, but these disjunctions can themselves enhance immersion. Four, the *Iliad*'s formal elements should be seen to exert an immersive force that makes for a distinct experience or prepares one to enter the storyworld.

---

[7] For additional work on "the eudaimonic turn" in literary and narrative studies, one can start with Moores 2013 and Reinecke and Oliver 2016. Moores usefully links eudaimonic reading to Sedgwick's reparative reading and Felski's postcritical reading (2013: 29–31).

# 9
# Conclusion

Menelaus declares, "There is satiety (*koros*) in all things, both sleep and love-making, and sweet song (*molpēs*) and blameless dance, of which someone hopes to send away their desire more than of war" (*Iliad* 13.636–9). Recognizing that audiences could in fact reach their limit and experience *koros* when listening to poetry, Pindar advocates for variation (*poikilia*) (Liebert 2017: 66–7, 72). Lauding epic for its "dissimilar (*anomoiois*) episodes," Aristotle avers, "similarity soon brings satiation (τὸ γὰρ ὅμοιον ταχὺ πληροῦν) and makes tragedies stumble" (*Poetics* 1459b28–31). Scholiastic commentary regularly praises Homer for his pursuit of variation in the presentation of his tale (Nünlist 2009: 198–202), and critics still applaud this feature of Homeric poetry (J. Porter 2015: 198):

> Not everything described by Homer is of one emotive tenor and deserving to go under the heading to which Longinus and others would later place his poetry, that of grand *pathos*. Homer may frequently be sublime, according to Longinian criteria, and he may even be this on balance, as Longinus believed, but he is not monotone. There is plenty of delicacy and humor and tragic sadness in Homer, as well as refined attention to exquisite sensuous detail, some of which could in turn be construed as sublime.

We should approach immersion and identification from this perspective as well. As a narrative unfolds, it does not immerse us all the time (Reinhard 2016: 224; Grethlein 2017a: 128; R. Allan 2020: 35; 2022a: 82) and does not ask us to identify with the characters all the time (see sections 2.2, pp. 25–6, and 4.4, p. 127). Likewise, as a narrative unfolds, it will alternately cue the different types of identification—from perceptual to motivational—and the various kinds of immersion—from spatial to artifact—offering different identificatory and immersive prompts at different times (Clercx 2018: 53; Consoli 2018: 89; R. Allan 2019b: 135–6). This diversity provides necessary respites. Audiences require breaks from identification lest the taxing endeavor lose its appeal (again, see sections 2.2, pp. 25–6, and 4.4, p. 127). When it comes to the distinct features that trigger immersion, the point of diminishing return is also quickly reached (Ryan 2015a: 98; Grethlein and Huitink 2017: 83–4; Grethlein 2021a: 58). For example, motor resonance prompts immersion, but recipients need moments away from such stimulation so as not to become numb to the stimulus. Suspense also prompts immersion, but already the scholiastic commentary on the *Iliad* recognizes the value in breaks from tension, including that engendered by suspense (Nünlist 2009: 58, 64, 147, 151-3; cf. section 5.2, p. 153).

At the same time, I have separated out identification from immersion and distinguished between kinds of identification and kinds of immersion for heuristic purposes, and they can arise discreetly. But they also interweave, co-occur, and build on one another (cf. Barker 2009: 92; Cave 2016: 120; Nilsson, Nordahl, and Serafin 2016: 121; section 2.1). For instance, following Murray Smith, who explores a connection between motor resonance and empathy (2017: 180–2), we might suggest that motor resonance triggered by a character's actions and the associated experience of spatio-temporal immersion makes one more apt to identify with a character. I noted in section 7.3 (p. 212) the likelihood that emotional identification and emotional immersion operate as a sort of feedback loop. One could also investigate for their immersive potential scenes I discussed under the rubric of identification, such as Andromache's appearance in *Iliad* 22 and Priam's appearance in *Iliad* 24.

The *Iliad*, then, offers a varied immersive and identificatory experience. On top of that, each recipient's experience of immersion and identification varies. In the first place, the obvious bears mention: several of the factors reviewed in previous chapters, such as the degree to which a text triggers personal memories, depend entirely on the recipient; a given moment in a text will not prompt the same response in every recipient. Second, context affects reception. Jonathan Cohen and Nurit Tal-Or point to how consuming media with other audience members affects identification: demographic similarity or dissimilarity matters. For instance, "a male co-viewer caused the viewer to identify more with a male protagonist in an action film than a female co-viewer" (2017: 147); when a Jewish viewer watched a clip favorable to Israel in the presence of an Arab co-viewer, they experienced greater identification with the Arab protagonist (147–8). Felix Budelmann et al. detected a significant correlation between subjects' feeling "connected to other viewers" and their identification with a film's two protagonists (2017: 240).

Third, much depends on the recipient's personality and attributes (cf. Wolf 2013: 29; R. Allan 2019b: 135; Myers 2019: 108). Some people have a greater "predisposition to be transported (transportability)" than others; they are simply more disposed than others to experience immersion in narratives: "participants who reported a greater tendency to become involved in narratives were more transported by the stories than were participants who reported a lesser tendency to become involved in narratives.... People vary in the extent to which they are transported by narratives" (Dal Cin, Zanna, and Fong 2004: 185–6; cf. Mazzocco et al. 2010: 362).

A number of other discrete traits impinge upon immersion and identification. Arthur Jacobs and Jana Lüdtke assemble earlier scholarship to compile the following list of factors affecting immersion (2017: 80):

higher need for affect scores
higher empathy
conscientiousness, openness, or neuroticism
a reader's mood
beliefs (e.g., whether they believe a text to be fact or fiction)
reading perspective, including knowledge and expectations about genre (effects) or motivations for mood management

Richard Gerrig and Matthew Bezdek flesh out the first item: "Individuals with high need for affect may enjoy watching emotionally-charged dramatic films whereas individuals with a low need for affect may find these types of programs aversive" (2013: 102; cf. Fitzgerald and Green 2017: 51; Oliver et al. 2017: 257). Mary Beth Oliver et al. note that recipients who possess "higher levels of trait empathy" dislike horror films and favor "dramas and more 'meaningful' types of content" (2017: 256–7; cf. Thompson et al. 2018: 214–16). Jacobs and Lüdtke find "that immersion rates are lower when neuroticism scores are bigger…, and higher when openness scores are bigger" (2017: 87). Researchers attend to still other factors. Bradford Owen and Matt Riggs tease out the connection between transportation and a recipient's "need for cognition, which refers to the degree to which we enjoy and engage in thinking, particularly that related to planning, analysis, and problem solving" (2012: 132). Oliver et al. posit that "searching for meaning in life appears to be a trait associated with heightened likelihood of absorption or engagement" (2017: 257) and that, if your own mortality is on your mind, you "are more touched by tragedies, and enjoy non-tragic content less" (263). Jacqueline Thompson et al.'s experiment suggests that "sensation seeking"—"a preference for disinhibited behavior and novel experiences"—predicts transportation (2018: 214–16).

Eva Koopman finds that "trait empathy" predicts both identification and absorption (2016: 89; cf. Wimmer et al. 2021). Observing differences in readers' interest in mind reading fictional characters, Jordan Carpenter, Melanie Green, and Kaitlin Fitzgerald find a positive correlation between one's motivation to mind read and one's experiences of transportation and identification (2018). Cohen and Tal-Or point to studies showing that extroverts and those who score high in "affective empathy (but not cognitive empathy)" readily identify with characters, whereas "those who tend to focus on themselves" do not (2017: 146). Jens Kjeldgaard-Christiansen et al. find an association, especially in young males, between "having a dark personality" and identifying with fictional villains (2021: section 6.3). For their part, Katalin Bálint and András Kovács examine how access to a character's mind interacts with a recipient's attachment style—"an important personality characteristic that regulates the quality and intensity of interpersonal relationships in real life"—to affect their degree of engagement with a character, a capacious concept that includes identification (2016, quotation from 193).

In short, a narrative can only offer the possibility of immersion and identification (cf. Wolf 2013: 32). Each recipient will have a unique experience of the *Iliad* based on a range of variables external to the text, from the distinct context in which they encounter the text to differences in personal qualities.

Turning to the performers of the poetry, I note another factor that will have varied in its implementation in antiquity. Homeric poets orally performed their poetry before an audience. The mode of performance changed over time (González 2013), and each performer's style of presentation would have been idiosyncratic to some degree. We should think about how watching and listening to someone perform the poetry affected the audience's immersion in the storyworld and identification with the characters (cf. Grethlein 2021a: 103–5, 163–4). Budelmann and Evert van Emde Boas pave the way here with their discussion of messenger speeches in Greek tragedies (2020). They start by noting that we might attend to the actor's bravura performance as a messenger or to the dynamics between the messenger and the other characters with whom he interacts, or we might find ourselves immersed in the tale the messenger tells (60–1). They ask how each factor impinges on the other, concluding that, although we can only attend consciously to one of the three, "an unconscious or half-conscious awareness of both the actor and the character may run in parallel with immersion in the narrative" (79). Jonas Grethlein extends their inquiry into the immersive features of the *paedogogus*'s speech in Sophocles's *Electra* (680–763), which functions like a messenger speech insofar as it reports (falsely) the death of Orestes (2021a: 56–67). Stipulating that we can be just as immersed in the storyworld when a live storyteller creates it as we can when reading silently, we can ask what features of live, embodied performance aid immersion and identification.

I begin with gestures, following Alex Purves in including "whole-body movement phrases," such as standing and running, in the category of gesture along with facial and hand movements (2019: 3–4, quotation from 3). Scholars continue to debate the degree to which Homeric performers gestured as they performed (Purves 2019: 29–32; Kretler 2020: 332–4), but we all should allow for some degree of movement. This allowance obtains even if we imagine a singer holding a lyre and a plectrum (Kretler 2020: 332; *pace* de Jong 2012c: 67, 69). Modern performers of oral epic who play an instrument move about, even when seated, like the bard of the Haya *enanga* epic tradition: "His gestures are confined to swaying of the body, particularly the head, rolling or closing the eyes, and manipulation of the mouth. Thus, the bard would enact a boat-rowing scene by swaying the body, eating by smacking, and drunkenness by a pretense of drowsiness" (Mulokozi 2002: 58). Holding a cithara and plectrum, the citharodes of ancient Greece engaged in "spectacular gesture and movement" and "dramatic posturing" and, with the advent of the so-called New Music in the late fifth century BCE, "mimetically sensational bodily expressions," including "a variety of stylized faces, even outlandish ones" (T. Power 2010: 136, 138, 145, 148).

Homerists try to divine from our texts where a performer may have used a gesture in support of the content. Alan Boegehold posits that gestures could accompany demonstratives and take the place of protases and apodoses of conditional sentences (1999: 36–47). Katherine Kretler finds a number of such hints in the text: when the priest Chryses prays to Apollo, the performer may "gesture with his arms in prayer" (2020: 33); he may use his staff to mimic Lycurgus's goad and Diomedes's spear (63, 65); he may pretend to pick up Deïpyrus's helmet as it rolls on the battlefield (80); he may use his staff to imitate Odysseus as he wields his sword to maintain order among the souls of the dead in the underworld (337). Mimetic gestures of this sort may contribute to immersion in the storyworld. First, they clarify, or at least make still more clear, what is going on in the storyworld. Second, because seeing someone do something activates the part of our brain that makes us do that thing, these gestures trigger motor resonance, perhaps even motor resonance that rises to the level of felt experience.

Not all gestures are so transparently linked to content. Harold Scheub distinguishes between the Xhosa storyteller's use of mimetic gestures (what he terms "complementary" gestures) and non-mimetic gestures (what he calls "supplementary" or "abstract" gestures) (1977; 2002). He details, for instance, how "the artist's hands form a miming gesture, then, the hands still miming, the gesture-word union ends, but the hands remain in the gesturing position—and continue to gesticulate. Now they move about as abstract gestures, with no mimed narrative content (no content that is obvious, anyway)" (1977: 361; cf. 2002: 208–9). Mimetic or not, gestures help impart to an utterance coherence (the utterance is understandable) and cohesion (the utterance holds together and has a discrete identity) (Ready 2019a: 19, 24–5, 161). To the extent that gestures impart coherence and cohesion, they enable us to devote our attention to the storyworld and not to be distracted by weaknesses in the presentation. If we are going to stipulate that the Homeric poet gestured mimetically, we should stipulate that he gestured abstractly as well, and we should recognize the ways both kinds of gestures enhanced immersion.

The paralinguistic component of speaking involves more than gestures. Speakers laugh, giggle, quake, whisper; they can sound breathy or husky, slurred, lax, tense, or precise; variations appear in stress, pitch, rhythm, speed, volume, and tempo (Reichl 2000a: 111). If those things happen when we all speak, performers are all the more conscious of vocal effects. Some performers modulate their voices dramatically. When a famous Kyrgyz poet performs an "elegiac poem sung by Manas's favorite wife," he deploys "expressive nuances: now an exclamation, now a simple cry, now a loud sigh, here he uses strong accents, there soft smooth transitions" (Reichl 2000b: 142, translating Vinogradov 1984: 494). In general, performers of Turkic oral epic "imitate different voices" of their characters: for instance, when "a nasty toothless old woman" participates in a singing contest in *Alpamish*, "some singers imitate the voice of the old woman and make fun of her pronunciation" (Reichl 2000b: 144). When a Black performer offers a so-called toast (a narrative poem told in rhyme, such as "Stackolee"), "his voice changes for the various personae of the poem, and sometimes there is another voice for the narrator. There are differences in stress, in accent, in clarity of articulation for various characters" (Jackson 2004: 5). Other modern performers (e.g., Reynolds 1994/1995: 78) also do what Socrates says Homer does: imitate a character in voice (*kata phōnēn*, Plato *Republic* 393c5). Let us assume the Homeric poet engaged in some sort of vocal discrimination between his characters—Richard Martin notes the large amount of epic correption in Thersites's speech in *Iliad* 2: "Thersites slurs his words" (1989: 112); Nancy Felson asks us to "imagine Homer or a rhapsode modulating his voice as he 'plays' Kalypso or Kirke, Nausikäa, Penelope, Athena" (1994: 137; cf. Grethlein 2021b: 219–20)—and that he had them speak in different ways depending on the situation in which they find themselves—Anna Bonifazi sees an opportunity for mimetic sobs as Telemachus speaks at *Odyssey* 1.243–4 (2012: 48) (cf. González 2013: 535, 643; Allen-Hornblower 2016: 75).

This strategy has the potential to affect identification. We might, for instance, connect knowing what a character sounds like with knowing what they look like, one of the antecedents to identification. Or we might connect both the differences in the way different characters sound and how the same character speaks differently on different occasions with the two components of perceived realism, another antecedent to identification (and immersion: see section 8.3, p. 226). That the same character consistently speaks in the same distinct way imparts a high degree of narrative realism. That people speak differently from one another and speak differently on different occasions jibes with our own experience in real life and thereby enhances the degree of external realism: as Irene de Jong notes, prompted by a different stimulus (the abundance of deictic pronouns in character speech), "Homer aims at *mimēsis*, at making his characters speak like real persons" (2012c: 79).

Of course, the manner of delivery injects emotional valence into an utterance, especially when paralinguistic components, be they bodily or vocal, vary. By making the emotional tenor of an utterance clear, the poet invites emotional identification and emotional immersion. I have been concentrating on character-text, but this point pertains to the narrator-text as well.

As alluded to on p. 242, Homeric performance included instrumental accompaniment and melody at some point (González 2013: 343–6, 419; C. Marshall 2021). Comparative perspectives help us speculate about the contribution Homeric music made to audiences' immersion and identification. To the untutored ear the music of oral epic poetry can appear simplistic and boring, but in truth variation abounds in any given presentation. The singer of the epic of Pabuji accompanies himself on the *ravanhattho* (a "spike-fiddle" with two strings that are bowed and between five and sixteen "sympathetic strings" (J. Smith 1991: 18, 27 n. 2)) and uses between three and six different tunes over a discrete section of verse (J. Smith 1991: 26). Accompanying himself on the *rabāb*—a "two-string spike-fiddle" (Reynolds 1994/1995: 57)—the Egyptian singer of Sīrat Banī Hilāl may present (66):

> two dozen or more melodies in the first half to full hour of performance, although the poet may settle into a pattern of much less rapid change later in the performance when it is not uncommon for a poet to use a single melody for a hundred or more lines. In addition, the melodies themselves are not strictly fixed, so that half-phrases and even smaller units are freely reset to create "new" melodic lines during performance.

Accompanying himself on the one-stringed *gusle* (Lord 2019: 34), the Bosniac singer Halil Bajgorić "relies on a melodic repertoire and a tool kit of variational devices with which he alters the musical landscape" (Foster 2004: 250). When performing the verse passages in the prosimetric epic of Edige, a Karakalpak singer accompanies himself on a two-string *qobïz* and routinely deploys twenty or more melodies (Reichl 2007: 166). Jumabay Bazarov, the Karakalpak singer studied by Karl Reichl, uses only "four basic tunes," but "no line is sung exactly like the other" (2007: 174, 177). Based on these analogues (cf. Franklin 2011), I would impute a similar degree of variation to the Homeric singer (cf. C. Marshall 2021: 103–7), whatever the precise nature of his instrument (a four-stringed lyre? (West 1981; C. Marshall 2021)) and however limited his repertoire of melodies. In all cases, the variation in the music keeps the recipient attentive and contributes in that essential way to immersion (see section 5.3, pp. 155–6, for the importance of attention to immersion).

The fact of variation should not blind us to the presence of melodic repetition of the sort we just saw in the quotation from Dwight Reynold's study of Sīrat Banī Hilāl. That repetition can itself be seen to contribute to immersion. I quote Reichl (2000b: 146):

> Anybody who has witnessed the performance of an epic in the style of a singer like the Karakalpak *zhyrau* is struck by the hypnotic effect that the repetition of the same or similar melodies has on listeners. The audience is as it were "taken into" the tale; there is no place for the detached stance of a reader who can pursue or leave off his reading whenever he or she feels the urge.

Reichl confirms Gregory Hutchinson's intuition that "accumulation can absorb the reader or listener into a pattern and a world" (2017: 152). One should imagine that the Homeric poet's melodic repetitions created a similar effect.

Poets use not only gestures but also their instrument to bring coherence and cohesion to their tale and thereby pave the way for an immersive experience. They might take advantage of the presence of the instrument to make up for restrictions on mimetic gestures. Egyptian singers "use a snap of the bow against the body of the *rabâb* to portray the sound of a heavy blow in battle" (Reynolds 1994/1995: 79). When relating the hero's fight with a snake, a griot in Mali slaps his lute (Seydou 2000: 215). Specific tunes with specific associations can make clear what is happening in the story. Egyptian singers might "play an instrumental phrase or two from a wedding song to mark a wedding scene in the story" (Reynolds 1994/1995: 79). The Malian griot aligns words and music: each hero has a "musical theme" or "motto" that played at the start of the performance alerts the audience to the protagonist of the tale (Seydou 2000: 215); moreover, specific musical themes and motifs pair with "muster drums, military cavalcades, vultures feeding on the dead on the battlefield, the implacable rhythm of destiny at work" (215; cf. 221). Yakut epic singers assign specific melodies to specific narrative situations and characters, such as "the hero of the Middle World, the figures of the Lower World" (Reichl 2000b: 141). Again, these documented features of modern oral performance should encourage us to attribute similar tactics to the Homeric poet.

I will not belabor the point that music, whether vocal or instrumental, can contribute to immersion and identification by clarifying a character's inner, mental state (M. Smith 1995: 151–2; Hoeckner et al. 2011) and by enhancing our emotional reactions to a narrative (Meineck 2018: 154–79; Brown, Howe, and Belyk 2020). I merely note that those who study the musical elements of oral epic highlight those elements' emotional impact. The music of the Egyptian singer's Sīrat Banī Hilāl can "produce emotional reactions among listeners" (Reynolds 1994/1995: 80). The music of the griot generates "in the listeners a shared emotion, an internalised exaltation" (Seydou 2000: 216). In the Haya *enanga* epic tradition, "short songs serve to heighten the emotional impact of the given incident or episode" (Mulokozi 2002: 74). Halil Bajgorić deploys music "for expressive effects" (Foster 2004: 250). We should assign the same understanding of music's power to the Homeric poet as well.

Martin West surmises that the Homeric singer routinely paused his singing and continued to play the lyre during those pauses, likely introducing more elaborate runs in those breaks (1981: 122; cf. C. Marshall 2021: 105). West finds support for this reconstruction in a performance by Salih Ugljanin recorded by Milman Parry and Albert Lord in Novi Pazar in 1934 (1981: 123), and one can now cite several other illustrative parallels from traditions of epic song, ranging from Rajasthani (J. Smith 1991: 18) to Egyptian (Reynolds 1994/1995: 75; 1995: 156–7) to Karakalpak (Reichl 2000b: 137–8; 2007: 165) traditions. An instrumental interlude in the midst of a suspenseful passage can function as a non-diegetic delay and ratchet up the suspense. Conversely, an instrumental interlude at a transitional point in the tale provides recipients with some respite from the taxing mental work of immersion and identification and allows them to re-engage in those efforts when the story resumes.

I have been looking at steps the orally performing Homeric poet could take to immerse the audience in the storyworld and to encourage them to identify with the characters. Yet audience members would only have had these reactions if they thought the performer was good. Athenian audiences booed bad acting (Demosthenes *On the Crown* 265; Pickard-Cambridge 1968: 272–3; Csapo and Slater 1995: 290; Farmer 2021: 3), and ancient Greek audiences judged performers of Homeric epic vigorously too, as evidenced in the existence of rhapsodic contests from the classical through the imperial periods (Tsagalis 2018a; 2018b; Gangloff 2018). Just as audiences of modern oral performers evaluate what a performer says and how they say it (Ready 2018: 84–111), so too did ancient audiences (González 2013: 381, 418–19, 464, 643): archaic Greek epic itself self-reflexively explores what makes for a good performance in terms of content and form (Ready 2018: 170–83). Audience members were unlikely to base their evaluations solely on impartial and technical analyses of poetic craft. We should imagine that one factor informing positive assessments of content was whether the poet said things with which a recipient agreed. Recall the Homeric narrator's judgments on the characters (section 7.3, p. 213; cf. section 2.2, p. 17) and many ancient recipients' assumption that the narrator and the poet were the same (section 4.6, p. 142). Audience members who imputed those opinions to the poet and who agreed with those opinions would consider the poet good.

Modern audiences, though, look beyond content and form. Ineffable qualities like charisma inform judgment (e.g., Greene 1996: 2), but modern audiences also draw on what they think about the performer outside of the performance context. In her study of Tuareg verbal art (Niger), Susan Rasmussen recalls (1992: 163):

> At a baby's nameday, a member of the audience commented that the singers were "bad." When I asked her what she meant, and what was necessary to be a good singer, she said "they must be well-reared," linking performance and competence to social and moral norms as well as technical training. For performing verbal art well, one must be well brought up in an ethical sense.

Exploring storytelling among Latter-day Saints, Tom Mould reports (2011: 135–6):

> The most important criteria for evaluating the narrative generally and belief specifically come from outside the performance event. Even before a person begins his or her narrative, audience members have begun their evaluation, training their focus on the narrator rather than the narrative.... The reputation of a person outside the performance event can weigh so heavily upon the evaluation of performance that it can make people question the truth of the story even when they feel the presence of the Holy Ghost.

Surely some performers of Homeric poetry were known in their local communities outside of their gigs as performers. What people thought of them when they were not performing affected how people responded to their performances, including their degree of immersion and identification. In the end—and here we follow up on an implication of a recipient's personality and attributes informing their response to a narrative (see pp. 240-1)—performers could only do so much to engage their audiences: some of it was out of their hands.

So much for caveats and speculation. Once recipients are immersed, their response to a text changes. Immersion cuts down on counterarguing, the propensity to question the information provided and the assertions made in a text (de Graaf and van Leeuwen 2017: 272-3; Consoli 2018: 89, 91; Krause and Appel 2020: 47-8, 50; cf. Dadlez 2011: 122-3; Grethlein 2021a: 266). When Alcinous, the Phaeacian king, declares that Odysseus is not a liar (*Odyssey* 11.363-6), he endorses the veracity of Odysseus's tale. Michael Power suggests, "Alkinoös, who was highly transported by Odysseus' narrative, is inherently less likely—indeed, less able—to question or contextualize the narrative content, and thus more likely to find the story realistic" (2006: 98). By contrast, Eumaeus labels "not in good order" (*ou kata kosmon*) and lies (*pseudethai, pseudessi*) the disguised Odysseus's account of the real Odysseus's imminent return to Ithaca (*Odyssey* 14.363-5, 387). Eumaeus allows that the disguised Odysseus "roused" his heart (*thuman orinas*, 14.361), but in nine of its ten other occurrences this phrase presages a character's being stirred to action; it does not by itself indicate immersion. That he argues against the veracity of a portion of Odysseus's account also suggests that he was not completely immersed during Odysseus's tale. Nonetheless, Eumaeus grants the possibility of being "bewitched by lies" (*pseudessi...thelge, Odyssey* 14.387). To be "bewitched" (*thelgō*) means to be wrapped up in a story, usually that presented by a poet (Ready 2018: 171). Eumaeus's words acknowledge that the immersed recipient will have trouble determining and be less inclined to determine the truth value of a tale. The same idea undergirds the Muses's declaration in Hesiod's *Theogony* that they speak "many false things similar to true things" (27): the point is not (or not only) that the Muses and so poets can make things up; the point is that the immersed recipient—for who could fail to be immersed when listening to the Muses?—is less inclined to counterargue and label the poetry lies.

The moments in which the Homeric poet stumbles (or nods) will tend not to catch the attention of an immersed recipient. Readers will find a litany of the *Iliad*'s infelicities and errors in, for example, Steven Reece's 2005 book chapter and Martin West's 2011 book. Pylaemenes falls to Menelaus at *Iliad* 5.576-9 but reappears at *Iliad* 13.658 in the company of those carrying his son's corpse from the battlefield (Reece 2005: 61). Apollo disarms Patroclus (*Iliad* 16.786-804), but at *Iliad* 17.125 Hector strips the previously naked Patroclus of his armor (Reece 2005: 59-60). Odysseus's declaring himself "the father of Telemachus" at *Iliad*

2.260 is "anachronistic" and "inorganic" (West 2011: 107). Assessing the portion of *Iliad* 7 wherein the Achaeans build a fortification wall, West writes (2011: 197):

> It is evident that this whole part of the poem is hastily composed, perhaps more of a draft than a fully finished version. We might suppose that 421–32 and 433–41 were blocks of text composed at different moments, that P [West's *Iliad* poet] never harmonized; or that he meant to put some extra lines after 432 in which the passage of a night was recorded.

Others have responded that some of the supposed mistakes are not mistakes at all (e.g., Nagy 2003: 49–71; González 2013: 25–7), but even if one grants that these mistakes qualify as mistakes, these lists of blunders simply prove that a battery of scholars who have spent a lifetime rereading the poems with all the advantages offered by modern technology can detect errors and that they are not immersed when they do so. To be fair, sometimes inconsistencies occur so close to one another that they are hard to ignore. Hypsenor, well and truly dead at *Iliad* 13.412, groans only a few verses later at 13.423, groans of this sort emanating from the wounded, tired, or hopeless, but not the dead (Reece 2005: 59). For the most part, though, an immersed recipient will not care about or notice these missteps.

Because immersion lessens counterarguing, it increases the tale's impact (Igartua 2010: 352; Sanford and Emmott 2012: 243–4; Consoli 2018: 89; Ma 2020: 867, 872). I return once more to the phenomenon of narrative impact discussed in section 3.3 (pp. 64–5) and section 4.5 (p. 137): to repeat, research into narrative impact finds that "highly transporting narratives have the potential to alter beliefs, attitudes, and behaviors" (Fitzgerald and Green 2017: 62) and that identification with characters makes an important contribution to this equation or causes similar changes. Gorgias, Plato, and Aristotle were right in their contentions that immersion in a narrative and identification with characters affect recipients after they stop reading or watching (Halliwell 2002: 93–4, 96; 2005: 397; Liebert 2017: 139, 156, 159, 168, 185, 189–90; Grethlein 2021a: 80–91, 98–9, 101, 247–8, 279; cf. Araújo 2018), and Rita Felski is right when she says that texts can "cause us to do things we had not anticipated" (2015: 84) and that the inability of artworks to "topple banks and bureaucracies, museums and markets, does not mean...that they are therefore doomed to be impotent and inert, stripped of all power to challenge perception or shake up the psyche" (2008: 109; cf. 16; 2015: 65, 177–80). I hasten to recall again that we are dealing with potentialities here, not inevitabilities. I stressed in section 4.5 the problems with assuming a direct line between identification and real-world actions as well as our limited knowledge about the lasting effects of engagement with a narrative. Isocrates's observation comes to mind: audiences cry (*dakruein*) over the misfortunes depicted by poets, but that response does not translate into feeling pity (*eleein*) when made to witness real suffering (*pathē*) (*Panegyricus* [4.]168 Usher; cf. Andocides, *Against Alcibiades* [4.]23; see Heath 2006: 272; Wohl 2015: 40 with 151 n. 4).

Scholarship on the *Odyssey* in particular has argued for its effects on audiences. Nancy Felson considers how audience members' changing assessment of Penelope's suitors might change them. First "identifying with" and then coming to detest the suitors, audience members—above all, the "laggards," those "lagging in the maturation process"—get "a chance to grow and learn through abandoning their own suitor-qualities" (1994: 109). Joel Christensen proposes that the *Odyssey* can offer coping strategies for dealing with the vagaries of chance and fate (2020). These are cast as possible outcomes. But we can also document the profound political, cultural, and social impact of Homeric poetry in antiquity, impact it will be otiose to belabor (e.g., Hunter 2018; Kim 2020). I cite just one example: Joseph Farrell observes, "Self-identification with the actions and characters depicted in Homer's epics and adoption of ideals embodied in those actions and characters, is characteristic not only of Roman but of other Italian elites as well" (2004: 270). These ancient fans of Homeric epic resemble those fans of modern fictional characters who try to behave like their favorites in a process that Carl Plantinga labels "projection" (2018: 201, 204). The impact, notional or historically attested, that scholars impute to the Homeric poems should be understood at least in part as narrative impact triggered by the species of immersion and identification explored in this book.

Homerists have also rigorously teased out the arguments embedded in the poems—for instance, that kings are best (or not); that aristocrats are best (or not); that mortals can outshine immortals in wisdom (e.g., Rose 1997; Janko 1998; Thalmann 1998; Ahrensdorf 2014; Scanlon 2018). William Thalmann can be taken to make explicit the implications of this sort of scholarship when he writes that the *Odyssey*'s defense of structural inequality "may well have carried over into daily life" (1998: 299). We come back to narrative impact, and, accordingly, I add that the immersion and identification offered by the epics make these lessons easier to absorb. As Felski observes, "any social knowledge we gain from reading ... requires that a text solicit and capture our attention"; one has to acknowledge "the co-dependence of ... enlightenment and enchantment" (2008: 133); as Carl Plantinga observes of popular movies, "whatever ideas they embody become salient and attractive to audiences in large part because they are affectively powerful to many spectators" (2009: 189).

But who today find themselves immersed in the *Iliad* and identifying with its characters? Most readers of the original language text in Greek, impeded by the need to consult dictionaries and commentaries, read too slowly to have these experiences. In any case, these readers and even those with exceptional facility in Homeric Greek likely read as they have been trained to read: interpreting and getting at meaning (Altieri 2003: 2; Gumbrecht 2004: 1–2) or in a suspicious manner, detecting the implicit and hidden (Felski 2015), or in a paranoid fashion, seeking to unmask power (Sedgwick 2003: e.g., 139–40, 143–4). Although I did note some important exceptions in Chapter 1, many of us might reflexively agree that other modes of analysis beyond a demystifying critique are "sappy and starry-eyed, compliant and complacent" and represent "a full-scale surrender to sentimentality, quietism, Panglossian optimism, or...the intellectual fluff of aesthetic appreciation" (Felski 2015: 150). After all, as I mentioned a moment ago (p. 248), the first thing the Muses say to Hesiod is that they know how to tell lies that seem true (*Theogony* 27): epic alerts us to be on guard (cf. Solon fragment 29 West 1972; Felski 2015: 42–3). Interpreters of Homeric epic may "become immersed in techniques of deciphering and diagnosing" and "enchanted by critique" (Felski 2015: 112, 134; cf. 2020b: 122–3, 127, 132–3), but, in their capacity as scholars, they tend not to approach the *Iliad* with the same mindset with which they read or watch *Game of Thrones*, becoming immersed in the storyworld and identifying with the characters (cf. Felski 2008: 12, 14; 2020b: 162).

It is no accident that the two empirical studies that have used Homeric poetry to query issues related to immersion and identification have done so by way of translations (Power 2006; Thissen, Menninghaus, and Schlotz 2020). For undergraduate students reading the epic in translation are far more likely than their professors to experience immersion and identification. Rita Felski describes what tends to happen in an undergraduate classroom: "critical caveats are interspersed with flashes of affinity or sympathy; bursts of romantic hope coexist with the deciphering of ideological subtexts" (2015: 4). Ask yourself how you tend to react to those flashes and bursts. I, for one, would typically work to steer the conversation back to the caveats and the deciphering. In fact, I use to lament what I called the students' desire to find characters they would want to have a beer with (cf. Halpern 2013: 112–13). I now see my mistake. Those of us who teach the *Iliad* in translation should capitalize on those apparently unsophisticated inclinations (cf. Knox 2021: 155–65). Talking with students about how they find themselves drawn into the storyworld and about how they identify with the characters validates their actual responses to the poem (cf. Felski 2015: 181). That validation makes them aware of, willing to acknowledge out loud, and even equipped to proclaim the immersive power of literature. The world only needs a handful of professional Homerists, but it needs many people who appreciate, value, and advocate for literary engagement. Telling students that their responses to a text matter and then delving into those responses in a rigorous fashion makes an important contribution to our larger project: enabling a life-long involvement with literature.

Simultaneously, if we take immersion and identification seriously, if we tell students that they are allowed to respond to the *Iliad* as they respond to *Game of Thrones*, we give them the chance to like the poem on their terms. This permission structure might even enable readers who find the poem confounding and inaccessible, filled with unpronounceable names, to get some purchase on the text. If we start by analyzing how students react to the poem and valuing that analysis, we can perhaps more easily move next to forms of interrogation with which they are less familiar—not better forms, just new ones (cf. Halpern 2013: 136).

This work differs little from the work in which we traditionally engage in the classroom. We have been looking at how texts function in the world by tracing their social and political engagements and entanglements. To pursue questions of immersion and identification is to query from another angle how texts function in the world, to investigate their "social lives" (Felski 2015: 184) from another angle. Nor need such explorations jettison the notion of historical variability and contingency. We can trace, as I have done in sections 2.4 and 5.2, how ancient readers themselves asked after and had their own ideas about what we call identification and immersion. Discussions of how immersion and identification work provide new vantage points from which to consider still other topics that we typically address in classes on Homeric epic and that I have pointed to in this concluding chapter, ranging from questions of composition and performance to questions of ideological operations and implicit violence.

I would not limit such discussions to the undergraduate classroom. We should train our graduate students in the features of immersion and identification (cf. Felski 2015: 180–2). Not only will they one day take our places in the undergraduate classes mentioned in the previous paragraphs. Graduate students in classical studies encounter one mystification after another: What commentary should I use? Am I supposed to cite this critical edition or that one? What does this abbreviation mean? Why do the four lines in this choral ode seem to be numbered as if they were five lines? What is a minus verse? Who is Pauly-Wissowa? Wait, I'm only just now learning that there is a dictionary devoted to Pindar? It may be refreshing and invigorating to study something so intuitively resonant as immersion and identification. Graduate seminars might also be the best place to pick up the discussion initiated in section 4.5 concerning the politics of identification. Alongside and related to that debate are scholarly disputes over the politics of immersion writ large (Plantinga 2018: e.g., 109, 117–22, 124, 151–3, 224, 230, 250), disputes that, unlike those pertaining to identification, have not yet found their way into classicists' investigations of immersion, as far as I can tell. Jonas Grethlein's examination of how ancient authors wrestled with "the ethics of enchantment" (that is, the ethics of aesthetic illusion or immersion) prepares the ground for such an exploration (2021a): authors explored how aesthetic illusion can deceive, how it can corrupt, and, even on occasion, how it can edify. The introductory course to literary theory that many departments offer might benefit too from considering the politics of immersion and identification. Such queries bring one to key texts of and approaches in twentieth- and twenty-first-century critical theory. Introducing students to those texts and approaches as they pertain to questions of immersion and identification may make those texts and approaches more accessible.

# Works Cited

Adkins, A. W. H. 1960. *Merit and Responsibility: A Study in Greek Values*. Oxford: Clarendon Press.
Ahrensdorf, P. J. 2014. *Homer on the Gods and Human Virtue: Creating the Foundations of Classical Civilization*. Cambridge: Cambridge University Press.
Alam, N. and So, J. 2020. "Contributions of Emotional Flow in Narrative Persuasion: An Empirical Test of the Emotional Flow Framework." *Communication Quarterly*, 68: 161–82.
Aldana Reyes, X. 2016. *Horror Film and Affect: Towards a Corporeal Model of Viewership*. New York: Routledge.
Alden, M. J. 2000. *Homer beside Himself: Para-Narratives in the Iliad*. Oxford: Oxford University Press.
Alden, M. J. 2017. *Para-Narratives in the Odyssey: Stories in the Frame*. Oxford: Oxford University Press.
Alejandro Aranda, M. 2016. "World Building." In H. Lowood and R. Guins (eds), *Debugging Game History: A Critical Lexicon*. Cambridge, MA: MIT Press, 419–24.
Alexiou, M. 2002. *The Ritual Lament in Greek Tradition*. 2nd edn. P. Roilos and D. Yatromanolakis (eds). Lanham, MD: Rowman and Littlefield.
Allan, R. J. 2019a. "Construal and Immersion: A Cognitive Linguistic Approach to Homeric Immersivity." In P. Meineck, W. M. Short, and J. Devereaux (eds), *The Routledge Handbook of Classics and Cognitive Theory*. London: Routledge, 59–78.
Allan, R. [J.] 2019b. "Herodotus and Thucydides: Distance and Immersion." In L. van Gils, I. de Jong, and C. Kroon (eds), *Textual Strategies in Ancient War Narrative: Thermopylae, Cannae and Beyond*. Leiden: Brill, 131–54.
Allan, R. J. 2020. "Narrative Immersion: Some Linguistic and Narratological Aspects." In J. Grethlein, L. Huitink, and A. Tagliabue (eds), *Experience, Narrative, and Criticism in Ancient Greece: Under the Spell of Stories*. Oxford: Oxford University Press, 15–35.
Allan, R. [J.] 2022a. "Metaleptic Apostrophe in Homer: Emotion and Immersion." In M. de Bakker, B. van der Berg, and J. Klooster (eds), *Emotions and Narrative in Ancient Literature and Beyond: Studies in Honour of Irene de Jong*. Leiden: Brill, 78–93.
Allan, R. J. 2022b. "Persuasion by Immersion: The *narratio* of Lysias 1, *On the Killing of Eratosthenes*." *Trends in Classics*, 14: 271–98.
Allan, R. J., de Jong, I. J. F., and de Jonge, C. C. 2017. "From *Enargeia* to Immersion: The Ancient Roots of a Modern Concept." *Style*, 51: 34–51.
Allan, W. 2004. "Religious Syncretism: The New Gods of Greek Tragedy." *Harvard Studies in Classical Philology*, 102: 113–55.
Allan, W. 2010. *Euripides: Helen*. Cambridge: Cambridge University Press. Reprinted with corrections.
Allen, J. J. and Anderson, C. A. 2019. "Does Avatar Identification Make Unjustified Video Game Violence More Morally Consequential?" *Media Psychology*, 24: 1–23. DOI: 10.1080/15213269.2019.1683030.
Allen-Hornblower, E. 2016. *From Agent to Spectator: Witnessing the Aftermath in Ancient Greek Epic and Tragedy*. Berlin: Walter de Gruyter.

Altieri, C. 2003. *The Particulars of Rapture: An Aesthetic of the Affects*. Ithaca, NY: Cornell University Press.
Altmann, U. et al. 2012. "The Power of Emotional Valence—From Cognitive to Affective Processes in Reading." *Frontiers in Human Neuroscience*, 6: Article 192. DOI: 10.3389/fnhum.2012.00192.
Ambler, W. 2015. *Xenophon: The Education of Cyrus*. Ithaca, NY: Cornell University Press.
Andersen, Ø. 1978. *Die Diomedesgestalt in der Ilias*. Oslo: Universitetsforlaget.
Anderson, A. 2019. "Thinking with Character." In A. Anderson, R. Felski, and T. Moi (eds), *Character: Three Inquiries in Literary Studies*. Chicago: University of Chicago Press, 127–70.
Anderson, W. L. 1953. "Of Gods and Men in the 'Iliad'." *College English*, 14: 391–5.
Andrews, A. D. 2005. "Homeric Recitation, with Input from Phonology and Philology." *Antichthon*, 39: 1–28.
Andringa, E. 2004. "The Interface between Fiction and Life: Patterns of Identification in Reading Autobiographies." *Poetics Today*, 25: 205–40.
Angelopoulou, A. 2020. "Problematizing *Aisthēsis*: The Disruption of Shared Affectivity in the *Ajax*." *Transactions of the American Philological Association*, 150: 39–64.
Anker, E. S. and Felski, R. 2017. "Introduction." In E. S. Anker and R. Felski (eds), *Critique and Postcritique*. Durham, NC: Duke University Press, 1–28.
Araújo, C. 2018. "Plato's *Republic* on Mimetic Poetry and Empathy." In H. Reid and J. DeLong (eds), *The Many Faces of Mimesis: Selected Essays from the 2017 Symposium on the Hellenic Heritage of Western Greece*. Sioux City, IA: Parnassos Press, 75–85.
Arft, J. 2014. "Immanent Thebes: Traditional Resonance and Narrative Trajectory in the *Odyssey*." *Trends in Classics*, 6: 399–411.
Armstrong, J. I. 1958. "The Arming Motif in the *Iliad*." *American Journal of Philology*, 79: 337–54.
Arnaud, P. 2019. *À quoi bon Achille? Une autre lecture de L'Iliade*. Paris: L'Harmattan.
Arthur, M. B. 1981. "The Divided World of *Iliad* VI." In H. Foley (ed.), *Reflections of Women in Antiquity*. New York: Gordon and Breach Science Publishers, 19–44.
Austin, N. 1966. "The Function of Digressions in the *Iliad*." *Greek, Roman, and Byzantine Studies*, 7: 295–312.
Auyoung, E. 2010. "The Sense of Something More in Art and Experience." *Style*, 44: 547–65.
Auyoung, E. 2015. "Rethinking the Reality Effect: Detail and the Novel." In L. Zunshine (ed.), *The Oxford Handbook of Cognitive Literary Studies*. Oxford: Oxford University Press, 581–92.
Bachvarova, M. R. 2016. *From Hittite to Homer: The Anatolian Background of Ancient Greek Epic*. Cambridge: Cambridge University Press.
Bakker, E. J. 1997. *Poetry in Speech: Orality and Homeric Discourse*. Ithaca, NY: Cornell University Press.
Bakker, E. J. 2005. *Pointing at the Past: From Formula to Performance in Homeric Poetics*. Washington, DC: Center for Hellenic Studies.
Bakker, E. J. 2013. *The Meaning of Meat and the Structure of the Odyssey*. Cambridge: Cambridge University Press.
Bal, P. M. and Veltkamp, M. 2013. "How Does Fiction Reading Influence Empathy? An Experimental Investigation on the Role of Emotional Transportation." *PLoS ONE*, 8.1: e55341. DOI: 10.1371/journal.pone.0055341.
Bálint, K. and Kovács, A. B. 2016. "Focalization, Attachment, and Film Viewers' Responses to Film Characters: Experimental Design with Qualitative Data Collection." In

C. D. Reinhard and C. J. Olson (eds), *Making Sense of Cinema: Empirical Studies into Film Spectators and Spectatorship*. New York: Bloomsbury Academic, 187–210.
Bálint, K, Kuijpers, M. K. and Doicaru, M. M. 2017. "The Effect of Suspense Structure on Felt Suspense and Narrative Absorption in Literature and Film." In F. Hakemulder et al. (eds), *Narrative Absorption*. Amsterdam: John Benjamins Publishing, 177–97.
Bálint, K. and Tan, E. 2019. "Absorbed Character Engagement: From Social Cognition Responses to the Experience of Fictional Constructions." In J. Riis and A. Taylor (eds), *Screening Characters: Theories of Character in Film, Television, and Interactive Media*. New York: Routledge, 209–30.
Banerjee, S. C. and Greene, K. 2012. "Role of Transportation in the Persuasion Process: Cognitive and Affective Responses to Antidrug Narratives." *Journal of Health Communication*, 17: 564–81.
Baragwanath, E. 2008. *Motivation and Narrative in Herodotus*. Oxford: Oxford University Press.
Barker, J. M. 2009. *The Tactile Eye: Touch and the Cinematic Experience*. Berkeley, CA: University of California Press.
Baroni, R. 2007. *La Tension narrative: Suspense, curiosité et surprise*. Paris: Éditions du Seuil.
Baroni, R. 2021. "Perspective narrative, focalisation et point de vue: Pour une synthèse." *Fabula LHT*, 25: http://www.fabula.org/lht/25/baroni.html.
Bassett, S. E. 1912. "The Palace of Odysseus." *American Journal of Archaeology*, 23: 288–311.
Bassett, S. E. 1938. *The Poetry of Homer*. Berkeley, CA: University of California Press.
Beck, D. 2005. *Homeric Conversation*. Washington, DC: Center for Hellenic Studies.
Beck, D. 2012. *Speech Presentation in Homeric Epic*. Austin, TX: University of Texas Press.
Beck, D. 2018. "Emotional and Thematic Meanings in a Repeating Homeric Motif: A Case Study." *Journal of Hellenic Studies*, 138: 150–72.
Beecher, D. 2007. "Suspense." *Philosophy and Literature*, 31: 255–79.
Benardete, S. 2005. *Achilles and Hector: The Homeric Hero*. R. Burger (ed.). South Bend, IN: St. Augustine's Press.
Bergren, A. L. T. 1975. *The Etymology and Usage of ΠΕΙΡΑΡ in Early Greek Poetry: A Study in the Interrelationship of Metrics, Linguistics and Poetics*. State College, PA: Commercial Printing [for] American Philological Association.
Bergren, A. [L. T.] 2008. *Weaving Truth: Essays on Language and the Female in Greek Thought*. Washington, DC: Center for Hellenic Studies.
Bernabé, A. 1987. *Poetarum epicorum Graecorum: Testimonia et fragmenta*, vol. 1. Leipzig: Teubner.
Bernaerts, L. et al. 2013. "Introduction: Cognitive Narrative Studies: Themes and Variations." In L. Bernaerts et al. (eds), *Stories and Minds: Cognitive Approaches to Literary Narratives*. Lincoln, NE: University of Nebraska Press, 1–20.
Bernstein, N. W. 2004. "*Auferte oculos*: Modes of Spectatorship in Statius *Thebaid* 11." *Phoenix*, 58: 62–85.
Bierl, A. 2019. "Agonistic Excess and Its Ritual Resolution in Hero Cult: The Funeral Games in *Iliad* 23 as a *mise en abyme*." In C. Damon and C. Pieper (eds), *Eris vs. Aemulatio: Valuing Competition in Classical Antiquity*. Leiden: Brill, 53–77.
Bilandzic, H. and Busselle, R. W. 2011. "Enjoyment of Films as a Function of Narrative Experience, Perceived Realism and Transportability." *Communications*, 36: 29–50.
Bilandzic, H. and Busselle, R. 2017. "Beyond Metaphors and Traditions: Exploring the Conceptual Boundaries of Narrative Engagement." In F. Hakemulder et al. (eds), *Narrative Absorption*. Amsterdam: John Benjamins Publishing, 11–27.

Blondell, R. 2013. *Helen of Troy: Beauty, Myth, Devastation*. Oxford: Oxford University Press.
Blundell, M. W. 1989. *Helping Friends and Harming Enemies: A Study in Sophocles and Greek Ethics*. Cambridge: Cambridge University Press.
Boegehold, A. L. 1999. *When a Gesture Was Expected: A Selection of Examples from Archaic and Classical Greek Literature*. Princeton: Princeton University Press.
Bonifazi, A. 2012. *Homer's Versicolored Fabric: The Evocative Power of Ancient Greek Epic Word-Making*. Washington, DC: Center for Hellenic Studies.
Bonifazi, A. 2018. "Embedded Focalization and Free Indirect Speech in Homer as Viewpoint Blending." In J. L. Ready and C. C. Tsagalis (eds), *Homer in Performance: Rhapsodes, Narrators, and Characters*. Austin, TX: University of Texas Press, 230–54.
Bonifazi, A. and Elmer, D. F. 2016. "Visuality in Bosniac and Homeric Epic." *Classics@*, 14. https://classics-at.chs.harvard.edu/classics14-bonifazi-and-elmer/.
Booth, W. C. 1961. *The Rhetoric of Fiction*. Chicago: University of Chicago Press.
Bopp, J. A. et al. 2019. "Exploring Emotional Attachment to Game Characters." In *CHI PLAY '19: Proceedings of the Annual Symposium on Computer-Human Interaction in Play*. New York: Association for Computing Machinery, 313–24.
Bortolussi, M. and Dixon, P. 2015. "Transport: Challenges to the Metaphor." In L. Zunshine (ed.), *The Oxford Handbook of Cognitive Literary Studies*. Oxford: Oxford University Press, 525–40.
Bourdieu, P. 1984. *Distinction: A Social Critique of the Judgement of Taste*. Trans. R. Nice. Cambridge, MA: Harvard University Press.
Breithaupt, F. 2011. "The Birth of Narrative out of the Spirit of the Excuse: A Speculation." *Poetics Today*, 32: 102–28.
Breithaupt, F. 2015. "Empathetic Sadism: How Readers Get Implicated." In L. Zunshine (ed.), *The Oxford Handbook of Cognitive Literary Studies*. Oxford: Oxford University Press, 440–59.
Breithaupt, F. 2018. "Empathy and Aesthetics." *Zeitschrift für Ästhetik und allgemeine Kunstwissenschaft*, 63: 45–60.
Breithaupt, F. 2019. *The Dark Sides of Empathy*. Ithaca, NY: Cornell University Press.
Bremer, J. M. 1986. "Four Similes in *Iliad* 22." In F. Cairns (ed.), *Papers of the Liverpool Latin Seminar*. Vol. 5: *1985*. Liverpool: Francis Cairns.
Brockliss, W. 2018. "Abject Landscapes of the *Iliad*." In D. Felson (ed.), *Landscapes of Dread in Classical Antiquity: Negative Emotion in Natural and Constructed Spaces*. London: Routledge, 15–37.
Brosch, R. 2017. "Experiencing Narratives: Default and Vivid Modes of Visualization." *Poetics Today*, 38: 255–72.
Brown, S., Howe, M., and Belyk, M. 2020. "Music Enhances Empathic Engagement with Character in Films." *Music and Arts in Action*, 7: 2–15.
Budelmann, F. 2000. *The Language of Sophocles: Communality, Communication and Involvement*. Cambridge: Cambridge University Press.
Budelmann, F. and Easterling, P. 2010. "Reading Minds in Greek Tragedy." *Greece and Rome*, 57: 289–303.
Budelmann, F. and Emde Boas, E. van. 2020. "Attending to Tragic Messenger Speeches." In J. Grethlein, L. Huitink, and A. Tagliabue (eds), *Experience, Narrative, and Criticism in Ancient Greece: Under the Spell of Stories*. Oxford: Oxford University Press, 59–80.
Budelmann, F. et al. 2017. "Cognition, Endorphins, and the Literary Response to Tragedy." *Cambridge Quarterly*, 46: 229–50.
Burgess, J. S. 2001. *The Tradition of the Trojan War in Homer and the Epic Cycle*. Baltimore, MD: Johns Hopkins University Press.

Burgess, J. S. 2009. *The Death and Afterlife of Achilles*. Baltimore, MD: Johns Hopkins University Press.
Burgess, J. S. 2015. *Homer*. London: I. B. Tauris.
Burgess, J. S. 2019. "The Corpse of Odysseus." *Yearbook of Ancient Greek Epic*, 3: 136–57.
Burke, M. et al. 2016. "Empathy at the Confluence of Neuroscience and Empirical Literary Studies." *Scientific Study of Literature*, 6: 6–41.
Busselle, R. and Bilandzic, H. 2009. "Measuring Narrative Engagement." *Media Psychology*, 12: 321–47.
Bussels, S. 2013. *The Animated Image: Roman Theory on Naturalism, Vividness and Divine Power*. Berlin: Akademie Verlag.
Büttner-Wobst, T. 2009. *Polybii historiae*. Vol. 1: *Libri I–III*. Berlin: Walter de Gruyter. Reprint; first published by Teubner, 1905.
Buxton, R. 2004. "Similes and Other Likenesses." In R. Fowler (ed.), *The Cambridge Companion to Homer*. Cambridge: Cambridge University Press, 139–55.
Bywater, I. 1894. *Aristotelis ethica Nicomachea*. Reprint 1962. Oxford: Clarendon Press.
Cairns, D. L. 2003. "Ethics, Ethology, Terminology: Iliadic Anger and the Cross-Cultural Study of Emotion." In S. M. Braund and G. Most (eds), *Ancient Anger: Perspectives from Homer to Galen*. Cambridge: Cambridge University Press, 11–49.
Cairns, D. [L.] 2008. "Look Both Ways: Studying Emotion in Ancient Greek." *Critical Quarterly*, 50.4: 43–62.
Cairns, D. L. 2009. "Weeping and Veiling: Grief, Display and Concealment in Ancient Greek Culture." In T. Fögen (ed.), *Tears in the Greco-Roman World*. Berlin: Walter de Gruyter, 37–57.
Cairns, D. L. 2011. "Veiling Grief on the Tragic Stage." In D. L. Munteanu (ed.), *Emotions, Genre and Gender in Classical Antiquity*. London: Bristol Classical Press, 15–33.
Cairns, D. L. 2012. " *Atē* in the Homeric Poems." In F. Cairns (ed.), *Papers of the Langford Latin Seminar: Fifteenth Volume 2012*. Prenton, UK: Francis Cairns.
Cairns, D. L. 2013. "A Short History of Shudders." In A. Chaniotis and P. Ducrey (eds), *Unveiling Emotions II. Emotions in Greece and Rome: Texts, Images, Material Culture*. Stuttgart: Franz Steiner Verlag, 85–107.
Cairns, D. [L.] 2016. "Metaphors for Hope in Archaic and Classical Greek Poetry." In R. R. Caston and R. A. Kaster (eds), *Hope, Joy, and Affection in the Classical World*. Oxford: Oxford University Press, 13–44.
Cairns, D. [L.] 2017. "Horror, Pity, and the Visual in Ancient Greek Aesthetics." In D. Cairns and D. Nelis (eds), *Emotions in the Classical World: Methods, Approaches, and Directions*. Stuttgart: Franz Steiner Verlag, 53–77.
Cairns, D. [L.] and Fulkerson, L. 2015. "Introduction." In D. Cairns and L. Fulkerson (eds), *Emotions between Greece and Rome*. London: Institute of Classical Studies, University of London, 1–22.
Cairns, D. [L.] and Nelis, D. 2017. "Introduction." In D. Cairns and D. Nelis (eds), *Emotions in the Classical World: Methods, Approaches, and Directions*. Stuttgart: Franz Steiner Verlag, 7–30.
Calarco, N. et al. 2017. "Absorption in Narrative Fiction and its Possible Impact on Social Abilities." In F. Hakemulder et al. (eds), *Narrative Absorption*. Amsterdam: John Benjamins Publishing, 293–313.
Campbell, D. A. 1990. *Greek Lyric I: Sappho and Alcaeus*. Cambridge, MA: Harvard University Press. Reprint with corrections.
Canevaro, L. G. 2018. *Women of Substance in Homeric Epic: Objects, Gender, Agency*. Oxford: Oxford University Press.

Caracciolo, M. 2014. *The Experientiality of Narrative: An Enactivist Approach*. Berlin: Walter de Gruyter.

Caracciolo, M. 2016. *Strange Narrators in Contemporary Fiction: Explorations in Readers' Engagement with Characters*. Lincoln, NE: University of Nebraska Press.

Caracciolo, M. 2018. "Degrees of Embodiment in Literary Reading: Notes for a Theoretical Model, with *American Psycho* as a Case Study." In S. Csábi (ed.), *Expressive Minds and Artistic Creations: Studies in Cognitive Poetics*. Oxford: Oxford University Press, 11–31.

Carpenter, J. M., Green, M. C., and Fitzgerald, K. 2018. "Mind-Reading Motivation: Individual Differences in Desire to Perspective-Take Influence Narrative Processing." *Scientific Study of Literature*, 8: 211–38.

Carroll, N. 2011. "On Some Affective Relations between Audiences and the Characters in Popular Fictions." In A. Coplan and P. Goldie (eds), *Empathy: Philosophical and Psychological Perspectives*. Oxford: Oxford University Press, 162–84.

Castiglioni, B. 2020. "Menelaus in the *Iliad* and the *Odyssey*: The Anti-Hero of πένθος." *Commentaria classica: Studi di filologia greca e latina*, 7: 219–32.

Cave, T. 2016. *Thinking with Literature: Towards a Cognitive Criticism*. Oxford: Oxford University Press.

Chamberlin, J. 2015. "Know Thyself: The Linguistics of Place." *Poets and Writers*, 43.5: 35–9.

Chen, M., Bell, R. A., and Taylor, L. D. 2016. "Narrator Point of View and Persuasion in Health Narratives: The Role of Protagonist-Reader Similarity, Identification, and Self-Referencing." *Journal of Health Communication*, 21: 908–18.

Chen, M., Bell, R. A., and Taylor, L. D. 2017. "Persuasive Effects of Point of View, Protagonist Competence, and Similarity in a Health Narrative about Type 2 Diabetes." *Journal of Health Communication*, 22: 707–12.

Chen, M., McGlone, M. S., and Bell, R. A. 2015. "Persuasive Effects of Linguistic Agency Assignments and Point of View in Narrative Health Messages about Colon Cancer." *Journal of Health Communication*, 20: 977–88.

Cho, H, Shen, L., and Wilson, K. 2014. "Perceived Realism: Dimensions and Roles in Narrative Persuasion." *Communication Research*, 41: 828–51.

Christensen, J. 2020. *The Many-Minded Man: The Odyssey, Psychology, and the Therapy of Epic*. Ithaca, NY: Cornell University Press.

Cingano, E. 2015. "Epigonoi." In M. Fantuzzi and C. Tsagalis (eds), *The Greek Epic Cycle and Its Ancient Reception: A Companion*. Cambridge: Cambridge University Press, 244–60.

Clarke, M. J. 1999. *Flesh and Spirit in the Songs of Homer: A Study of Words and Myths*. Oxford: Oxford University Press.

Clavel-Vazquez, A. 2018. "Sugar and Spice, and Everything Nice: What Rough Heroines Tell Us about Imaginative Resistance." *Journal of Aesthetics and Art Criticism*, 76: 201–12.

Clay, J. S. 2006. *The Politics of Olympus: Form and Meaning in the Major Homeric Hymns*. 2nd edn. London: Bristol Classical Press. First published by Princeton University Press, 1989.

Clay, J. S. 2011. *Homer's Trojan Theater: Space, Vision, and Memory in the Iliad*. Cambridge: Cambridge University Press.

Clercx, S. G. 2018. "Silent Witnesses: Cases of Audience Immersion in Sarpedon's and Patroclus' Death Scenes of *Iliad* 16." *Eisodos—Zeitschrift für Literatur und Theorie*, 2018.2: 41–55.

Cohen, J. 2001. "Defining Identification: A Theoretical Look at the Identification of Audiences with Media Characters." *Mass Communication and Society*, 4: 245–64.

Cohen, J. 2006. "Audience Identification with Media Characters." In J. Bryant and P. Vorderer (eds), *Psychology of Entertainment*. Mahwah, NJ: Lawrence Erlbaum Associates, 183–97.

Cohen, J. 2014. "Mediated Relationships and Social Life: Current Research on Fandom, Parasocial Relationships, and Identification." In M. B. Oliver and A. A. Raney (eds), *Media and Social Life*. New York: Routledge, 142–56.

Cohen, J. and Hershman-Shitrit, M. 2017. "Mediated Relationships with TV Characters: The Effect of Perceived and Actual Similarity in Personality Traits." *Scientific Study of Literature*, 7: 109–28.

Cohen, J., Oliver, M. B., and Bilandzic, H. 2019. "The Differential Effects of Direct Address on Parasocial Experience and Identification: Empirical Evidence for Conceptual Difference." *Communication Research Reports*, 36: 78–83.

Cohen, J. and Ribak, R. 2003. "Sex Differences in Pleasure from Television Texts: The Case of *Ally McBeal*." *Women's Studies in Communication*, 26: 118–34.

Cohen, J. and Tal-Or, N. 2017. "Antecedents of Identification: Character, Text, and Audiences." In F. Hakemulder et al. (eds), *Narrative Absorption*. Amsterdam: John Benjamins Publishing, 133–53.

Cohen, J., Tal-Or, N., and Mazor-Tregerman, M. 2015. "The Tempering Effect of Transportation: Exploring the Effects of Transportation and Identification during Exposure to Controversial Two-Sided Narratives." *Journal of Communication*, 65: 237–58.

Cohen, J., Weimann-Saks, D., and Mazor-Tregerman, M. 2018. "Does Character Similarity Increase Identification and Persuasion?" *Media Psychology*, 21: 506–28.

Collard, C. and Cropp, M. 2008. *Euripides. Fragments: Aegeus—Meleager*. Cambridge, MA: Harvard University Press.

Consoli, G. 2018. "Preliminary Steps towards a Cognitive Theory of Fiction and Its Effects." *Journal of Cultural Cognitive Science*, 2: 85–100.

Cook, E. 2003. "Agamemnon's Test of the Army in *Iliad* Book 2 and the Function of Homeric *Akhos*." *American Journal of Philology*, 124: 165–98.

Cook, E. 2004. "Near Eastern Sources for the Palace of Alkinoos." *American Journal of Archaeology*, 108: 43–77.

Cook, E. 2009. "On the 'Importance' of *Iliad* Book 8." *Classical Philology*, 104: 133–61.

Cook, E. 2018. "Homeric Time Travel." *Literary Imagination*, 20: 113–25.

Coray, M., Krieter-Spiro, M., and Visser, E. 2017. *Homers Ilias: Gesamtkommentar*. Band XIII: *Vierter Gesang (Δ). Faszikel 2: Kommentar*. Berlin: Walter de Gruyter.

Cornell, T. J. 2002. "On War and Games in the Ancient World." In R. K. Barney, S. G. Martyn, and K. B. Warmsley (eds), *The Globel Nexus Engaged: Past, Present, Future Interdisciplinary Olympic Studies*. London, Ont.: International Centre for Olympic Studies, University of Western Ontario, 29–40.

Crielaard, J. P. 2020. "Homeric Communities." In C. O. Pache (ed.), *The Cambridge Guide to Homer*. Cambridge: Cambridge University Press, 227–44.

Cruse, D. A. 2008. "Metaphor, Simile and Metonymy: Aspects of Conceptual Blending in Figurative Language." *Jornados de Lingüística*, X: 137–60.

Csapo, E. and Slater, W. J. 1995. *The Context of Athenian Drama*. Ann Arbor, MI: University of Michigan Press.

Cullhed, E. 2014. "Movement and Sound on the Shield of Achilles in Ancient Exegesis." *Greek, Roman, and Byzantine Studies*, 54: 192–219.

Currie, B. 2016. *Homer's Allusive Art*. Oxford: Oxford University Press.

Cuypers, M. 2002/2003. "Ptoliporthos Akhilleus: The Sack of Methymna in the *Lesbou Ktisis.*" *Hermathena*, 173/174: 117–35.
Dadlez, E. 2011. "Ideal Presence: How Kames Solved the Problem of Fiction and Emotion." *Journal of Scottish Philosophy*, 9: 115–33.
Dal Cin, S., Zanna, M. P., and Fong, G. T. 2004. "Narrative Persuasion and Overcoming Resistance." In E. S. Knowles and J. A. Linn (eds), *Resistance and Persuasion*. Mahwah, NJ: Lawrence Erlbaum Associates, 175–91.
Dancygier, B. and Sweetser, E. 2014. *Figurative Language*. Cambridge: Cambridge University Press.
Davidson, J. 2002. "Arrival at the Cave: The *Odyssey* and Greek Drama." *Wiener Studien*, 115: 45–57.
Davies, M. 2002. "The Folk-Tale Origins of the *Iliad* and *Odyssey.*" *Wiener Studien*, 115: 5–43.
Davis, K. C. 2007. *Postmodern Texts and Emotional Audiences*. West Lafayette, IN: Purdue University Press.
Davis, K. C. 2014. *Beyond the White Negro: Empathy and Anti-Racist Reading*. Urbana, IL: University of Illinois Press.
de Bakker, M., van der Berg, B., and Klooster, J. 2022. "Introduction: The Narratology of Emotions in Ancient Literature." In M. de Bakker, B. van der Berg, and J. Klooster (eds), *Emotions and Narrative in Ancient Literature and Beyond: Studies in Honour of Irene de Jong*. Leiden: Brill, 1–24.
de Graaf, A. and van Leeuwen, L. 2017. "The Role of Absorption Processes in Narrative Health Communication." In F. Hakemulder et al. (eds), *Narrative Absorption*. Amsterdam: John Benjamins Publishing, 271–92.
de Graaf, A. et al. 2012. "Identification as a Mechanism of Narrative Persuasion." *Communication Research*, 39: 802–23.
de Jong, I. J. F. 1994. "Between Word and Deed: Hidden Thoughts in the *Odyssey.*" In I. J. F. de Jong and J. P. Sullivan (eds), *Modern Critical Theory and Classical Literature*. Leiden: Brill, 27–50.
de Jong, I. J. F. 2001. *A Narratological Commentary on the Odyssey*. Cambridge: Cambridge University Press.
de Jong, I. J. F. 2004. *Narrators and Focalizers: The Presentation of the Story in the Iliad*. 2nd edn. London: Bristol Classical Press.
de Jong, I. J. F. 2005. "Convention versus Realism in the Homeric Epics." *Mnemosyne*, 58: 1–22.
de Jong, I. J. F. 2007. "Homer." In I. J. F. de Jong and R. Nünlist (eds), *Time in Ancient Greek Literature*. Leiden: Brill, 17–37.
de Jong, I. J. F. 2009. "Metalepsis in Ancient Greek Literature." In J. Grethlein and A. Rengakos (eds), *Narratology and Interpretation: The Content of Narrative Form in Ancient Literature*. Berlin: Walter de Gruyter, 87–116.
de Jong, I. J. F. 2012a. "Homer." In I. J. F. de Jong (ed.), *Space in Ancient Greek Literature*. Leiden: Brill, 21–38.
de Jong, I. J. F. 2012b. "The Homeric Hymns." In I. J. F. de Jong (ed.), *Space in Ancient Greek Literature*. Leiden: Brill, 39–53.
de Jong, I. J. F. 2012c. "Double Deixis in Homeric Speech: On the Interpretation of ὅδε and οὗτος." In M. Meier-Brügger (ed.), *Homer, gedeutet durch ein großes Lexikon*. Berlin: Walter de Gruyter, 63–83.
de Jong, I. J. F. 2012d. *Homer: Iliad, Book XXII*. Cambridge: Cambridge University Press.
de Jong, I. J. F. 2018a. "Homer." In K. De Temmerman and E. van Emde Boas (eds), *Characterization in Ancient Greek Literature*. Leiden: Brill, 27–45.

de Jong, I. J. F. 2018b. "The Birth of the Princes' Mirror in the Homeric Epics." In J. Klooster and B. van den Berg (eds), *Homer and the Good Ruler in Antiquity and Beyond*. Leiden: Brill, 20–37.

de Jong, I. J. F. and Nünlist, R. 2004. "From Bird's Eye View to Close-Up: The Standpoint of the Narrator in the Homeric Epics." In A. Bierl, A. Schmitt, and A. Willi (eds), *Antike Literatur in neuer Deutung: Festschrift für Joachim Latacz anlässlich seines 70. Geburtstages*. Munich: K. G. Saur, 63–83.

de Jonge, C. C. 2012. "Dionysius and Longinus on the Sublime: Rhetoric and Religious Language." *American Journal of Philology*, 133: 271–300.

de Jonge, C. C. 2020. "Ps.-Longinus on Ecstasy: Author, Audience, and Text." In J. Grethlein, L. Huitink, and A. Tagliabue (eds), *Experience, Narrative, and Criticism in Ancient Greece: Under the Spell of Stories*. Oxford: Oxford University Press, 148–71.

Delacruz, M. 2021. "Echoes of the Tragic in the Sacred Landscape of Ancient Salamis: A Geospatial Analysis of Hero Cult." *Journal of Greek Archaeology*, 6: 249–91.

de Lacy, P. H. and Einarson, B. 1959. *Plutarch Moralia: Volume II*. Cambridge, MA: Harvard University Press.

De Temmerman, K. 2014. *Crafting Characters: Heroes and Heroines in the Ancient Greek Novel*. Oxford: Oxford University Press.

De Temmerman, K. and Emde Boas, E. van. 2018. "Character and Characterization in Ancient Greek Literature: An Introduction." In K. De Temmerman and E. van Emde Boas (eds), *Characterization in Ancient Greek Literature*. Leiden: Brill, 1–23.

Dickson, K. 1995. *Nestor: Poetic Memory in Greek Epic*. New York: Garland Publishing.

Diels, H. and Kranz, W. 1972. *Die Fragmente der Vorsokratiker*, vol. 2. 6th edn. Berlin: Weidmann.

Diggle, J. 1984. *Euripidis fabulae*, vol. 1. Oxford: Clarendon Press.

Diggle, J. 1994. *Euripidis fabulae*, vol. 3. Oxford: Clarendon Press.

Dimock, W. C. 1997. "A Theory of Resonance." *PMLA*, 112: 1060–71.

Dindorf, G. 1855. *Scholia Graeca in Homeri Odysseam ex codicibus aucta et emendata*. 2 vols. Oxford: Clarendon Press.

Dixon, P. and Bortolussi, M. 2017. "Elaboration, Emotion, and Transportation: Implications for Conceptual Analysis and Textual Features." In F. Hakemulder et al. (eds), *Narrative Absorption*. Amsterdam: John Benjamins Publishing, 199–215.

Docherty, M. 2021. "Felskian Phenomenopolitics: Decolonial Reading through Postcritical Singularities." *Textual Practice*, 36: 953–71. DOI: 10.1080/0950236X.2021.1900358.

Doherty, L. E. 1995. *Siren Songs: Gender, Audiences, and Narrators in the Odyssey*. Ann Arbor, MI: University of Michigan Press.

Doicaru, M. M. 2016. *Gripped by Movies: From Story-World to Artifact Absorption*. Dissertation, University of Amsterdam.

Donadi, F., ed. 2016. *Gorgias Helenae Encomium*. Berlin: Walter de Gruyter.

Donlan, W. 1999. *The Aristocratic Ideal and Selected Papers*. Wauconda, IL: Bolchazy-Carducci Publishers.

Dougherty, C. 2001. *The Raft of Odysseus: The Ethnographic Imagination in Homer's Odyssey*. Oxford: Oxford University Press.

Douglass, E. 2018. *Interpreting New Testament Narratives: Recovering the Author's Voice*. Leiden: Brill.

Dräger, P. 2005. *Apollodor: Bibliotheke, Götter- und Heldensagen*. Düsseldorf: Artemis and Winkler.

Duckworth, G. E. 1933. *Foreshadowing and Suspense in the Epics of Homer, Apollonius, and Vergil*. Princeton: Princeton University Press.

Dué, C. 2019. *Achilles Unbound: Multiformity and Tradition in the Homeric Epics.* Washington, DC: Center for Hellenic Studies.

Dunkle, R. 1987. "Nestor, Odysseus, and the *Mētis–Biē* Antithesis: The Funeral Games, *Iliad* 23." *Classical World*, 81: 1–17.

Eder, J. 2006. "Ways of Being Close to Characters." *Film Studies*, 8: 68–80.

Eder, J., Hanich, J., and Stadler, J. 2019. "Media and Emotion: An Introduction." *NECSUS: European Journal of Media Studies*, 8: 91–104.

Eder, J., Jannidis, F. and Schneider, R. 2010. "Characters in Fictional Worlds: An Introduction." In J. Eder, F. Jannidis, and R. Schneider (eds), *Characters in Fictional Worlds: Understanding Imaginary Beings in Literature, Film, and Other Media*. Berlin: Walter de Gruyter, 3–64.

Eder, S. 2019. *Identifikationspotenziale in den Psalmen: Emotionen, Metaphern und Textdynamik in den Psalmen 30, 64, 90 und 147*. Gottingen: Vandenhoeck and Ruprecht.

Edmunds, L. 2016. *Stealing Helen: The Myth of the Abducted Wife in Comparative Perspective*. Princeton: Princeton University Press.

Edmunds, L. 2019. *Toward the Characterization of Helen in Homer: Appellatives, Periphrastic Denominations, and Noun-Epithet Formulas*. Berlin: Walter de Gruyter.

Edmunds, L. 2021. *Greek Myth*. Berlin: Walter de Gruyter.

Edmunds, S. T. 2012. "Picturing Homeric Weaving." In V. Bers, D. Elmer, and L. Muellner (eds), *Donum natalicum digitaliter confectum Gregorio Nagy septuagenario a discipulis collegis familiaribus oblatum*. Washington, DC: Center for Hellenic Studies. https://chs.harvard.edu/susan-t-edmunds-picturing-homeric-weaving.

Edwards, M. W. 1987. *Homer: Poet of the Iliad*. Baltimore, MD: Johns Hopkins University Press.

Edwards, M. W. 1991. *The Iliad: A Commentary*. Vol. 5: *Books 17–20*. Cambridge: Cambridge University Press.

Edwards, M. W. 2002. *Sound, Sense, and Rhythm: Listening to Greek and Latin Poetry*. Princeton: Princeton University Press.

Elmer, D. F. 2013. *The Poetics of Consent: Collective Decision Making and the Iliad*. Baltimore, MD: Johns Hopkins University Press.

Elmer, D. F. 2022. "Textual Jealousies in Chariton's *Callirhoe*." *Classical Antiquity*, 41: 180–220.

Elsner, J. 2006. "Reflections on the 'Greek Revolution' in Art: From Changes in Viewing to the Transformation of Subjectivity." In S. Goldhill and R. Osborne (eds), *Rethinking Revolutions through Ancient Greece*. Cambridge: Cambridge University Press, 68–95.

Erbse, H. 1969–88. *Scholia graeca in Homeri Iliadem (scholia vetera)*. 7 vols. Berlin: Walter de Gruyter.

Esrock, E. J. 2018. "Einfühlung as the Breath of Art: Six Modes of Embodiment." *Cognitive Processing*, 19: 187–99.

Esrock, E. J. 2019. "Body Forth in Narrative." In M. Grishakova and M. Poulaki (eds), *Narrative Complexity: Cognition, Embodiment, Evolution*. Lincoln, NE: University of Nebraska Press, 270–90.

Eyal, K. and Rubin, A. M. 2003. "Viewer Aggression and Homophily, Identification, and Parasocial Relationships with Television Characters." *Journal of Broadcasting and Electronic Media*, 47: 77–98.

Fanfani, G. 2017. "Weaving a Song: Convergences in Greek Poetic Imagery between Textile and Musical Terminology. An Overview on Archaic and Classical Literature." In S. Gaspa, C. Michel, and M.-L. Nosch (eds), *Textile Terminologies from the Orient to the Mediterranean and Europe, 1000 BC to 1000 AD*. Lincoln, NE: Zea Books, 421–36.

Farmer, M. C. 2021. "Once More a Weasel: Actors' Mistakes and Parody in Greek Drama." *Mnemosyne*, 75: 1–20.
Farner, G. 2014. *Literary Fiction: The Ways We Read Narrative Literature*. New York: Bloomsbury.
Farrell, J. 2004. "Roman Homer." In R. Fowler (ed.), *The Cambridge Companion to Homer*. Cambridge: Cambridge University Press, 254–71.
Fearn, D. 2020. "The Allure of Narrative in Greek Lyric Poetry." In J. Grethlein, L. Huitink, and A. Tagliabue (eds), *Experience, Narrative, and Criticism in Ancient Greece: Under the Spell of Stories*. Oxford: Oxford University Press, 37–58.
Feeney, D. C. 1991. *The Gods in Epic: Poets and Critics of the Classical Tradition*. Oxford: Clarendon Press.
Feldherr, A. 2010. *Playing Gods: Ovid's Metamorphoses and the Politics of Fiction*. Princeton: Princeton University Press.
Felski, R. 2008. *Uses of Literature*. Malden, MA: Blackwell Publishing.
Felski, R. 2015. *The Limits of Critique*. Chicago: University of Chicago Press.
Felski, R. 2020a. "Postcritical." In *Oxford Handbooks Online: Scholarly Research Reviews*. Oxford: Oxford University Press.
Felski, R. 2020b. *Hooked: Art and Attachment*. Chicago: University of Chicago Press.
Felson, N. 1994. *Regarding Penelope: From Character to Poetics*. Princeton: Princeton University Press.
Felson, N. 1999. "Vicarious Transport: Fictive Deixis in Pindar's *Pythian* Four." *Harvard Studies in Classical Philology*, 99: 1–31.
Fenik, B. 1968. *Typical Battle Scenes in the Iliad: Studies in the Narrative Technique of Homeric Battle Description*. Wiesbaden: Franz Steiner Verlag.
Fenik, B. 1986. *Homer and the Nibelungenlied: Comparative Studies in Epic Style*. Cambridge, MA: Harvard University Press.
Ferchaud, A. et al. 2020. "Reducing Mental Health Stigma Through Identification with Video Game Avatars with Mental Illness." *Frontiers in Psychology*, 11: Article 2240. DOI: 10.3389/fpsyg.2020.02240.
Fernandez-Quintanilla, C. 2020. "Textual and Reader Factors in Narrative Empathy: An Empirical Reader Response Study Using Focus Groups." *Language and Literature*, 29: 124–46.
Ferrari, G. R. F. 1999. "Aristotle's Literary Aesthetics." *Phronesis*, 44: 181–98.
Ferrari, G. R. F. 2019. "Aristotle on Musical Catharsis and the Pleasure of a Good Story." *Phronesis*, 64: 117–71.
Finglass, P. J. 2011. *Sophocles: Ajax*. Cambridge: Cambridge University Press.
Finkelberg, M. 1998. *The Birth of Literary Fiction in Ancient Greece*. Oxford: Oxford University Press.
Finkelberg, M. 2006. "Aristotle and Episodic Tragedy." *Greece and Rome*, 53: 60–72.
Finkelberg, M. 2022. "The Joys and Sorrows of the Argument: Emotions and Emotional Involvement in Plato's Narratives of Philosophical Reasoning." In M. de Bakker, B. van der Berg, and J. Klooster (eds), *Emotions and Narrative in Ancient Literature and Beyond: Studies in Honour of Irene de Jong*. Leiden: Brill, 428–41.
Fitzgerald, K. and Green, M. C. 2017. "Narrative Persuasion: Effects of Transporting Stories on Attitudes, Beliefs, and Behaviors." In F. Hakemulder et al. (eds), *Narrative Absorption*. Amsterdam: John Benjamins Publishing, 49–67.
Flesch, W. 2015. "Reading and Bargaining." In L. Zunshine (ed.), *The Oxford Handbook of Cognitive Literary Studies*. Oxford: Oxford University Press, 369–89.

Fletcher, A. and Monterosso, J. 2016. "The Science of Free-Indirect Discourse: An Alternative Cognitive Effect." *Narrative*, 24: 82–103.
Fludernik, M. 2011. "The Category of 'Person' in Fiction: *You* and *We* Narrative-Multiplicity and Indeterminacy of Reference." In G. Olson (ed), *Current Trends in Narratology*. Berlin: Walter de Gruyter, 101–41.
Fludernik, M. 2015. "Plotting Experience: A Comment on Jonas Grethlein's 'Heliodorus against Palmer, Zunshine and Co.'" *Style*, 45: 288–92.
Foley, H. P., ed. 1999. *The Homeric Hymn to Demeter: Translation, Commentary, and Interpretative Essays*. Princeton: Princeton University Press. 3rd printing with bibliographical addendum.
Foley, J. M. 1991. *Immanent Art: From Structure to Meaning in Traditional Oral Epic*. Bloomington, IN: Indiana University Press.
Forbes, R. J. 1964. *Studies in Ancient Technology*, vol. 4. 2nd edn. Leiden: Brill.
Ford, A. 1992. *Homer: The Poetry of the Past*. Ithaca, NY: Cornell University Press.
Forte, A. S. W. 2018. "The Cognitive Linguistics of Homeric Surprise." In P. Meineck, W. M. Short, and J. Devereaux (eds), *The Routledge Handbook of Classics and Cognitive Theory*. London: Routledge, 39–58.
Forte, A. S. W. 2019. "The Disappearing Turn of *Iliad* 23.373." *Classical Philology*, 114: 120–5.
Forte, A. [S. W.] 2020. "Reach and Reunion in the *Odyssey*: An Enactive Narratology." *Helios*, 47: 1–38.
Foster, H. W. 2004. "The Role of Music." In J. M. Foley, *The Wedding of Mustajbey's Son Bećirbey as Performed by Halil Bajgorić*. Helsinki: Suomalainen Tiedeakatemia, 223–60.
Frade, S. 2022. "Retelling the War of Troy: Tragedy, Emotions, and Catharsis." In M. de Bakker, B. van der Berg, and J. Klooster (eds), *Emotions and Narrative in Ancient Literature and Beyond: Studies in Honour of Irene de Jong*. Leiden: Brill, 324–36.
Frame, D. 2009. *Hippota Nestor*. Washington, DC: Center for Hellenic Studies.
Franklin, J. C. 2011. "Music." In M. Finkelberg (ed.), *The Homer Encyclopedia*. Chichester, West Sussex: Wiley-Blackwell. Electronic.
Friedrich, P. 2001. "Lyric Epiphany." *Language in Society*, 30: 217–47.
Friedrich, R. 2019. *Postoral Homer: Orality and Literacy in the Homeric Epic*. Stuttgart: Franz Steiner Verlag.
Friedrich, W.-H. 2003. *Wounding and Death in the Iliad: Homeric Techniques of Description*. Trans. G. Wright and P. Jones. London: Duckworth.
Friend, S. 2020. "Fiction and Emotion: The Puzzle of Divergent Norms." *British Journal of Aesthetics*, 60: 403–18.
Frijda, N. H. and Scherer, K. R. 2009. "Affect (Psychological Perspectives)." In D. Sander and K. R. Scherer (eds), *The Oxford Companion to Emotion and the Affective Sciences*. Oxford: Oxford University Press, 10.
Frisone, F. 2011. "Construction of Consensus: Norms and Change in Greek Funerary Rituals." In A. Chaniotis (ed.), *Ritual Dynamics in the Ancient Mediterranean: Agency, Emotion, Gender, Representation*. Stuttgart: Franz Steiner Verlag, 179–201.
Frost, R. 2002. "Perfect Day—A Day of Prowess." In N. Dawidoff (ed.), *Baseball: A Literary Anthology*. New York: Library of America, 260–3.
Frow, J. 2014. *Character and Person*. Oxford: Oxford University Press.
Frow, J. 2018. "Character." In M. Garrett (ed.), *The Cambridge Companion to Narrative Theory*. Cambridge: Cambridge University Press, 105–19.
Fuxjäger, A. 2002. *Deadline/Time Lock/Ticking Clock und Last Minute Rescue: Zur Dramaturgie von Fristen und Zeitdruck im populären Film*. Dissertation, Universität Wien.

Gabriel, S. and Young, A. F. 2011. "Becoming a Vampire without Being Bitten: The Narrative Collective-Assimilation Hypothesis." *Psychological Science*, 22: 990–4.

Gagarin, M. 1983. "Antilochus' Strategy: The Chariot Race in Iliad 23." *Classical Philology*, 78: 35–9.

Gallagher, C. 2006. "The Rise of Fictionality." In F. Moretti (ed.), *The Novel*. Vol. 1: *History, Geography, and Culture*. Princeton: Princeton University Press, 336–63.

Gallese, V. and Wojciehowski, H. 2011. "How Stories Make Us Feel: Toward an Embodied Narratology." *California Italian Studies* 2.1: https://escholarship.org/uc/item/3jg726c2.

Gangloff, A. 2018. "Rhapsodes and Rhapsodic Contests in the Imperial Period." In J. L. Ready and C. C. Tsagalis (eds), *Homer in Performance: Rhapsodes, Narrators, and Characters*. Austin, TX: University of Texas Press, 130–50.

Gantz, T. 1996. *Early Greek Myth*. 2 vols. Baltimore, MD: Johns Hopkins University Press. Paperback.

Garcia, L. F., Jr. 2013. *Homeric Durability: Telling Time in the Iliad*. Washington, DC: Center for Hellenic Studies.

Garcia, L. F., Jr. 2018. "Hektor, the Marginal Hero: Performance Theory and the Homeric Monologue." In J. L. Ready and C. C. Tsagalis (eds), *Homer in Performance: Rhapsodes, Narrators, and Characters*. Austin, TX: University of Texas Press, 299–319.

Gaut, B. 1999. "Identification and Emotion in Narrative Film." In C. Plantinga and G. M. Smith (eds), *Passionate Views: Film, Cognition, and Emotion*. Baltimore, MD: Johns Hopkins University Press, 200–16.

Gazis, G. A. 2018. *Homer and the Poetics of Hades*. Oxford: Oxford University Press.

Genette, G. 1980. *Narrative Discourse: An Essay in Method*. Trans. J. E. Lewin. Ithaca, NY: Cornell University Press.

Gerrig, R. [J.] 1993. *Experiencing Narrative Worlds: On the Psychological Activities of Reading*. New Haven: Yale University Press.

Gerrig, R. J. and Allbritton, D. W. 1990. "The Construction of Literary Character: A View from Cognitive Psychology." *Style*, 24: 380–91.

Gerrig, R. J. and Bezdek, M. A. 2013. "The Role of Participation in Aesthetic Illusion." In W. Wolf, W. Bernhart, and A. Mahler (eds), *Immersion and Distance: Aesthetic Illusion in Literature and Other Media*. Amsterdam: Rodopi, 89–111.

Gervais, K. 2013. "Viewing Violence in Statius' *Thebaid* and the Films of Quentin Tarantino." In H. Lovatt and C. Vout (eds), *Epic Visions: Visuality in Greek and Latin Epic and Its Reception*. Cambridge: Cambridge University Press, 139–67.

Gervais, K. 2017. *Statius, Thebaid 2: Edited with an Introduction, Translation, and Commentary*. Oxford: Oxford University Press.

Gill, C. 1984. "The *Ēthos/Pathos* Distinction in Rhetorical and Literary Criticism." *Classical Quarterly*, 34: 149–66.

Gill, C. 1990. "The Character-Personality Distinction." In C. Pelling (ed.), *Characterization and Individuality in Greek Literature*. Oxford: Clarendon Press, 1–31.

Gill, C. 2002. *Personality in Greek Epic, Tragedy, and Philosophy: The Self in Dialogue*. Oxford: Oxford University Press. Paperback. First published in 1996.

Giordano, M. 2022. "From Oral Theory to Neuroscience: A Dialogue on Communication." In A. Ercolani and L. Lulli (eds), *Rethinking Orality I: Codification, Transcodification and Transmission of "Cultural Messages."* Berlin: Walter de Gruyter, 167–97.

Giuliani, L. 2013. *Image and Myth: A History of Pictorial Narration in Greece*. Trans. J. O'Donnell. Chicago: University of Chicago Press.

Gleason, M. 2020. "Aretaeus and the Ekphrasis of Agony." *Classical Antiquity*, 39: 153–87.

Glenn, J. 1971. "The Polyphemus Folktale and Homer's *Kyklôpeia.*" *Transactions and Proceedings of the American Philological Association*, 102: 133–81.
Goffin, K. and Friend, S. 2022. "Learning Implicit Biases from Fiction." *Journal of Aesthetics and Art Criticism*, 80: 129–39.
González, J. M. 2013. *The Epic Rhapsode and His Craft: Homeric Performance in a Diachronic Perspective.* Washington, DC: Center for Hellenic Studies.
Gorman, D. 2010. "Character and Characterization." In D. Herman, B. McHale, and J. Phelan (eds), *Teaching Narrative Theory.* New York: Modern Language Association of America, 165–77.
Grau, C. 2010. "*American History X*, Cinematic Manipulation, and Moral Conversion." *Midwest Studies in Philosophy*, 34: 52–76.
Gray, J. 2005. "Antifandom and the Moral Text: *Television Without Pity* and Textual Dislike." *American Behavioral Scientist*, 48: 840–58.
Graziosi, B. 2013. "The Poet in the *Iliad.*" In A. Marmodoro and J. Hill (eds), *The Author's Voice in Classical and Late Antiquity.* Oxford: Oxford University Press, 9–38.
Graziosi, B. and Haubold, J. 2003. "Homeric Masculinity: *HNOPEH* and *AΓHNOPIH.*" *Journal of Hellenic Studies*, 123: 60–76.
Graziosi, B. and Haubold, J. 2010. *Homer Iliad: Book VI.* Cambridge: Cambridge University Press.
Green, M. C. 2004. "Transportation into Narrative Worlds: The Role of Prior Knowledge and Perceived Realism." *Discourse Processes*, 38: 247–66.
Green, M. C. and Brock, T. C. 2000. "The Role of Transportation in the Persuasiveness of Public Narratives." *Journal of Personality and Social Psychology*, 79: 701–21.
Green, M. C. and Brock, T. C. 2002. "In the Mind's Eye: Transportation-Imagery Model of Narrative Persuasion." In M. C. Green, J. J. Strange, and T. C. Brock (eds), *Narrative Impact: Social and Cognitive Functions.* Mahwah, NJ: Lawrence Erlbaum Associates, 315–41.
Greene, E. 1996. *Storytelling: Art and Technique.* 3rd edn. New Providence, NJ: R. R. Bowker.
Gregory, J. 2018. *Cheiron's Way: Youthful Education in Homer and Tragedy.* Oxford: Oxford University Press.
Grethlein, J. 2006. *Das Geschichtsbild der Ilias: Eine Untersuchung aus phänomenologischer und narratologischer Perspektive.* Göttingen: Vandenhoeck and Ruprecht.
Grethlein, J. 2007a. "Epic Narrative and Ritual: The Case of the Funeral Games in *Iliad* 23." In A. Bierl, R. Lämmle, and K. Wesselman (eds), *Literatur und Religion 1: Wege zu einer mythisch-rituellen Poetik bei den Griechen.* Berlin: Walter de Gruyter, 151–77.
Grethlein, J. 2007b. "The Poetics of the Bath in the *Iliad.*" *Harvard Studies in Classical Philology*, 103: 25–49.
Grethlein, J. 2013. *Experience and Teleology in Ancient Historiography: "Futures Past" from Herodotus to Augustine.* Cambridge: Cambridge University Press.
Grethlein, J. 2015. "Is Narrative 'The Description of Fictional Mental Functioning'? Heliodorus against Palmer, Zunshine, and Co." *Style*, 49: 257–84.
Grethlein, J. 2017a. *Aesthetic Experiences and Classical Antiquity: The Significance of Form in Narratives and Pictures.* Cambridge: Cambridge University Press.
Grethlein, J. 2017b. *Die Odyssee: Homer und die Kunst des Erzählens.* Munich: C. H. Beck.
Grethlein, J. 2018. "Homeric Motivation and Modern Narratology: The Case of Penelope." *Cambridge Classical Journal*, 64: 70–90.
Grethlein, J. 2020. "Odysseus and His Bed: From Significant Object to Thing Theory in Homer." *Classical Quarterly*, 69: 467–82.

Grethlein, J. 2021a. *The Ancient Aesthetics of Deception: The Ethics of Enchantment from Gorgias to Heliodorus*. Cambridge: Cambridge University Press.
Grethlein, J. 2021b. "Author and Characters: Ancient, Narratological, and Cognitive Views on a Tricky Relationship." *Classical Philology*, 116: 208–30.
Grethlein, J. and Huitink, L. 2017. "Homer's Vividness: An Enactive Approach." *Journal of Hellenic Studies*, 137: 67–91.
Grethlein, J., Huitink, L., and Tagliabue, A. 2020. "Introduction: Narrative and Aesthetic Experience in Ancient Greece." In J. Grethlein, L. Huitink, and A. Tagliabue (eds), *Experience, Narrative, and Criticism in Ancient Greece*. Oxford: Oxford University Press, 1–12.
Griesinger, R. 1907. *Die ästhetischen Anschauungen der alten Homererklärer dargestellt nach den Homerscholien*. Tübingen: H. Laupp, Jr.
Griffin, J. 1977. "The Epic Cycle and the Uniqueness of Homer." *Journal of Hellenic Studies*, 97: 39–53.
Griffin, J. 1980. *Homer on Life and Death*. Oxford: Clarendon Press.
Griffin, J. 1998. "The Social Function of Attic Tragedy." *Classical Quarterly*, 48: 39–61.
Griffin, J. 1999. "Sophocles and the Democratic City." In J. Griffin (ed.), *Sophocles Revisited: Essays Presented to Sir Hugh Lloyd-Jones*. Oxford: Oxford University Press, 73–94.
Griffith, M. 1999a. *Sophocles: Antigone*. Cambridge: Cambridge University Press.
Griffith, M. 1999b. "The King and Eye: The Rule of the Father in Greek Tragedy." *Proceedings of the Cambridge Philological Society*, 44: 20–84.
Griffith, M. 2010. "Psychoanalysing *Antigone*." In S. E. Wilmer and A. Žukauskaitė (eds), *Interrogating Antigone in Postmodern Philosophy and Criticism*. Oxford: Oxford University Press, 110–34.
Griffith, M. 2015. *Greek Satyr Play: Five Studies*. Berkeley, CA: California Classical Studies.
Gumbrecht, H. U. 2004. *Production of Presence: What Meaning Cannot Convey*. Stanford, CA: Stanford University Press.
Gurd, S. 2016. *Dissonance: Auditory Aesthetics in Ancient Greece*. New York: Fordham University Press.
Hainsworth, J. B. 1990. "Books V–VIII." In A. Heubeck, S. West, and J. B. Hainsworth, *A Commentary on Homer's Odyssey*. Vol. 1: *Introduction and Books I–VIII*. Oxford: Clarendon Press, 249–385. Paperback.
Hainsworth, [J.] B. 1993. *The Iliad: A Commentary*. Vol. 3: *Books 9–12*. Cambridge: Cambridge University Press.
Hakemulder, F. 2013. "Travel Experiences: A Typology of Transportation and Other Absorption States in Relation to Types of Aesthetic Responses." In M. Baisch, A. Degen, and J. Lüdtke (eds), *Wie gebannt: Ästhetische Verfahren der affektiven Bindung von Aufmerksamkeit*. Freiburg: Rombach Verlag, 163–82.
Hakemulder, F. and van Peer, W. 2016. "Empirical Stylistics." In V. Sotirova (ed.), *The Bloomsbury Companion to Stylistics*. London: Bloomsbury, 189–207.
Haller, B. S. 2007. *Landscape Description in Homer's Odyssey*. Dissertation, University of Pittsburgh.
Halleran, M. 2004. "The *Heracles*: An Interpretation." In S. Esposito (ed.), *Euripides: Four Plays. Medea, Hippolytus, Heracles, Bacchae*. Newburyport, MA: Focus Publishing.
Halliwell, S. 1986. *Aristotle's Poetics*. Chapel Hill: University of North Carolina Press.
Halliwell, S. 1995. "Aristotle: Poetics." In S. Halliwell et al. (eds and trans.), *Aristotle, Longinus, Demetrius: Poetics, Longinus: On the Sublime, Demetrius: On Style*. Cambridge, MA: Cambridge University Press, 1–141.
Halliwell, S. 2002. *The Aesthetics of Mimesis: Ancient Texts and Modern Problems*. Princeton: Princeton University Press.

Halliwell, S. 2005. "Learning from Suffering: Ancient Responses to Tragedy." In J. Gregory (ed.), *A Companion to Greek Tragedy*. Malden, MA: Blackwell Publishing, 394–412.

Halliwell, S. 2011. *Between Ecstasy and Truth: Interpretations of Greek Poetics from Homer to Longinus*. Oxford: Oxford University Press.

Halliwell, S. 2017. "The Poetics of Emotional Expression: Some Problems of Ancient Theory." In D. Cairns and D. Nelis (eds), *Emotions in the Classical World: Methods, Approaches, and Directions*. Stuttgart: Franz Steiner Verlag, 105–23.

Halliwell, S. 2021. *Sul Sublime*. Trans. L. Lulli. Milan: Fondazione Lorenzo Valla.

Halpern, F. 2013. *Sentimental Readers: The Rise, Fall, and Revival of a Disparaged Rhetoric*. Iowa City, IA: University of Iowa Press.

Hame, K. J. 2008. "Female Control of Funeral Rites in Greek Tragedy: Klytaimestra, Medea, and Antigone." *Classical Philology*, 103: 1–15.

Harold, J. 2000. "Empathy with Fictions." *British Journal of Aesthetics*, 40: 340–55.

Harris, J. P. 2018. "Flies, Wasps, and Gadflies: The Role of Insect Similes in Homer, Aristophanes, and Plato." *Mouseion: Journal of the Classical Association of Canada*, 15: 475–500.

Hastall, M. R. 2013. "Spannung." In W. Schweiger and A. Fahr (eds), *Handbuch Medienwirkungsforschung*. Wiesbaden: VS Verlag, 262–78.

Haubold, J. 2014. "Beyond Auerbach: Homeric Narrative and the *Epic of Gilgamesh*." In D. Cairns and R. Scodel (eds), *Defining Greek Narrative*. Edinburgh: Edinburgh University Press.

Hawhee, D. 2005. *Bodily Arts: Rhetoric and Athletics in Ancient Greece*. Austin, TX: University of Texas Press.

Heath, M. 1987. *The Poetics of Greek Tragedy*. London: Duckworth.

Heath, M. 2006. "The 'Social Function' of Tragedy: Clarifications and Questions." In D. Cairns and V. Liapis (eds), *Dionysalexandros: Essays on Aeschylus and His Fellow Tragedians in Honour of Alexander F. Garvie*. Swansea: The Classical Press of Wales, 253–81.

Heiden, B. 1998. "The Simile of the Fugitive Homicide, *Iliad* 24.480–84: Analogy, Foiling, and Allusion." *American Journal of Philology*, 119: 1–10.

Heidenreich, S. M and Roth, J. P. 2020. "The Neurophysiology of Panic on the Ancient Battlefield." In L. B. Brice (ed.), *New Approaches to Greek and Roman Warfare*. Hoboken, NJ: Wiley-Blackwell, 127–38.

Herington, C. J. 1972. *The Older Scholia on the Prometheus Bound*. Leiden: Brill.

Herrero de Jáuregui, M. 2011. "Priam's Catabasis: Traces of the Epic Journey to Hades in *Iliad* 24." *Transactions of the American Philological Association*, 141: 37–68.

Hesk, J. 2013. "Seeing in the Dark: *Kleos*, Tragedy and Perception in *Iliad* 10." In H. Lovatt and C. Vout (eds), *Epic Visions: Visuality in Greek and Latin Epic and Its Reception*. Cambridge: Cambridge University Press, 32–59.

Hinckley, L. V. 1986. "Patroclus' Funeral Games and Homer's Character Portrayal." *Classical Journal*, 81: 209–21.

Hitch, S. 2018. "Tastes of Greek Poetry: From Homer to Aristophanes." In K. C. Rudolph (ed.), *Taste and the Ancient Senses*. New York: Routledge, 22–44.

Hoeckner, B. et al. 2011. "Film Music Influences How Viewers Relate to Movie Characters." *Psychology of Aesthetics, Creativity, and the Arts*, 5: 146–53.

Hoeken, H. and Fikkers, K. M. 2014. "Issue-Relevant Thinking and Identification as Mechanisms of Narrative Persuasion." *Poetics*, 44: 84–99.

Hoeken, H., Kolthoff, M., and Sanders, J. 2016. "Story Perspective and Character Similarity as Drivers of Identification and Narrative Persuasion." *Human Communication Research*, 42: 292–311.

Hoeken, H. and Sinkeldam, J. 2014. "The Role of Identification and Perception of Just Outcome in Evoking Emotions in Narrative Persuasion." *Journal of Communication*, 64: 935–55.
Hogan, P. C. 2003. *The Mind and Its Stories: Narrative Universals and Human Emotion.* Cambridge: Cambridge University Press.
Hogan, P. C. 2011. *Affective Narratology: The Emotional Structure of Stories.* Lincoln, NE: University of Nebraska Press.
Hogan, P. C. 2018. *Literature and Emotion.* London: Routledge.
Holladay, H. W. and Click, M. A. 2019. "Hating Skyler White: Gender and Anti-Fandom in AMC's *Breaking Bad.*" In M. A. Click (ed.), *Anti-Fandom: Dislike and Hate in the Digital Age.* New York: New York University Press, 147–65.
Holmes, B. 2015. "Situating Scamander: 'Natureculture' in the *Iliad.*" *Ramus*, 44: 29–51.
Hölscher, U. 1988. *Die Odyssee: Epos zwischen Märchen und Roman.* Munich: C. H. Beck.
Hoorn, J. F. and Konijn, E. A. 2003. "Perceiving and Experiencing Fictional Characters: An Integrative Account." *Japanese Psychological Research*, 45: 250–68.
Horrell, M. A. 2017. *Epic Hyperbole in Homer.* Dissertation, University of Iowa.
Huitink, L. 2019. "*Enargeia*, Enactivism and the Ancient Readerly Imagination." In M. Anderson, D. Cairns, and M. Sprevak (eds), *Distributed Cognition in Classical Antiquity.* Edinburgh: Edinburgh University Press, 169–89.
Huitink, L. 2020. "*Enargeia* and Bodily *Mimesis.*" In J. Grethlein, L. Huitink, and A. Tagliabue (eds), *Experience, Narrative, and Criticism in Ancient Greece: Under the Spell of Stories.* Oxford: Oxford University Press, 188–209.
Hunter, R. 2018. *The Measure of Homer: The Ancient Reception of the Iliad and the Odyssey.* Cambridge: Cambridge University Press.
Hunter, R. and Russell, D. 2011. *Plutarch: How to Study Poetry.* Cambridge: Cambridge University Press.
Hutchinson, G. O. 2017. "Repetition, Range, and Attention: The *Iliad.*" In C. Tsagalis and A. Markantonatos (eds), *The Winnowing Oar—New Perspectives in Homeric Studies.* Berlin: Walter de Gruyter, 145–70.
Hutchinson, G. O. 2020. *Motion in Classical Literature: Homer, Parmenides, Sophocles, Ovid, Seneca, Tacitus, Art.* Oxford: Oxford University Press.
Hutton, J. 1982. *Aristotle's Poetics.* New York: W. W. Norton.
Igartua, J.-J. 2010. "Identification with Characters and Narrative Persuasion through Fictional Feature Films." *Communications*, 35: 347–73.
Igartua, J.-J. and Barrios, I. 2012. "Changing Real-World Beliefs with Controversial Movies: Processes and Mechanisms of Narrative Persuasion." *Journal of Communication*, 62: 514–31.
Igartua, J.-J. and Fiuza, D. 2018. "Persuading with Narratives against Gender Violence: Effect of Similarity with the Protagonist on Identification and Risk-Perception." *Palabra Clave*, 21: 499–523.
Ingalls, J. 1947. "Structural Unity of the *Iliad.*" *Classical Journal*, 42: 399–406.
Innes, D. C. 1995. "Demetrius: On Style." In S. Halliwell et al. (eds and trans), *Aristotle, Longinus, Demetrius: Poetics, Longinus: On the Sublime, Demetrius: On Style.* Cambridge, MA: Cambridge University Press, 307–521.
Ione, A. 2016. *Art and the Brain: Plasticity, Embodiment, and the Unclosed Circle.* Leiden: Brill.
Jackson, B. 2004. *Get Your Ass in the Water and Swim Like Me: African American Narrative Poetry from Oral Tradition.* 2nd edn. New York: Routledge. First published by Harvard University Press, 1974.

Jacobs, A. M. and Lüdtke, J. 2017. "Immersion into Narrative and Poetic Worlds: A Neurocognitive Poetics Perspective." In F. Hakemulder et al. (eds), *Narrative Absorption*. Amsterdam: John Benjamins Publishing, 69–96.

Jane, E. A. 2019. "Hating 3.0: Should Anti-Fan Studies Be Renewed for Another Season?" In M. A. Click (ed.), *Anti-Fandom: Dislike and Hate in the Digital Age*. New York: New York University Press, 42–61.

Janko, R. 1992. *The Iliad: A Commentary*. Vol. 4: *Books 13–16*. Cambridge: Cambridge University Press.

Janko, R. 1998. "The Homeric Poems as Oral Dictated Texts." *Classical Quarterly*, 38: 1–13.

Janko, R. 2020a. *Philodemus: On Poems, Books Three and Four. With the Fragments of Aristotle On Poets*. Oxford: Oxford University Press. Corrected paperback version.

Janko, R. 2020b. *Philodemus: On Poems, Book 2. With the Fragments of Heracleodorus and Pausimachus*. Oxford: Oxford University Press.

Jauss, H. R. 1974. "Levels of Identification of Hero and Audience." *New Literary History*, 5: 283–317.

Jauss, H. R. 1982. *Aesthetic Experience and Literary Hermeneutics*. Trans. M. Shaw. Minneapolis, MN: University of Minnesota Press.

Jensen, M. S. 2011. *Writing Homer: A Study Based on Results from Modern Fieldwork*. Copenhagen: Royal Danish Academy of Sciences and Letters.

Johnson, B. K. and Rosenbaum, J. E. 2015. "Spoiler Alert: Consequences of Narrative Spoilers for Dimensions of Enjoyment, Appreciation, and Transportation." *Communication Research*, 42: 1068–88.

Johnston, S. I. 2018. *The Story of Myth*. Cambridge, MA: Harvard University Press.

Jollimore, T. and Barrios, S. 2004. "Beauty, Evil, and *The English Patient*." *Philosophy and Literature*, 28: 23–40.

Jose, P. E. and Brewer, W. F. 1984. "Development of Story Liking: Character Identification, Suspense, and Outcome Resolution." *Developmental Psychology*, 20: 911–24.

Jurriaans-Helle, G. 2022. "*Sunt lacrimae rerum*: Emotions at the Deaths of Troilus, Priam, and Astyanax in Athenian Black-Figure Vase-Painting." In M. de Bakker, B. van der Berg, and J. Klooster (eds), *Emotions and Narrative in Ancient Literature and Beyond: Studies in Honour of Irene de Jong*. Leiden: Brill, 230–54.

Karanika, A. 2014. *Voices at Work: Women, Performance, and Labor in Ancient Greece*. Baltimore, MD: Johns Hopkins University Press.

Kassel, R. 1976. *Aristotelis ars rhetorica*. Berlin: Walter de Gruyter.

Keaney, J. J. and Lamberton, R., eds. 1996. *[Plutarch]: Essay on the Life and Poetry of Homer*. Atlanta, GA: Scholars Press.

Keen, S. 2006. "A Theory of Narrative Empathy." *Narrative*, 14: 207–36.

Keen, S. 2007. *Empathy and the Novel*. Oxford: Oxford University Press.

Keen, S. 2014. "Novel Readers and the Empathetic Angel of Our Nature." In M. M. Hammond and S. J. Kim (eds), *Rethinking Empathy through Literature*. London: Routledge, 21–33.

Kelly, A. 2007. *A Referential Commentary and Lexicon to Homer, Iliad VIII*. Oxford: Oxford University Press.

Kelly, A. 2012. "The Mourning of Thetis: 'Allusion' and the Future in the *Iliad*." In F. Montanari, A. Rengakos, and C. Tsagalis (eds), *Homeric Contexts: Neoanalysis and the Interpretation of Oral Poetry*. Berlin: Walter de Gruyter, 221–65.

Kelly, A. 2017. "Achilles in Control? Managing Oneself and Others in the Funeral Games." In P. Bassino, L. Grace Canevaro, and B. Graziosi (eds), *Conflict and Consensus in Early Greek Hexameter Poetry*. Oxford: Oxford University Press, 87–108.

Kelly, A. 2018. "Homer's Rivals? Internal Narrators in the *Iliad*." In J. L. Ready and C. C. Tsagalis (eds), *Homer in Performance: Rhapsodes, Narrators, and Characters*. Austin, TX: University of Texas Press, 351–77.

Kharroub, T. and Weaver, A. J. 2019. "Selective Exposure and Perceived Identification with Characters in Transnational Arabic Television." *International Journal of Communication*, 13: 653–73.

Kim, L. 2014. "Archaizing and Classicism in the Literary Historical Thinking of Dionysius of Halicarnassus." In J. Ker and C. Pieper (eds), *Valuing the Past in the Greco-Roman World*. Leiden: Brill, 357–87.

Kim, L. 2020. "Homer in Antiquity." In C. O. Pache (ed.), *The Cambridge Guide to Homer*. Cambridge: Cambridge University Press, 417–34.

Kirk, G. S. 1985. *The Iliad: A Commentary*. Vol. 1: Books 1–4. Cambridge: Cambridge University Press.

Kirk, G. S. 1990. *The Iliad: A Commentary*. Vol. 2: Books 5–8. Cambridge: Cambridge University Press.

Kirstein, R. 2022. "Emotions and Politeness in Homer's *Odyssey*." In M. de Bakker, B. van der Berg, and J. Klooster (eds), *Emotions and Narrative in Ancient Literature and Beyond: Studies in Honour of Irene de Jong*. Leiden: Brill, 119–34.

Kjeldgaard-Christiansen, J. et al. 2021. "Do Dark Personalities Prefer Dark Characters? A Personality Psychological Approach to Positive Engagement with Fictional Villainy." *Poetics*, 85: 101511. Electronic.

Klimmt, C., Hefner, D., and Vorderer, P. 2009. "The Video Game Experience as 'True' Identification: A Theory of Enjoyable Alterations of Players' Self-Perception." *Communication Theory*, 19: 351–73.

Knights, L. C. 1933. *How Many Children Had Lady Macbeth? An Essay in the Theory and Practice of Shakespeare Criticism*. Cambridge: Gordon Fraser, The Minority Press.

Knox, M. P. 2021. *Victorian Women and Wayward Reading: Crises of Identification*. Cambridge: Cambridge University Press.

Köhnken, A. 2003. "Herakles und Orpheus als mythische Referenzfiguren (‚Identifikations-‛ bzw., Integrationsfigur‛) im hellenistischen Epos." In B. Aland, J. Hahn, and C. Ronning (eds), *Literarische Konstituierung von Identifikationsfiguren in der Antike*. Tübingen: Mohr Siebeck, 19–27.

Kokolakis, M. M. 1981. "Homeric Animism." *Museum Philologum Londiniense*, 4: 89–113.

Konrad, E.-M., Petraschka, T., and Werner, C. 2018. "The Paradox of Fiction—A Brief Introduction into Recent Developments, Open Questions, and Current Areas of Research, including a Comprehensive Bibliography from 1975 to 2018." *Journal of Literary Theory*, 12: 193–203.

Konstan, D. 1999. "The Tragic Emotions." *Comparative Drama*, 33: 1–21.

Konstan, D. 2006. *The Emotions of the Ancient Greeks: Studies in Aristotle and Classical Literature*. Toronto: University of Toronto Press.

Koopman, E. M. 2016. "Effects of 'Literariness' on Emotions and on Empathy and Reflection after Reading." *Psychology of Aesthetics, Creativity, and the Arts*, 10: 82–98.

Koopman, E. M. and Hakemulder, F. 2015. "Effects of Literature on Empathy and Self-Reflection: A Theoretical-Empirical Framework." *Journal of Literary Theory*, 9: 79–111.

Köppe, T. and Klauk, T. 2013. "Puzzles and Problems for the Theory of Focalization." In P. Hühn (ed.), *Living Handbook of Narratology*. Berlin: Walter de Gruyter. Electronic.

Kotovych, M. et al. 2011. "Textual Determinants of a Component of Literary Identification." *Scientific Study of Literature*, 1: 260–91.

Kozak, L. 2017. *Experiencing Hektor: Character in the Iliad*. London: Bloomsbury.

Kramer-Hajos, M. 2012. "The Land and the Heroes of Lokris in the *Iliad*." *Journal of Hellenic Studies*, 132: 87–105.

Krause, S. and Appel, M. 2020. "Stories and the Self: Assimilation, Contrast, and the Role of Being Transported into the Narrative World." *Journal of Media Psychology*, 32.2: 47–58.

Kretler, K. 2020. *One Man Show: Poetics and Presence in the Iliad and Odyssey*. Washington, DC: Center for Hellenic Studies.

Kühn, S. et al. 2019. "Does Playing Violent Video Games Cause Aggression? A Longitudinal Intervention Study." *Molecular Psychiatry*, 24: 1220–34.

Kuijpers, M. [M.] and Miall, D. 2011. "Bodily Involvement in Literary Reading: An Experimental Study of Readers' Bodily Experiences during Reading." In F. Hakemulder (ed.), *De stralende lezer: Wetenschappelijk onderzoek naar de invloed van het lezen*. Delft: Eburon, 160–74.

Kuijpers, M. M. et al. 2014. "Exploring Absorbing Reading Experiences: Developing and Validating a Self-Report Scale to Measure Story-World Absorption." *Scientific Study of Literature*, 4: 89–122.

Kuijpers, M. M. et al. 2017. "Towards a New Understanding of Absorbing Reading Experiences." In F. Hakemulder et al. (eds), *Narrative Absorption*. Amsterdam: John Benjamins Publishing, 29–47.

Kuiken, D. and Douglas, S. 2017. "Forms of Absorption That Facilitate the Aesthetic and Explanatory Effects of Literary Reading." In F. Hakemulder et al. (eds), *Narrative Absorption*. Amsterdam: John Benjamins Publishing, 217–49.

Kuiken, D., Miall, D. S., and Sikora, S. 2004. "Forms of Self-Implication in Literary Reading." *Poetics Today*, 25: 171–203.

Kukkonen, K. and Caracciolo, M. 2014. "Introduction: What Is the 'Second Generation'?" *Style*, 48: 261–74.

Kuzmičová, A. 2012. "Presence in the Reading of Literary Narrative: A Case for Motor Enactment." *Semiotica*, 189: 23–48.

Kuzmičová, A. 2013. "The Words and World of Literary Narrative: The Trade-Off between Verbal Presence and Direct Presence in the Activity of Reading." In L. Bernaerts et al. (eds), *Stories and Minds: Cognitive Approaches to Literary Narrative*. Lincoln, NE: University of Nebraska Press, 107–28.

Kuzmičová, A. and Bálint, K. 2019. "Personal Relevance in Story Reading: A Research Review." *Poetics Today*, 40: 429–51.

Kyle, D. G. 2015. *Sport and Spectacle in the Ancient World*. 2nd edn. Chichester: Wiley-Blackwell.

Lacey, J. 2002. "One for the Boys? *The Sopranos* and Its Male, British Audience." In D. Lavery (ed.), *This Thing of Ours: Investigating the Sopranos*. New York: Columbia University Press, 95–108.

Lada, I. 1993. "'Empathetic Understanding': Emotion and Cognition in Classical Dramatic Audience-Response." *Proceedings of the Cambridge Philological Society*, 39: 94–140.

Lamberton, R. 2012. *Proclus the Successor on Poetics and the Homeric Poems: Essays 5 and 6 of His Commentary On the Republic of Plato*. Atlanta, GA: Society of Biblical Literature.

Langella, E. 2018. "Il personaggio omerico di Epeo: Dall'etimologia del nome all'individuazione delle prerogative." In M. Tulli (ed.), *In dialogo con Omero*. Pisa: Fabrizio Serra Editore, 11–30.

Lateiner, D. 1995. *Sardonic Smile: Nonverbal Behavior in Homeric Epic*. Ann Arbor, MI: University of Michigan Press.

Lateiner, D. 2011. "Bathing." In M. Finkelberg (ed.), *The Homer Encyclopedia*. Chichester, West Sussex: Wiley-Blackwell. Electronic.

Lateiner, D. 2017. "The Emotion of Disgust, Provoked and Expressed in Earlier Greek Literature." In D. Cairns and D. Nelis (eds), *Emotions in the Classical World: Methods, Approaches, and Directions*. Stuttgart: Franz Steiner Verlag, 31–51.

Lateiner, D. and Spatharas, D. 2017. "Introduction: Ancient and Modern Modes of Understanding and Manipulating Disgust." In D. Lateiner and D. Spatharas (eds), *The Ancient Emotion of Disgust*. Oxford: Oxford University Press, 1–42.

Lather, A. 2020. "Epic Matter: Iliadic Dust, Sand, and the Limits of the Human." *Transactions of the American Philological Association*, 150: 263–86.

Lawrence, S. 2013. *Moral Awareness in Greek Tragedy*. Oxford: Oxford University Press.

Lesser, R. H. 2021. "Sappho's Mythic Models for Female Homoeroticism." *Arethusa*, 54: 121–61.

Lesser, R. H. 2022. *Desire in the Iliad: The Force That Moves the Epic and Its Audience*. Oxford: Oxford University Press.

LeVen, P. A. 2014. *The Many-Headed Muse: Tradition and Innovation in Late Classical Greek Lyric Poetry*. Cambridge: Cambridge University Press.

Levett, B. 2018. "Assessing the Character of Creon." In D. Stuttard (ed.), *Looking at Antigone*. London: Bloomsbury Academic, 37–46.

Liebert, R. S. 2010. "Fact and Fiction in Plato's *Ion*." *American Journal of Philology*, 131: 179–218.

Liebert, R. S. 2017. *Tragic Pleasure from Homer to Plato*. Cambridge: Cambridge University Press.

Liotsakis, V. 2021. "Introduction." In I. M. Konstantakos and V. Liotsakis (eds), *Suspense in Ancient Greek Literature*. Berlin: Walter de Gruyter, 1–28.

Lloyd, Matthew. 2020. "Weapons and Armor." In C. O. Pache (ed.), *The Cambridge Guide to Homer*. Cambridge: Cambridge University Press, 402–4.

Lloyd, Michael. 2018. "Sophocles." In K. De Temmerman and E. van Emde Boas (eds), *Characterization in Ancient Greek Literature*. Leiden: Brill, 337–54.

Lord, A. B. 2019. *The Singer of Tales*. 3rd edn. D. F. Elmer (ed.). Washington, DC: Center for Hellenic Studies.

Lovatt, H. 2013. *The Epic Gaze: Vision, Gender and Narrative in Ancient Epic*. Cambridge: Cambridge University Press.

Lucas, D. W. 1968. *Aristotle Poetics*. Oxford: Oxford University Press. Reprint 2002.

Lynch, D. S. 2015. *Loving Literature: A Cultural History*. Chicago: University of Chicago Press.

Lyne, R. O. A. M. 1989. *Words and the Poet: Characteristic Techniques of Style in Vergil's Aeneid*. Oxford: Clarendon Press.

Ma, Z. 2020. "Effects of Immersive Stories on Prosocial Attitudes and Willingness to Help: Testing Psychological Mechanisms." *Media Psychology*, 23: 865–90.

Mackey, M. 2019. "Visualization and the Vivid Reading Experience." *Jeunesse: Young People, Texts, Cultures*, 11: 38–58.

Mackie, C. J. 2013. "*Iliad* 24 and the Judgement of Paris." *Classical Quarterly*, 63: 1–16.

Mackie, H. 1997. "Song and Storytelling: An Odyssean Perspective." *Transactions of the American Philological Association*, 127: 77–95.

Macleod, C. W. 1982. *Homer Iliad: Book XXIV*. Cambridge: Cambridge University Press.

MacPhail, J. A., Jr. 2011. *Porphyry's Homeric Questions on the Iliad: Text, Translation, and Commentary*. Berlin: Walter de Gruyter.

Mahler, A. 2013. "Aesthetic Illusion in Theatre and Drama: An Attempt at Application." In W. Wolf, W. Bernhart, and A. Mahler (eds), *Immersion and Distance: Aesthetic Illusion in Literature and Other Media*. Amsterdam: Rodopi, 151–81.

Makris, S. and Cazzato, V. 2020. "Implicit Visual Sensitivity towards Slim versus Overweight Bodies Modulates Motor Resonance in the Primary Motor Cortex: A tDCS Study." *Cognitive, Affective, and Behavioral Neuroscience*, 21: 93–104.

Maloney, K. 2020. "All the News That's Fit to Push: The New York Times Company and Transmedia Daily News." *International Journal of Communication*, 14: 4683–702.

Manieri, A. 1998. *L'immagine poetica nella teoria degli antichi*. Pisa: Istituti editoriali e poligrafici internazionali.

Mar, R. A. 2018. "Evaluating Whether Stories Can Promote Social Cognition: Introducing the Social Processes and Content Entrained by Narrative (SPaCEN) Framework." *Discourse Processes*, 55: 454–79.

Mar, R. A. et al. 2011. "Emotion and Narrative Fiction: Interactive Influences before, during, and after Reading." *Cognition and Emotion*, 25: 818–33.

Marchant, E. C. 1910. *Xenophontis omnia opera*, vol. 4. Oxford: Clarendon Press. Reprint 1951.

Margolin, U. 2007. "Character." In D. Herman (ed.), *The Cambridge Companion to Narrative*. Cambridge: Cambridge University Press, 66–79.

Margolin, U. 2008. "Studying Literature and Being Empirical: A Multifaceted Comparison." In S. Zyngier et al. (eds), *Directions in Empirical Literary Studies: In Honor of Willie van Peer*. Amsterdam: John Benjamins Publishing Company.

Marini, N. 2007. *Demetrio: Lo stile*. Rome: Edizioni di storia e letteratura.

Marks, J. 2008. *Zeus in the Odyssey*. Washington, DC: Center for Hellenic Studies.

Marks, J. 2010. "Context as Hypertext: Divine Rescue Scenes in the *Iliad*." *Trends in Classics*, 2: 300–22.

Marshall, C. W. 2021. "The Melody of Homeric Performance." In J. J. Price and R. Zelnick-Abramovitz (eds), *Text and Intertext in Greek Epic and Drama: Essays in Honor of Margalit Finkelberg*. London: Routledge, 102–17.

Marshall, P. K. 2002. *Hygini fabulae*. 2nd edn. Munich: K. G. Saur.

Martin, R. P. 1989. *The Language of Heroes: Speech and Performance in the Iliad*. Ithaca, NY: Cornell University Press.

Martin, R. P. 1993. "Telemachus and the Last Hero Song." *Colby Quarterly*, 29: 222–40.

Martin, R. P. 2000. "Wrapping Homer Up: Cohesion, Discourse, and Deviation in the *Iliad*." In A. Sharrock and H. Morales (eds), *Intratextuality: Greek and Roman Textual Relations*. Oxford: Oxford University Press, 43–65.

Martin, R. P. 2016. "Poseidon in the *Odyssey*." In J. J. Clauss, M. Cuypers, and A. Kahane (eds), *The Gods of Greek Hexameter Poetry: From the Archaic Age to Late Antiquity and Beyond*. Stuttgart: Franz Steiner Verlag, 76–94.

Martínez, M.-Á. 2018. *Storyworld Possible Selves*. Berlin: Walter de Gruyter.

Mastronarde, D. J. 2010. *The Art of Euripides: Dramatic Technique and Social Context*. Cambridge: Cambridge University Press.

Mazzocco, P. J. et al. 2010. "This Story Is Not for Everyone: Transportability and Narrative Persuasion." *Social Psychological and Personality Science*, 1: 361–8.

McCarthy, K. 2019. *I, the Poet: First-Person Form in Horace, Catullus, and Propertius*. Ithaca, NY: Cornell University Press.

Meineck, P. 2018. *Theatrocracy: Greek Drama, Cognition, and the Imperative for Theatre*. London: Routledge.

Mellmann, K. 2010. "Objects of 'Empathy': Characters (and Other Such Things) as Psycho-Poetic Effects." In J. Eder, F. Jannidis, and R. Schneider (eds), *Characters in Fictional Worlds: Understanding Imaginary Beings in Literature, Film, and Other Media*. Berlin: Walter de Gruyter, 416–41.

Menninghaus, W. et al. 2017. "The Distance-Embracing Model of the Enjoyment of Negative Emotions in Art Reception." *Behavioral and Brain Sciences*, 40: E347. DOI: 10.1017/s0140525x17000309.

Miall, D. S. and Kuiken, D. 2002. "A Feeling for Fiction: Becoming What We Behold." *Poetics*, 30: 221–41.

Miltsios, N. 2021. "Suspense in Conspiracy Narratives: Polybius and Appian." In I. M. Konstantakos and V. Liotsakis (eds), *Suspense in Ancient Greek Literature*. Berlin: Walter de Gruyter, 285–302.

Minchin, E. 1991. "Speaker and Listener, Text and Context: Some Notes on the Encounter of Nestor and Patroklos in *Iliad* 11." *Classical World*, 84: 273–85.

Minchin, E. 1999. "Describing and Narrating in Homer's *Iliad*." In E. A. Mackay (ed.), *Signs of Orality: The Oral Tradition and Its Influence in the Greek and Roman World*. Leiden: Brill, 49–62.

Minchin, E. 2001. *Homer and the Resources of Memory: Some Applications of Cognitive Theory to the Iliad and the Odyssey*. Oxford: Oxford University Press.

Minchin, E. 2008a. "Spatial Memory and the Composition of the *Iliad*." In E. A. Mackay (ed.), *Orality, Literacy, Memory in the Ancient Greek and Roman World*. Leiden: Brill, 9–34.

Minchin, E. 2008b. "Communication without Words: Body Language, 'Pictureability', and Memorability in the *Iliad*." *Ordia prima*, 7: 17–38.

Minchin, E. 2018. "The Battleground of Troy in the Mind's Eye: Homer's Landscape of War." *Humanities Australia*, 9: 48–56.

Minchin, E. 2019a. "Odysseus, Emotional Intelligence, and the Plot of the *Odyssey*." *Mnemosyne*, 72: 351–68.

Minchin, E. 2019b. "The Cognition of Deception: Falsehoods in Homer's *Odyssey* and Their Audiences." In P. Meineck, W. M. Short, and J. Devereaux (eds), *The Routledge Handbook of Classics and Cognitive Theory*. London: Routledge, 109–21.

Minchin, E. 2021a. "Visualizing the Shield of Achilles: Approaching Its Landscapes via Cognitive Paths." *Classical Quarterly*, 70: 473–84.

Minchin, E. 2021b. "Reading Emotional Intelligence: Antilochus and Achilles in the *Iliad*." In J. J. Price and R. Zelnick-Abramovitz (eds), *Text and Intertext in Greek Epic and Drama: Essays in Honor of Margalit Finkelberg*. London: Routledge, 52–64.

Moi, T. 2019. "Rethinking Character." In A. Anderson, R. Felski, and T. Moi (eds), *Character: Three Inquiries in Literary Studies*. Chicago: University of Chicago Press, 27–75.

Moores, D. J. 2013. "The Eudaimonic Turn in Literary Studies." In J. O. Pawelski and D. J. Moores (eds), *The Eudaimonic Turn: Well-Being in Literary Studies*. Madison, NJ: Fairleigh Dickinson University Press, 26–54.

Morrison, J. V. 1992. *Homeric Misdirection: False Predictions in the Iliad*. Ann Arbor, MI: University of Michigan Press.

Most, G. 2003. "Anger and Pity in Homer's *Iliad*." In S. M. Braund and G. W. Most (eds), *Ancient Anger: Perspectives from Homer to Galen*. Cambridge: Cambridge University Press, 50–75.

Most, G. W. 2006. *Hesiod: Theogony, Works and Days, Testimonia*. Cambridge, MA: Cambridge University Press.

Most, G. W. 2007. *Hesiod: The Shield, Catalogue of Women, Other Fragments*. Cambridge, MA: Cambridge University Press.

Mouffe, C. 2013. *Agonistics: Thinking the World Politically*. London: Verso.

Mould, T. 2011. "A Backdoor into Performance." In R. Cashman, T. Mould, and P. Shukla (eds), *The Individual and Tradition: Folkloristic Perspectives*. Bloomington, IN: Indiana University Press, 127–43.

Mousley, A. 2011. "Introduction." In A. Mousley (ed.), *Towards a New Literary Humanism*. Basingstoke: Palgrave Macmillan, 1–19.

Mueller, Martin. 2009. *The Iliad*. 2nd edn. London: Bloomsbury. First published by G. Allen and Unwin, 1984.

Mueller, Melissa. 2016. *Objects as Actors: Props and the Poetics of Performance in Greek Tragedy*. Chicago: University of Chicago Press.

Muellner, L. 1996. *The Anger of Achilles: Mēnis in Greek Epic*. Ithaca, NY: Cornell University Press.

Muellner, L. 2012. "Grieving Achilles." In F. Montanari, A. Rengakos, and C. Tsagalis (eds), *Homeric Contexts: Neoanalysis and the Interpretation of Oral Poetry*. Berlin: Walter de Gruyter, 197–220.

Mulokozi, M. M. 2002. *The African Epic Controversy: Historical, Philosophical, and Aesthetic Perspectives on Epic Poetry and Performance*. Dar es Salaam: Mkuki Na Nyota Publishers.

Mumper, M. L. and Gerrig, R. J. 2017. "Leisure Reading and Social Cognition: A Meta-Analysis." *Psychology of Aesthetics, Creativity, and the Arts*, 11: 109–20.

Munteanu, D. L. 2009. "*Qualis tandem misericodia in rebus fictis?*: Aesthetic and Ordinary Emotion." *Helios*, 36: 117–47.

Munteanu, D. L. 2012. *Tragic Pathos: Pity and Fear in Greek Philosophy and Tragedy*. Cambridge: Cambridge University Press.

Munteanu, D. L. 2017. "Grief: The Power and Shortcomings of Greek Tragic Consolation." In D. Cairns and D. Nelis (eds), *Emotions in the Classical World: Methods, Approaches, and Directions*. Stuttgart: Franz Steiner Verlag, 79–103.

Murnaghan, S. 1999. "The Poetics of Loss in Greek Epic." In M. Beissinger, J. Tylus, and S. Wofford (eds), *Epic Traditions in the Contemporary World: The Poetics of Community*. Berkeley, CA: University of California Press, 203–20.

Murray, P. 1996. *Plato on Poetry: Ion; Republic 376e-398b9; Republic 595-608b10*. Cambridge: Cambridge University Press.

Myers, T. 2019. *Homer's Divine Audience: The Iliad's Reception on Mount Olympus*. Oxford: Oxford University Press.

Nabi, R. L. and Green, M. C. 2015. "The Role of a Narrative's Emotional Flow in Promoting Persuasive Outcomes." *Media Psychology*, 18: 137–62.

Nachstädt, W. 1935. *Plutarchi moralia*, vol. 2. Leipzig: Teubner.

Nagy, G. 1999. *The Best of the Achaeans: Concepts of the Hero in Ancient Greek Poetry*. Revised edn. Baltimore, MD: Johns Hopkins University Press.

Nagy, G. 2003. *Homeric Responses*. Austin, TX: University of Texas Press.

Nagy, G. 2009. *Homer the Classic*. Washington, DC: Center for Hellenic Studies.

Nagy, G. 2010. *Homer the Preclassic*. Berkeley, CA: University of California Press.

Neer, R. and Kurke, L. 2019. *Pindar, Song, and Space: Towards a Lyric Archaeology*. Baltimore, MD: Johns Hopkins University Press.

Newby, Z. 2009. "Absorption and Erudition in Philostratus' *Imagines*." In E. Bowie and J. Elsner (eds), *Philostratus*. Cambridge: Cambridge University Press, 322–42.

Nightingale, A. 2006. "Mimesis: Ancient Greek Literary Theory." In P. Waugh (ed.), *Literary Theory and Criticism: An Oxford Guide*. Oxford: Oxford University Press, 37–47.

Nilsson, N. C., Nordahl, R., and Serafin, S. 2016. "Immersion Revisited: A Review of Existing Definitions of Immersion and Their Relation to Different Theories of Presence." *Human Technology*, 12: 108–34.

Nimis, S. A. 1987. *Narrative Semiotics in the Epic Tradition: The Simile*. Bloomington, IN: Indiana University Press.

Nosch, M.-L. 2014. "Voicing the Loom: Women, Weaving, and Plotting." In D. Nikassis, J. Gulizio, and S. A. James (eds), *KE-RA-ME-JA: Studies Presented to Cynthia W. Shelmerdine*. Philadelphia: INSTAP Academic Press, 91–101.

Novokhatko, A. 2021. "ἵνα ὁ θεατὴς προσδοκῶν καθῆτο: What Did Ancient Critics Know of 'Suspense'." In I. M. Konstantakos and V. Liotsakis (eds), *Suspense in Ancient Greek Literature*. Berlin: Walter de Gruyter, 31–51.

Nünlist, R. 2002. "Some Clarifying Remarks on 'Focalization'." In F. Montanari (ed.), *Omero tremila anni dopo: Atti del congresso di Genova 6-8 Luglio 2000*. Rome: Edizioni di storia e letteratura, 445–53.

Nünlist, R. 2009. *The Ancient Critic at Work: Terms and Concepts of Literary Criticism in Greek Scholia*. Cambridge: Cambridge University Press.

Nussbaum, M. C. 1995. *Poetic Justice: The Literary Imagination and Public Life*. Boston: Beacon Press.

Oatley, K. 1994. "A Taxonomy of the Emotions of Literary Response and a Theory of Identification in Fictional Narrative." *Poetics*, 23: 53–74.

Oatley, K. 1999a. "Why Fiction May Be Twice as True as Fact: Fiction as Cognitive and Emotional Simulation." *Review of General Psychology*, 3: 101–17.

Oatley, K. 1999b. "Meetings of Minds: Dialogue, Sympathy, and Identification in Reading Fiction." *Poetics*, 26: 439–54.

Oatley, K. 2012. *The Passionate Muse: Exploring Emotion in Stories*. Oxford: Oxford University Press.

Oatley, K. 2016. "Fiction: Simulation of Social Worlds." *Trends in Cognitive Science*, 20: 618–28.

Oatley, K. and Djikic, M. 2018. "Psychology of Narrative Art." *Review of General Psychology*, 22: 161–8.

Oatley, K. and Gholamain, H. 1997. "Emotions and Identification: Connections between Readers and Fiction." In M. Hjort and S. Laver (eds), *Emotion and the Arts*. Oxford: Oxford University Press, 263–81.

O'Connell, P. A. 2017a. "*Enargeia*, Persuasion, and the Vividness Effect in Athenian Forensic Oratory." *Advances in the History of Rhetoric*, 20: 225–51.

O'Connell, P. A. 2017b. *The Rhetoric of Seeing in Attic Forensic Oratory*. Austin, TX: University of Texas Press.

O'Hara, J. J. 2007. *Inconsistency in Roman Epic: Studies in Catullus, Lucretius, Vergil, Ovid and Lucan*. Cambridge: Cambridge University Press.

Oliver, M. B. et al. 2017. "Absorption and Meaningfulness: Examining the Relationship between Eudaimonic Media Use and Engagement." In F. Hakemulder et al. (eds), *Narrative Absorption*. Amsterdam: John Benjamins Publishing Company, 253–69.

Oliver, M. B. et al. 2019. "A Penchant for the Immoral: Implications of Parasocial Interaction, Perceived Complicity, and Identification on Liking of Anti-Heroes." *Human Communication Research*, 45: 169–201.

Olsen, S. 2017. "Kinesthetic *Choreia*: Empathy, Memory, and Dance in Ancient Greece." *Classical Philology*, 112: 153–74.

Olsen, S. 2020. "Pindar, *Paean* 6: Genre as Embodied Cultural Knowledge." In M. Foster, L. Kurke, and N. Weiss (eds), *Genre in Archaic and Classical Greek Poetry*. Leiden: Brill, 325–46.

Olson, S. D. 2008. *Athenaeus, The Learned Banqueters: Books VI–VIII*. Cambridge, MA: Harvard University Press.

O'Maley, J. 2014. "Controlling the Web: Hypertextuality, the *Iliad*, and the Crimes of Previous Generations." In R. Scodel (ed.), *Between Orality and Literacy: Communication and Adaptation in Antiquity*. Leiden: Brill, 6–28.

O'Maley, J. 2018. "Diomedes as Audience and Speaker in the *Iliad*." In J. L. Ready and C. C. Tsagalis (eds), *Homer in Performance: Rhapsodes, Narrators, and Characters*. Austin, TX: University of Texas Press, 278-98.

Ooms, J., Hoeks, J., and Jansen, C. 2019. "Hey, That Could Be Me": The Role of Similarity in Narrative Persuasion." *PLoS ONE*, 14.4: e0215359. DOI: 10.1371/journal.pone.0215359.

Ooms, S. and de Jonge, C. C. 2013. "The Semantics of ΕΝΑΓΩΝΙΟΣ in Greek Literary Criticism." *Classical Philology*, 108: 95-110.

Ortony, A., Clore, G., and Collins, A. 1988. *The Cognitive Structure of Emotions*. Cambridge: Cambridge University Press.

Otis, L. 2015. "The Value of Qualitative Research for Cognitive Literary Studies." In L. Zunshine (ed.), *The Oxford Handbook of Cognitive Literary Studies*. Oxford: Oxford University Press, 505-24.

Otto, N. 2009. *Enargeia: Untersuchung zur Charakteristik alexandrinischer Dichtung*. Stuttgart: Franz Steiner Verlag.

Owen, B. and Riggs, M. 2012. "Transportation, Need for Cognition, and Affective Disposition as Factors in Enjoyment of Film Narratives." *Scientific Study of Literature*, 2: 128-49.

Packard, D. W. 1974. "Sound-Patterns in Homer." *Transactions of the American Philological Association*, 104: 239-60.

Pagani, L. 2018. "Interpretazioni di Omero in chiave tragica negli scolii all'*Iliade*." In F. C. Bizzarro (ed.), *ΛΕΞΙΚΟΝ ΓΡΑΜΜΑΤΙΚΗΣ: Studi di lessicografia e grammatica greca*. Naples: Satura Editrice. 67-95.

Page, D. L. 1962. *Poetae melici graecae*. Oxford: Oxford University Press.

Palmer, A. 2011. "1945-: Ontologies of Consciousness." In D. Herman (ed.), *The Emergence of Mind: Representations of Consciousness in Narrative Discourse in English*. Lincoln, NE: University of Nebraska Press, 273-97.

Pantelia, M. 1993. "Spinning and Weaving: Ideas of Domestic Order in Homer." *Transactions of the American Philological Association*, 114: 493-501.

Patzer, H. 1996. *Die Formgesetze des homerischen Epos*. Stuttgart: Franz Steiner Verlag.

Payne, M. 2007. *Theocritus and the Invention of Fiction*. Cambridge: Cambridge University Press.

Pelliccia, H. 2021. "Seeing the Unseen in the *Iliad*." In J. J. Price and R. Zelnick-Abramovitz (eds), *Text and Intertext in Greek Epic and Drama: Essays in Honor of Margalit Finkelberg*. London: Routledge, 78-100.

Peradotto, J. 1990. *Man in the Middle Voice: Name and Narration in the Odyssey*. Princeton: Princeton University Press.

Peradotto, J. 2002. "Prophecy and Persons: Reading Character in the *Odyssey*." *Arethusa*, 35: 3-15.

Peretti, D. 2017. *Superman in Myth and Folklore*. Jackson, MI: University of Mississippi Press.

Perkell, C. 2008. "Reading the Laments of *Iliad* 24." In A. Suter (ed.), *Lament: Studies in the Ancient Mediterranean and Beyond*. Oxford: Oxford University Press, 93-117.

Petraschka, T. 2021. "How Empathy with Fictional Characters Differs from Empathy with Real Persons." *Journal of Aesthetics and Art Criticism*, 79: 227-32.

Petridou, G. 2015. *Divine Epiphany in Greek Literature and Culture*. Oxford: Oxford University Press.

Phillips, W. 2019. "Like Gnats to a Forklift Foot: TLC's *Here Comes Honey Boo Boo* and the Conservative Undercurrent of Ambivalent Fan Laughter." In M. A. Click (ed.), *Anti-Fandom: Dislike and Hate in the Digital Age*. New York: New York University Press, 249-70.

Pickard-Cambridge, A. 1968. *The Dramatic Festivals of Athens.* 2nd edn. Rev. by J. Gould and D. M. Lewis. Oxford: Oxford University Press.

Pitts, A. 2019. "The *Iliad*, Force, and the Soundscapes of War." *Environment, Space, Place,* 11: 1–37.

Plantinga, C. 2009. *Moving Viewers: American Film and the Spectator's Experience.* Berkeley, CA: University of California Press.

Plantinga, C. 2010. "'I Followed the Rules, and They All Loved You More': Moral Judgment and Attitudes toward Fictional Characters in Film." *Midwest Studies in Philosophy,* 34: 34–51.

Plantinga, C. 2018. *Screen Stories: Emotions and the Ethics of Engagement.* Oxford: Oxford University Press.

Plantinga, C. 2019. "Brecht, Emotion, and the Reflective Spectator: The Case of *BlacKkKlansman*." *NECSUS: European Journal of Medea Studies,* 8: 151–69.

Plett, H. F. 2012. *Enargeia in Classical Antiquity and the Early Modern Age: The Aesthetics of Evidence.* Leiden: Brill.

Plotz, J. 2018. *Semi-Detached: The Aesthetics of Virtual Experience since Dickens.* Princeton: Princeton University Press.

Pontani, F. 2007a. *Scholia graeca in Odysseam: Scholia ad libros α–β.* Rome: Edizioni di storia e letteratura.

Pontani, F. 2007b. *Scholia graeca in Odysseam: Scholia ad libros γ–δ.* Rome: Edizioni di storia e letteratura.

Porter, A. 2011. "'Stricken to Silence': Authoritative Response, Homeric Irony,and the Peril of a Missed Language Cue." *Oral Tradition,* 26: 493–520.

Porter, A. 2019. *Agamemnon, the Pathetic Despot: Reading Characterization in Homer.* Washington, DC: Center for Hellenic Studies.

Porter, J. I. 2011. "Making and Unmaking: The Achaean Wall and the Limits of Fictionality in Homeric Criticism." *Transactions of the American Philological Association,* 141: 1–36.

Porter, J. I. 2015. "Homer and the Sublime." *Ramus,* 44: 184–99.

Porter, J. I. 2016. *The Sublime in Antiquity.* Cambridge: Cambridge University Press.

Power, M. O. 2006. *Transportation and Homeric Epic.* Dissertation, The Australian National University.

Power, T. 2010. *The Culture of Kitharôidia.* Washington, DC: Center for Hellenic Studies. Electronic.

Pratt, L. 2007. "The Parental Ethos of the *Iliad*." In A. Cohen and J. B. Rutter (eds), *Constructions of Childhood in Ancient Greece and Italy.* Princeton: The American School of Classical Studies, 25–40.

Prescott, A. T., Sargent, J. D., and Hull, J. G. 2018. "Metaanalysis of the Relationship between Violent Video Game Play and Physical Aggression over Time." *Proceedings of the Nartional Academy of Sciences of the United States of America,* 115: 9882–8.

Prier, R. A. 1989. *Thauma idesthai: The Phenomenology of Sight and Appearance in Archaic Greek.* Tallahassee: Florida State University Press.

Pucci, P. 2002. "Theology and Poetics in the *Iliad*." *Arethusa,* 35: 17–34.

Purves, A. [C.] 2006. "Falling into Time in Homer's *Iliad*." *Classical Antiquity,* 25: 179–209.

Purves, A. C. 2010. *Space and Time in Ancient Greek Narrative.* Cambridge: Cambridge University Press.

Purves, A. [C.] 2014. "Thick Description: From Auerbach to the Boar's Lair (*Od.* 19.388–475)." In M. Skempis and I. Ziogas (eds), *Geography, Topography, Landscape: Configurations of Space in Greek and Roman Epic.* Berlin: Walter de Gruyter, 37–61.

Purves, A. [C.] 2015. "Ajax and Other Objects: Homer's Vibrant Materialism." *Ramus,* 44: 75–94.

Purves, A. C. 2019. *Homer and the Poetics of Gesture.* Oxford: Oxford University Press.

Purves, A. [C.] 2020. "Rough Reading: Tangible Language in Dionysius' Criticism of Homer." In J. Grethlein, L. Huitink, and A. Tagliabue (eds), *Experience, Narrative, and Criticism in Ancient Greece.* Oxford: Oxford University Press, 172–87.

Rahmstorf, L. 2015. "An Introduction to the Investigation of Archaeological Textile Tools." In E. Andersson Strand and M.-L. Nosch (eds), *Tools, Textiles and Contexts: Investigating Textile Production in the Aegean and Eastern Mediterranean Bronze Age.* Oxford: Oxbow Books, 1–23.

Raney, A. A. and Janicke, S. H. 2013. "How We Enjoy and Why We Seek Out Morally Complex Characters in Media Entertainment." In R. Tamborini (ed.), *Media and the Moral Mind.* New York: Routledge, 152–69.

Rapp, C. 2015. "Tragic Emotions." In P. Destrée and P. Murray (eds), *A Companion to Ancient Aesthetics.* Malden, MA: Wiley-Blackwell, 438–54.

Rasmussen, S. J. 1992. "Speech by Allusion: Voice and Authority in Tuareg Verbal Art." *Journal of Folklore Research,* 29: 155–75.

Ready, J. L. 2004. "A Binding Song: The Similes of *Catullus* 61." *Classical Philology,* 99: 153–63.

Ready, J. L. 2007. "Toil and Trouble: The Acquisition of Spoils in the *Iliad.*" *Transactions of the American Philological Association,* 137: 3–43.

Ready, J. L. 2010. "Why Odysseus Strings His Bow." *Greek, Roman, and Byzantine Studies,* 50: 133–57.

Ready, J. L. 2011. *Character, Narrator, and Simile in the Iliad.* Cambridge: Cambridge University Press.

Ready, J. L. 2012. "Zeus, Ancient Near Eastern Notions of Divine Incomparability, and Similes in the Homeric Epics." *Classical Antiquity,* 31: 56–91.

Ready, J. L. 2017. "The Epiphany at *Iliad* 4.73–84." *Hermes,* 145: 25–40.

Ready, J. L. 2018. *The Homeric Simile in Comparative Perspectives: Oral Traditions from Saudi Arabia to Indonesia.* Oxford: Oxford University Press.

Ready, J. L. 2019a. *Orality, Textuality, and the Homeric Epics: An Interdisciplinary Study of Oral Texts, Dictated Texts, and Wild Texts.* Oxford: Oxford University Press.

Ready, J. L. 2019b. "Odysseus and the Suitors Relatives." *Yearbook of Ancient Greek Epic,* 3: 117–35.

Ready, J. L. 2020. "Minor Characters in Homer's *Iliad.*" *Classical Antiquity,* 39: 284–329.

Redfield, J. M. 1975. *Nature and Culture in the Iliad: The Tragedy of Hector.* Chicago: University of Chicago Press.

Reece, S. 2005. "Homer's *Iliad* and *Odyssey*: From Oral Performance to Written Text." In M. C. Amodio (ed.), *New Directions in Oral Theory.* Tempe, AZ: Arizona Center for Medieval and Renaissance Studies, 43–89.

Reichel, M. 1990. "Retardationstechniken in der Ilias." In W. Kullmann and M. Reichel (eds), *Der Übergang von der Mündlichkeit zur Literatur bei den Griechen.* Tübingen: Gunter Narr Verlag, 125–51.

Reichl, K. 2000a. "Silencing the Voice of the Singer: Problems and Strategies in the Editing of Turkic Oral Epics." In L. Honko (ed.), *Textualization of Oral Epics.* Berlin: Mouton de Gruyter, 103–27.

Reichl, K. 2000b. "The Performance of the Karakalpak *Zhyrau.*" In K. Reichl (ed.), *The Oral Epic: Performance and Music.* Berlin: Verlag für Wissenschaft und Bildung, 129–50.

Reichl, K. 2007. *Edige: A Karakalpak Oral Epic as Performed by Jumabay Bazarov.* Helsinki: Suomalainen Tiedeakatemia.

Reinecke, L. and Oliver, M. B. 2016. "Media Use and Well-Being: Status Quo and Open Questions." In L. Reinecke and M. B. Oliver (eds), *The Routledge Handbook of Media Use and Well-Being: International Perspectives on Theory and Research on Positive Media Effects*. New York: Routledge, 3–13.

Reinhard, C. D. 2016. "Making Sense of the American Superhero Film: Experiences of Entanglement and Detachment." In C. D. Reinhard and C. J. Olson (eds), *Making Sense of Cinema: Empirical Studies into Film Spectators and Spectatorship*. New York: Bloomsbury Academic, 211–34.

Reinhardt, K. 1961. *Die Ilias und ihr Dichter*. Göttingen: Vandenhoeck und Ruprecht.

Rengakos, A. 1999. "Spannungsstrategien in den homerischen Epos." In J. N. Kazazis and A. Rengakos (eds), *Euphrosyne: Studies in Ancient Epic and Its Legacy in Honor of Dimitris N. Maronitis*. Stuttgart: Franz Steiner Verlag, 308–38.

Reyes, G. M. 2002. "Sources of Persuasion in the *Iliad*." *Rhetorical Review*, 21: 22–39.

Reynolds, D. F. 1994/1995. "Musical Dimensions of an Arabic Oral Epic Tradition." *Asian Music*, 26: 53–94.

Reynolds, D. F. 1995. *Heroic Poets, Poetic Heroes: The Ethnography of Performance in an Arabic Oral Epic Tradition*. Ithaca, NY: Cornell University Press.

Richardson, N. J. 1980. "Literary Criticism in the Exegetical Scholia to the *Iliad*: A Sketch." *Classical Quarterly*, 30: 265–87.

Richardson, N. [J.] 1993. *The Iliad: A Commentary*. Vol 6: *Books 21–24*. Cambridge: Cambridge University Press.

Richardson, N. [J.] 2011. "The *Homeric Hymn to Demeter*: Some Central Questions Revisited." In A. Faulkner (ed.), *The Homeric Hymns: Interpretative Essays*. Oxford: Oxford University Press, 44–58.

Richardson, S. 1990. *The Homeric Narrator*. Nashville, TN: Vanderbilt University Press.

Rijksbaron, A. 2007. *Plato Ion or: On the Iliad*. Leiden: Brill.

Rinon, Y. 2007. "The Pivotal Scene: Narration, Colonial Focalization, and Transition in *Odyssey* 9." *American Journal of Philology*, 128: 301–34.

Roberts, S. D. 2018. "Expanding Our Present Knowledge of the Non-Fictional World: An Analysis of Transportation and Identification with Victims and Perpetrators." Masters Thesis, Cleveland State University.

Robinson, J. 2005. *Deeper than Reason: Emotion and Its Role in Literature, Music, and Art*. Oxford: Oxford University Press.

Robinson, J. 2014. "Aesthetic Disgust?" *Royal Institute of Philosophical Supplement*, 75: 51–84.

Roisman, H. 1988. "Nestor's Advice and Antilochus' Tactics." *Phoenix*, 42: 114–20.

Roller, D. W. and Roller, L. K. 1994. "Penelope's Thick Hand (*Odyssey* 21.6)." *Classical Journal*, 90: 9–19.

Ronning, C. 2003. "Soziale Identität—Identifikation—Identifikationsfigur: Versuch eine Synthese." In B. Aland, J. Hahn, and C. Ronning (eds), *Literarische Konstituierung von Identifikationsfiguren in der Antike*. Tübingen: Mohr Siebeck, 233–51.

Rood, T. 2022. "Emotions in Thucydides: Revisiting the Final Battle in Syracuse Harbour." In M. de Bakker, B. van der Berg, and J. Klooster (eds), *Emotions and Narrative in Ancient Literature and Beyond: Studies in Honour of Irene de Jong*. Leiden: Brill, 381–96.

Rose, P. W. 1997. "Ideology in the *Iliad*: Polis, Basileus, Theoi." *Arethusa*, 30: 151–99.

Rudd, N. 1989. *Horace: Epistles, Book II and Epistle to the Pisones ("Ars poetica")*. Cambridge: Cambridge University Press.

Russo, J. 2012. "Re-Thinking Homeric Psychology: Snell, Dodd and Their Critics." *Quaderni urbinati di cultura classica*, 101: 11–28.

Rutherford, R. B. 1982. "Tragic Form and Feeling in the *Iliad*." *Journal of Hellenic Studies*, 102: 145–60.

Rutherford, R. [B.] 2013. *Homer*. 2nd edn. Cambridge: Cambridge University Press.

Ryan, M.-L. 2001. *Narrative as Virtual Reality: Immersion and Interactivity in Literature and Electronic Media*. Baltimore, MD: Johns Hopkins University Press.

Ryan, M.-L. 2007. "Toward a Definition of Narrative." In D. Herman (ed.), *The Cambridge Companion to Narrative*. Cambridge: Cambridge University Press, 22–35.

Ryan, M.-L. 2013. "Impossible Worlds and Aesthetic Illusion." In W. Wolf, W. Bernhart, and A. Mahler (eds), *Immersion and Distance: Aesthetic Illusion in Literature and Other Media*. Amsterdam: Rodopi, 131–48.

Ryan, M.-L. 2015a. *Narrative as Virtual Reality 2: Revisiting Immersion and Interactivity in Literature and Electronic Media*. Baltimore, MD: Johns Hopkins University Press.

Ryan, M.-L. 2015b. "Response to Jonas Grethlein's Essay 'Is Narrative "the Description of Fictional Mental Functioning"? Heliodorus against Palmer, Zunshine, and Co.'" *Style*, 49: 293–8.

Ryan, M.-L. 2018. "Narrative Mapping as Cognitive Activity and as Active Participation in Storyworlds." *Frontiers of Narrative Studies*, 4: 232–47.

Ryan, M.-L. 2019. "From Possible Worlds to Storyworlds: On the Worldness of Narrative Representation." In A. Bell and M.-L. Ryan (eds), *Possible Worlds Theory and Contemporary Narratology*. Lincoln, NE: University of Nebraska Press, 62–87.

Ryan, M.-L., Foote, K, and Azaryahu, M. 2016. *Narrating Space/Spatializing Narrative: Where Narrative Theory and Geography Meet*. Columbus, OH: Ohio State University Press.

Sale, W. M. 1994. "The Government of Troy: Politics in the *Iliad*." *Greek, Roman, and Byzantine Studies*, 35: 5–102.

Sammons, B. 2009a. "Agamemnon and His Audiences." *Greek, Roman, and Byzantine Studies*, 49: 159–85.

Sammons, B. 2009b. "Brothers in the Night: Agamemnon and Menelaus in Book 10 of the *Iliad*." *Classical Bulletin*, 85.1: 27–47.

Sammons, B. 2010. *The Art and Rhetoric of the Homeric Catalogue*. Oxford: Oxford University Press.

Sammons, B. 2014. "A Tale of Tydeus: Exemplarity and Structure in Two Homeric Insets." *Trends in Classics*, 6: 297–318.

Sammons, B. 2017. *Device and Composition in the Greek Epic Cycle*. Oxford: Oxford University Press.

Sanders, E. 2014. *Envy and Jealousy in Classical Athens: A Socio-Psychological Approach*. Oxford: Oxford University Press.

Sanford, A. J. and Emmott, C. 2012. *Mind, Brain and Narrative*. Cambridge: Cambridge University Press.

Saunders, D. 2008. "Dead Warriors and Their Wounds in Black-Figure Vase Painting." In D. C. Kurtz, H.-C. Meyer, and E. Hatzivassiliou (eds), *Essays in Classical Archaeology for Eleni Hatzivassiliou 1977–2007*. Oxford: Archaeopress, 85–94.

Saunders, D. 2010. "Warriors' Injuries on Red-Figure Vases." *Mouseion: Journal of the Classical Association of Canada*, 10: 1–21.

Saunders, K. B. 2003. "Appendix." In W.-H. Friedrich, *Wounding and Death in the Iliad: Homeric Techniques of Description*. Trans. G. Wright and P. Jones. London: Duckworth.

Scanlon, T. F. 2018. "Class Tensions in the Games of Homer: Epeius, Euryalus, Odysseus and Iros." *Bulletin of the Institute of Classical Studies*, 61: 5–20.

Scarry, E. 1995. "On Vivacity: The Difference between Daydreaming and Imagining-Under-Authorial-Instruction." *Representations*, 52: 1–26.

Schein, S. 2013. *Sophocles: Philoctetes*. Cambridge: Cambridge University Press.

Scherer, K. R. and Ellsworth, P. C. 2009. "Appraisal Theories." In D. Sander and K. R. Scherer (eds), *The Oxford Companion to Emotion and the Affective Sciences*. Oxford: Oxford University Press, 45–9.

Scheub, H. 1977. "Body and Image in Oral Narrative Performance." *New Literary History*, 8: 345–67.

Scheub, H. 2002. *The Poem in the Story: Music, Poetry, and Narrative*. Madison, WI: University of Wisconsin Press.

Schironi, F. 2018. *The Best of the Grammarians: Aristarchus of Samothrace on the Iliad*. Ann Arbor, MI: University of Michigan Press.

Schmitz, T. [A.] 1994. "Ist die *Odyssee* 'Spannend'? Anmerkungen zur Erzähltechnik des homerischen Epos." *Philologus*, 138: 3–23.

Schmitz, T. A. 2019. "Epic Apostrophe from Homer to Nonnus." *Symbolae Osloenses*, 93: 37–57.

Schoenmakers, H. 1988. "To Be, Wanting to Be, and Forced to Be: Identification Processes in Theatrical Situations." In W. Sauter (ed.), *New Directions in Audience Research*. Utrecht: Instituut voor Theaterwetenschap, 138–63.

Scodel, R. 1999. *Credible Impossibilities: Conventions and Strategies of Verisimilitude in Homer and Greek Tragedy*. Stuttgart: Teubner.

Scodel, R. 2008. *Epic Facework: Self-Presentation and Social Interaction in Homer*. Swansea: The Classical Press of Wales.

Scodel, R. 2012. "ἦ and Theory of Mind in the *Iliad*." In M. Meier-Brügger (ed.), *Homer, gedeutet durch ein großes Lexikon*. Berlin: Walter de Gruyter, 319–34.

Scodel, R. 2014. "Narrative Focus and Elusive Thought in Homer." In D. Cairns and R. Scodel (eds), *Defining Greek Narrative*. Edinburgh: Edinburgh University Press, 55–74.

Scodel, R. 2015. "*Sunt lacrimae rerum*." *Classical Journal*, 111: 219–30.

Scodel, R. 2018. "Homeric Attribution of Outcomes and Divine Causation." *Syllecta Classica*, 29: 1–27.

Scodel, R. 2021. "Homeric Suspense." In I. M. Konstantakos and V. Liotsakis (eds), *Suspense in Ancient Greek Literature*. Berlin: Walter de Gruyter, 55–72.

Scott, M. 1979. "Pity and Pathos in Homer." *Acta classica*, 22: 1–14.

Scott, W. C. 1997. "The Etiquette of Games in *Iliad* 23." *Greek, Roman, and Byzantine Studies*, 38: 213–27.

Scully, S. 1990. *Homer and the Sacred City*. Ithaca, NY: Cornell University Press.

Sedgwick, E. K. 2003. *Touching Feeling: Affect, Pedagogy, Performativity*. Durham, NC: Duke University Press.

Segal, C. 1971. "Andromache's *Anagnorisis*: Formulaic Artistry in *Iliad* 22.437–76." *Harvard Studies in Classical Philology*, 75: 33–57.

Segal, C. 1994. *Singers, Heroes, and Gods in the Odyssey*. Ithaca, NY: Cornell University Press.

Seo, J. M. 2013. *Exemplary Traits: Reading Characterization in Roman Poetry*. Oxford: Oxford University Press.

Seppänen, S. et al. 2021. "The Paradox of Fiction Revisited—Improvised Fictional and Real-Life Social Rejections Evoke Associated and Relatively Similar Psychophysiological Responses." *Brain Sciences*, 11: 1463. DOI: 10.3390/brainsci11111463.

Sestir, M. and Green, M. C. 2010. "You Are Who You Watch: Identification and Transportation Effects on Temporary Self-Concept." *Social Influence*, 5: 272–88.
Seydou, C. 2000. "Word and Music: The Epic Genre of the *Fulɓe* of Massina (Mali)." In K. Reichl (ed.), *The Oral Epic: Performance and Music*. Berlin: Verlag für Wissenschaft und Bildung, 211–24.
Shackleton Bailey, D. R. 1991. *Q. Horati Flacci opera*. Stuttgart: Teubner.
Sheppard, A. 2014. *The Poetics of Phantasia: Imagination in Ancient Aesthetics*. London: Bloomsbury.
Silk, M. 2004. *Homer: The Iliad*. 2nd edn. Cambridge: Cambridge University Press.
Slater, M. D. and Cohen, J. 2016. "Identification, TEBOTS, and Vicarious Wisdom of Experience: Narrative and the Self." In L. Reinecke and M. B. Oliver (eds), *The Routledge Handbook of Media Use and Well-Being: International Perspectives on Theory and Research on Positive Media Effects*. New York: Routledge, 118–30.
Slater, M. D. et al. 2014. "Temporarily Expanding the Boundaries of the Self: Motivations for Entering the Story World and Implications for Narrative Effects." *Journal of Communication*, 64: 439–55.
Slatkin, L. M. 1991. *The Power of Thetis: Allusion and Interpretation in the Iliad*. Berkeley, CA: University of California Press.
Slatkin, L. M. 2007. "Notes on Tragic Visualizing in the *Iliad*." In C. Kraus et al. (eds), *Visualizing the Tragic: Drama, Myth, and Ritual in Greek Art and Literature*. Oxford: Oxford University Press, 19–34.
Slings, S. R. 2003. *Platonis rempublicam*. Oxford: Oxford University Press.
Smith, J. D. 1991. *The Epic of Pābūjī: A Study, Transcription and Translation*. Cambridge: Cambridge University Press.
Smith, M. 1995. *Engaging Characters: Fiction, Emotion, and the Cinema*. Oxford: Oxford University Press.
Smith, M. 1999. "Gangsters, Cannibals, Aesthetes, or Apparently Perverse Allegiances." In C. Plantinga and G. M. Smith (eds), *Passionate Views: Film, Cognition, and Emotion*. Baltimore, MD: Johns Hopkins University Press, 217–38.
Smith, M. 2017. *Film, Art and the Third Culture: A Naturalized Aesthetics of Film*. Oxford: Oxford University Press.
Sobak, R. 2013. "Dance, Deixis, and the Performance of Kyrenean Identity: A Thematic Commentary on Pindar's *Fifth Pythian*." *Harvard Studies in Classical Philology*, 107: 99–153.
Sorabji, R. 2006. *Self: Ancient and Modern Insights about Individuality, Life, and Death*. Chicago: University of Chicago Press.
Sorabji, R. 2008. "Graeco-Roman Varieties of Self." In P. Remes and J. Sihvola (eds), *Ancient Philosophy of the Self*. Dordrecht: Springer, 13–34.
Spantidaki, S. 2016. *Textile Production in Classical Athens*. Oxford: Oxbow Books.
Spatharas, D. 2019. *Emotions, Persuasion, and Public Discourse in Classical Athens*. Berlin: Walter de Gruyter.
Spatharas, D. 2021. "Projective Disgust and Its Uses in Ancient Greece." In A. Chaniotis (ed.), *Unveiling Emotions III: Arousal, Display, and Performance of Emotions in the Greek World*. Stuttgart: Franz Steiner Verlag, 33–73.
Spaulding, S. 2018. *How We Understand Others: Philosophy and Social Cognition*. Abingdon: Routledge.
Speer, N. K. et al. 2009. "Reading Stories Activates Neural Representations of Visual and Motor Experiences." *Psychological Science*, 20: 989–99.

Stallbaum, G. 1960. *Eustathii, archiepiscopi thessalonicensis, commentarii ad Homeri Odysseam*. Hildesheim: Georg Olms Verlagsbuchhandlung.
Stanford, W. B. 1967. *The Sound of Greek: Studies in the Greek Theory and Practice of Euphony*. Berkeley, CA: University of California Press.
Stanford, W. B. 1976. "Varieties of Sound-Effects in the Homeric Poems." *College Literature*, 3: 219–27.
Stanford, W. B. 1983. *Greek Tragedy and the Emotions: An Introductory Study*. London: Routledge and Kegan Paul.
Stanley, K. 1993. *The Shield of Homer*. Princeton: Princeton University Press.
Stelow, A. R. 2020. *Menelaus in the Archaic Period: Not Quite the Best of the Achaeans*. Oxford: Oxford University Press.
Stockwell, P. 2002. *Cognitive Poetics: An Introduction*. London: Routledge.
Stoevesandt, M. 2004. *Feinde–Gegner–Opfer: Zur Darstellung der Troianer in den Kampfszenen der Ilias*. Basel: Schwabe Verlag.
Stoevesandt, M. 2008. *Homers Ilias: Gesamtkommentar*. Band IV: *Sechster Gesang (Z)*. Faszikel 2: *Kommentar*. Berlin: Walter de Gruyter.
Sukalla, F. et al. 2016. "Embodiment of Narrative Engagement: Connecting Self-Reported Narrative Engagement to Psychophysiological Measures." *Journal of Media Psychology*, 28: 175–86.
Susemihl, F. 1967. *Aristotelis ethica Eudemia*. Amsterdam: Hakkert. First published by Teubner, 1884.
Tal-Or, N. and Cohen, J. 2010. "Understanding Audience Involvement: Conceptualizing and Manipulating Identification and Transportation." *Poetics*, 38: 402–18.
Tan, E. 1994. "Film-Induced Affect as Witness Emotion." *Poetics*, 23: 7–23.
Tan, E. 1996. *Emotion and the Structure of Narrative Film: Film as an Emotion Machine*. Trans. B. Fasting. Mahwah, NJ: Lawrence Erlbaum Associates.
Tan, E. et al. 2017. "Into Film: Does Absorption in a Movie's Story World Pose a Paradox?" In F. Hakemulder et al. (eds), *Narrative Absorption*. Amsterdam: John Benjamins Publishing Company, 97–118.
Taplin, O. 1992. *Homeric Soundings: The Shaping of the Iliad*. Oxford: Clarendon Press.
Tarán, L. and Gutas, D. 2012. *Aristotle Poetics: Editio Maior of the Greek Text with Historical Introductions and Philological Commentaries*. Leiden: Brill.
Teffeteller, A. 2003. "Homeric Excuses." *Classical Quarterly*, 53: 15–31.
Telò, M. 2020. "Iambic Horror: Shivers and Brokenness in Archilochus and Hipponax." In M. Foster, L. Kurke, and N. Weiss (eds), *Genre in Archaic and Classical Greek Poetry: Theories and Models*. Leiden: Brill, 271–97.
Thalmann, W. G. 1998. *The Swineherd and the Bow: Representations of Class in the Odyssey*. Ithaca, NY: Cornell University Press.
Thissen, B. A. K., Menninghaus, W., and Schlotz, W. 2018. "Measuring Optimal Reading Experiences: The Reading Flow Short Scale." *Frontiers in Psychology*, 9: Article 2542. https://link.gale.com/apps/doc/A565570853/AONE?u=umuser&sid=summon&xid=c215dc7e.
Thissen, B. A. K., Menninghaus, W., and Schlotz, W. 2020. "The Pleasures of Reading Fiction Explained by Flow, Presence, Identification, Suspense, and Cognitive Involvement." *Psychology of Aesthetics, Creativity, and the Arts*, 15: 710–24.
Thompson, J. M. et al. 2018. "Individual Differences in Transportation into Narrative Drama." *Review of General Psychology*, 22: 210–19.
Todd, A. R. et al. 2015. "Anxious and Egocentric: How Specific Emotions Influence Perspective Taking." *Journal of Experimental Psychology: General*, 144: 374–91.

Tsagalis, C. [C.] 2001. "Style and Construction, Sound and Rhythm: Thetis' Supplication to Zeus (*Iliad* 1.493–516)." *Arethusa*, 34: 1–29.

Tsagalis, C. [C.] 2004. *Epic Grief: Personal Laments in Homer's Iliad*. Berlin: Walter de Gruyter.

Tsagalis, C. [C.] 2010a. "Epic Space Revisited: Narrative and Intertext in the Episode between Diomedes and Glaucus (*Il.* 6.119–236)." In P. Mitsis and C. Tsagalis (eds), *Allusion, Authority, and Truth: Critical Perspectives on Greek Poetic and Rhetorical Praxis*. Berlin: Walter de Gruyter, 87–113.

Tsagalis, C. [C.] 2010b. "Dynamic Hypertext: Lists and Catalogues in the Homeric Epics." *Trends in Classics*, 2: 323–47.

Tsagalis, C. [C.] 2012. *From Listeners to Viewers: Space in the Iliad*. Washington, DC: Center for Hellenic Studies.

Tsagalis, C. [C.] 2017. "Sound-Play in the Hesiodic *Catalogue of Women*." In C. Tsagalis (ed.), *Poetry in Fragments: Studies on the Hesiodic Corpus and Its Afterlife*. Berlin: Walter de Gruyter, 191–215.

Tsagalis, C. C. 2018a. "Performance Contexts for Rhapsodic Recitals in the Archaic and Classical Periods." In J. L. Ready and C. C. Tsagalis (eds), *Homer in Performance: Rhapsodes, Narrators, and Characters*. Austin, TX: University of Texas Press, 29–75.

Tsagalis, C. C. 2018b. "Performance Contexts for Rhapsodic Recitals in the Hellenistic Period." In J. L. Ready and C. C. Tsagalis (eds), *Homer in Performance: Rhapsodes, Narrators, and Characters*. Austin, TX: University of Texas Press, 98–129.

Tsagalis, C. [C.] 2020. "The Homeric Question: A Historical Sketch." *Yearbook of Ancient Greek Epic*, 4: 122–62.

Tukachinsky, R., Walter, N., and Saucier, C. J. 2020. "Antecedents and Effects of Parasocial Relationships: A Meta-Analysis." *Journal of Communication*, 70: 868–94.

Turkeltaub, D. 2005. "The Syntax and Semantics of Homeric Glowing Eyes: *Iliad* 1.200." *American Journal of Philology*, 126: 157–86.

Turkeltaub, D. 2010. "Reading the Epic Past: The *Iliad* on Heroic Epic." In P. Mitsis and C. Tsagalis (eds), *Allusion, Authority, and Truth: Critical Perspectives on Greek Poetic and Rhetorical Praxis*. Berlin: Walter de Gruyter, 129–52.

Turner, R. and Felisberti, F. M. 2017. "Measuring Mindreading: A Review of Behavioral Approaches to Testing Cognitive and Affective Mental State Attribution in Neurologically Typical Adults." *Frontiers in Psychology*, 8: Article 47. DOI: 10.3389/fpsyg.2017.00047.

Tyrell, E. 2020. *Strategies of Persuasion in Herodotus' Histories and Genesis–Kings: Evoking Reality in Ancient Narratives of a Past*. Leiden: Brill.

Usher, S. 1974. *Dionysius of Halicarnassus: Critical Essays*, vol. 1. Cambridge, MA: Harvard University Press.

Usher, S. 1985. *Dionysius of Halicarnassus: Critical Essays*, vol. 2. Cambridge, MA: Harvard University Press.

Usher, S. 1990. *Isocrates: Panegyricus and To Nicocles*. Warminster: Aris and Phillips.

Vaage, M. B. 2016. *The Antihero in American Television*. New York: Routledge.

van der Plas, M. 2020. "Corpse Mutilation in the *Iliad*." *Classical Quarterly*, 70: 459–72.

van Gils, L. and Kroon, C. 2022. "Common Ground and the Presentation of Emotions: Fright and Horror in Livy's Historiography." In M. de Bakker, B. van der Berg, and J. Klooster (eds), *Emotions and Narrative in Ancient Literature and Beyond: Studies in Honour of Irene de Jong*. Leiden: Brill, 523–39.

van Krieken, K., Hoeken, H., and Sanders, J. 2017. "Evoking and Measuring Identification with Narrative Characters—A Linguistic Cues Framework." *Frontiers in Psychology*, 8: 1190. DOI: 10.3389/fpsyg.2017.01190.

Van Lissa, C. J. et al. 2016. "Difficult Empathy: The Effect of Narrative Perspective on Readers' Engagement with a First-Person Narrator." *Diegesis*, 5: 43–62.
van Thiel, H. 1991. *Homeri Odyssea*. Hildesheim: Georg Olms Verlag.
van Thiel, H. 2010. *Homeri Ilias*. 2nd edn. Hildesheim: Georg Olms Verlag.
van Thiel, H. 2014. *Scholia D in Iliadem. Proecdosis aucta et correctior 2014: Secundum codices manu scriptos*. Cologne: Universitäts- und Stadt Bibliothek.
van Vught, J. and Schott, G. 2017. "Identifying with In-Game Characters: Exploring Player Articulations of Identification and Presence." In F. Hakemulder et al. (eds), *Narrative Absorption*. Amsterdam: John Benjamins Publishing, 157–76.
van Wees, H. 1994. "The Homeric Way of War: The *Iliad* and the Hoplite Phalanx (II)." *Greece and Rome*, 41: 131–55.
van Wees, H. 2005. "Clothes, Class and Gender in Homer." In D. L. Cairns (ed.), *Body Language in the Greek and Roman Worlds*. Swansea: Classical Press of Wales, 1–36.
Vatri, A. 2020. "Asyndeton, Immersion, and *Hypokrisis* in Ancient Greek Rhetoric." In J. Grethlein, L. Huitink, and A. Tagliabue (eds), *Experience, Narrative, and Criticism in Ancient Greece: Under the Spell of Stories*. Oxford: Oxford University Press, 210–32.
Verheij, M. J. O. 2014. "Selves in Conflict: Gill vs. Sorabji on the Conception of Selfhood in Antiquity: A Reconciliatory Review." *Classical World*, 107: 169–97.
Vermeule, B. 2010. *Why Do We Care about Literary Characters?* Baltimore, MD: Johns Hopkins University Press.
Vermeule, E. 1979. *Aspects of Death in Early Greek Art and Poetry*. Berkeley, CA: University of California Press.
Vezzali, L. et al. 2015. "The Greatest Magic of Harry Potter: Reducing Prejudice." *Journal of Applied Social Psychology*, 45: 105–21.
Viggiano, G. F. and van Wees, H. 2013. "The Arms, Armor, and Iconography of Early Greek Hoplite Warfare." In D. Kagan and G. F. Viggiano (eds), *Men of Bronze: Hoplite Warfare in Ancient Greece*. Princeton: Princeton University Press, 57–73.
Vinogradov, V. S. 1984. "Napevy 'Manasa'." In A. S. Sadykov et al. (eds and trans.), *Manas: Kirgizskiy geroicheskiy èpos*, vol. 1. Moscow: Nauka: 492–509.
Visvardi, E. 2015. *Emotion in Action: Thucydides and the Tragic Chorus*. Leiden: Brill.
Wace, A. J. B. 1948. "Weaving or Embroidery?" *American Journal of Archaeology*, 52: 51–5.
Wakker, G. 2022. "Self-Description of Emotions in Ancient Greek Drama: A First Exploration." In M. de Bakker, B. van der Berg, and J. Klooster (eds), *Emotions and Narrative in Ancient Literature and Beyond: Studies in Honour of Irene de Jong*. Leiden: Brill, 307–23.
Walker, H. J. 2016. "Horse Riders and Chariot Drivers." In P. A. Johnston, A. Mastrocinque, and S. Papaioannou (eds), *Animals in Greek and Roman Religion and Myth: Proceedings of the Symposium Grumentinum Grumento Nova (Potenza) 5–7 June 2013*. Newcastle upon Tyne: Cambridge Scholars Publishing, 309–33.
Walsh, R. 2017. "Beyond Fictional Worlds: Narrative and Spatial Cognition." In P. K. Hansen et al. (eds), *Emerging Vectors of Narratology*. Berlin: Walter de Gruyter, 461–78.
Walsh, T. R. 2005. *Fighting Words and Feuding Words: Anger and the Homeric Poems*. Lanham, MD: Lexington Books.
Walton, K. L. 1990. *Mimesis as Make-Believe: On the Foundations of the Representational Arts*. Cambridge, MA: Harvard University Press.
Ward, D., Silverman, D., and Villalobos, M. 2017. "Introduction: The Varieties of Enactivism." *Topoi*, 36: 365–75.
Webb, R. 2009. *Ekphrasis, Imagination and Persuasion in Ancient Rhetorical Theory and Practice*. Farnham: Ashgate.

Webb, R. 2016. "Sight and Insight: Theorizing Vision, Emotion and Imagination in Ancient Rhetoric." In M. Squire (ed.), *Sight and the Ancient Senses*. London: Routledge, 205–19.

Webb, R. 2020. "As If You Were There: *Enargeia* and Spatiality in Lysias 1." In M. Edwards and D. Spatharas (eds), *Forensic Narratives in Athenian Courts*. London: Routledge, 157–69.

Węcowski, M. 2020. "Feasting and Drinking in Homer." In C. O. Pache (ed.), *The Cambridge Guide to Homer*. Cambridge: Cambridge University Press, 332–5.

Weiss, N. 2016. "The Choral Architecture of Pindar's Eighth Paean." *Transactions of the American Philological Association*, 146: 237–55.

Weiss, N. 2018a. *The Music of Tragedy: Performance and Imagination in Euripidean Theater*. Oakland, CA: University of California Press.

Weiss, N. 2018b. "Speaking Sights and Seen Sounds in Aeschylean Tragedy." In M. Telò and M. Mueller (eds), *The Materialities of Greek Tragedy: Objects and Affect in Aeschylus, Sophocles, and Euripides*. London: Bloomsbury Academic, 169–84.

Weiss, N. 2020. "Opening Spaces: Prologic Phenomenologies of Greek Tragedy and Comedy." *Classical Antiquity*, 39: 330–67.

Weiss, N. 2023. *Seeing Theater: The Phenomenology of Classical Greek Drama*. Oakland, CA: University of California Press.

West, M. L. 1972. *Iambi et elegi graeci: Ante Alexandrum cantati*, vol. 2. Oxford: Oxford University Press.

West, M. L. 1981. "The Singing of Homer and the Modes of Early Greek Music." *Journal of Hellenic Studies*, 101: 113–29.

West, M. L. 1990. *Aeschyli tragodiae cum incerti poetae Prometheo*. Stuttgart: Teubner.

West, M. L. 1998. *HomerusIlias*, vol. 1. Stuttgart. Teubner.

West, M. L. 2000. *Homerus Ilias*, vol. 2. Stuttgart: Teubner.

West, M. L. 2003a. *Homeric Hymns, Homeric Apocrypha, Lives of Homer*. Cambridge, MA: Harvard University Press.

West, M. L. 2003b. *Greek Epic Fragments*. Cambridge, MA: Cambridge University Press.

West, M. L. 2011. *The Making of the Iliad: Disquisition and Analytical Commentary*. Oxford: Oxford University Press.

West, M. L. 2013. *The Epic Cycle: A Commentary on the Lost Troy Epics*. Oxford: Oxford University Press.

Whitely, S. 2011. "Text World Theory, Real Readers and Emotional Responses to *The Remains of the Day*." *Language and Literature*, 20: 23–42.

Whitley, J. 2013. "Homer's Entangled Objects: Narrative, Agency, and Personhood In and Out of Iron Age Texts." *Cambridge Archaeological Journal*, 23: 395–416.

Whitley, J. 2020. "Homer and History." In C. O. Pache (ed.), *The Cambridge Guide to Homer*. Cambridge: Cambridge University Press, 257–66.

Whitman, C. H. 1958. *Homer and the Heroic Tradition*. Cambridge, MA: Harvard University Press.

Whitmarsh, T. 2022. "Emotions and Narrativity in the Greek Romance." In M. de Bakker, B. van der Berg, and J. Klooster (eds), *Emotions and Narrative in Ancient Literature and Beyond: Studies in Honour of Irene de Jong*. Leiden: Brill, 633–49.

Wilson, D. F. 2002. *Ransom, Revenge, and Heroic Identity in the Iliad*. Cambridge: Cambridge University Press.

Wilson, N. G. 2015. *Herodoti historiae*. Oxford: Clarendon Press.

Wimmer, L. et al. 2021. "Reading Fictional Narratives to Improve Social and Moral Cognition: The Influence of Narrative Perspective, Transportation, and Identification." *Frontiers in Communication*, 5: 611935. DOI: 10.3389/fcomm.2020.611935.

Winkler, M. M. 2007. "The *Iliad* and the Cinema." In M. M. Winkler (ed.), *Troy: From Homer's Iliad to Hollywood Epic*. Malden, MA: Blackwell Publishing, 43–67.

Wohl, V. 2015. *Euripides and the Politics of Form*. Princeton: Princeton University Press.

Wolf, W. 1993. *Ästhetische Illusion und Illusionsdurchbrechung in der Erzählkunst: Theorie und Geschichte mit Schwerpunkt auf englischem illusionsstörenden Erzählen*. Tübingen: Niemeyer.

Wolf, W. 2013. "Aesthetic Illusion." In W. Wolf, W. Bernhart, and A. Mahler (eds), *Immersion and Distance: Aesthetic Illusion in Literature and Other Media*. Amsterdam: Rodopi, 1–63.

Wolf, W. 2014. "Illusion (Aesthetic)." In P. Hühn (ed.), *Living Handbook of Narratology*. Berlin: Walter de Gruyter. Electronic.

Woloch, A. 2003. *The One vs. the Many: Minor Characters and the Space of the Protagonist in the Novel*. Princeton: Princeton University Press.

Woloch, A. 2006. "Minor Characters." In F. Moretti (ed.), *The Novel*. Vol. 2: *Forms and Themes*. Princeton: Princeton University Press, 295–323.

Woodruff, P. 2008. *The Necessity of Theater: The Art of Watching and Being Watched*. Oxford: Oxford University Press.

Worman, N. 2018. "Touching, Proximity, and the Aesthetics of Pain in Sophocles." In A. Purves (ed.), *Touch and the Ancient Senses*. London: Routledge, 34–49.

Xian, R. 2017. "Geschlossener Raum und narrative Spannung in der *Odyssee*." *Materiali et discussioni per l'analisi dei testi classici*, 79: 9–29.

Xian, R. 2020. "The Dramatization of Emotions in *Iliad* 24.552–658." *Philologus*, 164: 181–96.

Yamagata, N. 2020. "Suicide in Homer and the *Tale of Heike*." *Yearbook of Ancient Greek Epic*, 4: 72–94.

Young, E. M. 2015. "The Touch of the *Cinaedus*: Unmanly Sensations in the *Carmina Priapea*." *Classical Antiquity*, 34: 183–208.

Young, E. M. 2018. "The Touch of Poetry in the *Carmina Priapea*." In A. Purves (ed.), *Touch and the Ancient Senses*. London: Routledge, 134–49.

Young, J. O. 2019. "Literary Fiction and the Cultivation of Virtue." *Croatian Journal of Philosophy*, 56: 315–30.

Zajko, V. 2006. "Hector and Andromache: Identification and Appropriation." In C. Martindale and R. Thomas (eds), *Classics and the Uses of Reception*. Malden, MA: Blackwell Publishing, 80–91.

Zajko, V. 2017. "Affective Interests: Ancient Tragedy, Shakespeare and the Concept of Character." *Arion*, 25: 53–78.

Zanker, A. T. 2019. *Metaphor in Homer: Time, Speech, and Thought*. Cambridge: Cambridge University Press.

Zanker, G. 1981. "*Enargeia* in the Ancient Criticism of Poetry." *Rheinisches Museum für Philologie*, 124: 291–311.

Zeitlin, F. 2018. "Constructing the Aesthetic Body in Homer and Beyond." In B. M. King and L. Doherty (eds), *Thinking the Greeks: A Volume in Honour of James M. Redfield*. London: Routledge, 53–69.

Ziegler, K. 1964. *Plutarchi vitae parallelae*, vol. 2.1. 2nd edn. Leipzig: Teubner.

Ziegler, K. and Gärtner, H. 1996. *Plutarchi vitae parallelae*, vol. 3.1. 2nd corrected edn. Stuttgart: Teubner.

Zillmann, D. 1996. "The Psychology of Suspense in Dramatic Exposition." In P. Vorderer, H. J. Wulff, and M. Friedrichsen (eds), *Suspense: Conceptualizations, Theoretical Analyses, and Empirical Explorations*. Mahwah, NJ: Lawrence Erlbaum Associates, 199–231.

Zunshine, L. 2003. "Theory of Mind and Experimental Representations of Fictional Consciousness." *Narrative*, 11: 270–91.

Zwaan, R. A. 2003. "The Immersed Experiencer: Toward an Embodied Theory of Language Comprehension." *Psychology of Learning and Motivation*, 44: 35–62.

# Index of Greek Passages

For the benefit of digital users, indexed terms that span two pages (e.g., 52–3) may, on occasion, appear on only one of those pages.

Aeschylus, *Agamemnon*
   3  175–6

Aeschylus, *Seven against Thebes*
   103  185–6
   151  185–6
   237–8  185–6
   246  185–6
   250  185–6
   262  185–6

*Aethiopis*
   argumentum 2 (West 2003b)  129

Apollodorus, *Library*
   3.15.7  69–70

Aristotle, *Art of Rhetoric*
   1386a25–6  40–1
   1386a33–4  147–8
   1408a23–4  36–7

Aristotle, *Eudemian Ethics*
   1240a37–8  39–40

Aristotle, *Nicomachean Ethics*
   1166a7–8  39–40

Aristotle, *Poetics*
   1448a4–14  40
   1448a16–18  40–1
   1453a5–6  36–7, 40–1
   1453a8–9  40–1
   1454a16–28  41–2
   1454a33–6  41–2
   1455a22–6  151–2
   1455a22–9  150–1
   1456a25–7  36–7
   1459b28–31  239
   1460a26–7  41–2
   1460a11–17  41–2

*Cypria*
   argumentum 9–20 (Bernabé)  129
   argumentum 10 (West 2003b)  90
   fragment 3 (Bernabé)  171–2

Demetrius, *On Style*
   216  37–8

Demosthenes, *On the Crown*
   265  247

Diodorus, *Library of History*
   4.65.4  67–8

Dionysius of Halicarnassus, *On Literary Composition*
   20  233–4
   23  153–4

Dionysius of Halicarnassus, *On Lysias*
   7.1–2  147–8
   9.6–8  44

Dionysius of Halicarnassus, *On the Style of Demosthenes*
   44  153–4
   45  153–4

Euripides, *Alcestis*
   369–70  39–40

Euripides, *Helen*
   726–7  39–40

Euripides, *Heracles*
   1395  98

Eustathius, *Commentary on the Odyssey*
   vol. 1, p. 432  107–8

Gorgias, fragments
   B 23  151

Gorgias, *Helen*
   7.49  130
   9.58–9  34–5

Heliodorus, *Ethiopian Story of Theagenes and Chariclea*
   4.3.3  176

Herodotus, *Histories*
   6.39.2  39–40

Hesiod, *Shield of Heracles*
   8  86
   47  86
   125  84
   140–3  86
   221  84

## 292  INDEX OF GREEK PASSAGES

Hesiod, *Theogony*
  27  248, 250–1
  98–103  148–9
  165  91
  173  91
  283  84
  516  74n.3
  980  86

Hesiod, *Works and Days*
  261  74n.3
  521  86

Homer, *Iliad*
  1.4–5  219
  1.29–31  43
  1.30  168–9
  1.31  95n.1
  1.34  163–4
  1.34–5  58–9
  1.37–42  58–9
  1.58  163–4
  1.67  163–4
  1.101  163–4
  1.104–5  54–5
  1.148  54–5
  1.154–7  171–2
  1.155  168–9
  1.185  135
  1.220  84, 176, 180
  1.224–5  99–100
  1.225  215–16
  1.240–4  198
  1.245–6  163–4
  1.246  84
  1.247  165–6, 211
  1.252  168–9
  1.287  188–9
  1.310–11  165–6
  1.331–2  54–5
  1.348–51  54–5
  1.352  122–3
  1.361  54–5
  1.362  121–2
  1.366  168–9
  1.380–1  58–9
  1.407–10  198
  1.407–12  58–9
  1.415–16  121–2
  1.416–18  122–3
  1.422  90–1
  1.423  170
  1.430  124
  1.431  168–9
  1.485  163–4

  1.505  121–3
  1.509–10  121–2
  1.561  215–16
  1.590–3  171–2
  1.595–6  54–5
  2.17  88
  2.45  84
  2.72–5  207
  2.73  57
  2.101–41  207
  2.241–2  212–13
  2.260  248–9
  2.270  49
  2.274  212–13
  2.303  172–3
  2.332  172–3
  2.484–6  113
  2.484–93  235–6
  2.496  172–3
  2.537–35  169–70
  2.589–90  91
  2.664  67–8
  2.697  68
  2.760  189
  2.722–5  172–3
  2.729–32  171–2
  2.738–47  107–8
  2.784–5  163–4
  2.816  54–5
  2.831  71
  2.844–5  129
  2.872–3  129
  3.9  59
  3.16–22  185
  3.17–18  85–6
  3.19–20  69
  3.21–37  213–14
  3.27–8  91
  3.29  163–4, 179
  3.46–9  129
  3.47  67–8
  3.54–5  215–16
  3.60–3  213–14
  3.74  169–70
  3.125–8  95–6
  3.135  165–6
  3.153–4  162–3
  3.205–7  90
  3.205–24  171–2
  3.220  215–16
  3.259  93
  3.271  165
  3.272  84–5
  3.306–7  93

## INDEX OF GREEK PASSAGES 293

3.310–12 165–6
3.322 181
3.328–38 88, 166
3.331 84
3.332 84
3.337 85
3.342 36
3.346 176
3.347 180
3.352 105
3.353–4 227–8
3.355 176
3.355–6 199–200
3.357 179–80
3.358 84
3.363 179
3.364–8 91
3.379 78
3.381 79
3.411 188–9
3.443–5 129
3.449 79
4.26–8 74–5
4.105–8 163–4
4.125 179
4.130–1 176–7
4.136 84
4.146–7 166
4.150–2 93
4.185 186–7
4.253 77
4.275–9 189–90
4.356 54–5
4.368–400 65–71
4.376–7 67–8
4.378 168–9
4.378–383 67–8
4.383 68, 168–9
4.384 67–8
4.385 67–8
4.390 70
4.397–8 70–1
4.404–10 227–8
4.406 171–2
4.419–20 163–4
4.451 163–4
4.452–5 189–90
4.482 163–4
4.490 166
4.493 97
4.494–5 77
4.495 179–80
4.498–9 199–200
4.502 179–80

4.522 180
4.525–6 218–19
4.535 181
4.539–42 187–8, 212–13
5.10–26 72–3
5.18–19 79
5.23 79
5.25–6 79
5.44 169–70
5.62–4 129
5.85–6 187
5.127–8 79
5.134–6 77
5.176 98n.4
5.182 85
5.197–205 213
5.216–327 72–3
5.237 72
5.253–4 216
5.260–73 89
5.273 89, 125
5.275 72
5.280–1 199–200
5.301–2 78–9
5.302 165, 176
5.304 56
5.307 105
5.308 180
5.314–18 121–2
5.319–27 89
5.344–5 79
5.354 93
5.361 93
5.432–5 79
5.434 92
5.436 8 78
5.438 92
5.439 79–80
5.471 106
5.473–4 106
5.482 75–6
5.485–6 92
5.493 211
5.509 84
5.530–2 59
5.576–9 248–9
5.576–89 72–3
5.585 179
5.608–9 72–3
5.620–1 176
5.626 181
5.661 179–80
5.694 176, 180
5.743 85

Homer, *Iliad (cont.)*
　5.848　88
　6.55–6　215–16
　6.55–60　130
　6.62　130, 176, 180, 213–14
　6.117–18　166
　6.141　227–8
　6.152　168–9
　6.168　168–9
　6.187–90　70
　6.201　168–9
　6.210　168–9
　6.216–21　227–8
　6.234–6　214–15
　6.237–51　161–2
　6.264–8　214–15
　6.266–8　54–5
　6.286　161–2
　6.288　160–2
　6.295　160
　6.296–8　161–2
　6.298　160
　6.313–18　161–2
　6.318–19　165
　6.321　161–2
　6.321–4　184–5
　6.322　165
　6.369–71　161–2
　6.375　161–2
　6.388–9　94
　6.390–4　161–2
　6.392　197–8
　6.404　54–5, 121
　6.407　215–16
　6.411–12　125–6
　6.414–28　99–100
　6.435　162–3
　6.444–6　58, 69
　6.456–7　172–3
　6.460–2　125–6
　6.469　85
　6.476–81　216
　6.480　219
　6.481　93
　6.484　49
　6.495　161–2
　6.497–8　161–2
　6.504　85
　6.521–2　87–8
　7.70　78–9
　7.91　125
　7.96–103　212–13
　7.109–10　212–13
　7.121　213–14

　7.135　168–9
　7.150　69
　7.191–2　93
　7.212　54–5
　7.213　181
　7.219–23　85
　7.224–5　199–200
　7.252　179–80
　7.285　69
　7.312　93
　7.389–90　129
　7.479　197–8
　8.38　54–5
　8.65　163–4
　8.87–90　197–8
　8.148–50　215–16
　8.191–8　89
　8.192–3　85
　8.195　84
　8.196–7　89
　8.217　197–8
　8.222–7　192–3
　8.229–34　106, 171–2
　8.252　179
　8.271–2　181
　8.273　235–6
　8.316–21　78–9
　8.320　179
　8.321　165, 176
　8.329　97, 179
　8.337　77
　8.342　73–4, 92
　8.343　179–80
　8.423　43
　8.473–6　198
　8.478–81　170
　8.493–4　165
　8.555–9　189–90
　9.46–9　70
　9.218–19　162–3
　9.223　224
　9.338　67–8
　9.360–1　58
　9.387　90–1
　9.410–16　122–3
　9.517　90–1
　9.530　168–9
　9.544　67–8
　9.568　180
　9.587–97　227–8
　9.618　186–7
　9.640–2　58
　9.650–3　227–8
　9.694　43–4

# INDEX OF GREEK PASSAGES 295

9.699  215–16
9.699–700  79–80
9.710–11  212–13
10.5–10  222
10.75–6  85
10.93–5  97–8
10.194  179–80
10.254–72  166
10.328  176
10.400  54–5
10.435–41  89
10.452  105
10.469  179–80
10.477  89
10.493–5  89
10.498–501  89
10.513  72
10.529  176
10.564–5  89
10.574–5  166
11.5–9  192–3
11.16  87–8
11.18  84
11.19–23  171–2
11.19–28  84
11.29  84
11.30  86
11.30–1  84–5
11.33–7  85
11.38  85
11.41–2  85
11.43  85–6, 166
11.44–5  86
11.46  86
11.64–5  92
11.91  88
11.91–147  72–3
11.100  89
11.101  88
11.110–12  89–90
11.137  90
11.142  90–2
11.154  92–3
11.165  92
11.166–7  163–4
11.168  92
11.177–8  92
11.178  73–4
11.181–2  88
11.191–4  198
11.195–209  199
11.217  88
11.218–20  235–6
11.226–7  72

11.227–30  128–9
11.237  180
11.248–50  127
11.254  93
11.274  93
11.275–9  93
11.296  77
11.299–300  235–6
11.320–4  73–4
11.329  168–9
11.335  73–4
11.341–2  77
11.349–50  199–200
11.349–56  199
11.352  180
11.362  79–80
11.395  98–9
11.400  93
11.403  222
11.404–10  202
11.408–10  215–16
11.435  179–80
11.462–3  185–6
11.465–84  203
11.544–7  79
11.546  36
11.597–9  185
11.630–1  164–5
11.633  84
11.636–7  165
11.671–81  73–4
11.672  74
11.673  168–9
11.674  74
11.676  75–6
11.683  75–6
11.684  75
11.688  74
11.688–702  74
11.697  73–4
11.703–5  74–6
11.707  74–5
11.711  168–9
11.713  75–6
11.714–16  74–5
11.717–21  71, 75
11.720  75–6
11.721  72–3
11.723  168–9
11.727–9  74–5
11.728–44  72
11.733  75–6
11.744  77
11.747–9  78–9

Homer, *Iliad* (*cont.*)
11.748 73–4
11.748–9 72–3
11.752 79
11.755 73–4
11.756 168–9
11.759 73–4
11.761 76
11.763 76
11.794–5 122–3
11.809–12.2 127–8
11.811–12 166
12.3–35 172–3
12.9–35 127–8
12.10 90–1
12.23 189
12.40–59 127–8
12.83 179
12.125 185
12.127–94 107–8
12.151 185
12.185 180
12.200 179–80
12.257 180
12.310–28 58, 113
12.335–8 192–3
12.338 185–6
12.384 105
12.396 185
12.465 180
13.148 181
13.282–3 97–8
13.295 85–6
13.352–3 93
13.363–9 171–2
13.384–401 72–3
13.399 179
13.412 249
13.423 249
13.434–6 92
13.437 177–8
13.442–4 129–30
13.471–6 176–7
13.504 181
13.505 179
13.507–8 218–19
13.519–20 179–80
13.521–5 113–14
13.530 163–4
13.548–9 163–4
13.563 109
13.583 181
13.613 166
13.619 89

13.619–23 91–2
13.628 78
13.636–9 239
13.648–9 36
13.658 248–9
13.726 215–16
14.1 185–6
14.16–21 222
14.153–65 118–19
14.164–5 120
14.179–86 119
14.188–9 193
14.197–210 119–20
14.200–1 170
14.222–3 120
14.225–30 120
14.262 79–80
14.281–5 120–1
14.301–2 170
14.393 185
14.401 185
14.405 84
14.413 177–8
14.414–17 189–90
14.451–2 179–80
14.465 180
14.493–5 218–19
14.508–10 235–6
14.517 218–19
15.1 179–80
15.52–71 198
15.79–83 113
15.110–42 113–14
15.147–8 43
15.297 180
15.313–14 179
15.314–15 177–8
15.335 168–9
15.347 73–4
15.362–4 176–7
15.370–1 92
15.421 97, 179
15.451 181
15.453 185
15.465 179
15.481 85
15.545 92
15.559 92
15.561–4 58
15.562–4 59
15.565 78
15.575–7 199–200
15.579–82 176–7
15.582–90 79

# INDEX OF GREEK PASSAGES 297

15.607–8  54–5
15.618  177–8
15.661–6  58
15.676  165–6
15.698  180
15.711  166
15.713  84
15.715  163–4
15.720  216
15.732  92
16.20  90
16.22  90
16.32–3  90
16.44–5  59
16.81  181
16.87  59
16.100  99
16.106–7  166
16.109–10  166
16.130–9  88
16.132  84
16.134  84
16.138  85
16.139  85–6
16.141–2  165–6
16.143–4  171–2
16.233–48  59
16.257  88
16.284–785  72–3
16.324  180
16.340  181
16.345–50  218–19
16.356–7  185–6
16.361  185–6
16.363  75–6
16.372  92
16.406–9  176–7
16.422  58
16.431–61  113–14
16.441  109
16.504  218–19
16.569–80  200–1
16.581–5  77
16.603–5  128–9
16.612  181
16.614  181
16.615  179
16.684–7  213–14
16.702  162–3
16.706  79–80
16.724  89
16.737  199–200
16.740  181
16.745  89

16.774  181
16.783–6  78–9
16.786–804  248–9
16.793  99
16.794  179
16.830  89
16.830–42  217
16.854  105
16.859–61  217
17.13–16  89
17.16  125
17.61–7  208–9
17.87–9  77, 185–6
17.91–101  213
17.123–4  77
17.125  248–9
17.142–3  104–5
17.144–59  58
17.186–7  89
17.197  122–3
17.205  212–13
17.212  88
17.232  125
17.301  168–9
17.314–15  218–19
17.314–18  219
17.350  168–9
17.356  92
17.389–93  208–9
17.389–95  176–7
17.478  79–80
17.516–17  199–200
17.523–4  129–30
17.524  181
17.528  181
17.562  180
17.617–18  180
17.666–714  112
18.5–37  124
18.23–7  110–11
18.29  78–9
18.35  124
18.39–48  236
18.39–49  123–5
18.50–1  125
18.51–64  124
18.53–4  125
18.56  125
18.59–60  125
18.59–64  121–3
18.65–6  125
18.71  122–3
18.73  121–2
18.95–6  121–3

Homer, *Iliad* (*cont.*)
  18.97  49
  18.107–11  49
  18.121  125
  18.128–37  121–2
  18.138–42  125
  18.207–14  78–9
  18.219–21  78–9
  18.228  78–9
  18.230–1  72–3, 78–9
  18.257  90–1
  18.276  186–7
  18.312  213–14
  18.432–5  121
  18.440–1  122–3
  18.444–56  126
  18.458  122–3
  18.461  121–2
  18.464–5  122–3
  18.466–7  188
  18.480  85
  18.496  160
  18.498–9  127–8
  18.509–40  127–8
  18.541–9  127–8
  18.610  84
  19.12  176
  19.12–19  178
  19.19  168–9
  19.24–6  219
  19.30–1  219
  19.35  90–1
  19.132–3  90
  19.143–4  112
  19.151–3  188
  19.208  90–2
  19.237–49  112
  19.252  165
  19.253  84–5
  19.326  172–3
  19.332  172–3
  19.338–9  59
  19.364–91  88
  19.365–6  54–5
  19.367–83  166
  19.370  84
  19.371  84
  19.372  85–6
  19.387  85–6
  19.396  176
  19.401–23  88
  19.416–17  122–3
  20.40–4  171–2
  20.127–8  122–3

20.158  88
20.226  162–3
20.258  186–7
20.259–66  213–14
20.261  165
20.274–81  43–4
20.277  185
20.284–5  78–9
20.285  165, 176
20.307–8  172–3
20.318–42  80
20.322–4  43–4
20.343  80
20.408–12  72
20.413–20  185, 218–19
20.423  181
20.442–3  78–9
20.443–5  79–80
20.448  79–80
20.449  79–80
20.469–70  218–19
20.481–3  218–19
20.484–9  72–3
20.494  163–4
21.9  185
21.20–6  72–3
21.33  78
21.60–1  186–7
21.82–3  79–80
21.103–5  209
21.114  98
21.123–4  98–9
21.136  214–15
21.145  85–6
21.174–5  85–6
21.174–8  163–4
21.180–1  218–19
21.277–8  122–3
21.284–97  121–2
21.304  121–2
21.328–41  121–2
21.387–9  185–6
21.408  91–2
21.412  91–2
21.425  98n.4
21.441–57  113–14
21.492  179
21.596–8  80
22.14  80
22.15  80
22.18  80
22.20  80
22.25–91  50–1
22.79  98–9

# INDEX OF GREEK PASSAGES 299

22.86–9 98–9
22.100 213
22.100–3 213
22.107 213
22.136 48–9
22.140 179
22.156 171–2
22.169–70 50–1
22.199–201 217–18
22.216–18 93
22.224 93
22.289–90 199–200
22.304–5 125
22.305 58
22.346–7 90–1, 219
22.357 215–16
22.359–60 122–3
22.371 186–7
22.373 186–7
22.391–4 91–2
22.395 214–15
22.406–7 99
22.410–11 113
22.412–13 111
22.414 111, 179
22.414–15 193
22.416–20 111
22.431–6 99
22.433 212–13
22.437 95
22.437–8 95–6
22.437–515 94–100
22.440 94–7
22.440–1 95–6
22.442 96–7
22.443–4 95–7
22.443–5 95
22.444 97
22.445 95–7
22.447 95
22.447–8 97
22.448 94–5, 179
22.448–56 55–6
22.452 97–9
22.453–4 98
22.454–9 98n.4
22.460–1 94, 98–9
22.460–3 94–5
22.463–4 95
22.463–5 19–20
22.465 95, 98–9
22.468 99–100
22.468–70 94–5
22.470–2 99–100

22.474 97
22.476 97
22.477–514 94
22.488–9 99–100
22.489 96–7
22.496 181
22.508–9 98–9
23.24 214–15
23.80–1 122–3
23.91–2 122–3
23.100–1 166
23.132 72–3
23.176 135
23.206 170
23.309–11 102
23.313–18 101
23.314 100–1
23.319–25 101
23.322 101
23.343 101
23.344 101
23.345 100–1
23.353–401 102
23.383–400 100–1
23.405–6 100–1
23.415–16 102
23.423–4 102–3
23.425–8 103
23.426 103
23.431–3 176–7
23.433–7 102–3
23.438–41 103
23.439–40 103–4, 215–16
23.449–98 102
23.478 215–16
23.510–11 100–1
23.517–23 208–9
23.555 54–5
23.560 84
23.581–95 103
23.632–3 69–70
23.634–42 69–70
23.647–9 89
23.664–5 104
23.667 69
23.667–75 104–5
23.670 104–5
23.673 180
23.673–5 105
23.676 106–7
23.677–84 106–7
23.680 69–70
23.682 100–1
23.685 106–7

Homer, *Iliad* (*cont.*)
  23.690 180
  23.702–5 135
  23.711–13 177–8
  23.736 107
  23.758 163–4
  23.760–3 108, 176–7
  23.764 163–4
  23.766–7 100–1, 108
  23.768–74 100–1
  23.774 176–7
  23.778–9 69–70
  23.784 100–1
  23.786 54–5
  23.797 176
  23.798–9 176
  23.809–10 107
  23.810 43–4
  23.822–3 105–6
  23.823 107
  23.826–9 99–100
  23.826–49 107
  23.839–40 104
  23.847 100–1
  23.852–8 108–9
  23.863–4 108–10
  23.863–5 100–1
  23.865–7 108–9
  23.870–1 109
  23.872–3 100–1, 109–10
  23.874 109
  23.881 212–13
  23.890–4 110
  24.83–6 122–3
  24.93–4 122–3
  24.130–1 43
  24.131–2 122–3
  24.163–5 54–5, 110
  24.171–87 111
  24.173–87 201–2
  24.189–90 113
  24.189–92 111
  24.197–9 111
  24.200–9 214–15
  24.201–10 111
  24.203–4 209
  24.207–8 209
  24.212–13 219
  24.212–14 99
  24.214–16 125
  24.218 111
  24.218–27 112
  24.220–4 111
  24.224–7 111–12

  24.228–35 112
  24.235–7 112
  24.236–7 111
  24.239–44 113
  24.239–46 112
  24.253–64 112
  24.263 113
  24.275–6 112
  24.431–6 125–6
  24.470 180
  24.478–9 209–10
  24.480–2 209–10
  24.568–70 209
  24.597–8 162–3
  24.602–19 227–8
  24.615 168–9
  24.640 179
  24.725–38 99–100
  24.733 90
  24.742 125–6

Homer, *Odyssey*
  1.7 74n.3
  1.34 74n.3
  1.239–40 125
  1.272–96 63–4
  1.296–302 63–4
  1.325–6 177–8
  1.326–7 62–3
  1.342–4 125–6
  1.350–2 62–3
  1.354–5 62–3
  2.41 67–8
  2.48–9 79–80, 99–100
  2.66–7 130–1
  2.76–8 99–100
  2.79–81 99–100
  2.220–3 98–9
  3.130–95 62–3
  3.132–6 62–3
  3.193 64
  3.205–7 91
  3.207 74
  3.260–1 98–9
  3.276–312 62–3
  4.113–16 110
  4.163–7 43
  4.341–4 107–8
  4.541 179
  4.584 125
  4.703 98
  4.724 125–6
  4.727 79–80
  4.814 125–6
  5.58–76 55–6, 182–3

## INDEX OF GREEK PASSAGES 301

5.129  79–80
5.297  98
5.299–312  201–2
5.311  125
5.406  98
5.426–7  105
6.2  88
6.232–5  177–8
7.40  179–80
7.81  124
7.86–102  55–6
7.105–6  95n.1
7.112–31  55–6
7.311–16  43
8.73–95  227–8
8.74  62–3
8.83–92  110
8.142  69
8.147  69
8.167–8  104–5
8.202–33  69–70
8.207  69–70
8.223–8  171–2
8.403–4  84
8.404  84–5
8.406  84
8.492–3  104
8.499–534  227–8
9.116–41  55–6
9.182–6  55–6
9.213–15, 57
9.219–23  55–6
9.264  62–3, 125
9.276  130–1
10.25–7  198
10.258–60  58–9
10.323–4  78–9
10.432–3  58–9
11.100–37  201–2
11.363–6  248
11.509  172–3
11.523  104
11.609–14  85
12.300  74n.3
12.412  105
12.416  97
13.102–12  55–6
13.125  124
13.125–38  113–14
13.133  57
13.187  124
13.265–6  89
13.345–50  55–6
13.429–38  54–5

14.5–16  55–6
14.31–2  97
14.211–45  89
14.229–34  74
14.306  97
14.339–59  179
14.363–5  248
14.369–70  125
14.361  248
14.387  248
16.105–9  90
16.214  116–17
17.182  124
17.216  130–1
17.233–4  130–1
17.251–3  130–1
17.588  74
17.596  78–9
18.21–2  105
18.28–9  105
18.73  106
18.83–7  105–6
18.91  105–6
18.95–6  180
18.96–7  105
18.105  180
18.308–9  109
18.347–9  90–1
19.231  178
19.257–8  125–6
19.438  181
19.439–43  55–6
20.49–51  70, 72–3
20.95  181
20.120–1  91
20.169–71  91–2
20.170  74, 74n.3
20.181  186–7
20.285–7  90–1
20.348  219
20.370  74
21.411  177–8
22.17  97
22.68  98
22.119  198
22.124  85
22.125  85–6
22.147  98
22.168  91–2
22.194  91–2
22.201  181
22.326–8  85–6
22.411–12  91–2
22.416  74n.3

Homer, *Odyssey* (cont.)
  22.498–9  116–17
  23.67  74n.3
  23.159–62  177–8
  23.205  98n.4
  23.207–8  116–17
  23.215–16  93
  23.355–8  74
  23.434–7  116–17
  24.32–3  125
  24.47–62  123–4
  24.179  36
  24.197–8  95–6
  24.316–17  110–11
  24.326  90–1
  24.345  98n.4
  24.351–2  74n.3
  24.498  181
  24.522–3  199–200
  24.538  179
  24.545  93

Homer, Scholia
  bT at *Iliad* 1.307b  43
  bT at *Iliad* 3.389b1  70–1
  bT at *Iliad* 4.154  152–3
  bT at *Iliad* 5.82  147–8
  bT at *Iliad* 5.370–2  42
  bT at *Iliad* 6.58–9b  130
  bT at *Iliad* 6.392  197–8
  bT at *Iliad* 6.467  42
  bT at *Iliad* 7.479  37, 197–8
  T at *Iliad* 8.87a1  197–8
  bT at *Iliad* 8.217a  197–8
  bT at *Iliad* 11.407–10  42
  bT at *Iliad* 14.226–7  148
  T at *Iliad* 16.463–7b  197–8
  bT at *Iliad* 16.762–3  152–3
  A at *Iliad* 18.22–35a  42
  bT at *Iliad* 21.269a  42
  T at *Iliad* 21.515–17  43
  bT at *Iliad* 22.463  94
  bT at *Iliad* 22.512–13  94
  T at *Iliad* 23.382  37
  D at *Iliad* 23.600  105–6
  bT at *Iliad* 23.685  108–9
  *Odyssey* 1.429a  43
  *Odyssey* 2.67g  130–1
  *Odyssey* 4.184a1  37
  *Odyssey* 9.276  130–1
  *Odyssey* 11.547  107–8

*Homeric Hymn* 9 (to Artemis)
  3  68

*Homeric Hymn* 20 (to Hephaestus)
  4  79

*Homeric Hymn* 28 (to Athena)
  6  86

*Homeric Hymn to Aphrodite*
  1  86
  9  86
  65  86

*Homeric Hymn to Apollo*
  123  84
  224  68

*Homeric Hymn to Demeter*
  4  84
  40–1  115
  44–6  115
  52–8  115–16
  60–3  115–16
  77–9  115–16
  82–7  115–16
  90–1  115–16
  111  116
  147–8  116
  188–9  116
  197–8  110
  212–15  116
  217  116
  243  116
  246  116
  255–8  116
  282  98
  304  117
  333  117
  356  116–17
  384  116–17
  385–90  116–17

*Homeric Hymn to Hermes*
  69–141  119–20
  88  68
  154–9  119–20
  213–14  119–20
  254–5  119–20
  260  119–20
  281  119–20
  302–3  119–20
  379  119–20
  389  119–20
  391–4  119–20

Horace, *Art of Poetry*
  102–4  39n.14

Hyginus, *Fabulae*
  XCI.5  69–70

## INDEX OF GREEK PASSAGES

Isocrates, *Panegyricus* [4]
  168 249–50
*Life of Aeschylus*
  5 153–4
  7 153–4
*Little Iliad*
  argumentum 10–11 (Bernabé) 172–3
  argumentum 14 (Bernabé) 104
Longinus, *On the Sublime*
  9.7 113–14
  9.10 38
  15.1 148
  15.2 38
  15.4 150
  20.2 38
  26.1–2 148, 187
  39.3 38
Lucian, *Fugitives*
  1 219–20
Lucian, *How to Write History*
  51 147–8
Lysias, *Against Eratosthenes*
  24 182
  24–6 164–5
Melanippides (*Poetae Melici Graecae*)
  757 184
Pindar, *Isthmian* 8
  29 121
Pindar, *Nemean* 8
  26–30 107–8
Plato, *Ion*
  535b7–c5 149
  535d8–e6 149–50
  535e1–6 151
  535e2–3 36, 217
  536a2 150
  537c5–8 36
Plato, *Republic*
  393c5 243–4
  462e2 39–40
  601a4–b4 232
  604e2 40
  605c9–d4 35–6
  607a4 150
Plutarch, *The Glory of Athens*, *Moralia*
  347a–c 38–9

Plutarch, *How to Study Poetry*, *Moralia*
  16b 44
  30d 230–1
Plutarch, *Life of Alexander*
  32.8–12 86–7
Plutarch, *Life of Artaxerxes*
  8.1 38–9
Plutarch, *Life of Cato Minor*
  68.6 36
Plutarch, *Life of Pyrrhus*
  34.6 36
Plutarch, *On Praising Oneself Inoffensively*, *Moralia*
  539a–547f 106
  544a 104–5
Polybius, *The Histories*
  2.56.8 147–8
Porphyry, *Homeric Questions on the Iliad*
  at 6.275 142
Proclus, *Commentary on the Republic of Plato*
  K163.24–6 152
  K164.2–5 38–9
  K164.5–6 152
Pseudo-Plutarch, *Essay on the Life and Poetry of Homer*
  217 147–8
Sophocles, *Ajax*
  1273–87 107–8
  1339–41 107–8
Sophocles, *Philoctetes*
  693 39–40
  792 39–40
  806 39–40
Statius, *Thebaid*
  2.687–8 70
*Thebaid*
  fragment 9 (Bernabé) 219
Timocles (in Athenaeus, *Scholars at Dinner*)
  223c 149
Thucydides, *History of the Peloponnesian War*
  4.32.3–4 223–4
Xenophon, *The Education of Cyrus*
  1.6.24.5–6 39–40

# Index of Terms

For the benefit of digital users, indexed terms that span two pages (e.g., 52–3) may, on occasion, appear on only one of those pages.

actor/observer bias 103–4, 215–16
Agamemnon 65–71, 83–94, 110
Ajax 58–60, 107–8
allegiance 4–5, 19–20, 25, 29–30, 134–6, 141, 203–4, 211
Andromache 19–20, 64, 94–100
Antilochus 101–4
*apatē* 153–4
Aristarchus 43–4
artifact absorption 233
Athena 63–4

character(s)
 accretive 60–1, 114–15
 definition of 45–6
 hatred of 130–1
 motivations of 70–1, 73–4
 plurimedial 60–1, 114–15
 transtextual 60–1, 113–14
 types of 46
 well-known 59–61
character virtue 30–1, 54, 68–9, 75, 95–6, 121–2
cognitive identification 26–8, 35–6, 58–9, 75, 113–16, 119–20, 125–6
 definition of 20–1
cognitive scripts 229
counterarguing 248–9

delay 67–8, 88, 102
 *see also* suspense
Demeter 115–18
Diomedes 65–71, 107–8, 213–14
disgust 218–20
disidentification 141–2
divine backing 70, 73

emotion
 appraisal theory and 211
 definition of 46–7
 theory of 47–9
emotional identification 24–5, 27–8, 34–40, 59, 76–81, 89–93, 96–100, 113, 116–17, 120
 definition of 20–1

emotional immersion
 definition of 155
 judgments and 211–17
 *see also* disgust, fear, suspense
empathy 24–5, 33, 112
 *see also* side-taking, staging
*enagōnios* 153
*enargeia* 152–3
Epeius 104–6
epistemic identification
 definition of 22
epithets 54
Euryalus 106–7
external realism 32, 56, 94–5

familiar material 229
fear 217–18
focalization 18–20, 26–8, 95

gestures 242–3
goals 24–5
graduate students 252
group membership 33, 58, 119, 125

Hera 118–21
how-suspense 198–201

identification
 addresses to the narratee and 18
 allegiance and 19–20
 apostrophe and 18
 appeal of 138–9, 141–2
 breaks from 127–8, 239–40
 characters and 17–18, 59
 components of 20–2, 135–6
 context of reception and 240
 dangers of 131–6, 139–40
 defense of 136–7, 140–1
 definition of 1–2
 discrepancies in knowledge and 31
 duration of 25–6
 effects of 137–8
 hypothetical focalization and 18

impediments to 128–31
likeability and 23–4
narrator and 142
nonfiction and 2
persuasion and 64
protagonists and 19–20, 32
relatability and 23–4
scenic narratorial standpoint and 18
*see also* character(s), character virtue, cognitive identification, emotional identification, empathy, epistemic identification, epithets, focalization, goals, group membership, motivational identification, music, narrative impact, parasocial interaction, perceived realism, perceptual identification, physical appearance, physical identification, point of view, recipient (traits of), setting, side-taking, similarity, staging, sympathy, transference, vocal effects
immersion
breaks from 152–3, 239–40
definition of 1–2
details and 152
distance and 151, 154–5
historical present tense and 153
meaningfulness and 236–7
models of 155–8
nonfiction and 2
plotting and 153–4
realism and 152–3
second person address and 153
sound and 153–4
suspense and 153
see also *apatē*, artifact absorption, cognitive scripts, emotion, emotional immersion, *enagōnios*, *enargeia*, familiar material, gestures, memories, mind reading, music, narrative impact, *phantasia*, place names, recipient (traits of), rhetorical devices, rhythm, similes, sound, spatial immersion, spatio-temporal immersion, speech presentation, suspense, temporal immersion, unfamiliarity, vocal effects
introspection 50–1, 61–2, 155, 159

Lapiths (Leonteus and Polypoetes) 107–8

Meriones 108–10
mass slaughter 70, 72–3
memories 226–8
metasuspense 210

mind reading 222–5
motivational identification 24–5, 27–8, 34–7, 59, 68, 75–6, 88, 101–14, 117–20
definition of 20–1
*see also* goals
music 244–6

narrated vs narrative time 117, 124–5, 190
narrative
definition of 1
narrative impact 64–5, 137–8, 249–50
narrative realism 32–3, 56–7, 94, 110–11, 120
typicality and 56, 71, 94, 120
Nestor 62–4, 71–81

objects 177–81
Odysseus 59–60, 107–8, 132–3, 136–7
Oilean Ajax 108
oral performance 242–8
evaluation of 247–8
*see also* gestures, music, vocal effects
Orestes 63–4

parasocial interaction 32
parents 71–2, 75–6
Patroclus 71–81
perceived realism 32–3, 41–4, 69–74
*see also* external realism, narrative realism
perceptual identification 26–8, 35–6, 183–4
definition of 22
*phantasia* 148, 152–3
Phemius 62–3
physical appearance 31–2, 54–5, 84–7, 94–5, 110, 119
physical identification 27–8, 36
definition of 22
place names 168–73
point of view 18–19, 32, 109, 112, 118–19
*see also* focalization
Priam 110–13

recipient
attention and 67–8, 84–6
definition of 2
recipient traits 240–1
rhetorical devices 235
rhythm 234–5

setting 31–2, 55–6, 68, 94–5
side-taking 33, 101, 103, 113, 115–16, 119–21
similarity 28–30, 40–1, 53–4, 68–9, 104–5, 121, 136–7
similes 176–7, 189–90, 207–10, 213–14, 227–8
sound 234–5

spatial immersion
    definition of 155, 160
    details and 160
    movement and 161–4
    place names and 168
    scene changes and 167
    solidity (of objects and people) and 165–7
spatio-temporal immersion
    definition of 155
    deictic shift and 188–9
    focalization and 182–7, 189–90
    inclusive forms of address and 187–8
    motor resonance and 173–82, 191–3
    speech introductions and 191–3
speech presentation 190–1
spotlight 67–8, 84, 88, 102, 106–9, 119
staging 58, 125
storyworld
    definition of 1–2
suspense 196–211
    delay and 206–10
    emotion and 196
    identification and 201–6
    types of 196–7
    typical structures and 199–201
    *see also* how-suspense, immersion, metasuspense, similes, what-suspense, when-suspense
sympathy 18–20, 23–4, 115

Telemachus 62–4
    identification and 64
temporal immersion
    definition of 155
Teucer 108–10
Thetis 121–7
traditional referentiality 76–7
transference 58–9
Tydeus 65–71

undergraduates 251–2
unfamiliarity 229–30

vocal effects 243–4

what-suspense 197–9
when-suspense 198–9